ROMNEY

A RECKONING

McKAY COPPINS

SCRIBNER

NEW YORK LONDON TORONTO SYDNEY NEW DELHI

Scribner

An Imprint of Simon & Schuster, Inc.

1230 Avenue of the Americas

New York, NY 10020

First Scribner hardcover edition October 2023

SCRIBNER and design are registered trademarks of The Gale Group, Inc.,
used under license by Simon & Schuster, Inc., the publisher of this work.

For information about special discounts for bulk purchases,
please contact Simon & Schuster Special Sales at 1-866-506-1949
or business@simonandschuster.com.

The Simon & Schuster Speakers Bureau can bring authors to
your live event. For more information or to book an event, contact
the Simon & Schuster Speakers Bureau at 1-866-248-3049
or visit our website at www.simonspeakers.com.

Manufactured in the United States of America

3   5   7   9   10   8   6   4   2

Library of Congress Cataloging-in-Publication Data has been applied for.

ISBN 978-1-9821-9620-2
ISBN 978-1-9821-9623-3 (ebook)

For Annie, Ellis, Alden, Margot, and Hewitt

"Do we weigh our own political fortunes more heavily than we weigh the strength of our republic, the strength of our democracy, and the cause of freedom? What is the weight of personal acclaim compared to the weight of conscience?"

—Mitt Romney, January 6, 2021

Contents

ROMNEY

Prologue

For most of his life, he has nursed a morbid fascination with his own death, suspecting that it might assert itself one day suddenly and violently.

He controls what he can, of course. He wears his seat belt, and diligently applies sunscreen, and stays away from secondhand smoke. For thirty years, he followed his doctor's recipe for longevity with monastic dedication—the lean meats, the low-dose aspirin, the daily thirty-minute sessions on the stationary bike, heartbeat at 140 or higher or it doesn't count. Then, one day, his doctor informed him that "low fat" was an anachronism now, that it was sugar he needed to avoid, and the revelation felt like a betrayal. How many months—or, heaven forbid, *years*—had he lost to what he thought was a harmless ice cream habit?

He would live to 120 if he could. "So much is going to happen!" he says when asked about this peculiar desire. "I want to be around to see it." But some part of him has always doubted he'll get anywhere close.

He has never really interrogated the cause of this preoccupation. There was the accident, yes, but it's more than that. Premonitions of death seem to follow him. Once, years ago, he boarded an airplane for a business trip to London and a flight attendant whom he'd never met saw him, gasped, and rushed from the cabin in horror. When she was asked what had so upset her, she confessed that she'd dreamt the night before about a man who looked like him—*exactly* like him—getting shot and killed at a rally in Hyde Park. He didn't know how to respond, other than to laugh and put it out of his mind. But when a few days later he happened to find himself on the park's edge and saw a crowd forming, he made a point not to linger.

All of which is to say there is something familiar about the unnerving sensation that Mitt Romney is feeling late on the afternoon of January 2, 2021.

It begins with a text message from Angus King, the junior senator from Maine: "Could you give me a call when you get a chance? Important."

He calls, and King informs him of a conversation he's just had with a high-ranking Pentagon official. They've been tracking online chatter from right-wing extremists who appear to be planning something bad on the day of Donald Trump's upcoming rally in Washington, D.C. The president has been telling them the election was stolen; now they're coming to steal it back. There's talk of gun smuggling, of bombs and arson, of targeting the traitors in Congress who are responsible for this travesty. Romney's name has been popping up in some frightening corners of the internet, which is why King needed to talk to him. He isn't sure Romney will be safe.

Romney hangs up and immediately begins typing out a text to Mitch McConnell, the Senate majority leader. Mitch has been indulgent of Trump's deranged behavior over the last four years, but he's not crazy. Mitch knows the election wasn't stolen, that his guy lost fair and square. He sees the posturing by Republican politicians for what it is. He'll want to know about this, Romney thinks. He'll want to protect his colleagues, and himself.

Romney sends his text: "In case you have not heard this, I just got a call from Angus King who said that he had spoken with a senior official at the Pentagon who reports that they are seeing very disturbing social media traffic regarding the protests planned on the 6th. There are calls to burn down your home, Mitch; to smuggle guns into DC, and to storm the Capitol. I hope that sufficient security plans are in place, but I am concerned that the instigator—the President—is the one who commands the reinforcements the DC and Capitol police might require."

McConnell never responds.

Ann doesn't want him to return to D.C. Romney's wife all but begs him to stay in Utah until the election is certified and the protest has passed. "Don't go back," she keeps saying. "Don't go back on January sixth." She has a bad feeling about all of this. She is worried something terrible might happen to him.

He assures her that he won't be in any physical danger, but says he'll take extra precautions all the same. He won't walk to the grocery store like he usually does, or pick up his dry cleaning. Plus, he reasons, "If I get shot, you can move on to a younger, more athletic husband." He, on the other hand, will be stuck attending "everlasting church" in the sky. Ann is not amused.

"This is too important," he finally tells her. "This is the certifying of the election. This is the peaceful transfer of power." Moments like this were the whole reason he came out of a very comfortable retirement to serve in the Senate.

"I'll be careful," he tells her, "but I've really got to go."

The truth is that he has a bad feeling, too. But he's also feeling something else, something that Romney—a walking amalgam of prep school manners and Mormon niceness and the practiced cool of the private equity set—has spent his life learning to control: anger. He is angry at the president for lying to so many Americans; angry at his Republican colleagues for cynically going along with the ploy. He is angry that the United States Senate, supposedly the world's greatest deliberative body, will be reduced to a pathetic spectacle of antidemocratic theater as lawmakers cast self-serving votes to overturn a presidential election. He wants to be there to tell them how wrong they are, how harmful this whole charade is to America's system of government. He has been working on his speech for days, and he is determined to deliver it—not angrily, but with conviction—on the floor of the Senate. Staying home is not an option.

Early on the morning of January 6, Romney slides into the back of an SUV and begins the short commute to his Senate office, with a Capitol Police car in tow. He appreciates the escort, but as he looks out the window at the streets of D.C. he can't help but question its utility. *If somebody wants to shoot me*, he thinks, *what good is it with these guys in a car behind you?*

He tries to go about his morning as usual. He has a meeting with Arizona senator Mark Kelly, and another with the chairman of the Federal Communications Commission. He goes to the basement of the Rayburn Building to receive his second dose of the COVID vaccine. But he's struggling to concentrate on his schedule.

Two miles away, at the White House Ellipse, thousands of angry people are gathering for a "Save America Rally." Trump is tweeting about widespread voting "irregularities" and "fraud" and calling on his vice president to block the certification of the electoral votes: "All Mike Pence has to do is send them back to the States, AND WE WIN. Do it Mike, this is a time for extreme courage!"

When Romney encounters a gaggle of reporters, he labors to contain his anger. "I'm confident we'll proceed as the Constitution demands and tell our supporters the truth, whether or not they want to hear it," he says.

In fact, he is not confident of this at all. He knows what Josh Hawley and Ted Cruz and the rest are planning to do, and he knows there's no dissuading them because he's tried. So, at 1:00 p.m., when Romney takes his seat in the chamber where the electoral college votes are to be counted, he's not surprised when Cruz and Congressman Paul Gosar formally object to certifying Arizona's election result. The joint session is adjourned, and Romney follows the rest of the senators to their own smaller chamber to debate the objection.

The Senate chamber is a cloistered place, with no television monitors or electronic devices, and strict rules that keep outsiders off the floor, so Romney doesn't know exactly what's happening outside. He doesn't know that the president has just directed his supporters to march down Pennsylvania Avenue—"We're going to the Capitol!" He doesn't know that pipe bombs have been discovered outside both parties' nearby headquarters. He doesn't know that Capitol Police are scrambling to evacuate the Library of Congress, or that rioters are crashing into police barricades outside the Capitol, or that officers are beginning to realize they're outmanned and won't be able to hold the line much longer.

Once the senators are seated, Cruz rises—his brow furrowed, his voice suffused with grave concern—and launches into a deeply cynical speech casting his own decision to perpetuate Trump's election lies as an act of patriotism. "Nearly half the country believes the 2020 election was rigged," he explains. "Even if you do not share that conviction, it is the responsibility, I believe, of this office to acknowledge that is a profound threat to this country."

At 2:08 p.m., Romney's phone buzzes with a text message from his aide Chris Marroletti, who's been communicating with Capitol Police: "Protestors [sic] getting closer. High intensity out there." He suggests Romney might want to move to his "hideaway," a little windowless room that the senator sometimes uses to rest during late-night votes.

Romney looks around the chamber. The hideaway is a few hundred yards and two flights of stairs away. He doesn't want to leave if he doesn't have to. He'll stay put, he decides, unless the protesters get inside the building.

A minute later, Romney's phone buzzes again.

"They're on the west front, overcame barriers."

Adrenaline surging, Romney stands and makes his way to the back of the chamber, where he pushes open the heavy, bronze-embroidered doors. He's expecting the usual crowd of reporters and staff aides, but nobody is there. A strange, unsettling quiet has engulfed the deserted corridor. He turns left and starts down the hall toward his hideaway, when suddenly he sees a Capitol Police officer sprinting toward him at full speed.

"Go back in!" the officer booms without breaking stride. "You're safer inside the chamber."

Romney turns around and starts to run.

He gets back in time to hear the gavel drop and see several men—Secret Service agents, presumably—rush into the chamber without explanation and pull the vice president out. Then, all at once, the room turns over to chaos: A man in a neon sash is bellowing from the middle of the Senate floor about a security breach. Officials are scampering around the room in a panic, slamming doors shut and barking at senators to move farther inside until they can be evacuated.

Something about the volatility of the moment causes Romney to lose his grip, and he finally vents the raw, primal anger he's been trying to contain. He turns to Hawley, who's huddled with some of his right-wing colleagues, and starts to yell.

Later, Romney will struggle to recall the exact wording of his rebuke. Sometimes he'll remember shouting, "You're the reason this is happening!" Other times, it will be something more terse: "You did this." At least one reporter in the chamber will recount seeing the senator throw up his hands in a fit of fury as he roared, "This is what you've gotten, guys!"

Whatever the words, the sentiment is the same: this violence, this crisis, this assault on democracy—this is your fault.

What Romney doesn't pause to consider in this moment is an uncomfortable question: *Is any of it my fault, too?*

We started meeting a few months after that. Sometimes we talked in his Senate office, after most of his staff had gone home for the night.

Sometimes we went to his hideaway. But most weeks, I drove to a stately brick townhome with perpetually drawn blinds on a quiet street a mile from the Capitol Building.

The place had not been Romney's first choice for a Washington residence. When he was first elected in 2018, he'd set his eye on a newly remodeled condo at the Watergate with glittering views of the Potomac. Ann fell in love at the viewing, and he was ready to make an offer. But when he asked his soon-to-be staffers and colleagues what they thought, they warned him that the commute would be a nightmare at rush hour, and suggested prioritizing easy access to the office. So, he grudgingly chose practicality over luxury and settled for the $2.4 million townhouse instead.

He tried to make it nice, so that Ann would be comfortable when she visited. A decorator filled the house with tasteful furniture and calming abstract art. He planted a garden in the small backyard patio. But his wife rarely came to Washington, and neither did his sons, and gradually the house took on an unkempt bachelor-pad quality. Crumbs littered the kitchen counter; soda and seltzer filled the otherwise empty fridge. Old campaign paraphernalia appeared on the mantel, clashing with the decorator's mid-tone color scheme, and a bar of "Trump's Small Hand Soap" (a gag gift from one of his sons) was placed in the powder room alongside the monogrammed hand towels. In the "dining room," a ninety-eight-inch TV went up on the wall and a leather recliner landed in front of it. Romney, who didn't have many real friends in Washington, ate dinner there most nights alone, watching *Ted Lasso* or *Better Call Saul* as he leafed through briefing materials. On the day of my first visit, he showed me his freezer, which was full of salmon filets that had been given to him by Lisa Murkowski, the senator from Alaska. He didn't especially like salmon but found that if he put them on hamburger buns and smothered them in ketchup, they made for serviceable meals.

When I first told Romney I wanted to write a book about him, my pitch was straightforward. Few political figures in the twenty-first century had undergone a more interesting transformation than his. In less than a decade, he'd gone from Republican standard-bearer and presidential nominee to party pariah; from careful and calculating politician to unlikely model of moral courage in politics. What had happened? Why had he changed? Were there lessons in his evolution that might benefit future leaders?

Still, I worried that he might not be ready to answer these questions honestly. I remembered his presidential campaigns, the tightly controlled talking points, the near-religious conviction in staying on message. Some of his friends tried to wave me off the project. "He's not going to give you what you need," said one. I figured he'd balk when I told him my conditions—full access, complete candor, and to yield no editorial control. (He'd get to read the manuscript before it was published, but I'd be the one to decide what went in it.)

To my surprise, Romney responded to my terms as if they were a dare. He instructed his scheduler to start blocking off evenings for interviews, and told me no subject would be off-limits. He handed over hundreds of pages of his private journals, and years' worth of personal correspondence, including sensitive emails with some of the most powerful Republicans in the country. When he couldn't find the key to an old filing cabinet that contained some of his personal papers, he took a crowbar to it and deposited stacks of campaign documents and legal pads on my lap. He'd kept all this stuff, he explained, because he thought he might write a memoir one day, but he'd decided against it. "I can't be objective about my own life," he said.

In the spring of 2021, we began meeting every week he was in Washington. Some nights he vented; other nights he dished. He's more puckish than his public persona suggests, attuned to the absurdist humor of political life and quick to share stories others might consider indiscreet. I got the feeling he liked the company—the conversations sometimes stretched for hours.

Sitting across from Romney at seventy-five, one can't help but become a little suspicious of his handsomeness. The jowl-free jawline.

The all-seasons tan. The just-so gray at the temples of that thick black coif that his barber once insisted he doesn't dye. It all seems a little uncanny. Only after studying him closely do the signs of age start to show. He shuffles a little when he walks now, hunches a little when he sits. At various points in recent years, he's gotten so thin that his staff has worried about him. Mostly, he looks tired.

In our conversations, he often sounded like a spy behind enemy lines. He hadn't told anyone he was talking to a biographer, and we kept our meetings discreet. The senator still had a day job to do, and he didn't want to give his Republican colleagues another reason to distrust him. But Romney's disillusionment and alienation during the Trump era had freed him to look at the GOP with clearer eyes—and he wasn't sure he liked what he saw.

"A very large portion of my party," he told me one day, "really doesn't believe in the Constitution." He'd realized this only recently, he said, and it came as a surprise. Romney had internalized the partisan idea that Democrats were the ones who abandoned Constitutional principles in the name of "progress," while Republicans were committed to conserving them. But it's hard to live through an attempted insurrection that was instigated by the leaders of your party and still believe they mean it when they talk about their reverence for America's founding documents.

Now he was wrestling with some difficult questions. Was the authoritarian element of his party a product of President Trump, or had it always been there, just waiting to be activated by a sufficiently shameless demagogue? Was the rot on the right new, or was it something very old just now bubbling to the surface? And what role had the members of the mainstream establishment—people like him, the *reasonable* Republicans—played in allowing that rot to fester? To find the answers, he would need to go back, to pick through his thirty-year political career, accounting for the compromises he'd made and looking for clues.

I had never encountered a politician so openly reckoning with what his pursuit of power had cost, much less one doing so while still in office. Candid introspection and crises of conscience are much less expensive in retirement. But Romney was thinking, perhaps for the first time, beyond his own political future.

Shortly after moving into his Senate office, Romney had hung a long rectangular map on the wall. First printed in 1931 by Rand McNally, the "histomap" attempted to chart the rise and fall of the world's most powerful civilizations through four thousand years of human history. When he first acquired the map, he saw it as a curiosity. After January 6, he became obsessed with it. He showed the map to visitors, brought it up in conversations and speeches. More than once, he found himself staring at it alone in his office at night. The Egyptian empire reigned for some nine hundred years before it was overtaken by the Assyrians. Then the Persians, the Romans, the Mongolians, the Turks—each civilization had its turn, and eventually collapsed in on itself. Maybe the falls were inevitable. But what struck Romney most about the map was how thoroughly it was dominated by tyrants of some kind—pharaohs, emperors, kaisers, kings. "A man gets some people around him and begins to oppress and dominate others," he said the first time he showed me the map. "It's a testosterone-related phenomenon, perhaps. I don't know. But in the history of the world, that's what happens." America's experiment in self-rule "is fighting against human nature."

"This is a very fragile thing," he told me. "Authoritarianism is like a gargoyle lurking over the cathedral, ready to pounce."

For the first time in his life, he wasn't sure if the cathedral would hold.

CHAPTER ONE

The Body Upstream

Even into his seventies, Mitt Romney would evince a childlike excitement when he talked about his father, eyes bright, voice hurried, each anecdote imbued with a boyish sense of awe. The rise and fall of George Wilcken Romney had long ago taken on an allegorical quality in his mind—a parable of courage and duty, of a great man beset by the forces of evil who overcame obstacles and stuck to his guns and paid a tragic price for his ideals.

This story began sixty miles south of the Mexican border, in a remote Mormon colony founded by exiled nineteenth-century polygamists. There, surrounded by rugged mountains and vast stretches of empty desert, George was born into a family with modest means, a strange past, and an uncertain future. When George was five, Mexican revolutionaries raided the colony and the Romneys were forced to flee to the States, where his unlucky father, Gaskell, dragged them across the country looking for work—an ill-fated construction job in El Paso, a failed carpentry business in Los Angeles, a potato farm in Idaho that went bankrupt. Life was not easy for George, who cycled through six different elementary schools in six years, but the adversity made him tough. By the time he hit puberty, he was doing hard physical labor, trimming sugar beet crops by hand and working lath and plaster on construction sites, where, according to family legend, he mastered the art of holding several nails in his mouth at once and spitting them out, pointy end forward, with such force that they stuck into the beams before he hammered them into place.

Traveling the Mormon West with his family, George developed a romantic attachment to his heritage. After visiting one Latter-day Saint temple in Utah, he wrote that it was as stylish as the White House. When he was old enough to serve a mission, the Church sent him to England, where he spent his days preaching from a soapbox. Competing for attention amid the cacophony of speakers in Tower Hill Square wasn't easy, but George proved resourceful. He partnered with a red-bearded socialist who frequented the square, and the two of them took turns heckling each other to stir up interest from the crowd.

After his mission, George dabbled in college, but dropped out to follow his high school girlfriend, Lenore LaFount, to Washington, D.C., where her father had taken a job in the Coolidge administration. Pretty and bright and blessed with a prosperous family, Lenore had always been a bit out of George's league, and for a while she resisted his proposals. She pursued an acting career in New York and Hollywood; MGM offered her a contract. But George was as relentless in courtship as he was in everything else. His persistence was charming in its way, as was his mesmerizing ambition. "I'll build you a round house with seven bathrooms along the Hudson River," he promised her. Lenore believed him and chose marriage over movie stardom. Every morning for the rest of his life, he would wake early and leave a rose on her bedside table.

True to his word, George was driven in his career. He parlayed a typist job on Capitol Hill into a lobbying gig for the auto industry and then a position at American Motors, the smallest of the major automakers, where he hustled up the company ladder. Once he became CEO, he waged a Davidian campaign against the industry Goliaths, touring the country as he preached against the popular "gas-guzzlers" sold by his competitors. At the time, American Motors' signature

offering was the Rambler, a relatively cheap compact car that con-
trasted starkly with the boat-size Cadillacs and Continentals, defined
by their bulky metal frames and noisy engines. George's decision to
double down on the Rambler went against every bit of conventional
wisdom in the auto industry, and drew more than a little snickering
from the executives at General Motors and Ford. But swimming
against the tide came naturally to George. "When a Romney drowns,"
a Mormon leader once observed of George's ancestors, "you look for
the body upstream."

Every family has its own mythology, the stories they choose to tell about
themselves. The Romneys' stories tend to be about stubbornness. There
was George's father, Gaskell, who sued the Mexican government—and
won—after losing his home during the revolution. There was George's
uncle Rey, who defied a Mexican ban on foreign ministers and turned
up in Chihuahua anyway, enthusiastically passing out Spanish copies
of the Book of Mormon, and George's other uncle Vernon who staged
a one-man walkout at the 1952 Republican convention when the party
nominated Eisenhower.

The pattern began with Miles Romney, the nineteenth-century
British carpenter who, upon hearing Mormon missionaries preach
in a town square, renounced the Church of England, converted to
Mormonism, crossed the Atlantic, and walked across the American
plains to join his fellow Saints in building their desert Zion.

Charged with designing a tabernacle in the southern Utah settle-
ment of St. George, Miles became fixated on erecting a grand spiral staircase that would lead up to the second-story dais. When the
Mormon prophet, Brigham Young, saw the plans, he concluded that
the podium would be too high and instructed Miles to cut down the
staircase. Miles balked. The prophet insisted. A standoff ensued, and
nearly two hundred years later the St. George Tabernacle—with its
grand spiral staircase that rises majestically to the building's second

story before awkwardly descending ten feet to the dais—stands as a testament to the lengths a Romney man will go when he believes he is right about something. *Romneys were not descended like other humans,* the family saying goes. *We descended from the mule.*

On March 12, 1947, Lenore gave birth to their youngest child and George promptly declared him a "miracle baby." In a letter to friends and family announcing the arrival of Willard Mitt Romney, George revealed that Lenore had been diagnosed with a health condition that was supposed to prevent her from giving birth again. After the baby was delivered, a doctor who examined her marveled, "I don't see how she became pregnant or how she carried the child." To George, the answer was clear: "We consider it a blessing for which we must thank the Creator of all."

As the family "caboose," Mitt was able to spend more time with his father than his much-older siblings ever did. George took him to the office, let him watch as he worked the phones and met with subordinates—sometimes stern in his approach, Mitt noticed, but always respectful, never assuming he was the smartest guy in the room. He taught his son about the intricacies of the Rambler's construction—the unibody frame that was more durable than other models on the market, the ceramic-coated muffler, the first-of-its-kind heating-and-air-conditioning unit—and Mitt became convinced of American Motors' superiority.

One day, when he was still in elementary school, he asked his dad, "We make the best cars, right?"

"Yes," George said.

"Then why doesn't everybody buy our cars?"

"You need to understand," George replied, "that just being right or just being best doesn't mean that most people will agree with you."

American Motors would never overtake its dominant competitors, but George's bet on the Rambler paid off. Before long, the company's surprising turnaround had landed him on the cover of *Time* and prompted speculation about a future in politics. He certainly looked the part. Sounded it, too. Tall and trim, with a prominent jawline and a courtly coif of graying hair, he spoke in a steady, rumbling-train cadence, which, combined with his Jimmy Stewart–esque Midwestern accent, made him sound sensible and earnest. And his tendency to frame every subject in moral terms—whether he was talking about the "twin evils of big labor and big business" or carburetors—added a righteous dimension to his character. (When the journalist Theodore White met him, he observed that George possessed "a sincerity so profound that, in conversation, one was almost embarrassed.") Perhaps most helpfully, he had an innate populist streak that enabled him to wade confidently into any crowd. As CEO, he fielded phone calls at home from Rambler owners who had mechanical questions. Once, when union bosses refused to let him into a Labor Day picnic, he hopped the fence and spent the afternoon hobnobbing with his employees.

George decided to run for governor of Michigan, but not before embarking on a day of private fasting and prayer to seek divine guidance. The practice was common in his faith, but less common among non-Mormon constituents, and when Mitt casually mentioned it to a reporter, the fasting became a front-page story, causing one labor leader to scoff, Romney "thinks he has a direct pipeline to God." George, who had a talent for defusing politically fraught situations, responded that *everyone* has a direct pipeline to God—it's called prayer.

Soon, Mitt was riding shotgun for his father's political ascent. When George mounted a campaign to amend Michigan's state constitution, he drove his thirteen-year-old son to baseball games and sent him into the bleachers with a clipboard to gather signatures. And when George's campaign began in earnest, Mitt dutifully set up booths with loudspeakers at county fairs to stump for his dad. The experience did not exactly instill in young Mitt a love of politics. On the contrary, he quickly learned that he didn't get the same charge from working a crowd that his dad seemed to get. "I would not have done it because it was fun," he'd tell me later. "But did I hate it? It was okay. I'd set up next to the hot tamale guy, because I loved hot tamales."

Governor George Romney took office in January 1963 and planted himself squarely in the liberal wing of the Republican Party. In his first State of the State address he declared, "Michigan's most urgent human rights problem is racial discrimination—in housing, public accommodations, education, administration of justice, and employment." He established the state's first civil rights commission, and marched with activists protesting racist housing policies. When Martin Luther King Jr. came to Detroit, the governor issued a proclamation announcing Freedom March Day (though George didn't attend himself because King's visit fell on the Sabbath).

George saw himself as carrying on a righteous tradition that had defined his party from Abraham Lincoln to Dwight Eisenhower. But tectonic shifts were taking place in the Grand Old Party. Insurgents were taking over. Just a year after George was sworn in, Barry Goldwater—a radical right-wing senator from Arizona who opposed the Civil Rights Act of 1964 and wanted to purge liberals from the Republican Party—shocked the political world by capturing the presidential nomination. George was appalled by Goldwater, but he was even more dismayed by his followers—a motley horde of John Birchers, conspiracy theorists, and overtly racist segregationists who had arrayed themselves under a banner they called "conservatism." They were, in his estimation, "extremists" and "purveyors of hate," noxious outsiders hell-bent on "infiltrating" his party.

Determined to hold the line against the Goldwater crowd, George traveled to San Francisco in the summer of 1964 for the Republican National Convention. He spent the week fighting to add two new planks to the party platform—one in favor of civil rights, the other a condemnation of extremism—but both efforts were defeated. Walking around the Cow Palace that week, he saw clearly for the first time that he was outnumbered. Thousands of unruly conservatives had turned the convention into a festival of vulgarity—booing and hissing and creating an atmosphere that drew comparisons in the press to a Nazi rally.

When his turn to speak arrived, George delivered a thundering indictment of the new right-wing movement's excesses and pointedly refused to endorse Goldwater. The Republican Party, he reminded delegates, was originally formed in rebellion against the "extremism and lily-white Protestantism" that had come to define the now-extinct Whigs. His message: Don't allow the GOP to be overrun by the same forces.

The warning went unheeded, and a couple nights later the delegates enthusiastically lined up to support Goldwater, who declared victory by needling his do-gooding detractors. "Extremism in the defense of liberty is no vice," he said in his speech. When the convention hall erupted in applause, George remained quietly seated. His teenage son, who'd traveled with him to San Francisco, an "associate delegate" badge dangling around his neck, had only a limited understanding of what was going on, but he was sure of one thing. "If thousands of people were cheering and Dad was standing alone, I knew he was right and they were wrong," Mitt would tell me.

Goldwater suffered a historic electoral wipeout in the 1964 election, and for a brief moment it seemed as if George's party might come around to his point of view. He was widely touted as a front-runner in the upcoming Republican presidential primaries, and the party's liberal wing quickly coalesced around his candidacy. But George was unwilling to do what it took to win in this new political climate.

While his chief rival, Richard Nixon, plotted a campaign through the South—channeling white grievance and courting conservatives with a law-and-order message—George insisted on launching his campaign with a tour of America's inner cities. He met with Black Panthers and new-left radicals; he posed for photos with Saul Alinsky and gave speeches pleading with white America to wake up to the injustices in their country. "We must rouse ourselves from our comfort, pleasure, and preoccupations," he said, "and listen to the voices from the ghetto."

When, in the summer of 1967, Detroit erupted into an apocalyptic week of race riots—with footage of bombed-out city blocks and violent clashes with police filling the nation's television screens—Governor Romney refused to change course. He would not distance himself from the civil rights movement, nor would he join his white constituents in demonizing the rioters. In a statewide televised address, he chastised those who ignored the inequality fueling the riots. "Some already are saying the answer is brute force such as would be used on mad dogs," he said. "Others are questioning present social and economic programs because they claim Negroes don't appreciate what has already been done. . . . As citizens of Michigan, as Americans, we must unhesitatingly reject all these divisive courses."

Nixon rose in the polls.

The final unraveling of George's presidential candidacy took place in the studio of WKBD-TV. It was late August in 1967, and he was sitting for an interview with a local news anchor named Lou Gordon. The host asked the candidate if he had changed his mind about the Vietnam War. Two years earlier, when the conflict was still relatively contained, George had visited Vietnam with a delegation of governors. They were briefed by some generals, introduced to some wounded soldiers, and George returned with a hazy impression that the war was "morally right." Foreign policy had never been his strong suit, but he had a patriotic instinct to support the troops and the commander in chief. Lately, though, he'd been critical of the escalation in Vietnam, and had taken to echoing the antiwar arguments of Martin Luther King Jr. The reversal had become conspicuous.

Now presented with a chance to explain himself, George responded to the interviewer's question with characteristic bluntness. "When I came back from Vietnam," he said, "I had just had the greatest brain-washing that anybody can get."

He was trying to make a point—about the pretenses being used to justify the war, about the dishonest story military leaders had been telling, about the complicity of America's diplomatic corps and political class who continued to mislead the public while young soldiers were shipped off to die in the jungle. But when the interview aired, nobody wanted to talk about the point George was making. They wanted to talk about that incendiary word—*brainwashing*—and the unsettling images it evoked. Manchurian candidates. Religious cultists. Communist propagandists.

All at once, the brainwashing quote consumed George's campaign. The *Detroit News* condemned him; Republican leaders piled on. His free fall in the polls—already underway before the fateful interview—accelerated, and before a single vote was cast, George was forced to drop out of the race.

By the time all this took place, Mitt was four thousand miles away, serving a Mormon mission in France. Largely cut off from American news, he didn't know about the political fallout from the Detroit riots, or the potency of Nixon's southern strategy, or the sweeping realignment taking place in U.S. politics as conservatives completed their conquest of the GOP. What he did know, and what would stick with him for the rest of his life, was that a single poorly chosen word in a local TV interview had abruptly cut short his dad's march to the White House.

Decades later, Mitt would still get agitated when he revisited the episode, the sheer injustice of it all surfacing long-buried grievances: "When you say, 'Hey, I got brainwashed on this,' it doesn't mean you *literally* got brainwashed," he said. "It's a metaphor, it's a term that you use. It's not unheard of. And yet, I mean, I remember the cartoons. They had a cartoon of him in a washing machine, you know, spinning around. . . . They had another one with bubbles coming out the top of his skull."

To Mitt, it was *so obvious* what his dad meant, should have been obvious to everyone. "He's saying that he had believed he was being told the truth by our generals, and then he realized . . . that they were lying to him. He was saying, 'Hey, I was wrong. What they told me were lies and this is the truth.'"

The rant felt like one he'd recited a thousand times before. And yet, some part of him—the part that saw his dad's story as not just a heroic parable but a cautionary tale—also knew that it didn't matter. George Romney's presidential campaign—noble, idealistic, maybe a little naive—was felled by his most admirable and self-destructive quality: a stubborn insistence on telling the truth.

CHAPTER TWO

"This Means Something"

Strictly speaking, Mitt Romney didn't know he was a rich kid. His parents didn't talk about money, and his dad was painfully frugal. When double-breasted suits went out of style, George refused to waste money buying new ones and instead had a tailor take scissors to the suit coats to make the lapels single-breasted. By the time Mitt was old enough to notice the status signifiers that might have tipped him off, his family had settled in Bloomfield Hills, a prosperous suburb of Detroit where *everyone* seemed to drive the same nice cars and live in the same big, stately houses. Within this bubble of affluence, Mitt sometimes felt he was less pampered than other kids. His parents made him mow the lawn and shovel the driveway and spend his summers working on an Idaho ranch or pulling the graveyard security shift at the Chrysler plant. And yet, he clearly understood something about his place in the world because from a young age he carried himself with a kind of rich-kid carelessness—the untroubled air of someone who knew he could get away with anything.

Skinny and good-looking, with an impish sense of humor, young Mitt glided through grade school, charming and exasperating his teachers. When he was in fifth grade, a dispute over a baseball game at recess resulted in a scrum of shouting and insults and vulgar gestures, requiring the teachers to step in and mediate. Once the warring students were gathered, a classmate accused Mitt's team of cheating. Mitt, who knew the swear word associated with the middle finger but not what the swear word actually meant, fired back with his own accusation: "That's nothing," Mitt announced to the teachers, "Rickie Snyder went around f-ing all the girls!" A moment of stunned silence fell over the classroom, at which point a classmate shouted, "Romney, run for your life!" He dashed down the hallway and locked himself in an empty art room with his friend, who filled him in on the birds and the bees for the first time. His mother was eventually summoned to the principal's office, but nothing came of it. The transgression had been innocent enough, and besides, that was just Mitt being Mitt.

The Romneys had high hopes for their precocious youngest son. They saw his potential, and in some ways, they saw themselves in him. George delighted in arguing with Mitt, their debates often dominating the family dinner table until both were laughing and gasping for breath. On road trips, Lenore read aloud from the poetry of Sam Walter Foss—*Bring me men to match my mountains*—and Tennyson's *Idylls of the King*. But the calls to greatness fell flat. Mitt loved his parents, but he felt little drive to rise to their expectations.

When he was twelve, he entered Cranbrook, the private boarding school to which Michigan's ruling class sent its children, and quickly learned that he wouldn't make it as a jock. The football team cut him at tryouts, and he spent his brief wrestling career getting his limbs bent in ways they were not meant to bend by boys much stronger than he was. Even track, that last refuge of the unathletic teenager, was ruled out after he discovered by way of the presidential fitness exam that he ran the slowest fifty-yard dash in his class. He spent time in the yearbook office and the glee club, and one year his mother even urged him—as a kind of Mormon *rumspringa*—to join the "smoking club." "If he wants to smoke," she insisted, "he can smoke." Mitt did not want to smoke, but he enrolled in the club anyway to appease his mom and never attended a meeting.

Mitt's true extracurricular passion was pranks. He was the kid who filled dorm rooms with shaving cream and blared obnoxious *ooga* horns during slow dances. He liked to dress up as a firefighter and run into stores pulling a hose and shouting, "This place is gonna blow!" After acquiring a siren and some blue lighting gels from the campus auditorium, he drove around town posing as a police officer and "pulling over" his friends.

He was not much of a partier—the one time he drank, he threw up, passed out, and swore off alcohol for the rest of his life—but he had a knack for getting into trouble with the law. By his own count, he was arrested three times between 1965 and 1968. None of the run-ins resulted in a criminal record, in part because they were relatively innocent—one included trespassing on a private hill for a late night of ice blocking—and in part because he was white and wealthy and the son of a governor.

Much later in life, he would recast these episodes as the acting out of a young man riven by insecurity. He wanted so badly to be an athlete, he would explain, but the sports he was good at, like waterskiing and paddle tennis, "don't really count, you know, in high school." So, he compensated with mischief.

Not everyone would buy this. Decades later, some classmates would recall Romney bullying a gay classmate at Cranbrook—pinning him down and forcibly cutting his hair while a "prep school posse" cheered him on. When the episode eventually wound up in the *Washington Post*, in the heat of his second presidential campaign, Romney had no memory of it, and found the accusation implausible. He barely knew what homosexuality was in 1965, he'd claim—in his cloistered suburban world, the only gay person he'd known was his mom's interior decorator. The idea that he would have suspected a student of being gay, let alone that he would have singled him out for humiliation based on that suspicion, struck him as absurd. He gave a vague apology during the campaign—"There's no question but that I did some stupid things when I was in high school"—and tried to forget about the whole thing.

But if he was being honest with himself, Romney also knew that he was capable of adolescent cruelty. Certain memories had clung to his conscience—pulling out a classmate's chair and watching him fall to the floor in tears while the rest of the class laughed; snickering at the boy in church with a cleft palate who blessed the sacrament and seeing the humiliation in his face. Even many decades later, he would think about those boys sometimes, wondering if they were still out there, wondering how he might say sorry, wondering who else he might have hurt.

By the time he reached his senior year of high school, Mitt was churning through girlfriends at a steady clip. He was outgoing and popular and he had a car. (His parents had left a Rambler in the garage when they moved into the governor's mansion in Lansing.) His pattern, not entirely novel among teenage boys, was to take an interest in a girl, pursue her tenaciously, and then move on as soon as she reciprocated his interest.

Then he met Ann Davies. He saw her for the first time at a party. She was beautiful and wholesome and slightly reserved in a way that intrigued him, not bubbly and loud like other girls. She was also fifteen, a sophomore at Cranbrook's sister school, which suggested to Mitt that she'd be easy to impress. For their first date, he took her out to dinner at the Detroit Athletic Club, where his dad was a member, and then to a screening of *The Sound of Music*. More dates followed, as well as regular nightly phone calls between dorms, but as Mitt became more infatuated she remained standoffish.

Shortly after they began dating, Mitt had to spend a few days in the hospital with appendicitis, during which time, he learned, Ann went on a date with another boy. When Mitt confronted her, expecting a sheepish apology, Ann was defiant. "Do you think you own me or something?" she demanded. "I've gone out with you a few times, that means I can't go out with someone else? I'm supposed to clear that with you?" Mitt was in love.

Ann eventually fell in love, too, but she had other things on her mind. One night, after a date, Mitt parked on a quiet hill near his family's house and leaned in to kiss her. She stopped him with a decidedly unsexy question: "What do Mormons believe?"

This was not a subject he was interested in discussing right at that moment, but he dutifully searched his mind for an answer. He recited the Church's first Article of Faith: "We believe in God, the Eternal Father, and in His Son Jesus Christ, and in the Holy Ghost." To Mitt's alarm, this led to a theological conversation about the nature of God. The subject had been bothering Ann ever since her Episcopal priest suggested to her that he didn't believe in a divine being so much as a general presence of good in the world—an abstract notion that had left Ann cold and searching. Now, as she listened to Mitt describe his church's teaching that God is a person, a literal heavenly father who knows and cares about each of His children, she was overwhelmed with emotion and began to cry. With the prospect of romance now fully evaporated, Mitt spent the rest of the evening reciting other passages of Mormon scripture to his intensely fascinated girlfriend.

Mitt took Ann to prom later that year and told her that he wanted to marry her one day. She said she felt the same way. But when he suggested that he might skip his Mormon mission so that they could start their lives together sooner, she balked. Somehow, she knew better than he did how important his faith would become to him.

"You'll resent me for the rest of your life," she told him. "You have to go."

Mitt spent a year studying at Stanford, and when the time came he submitted his papers to serve a thirty-month mission. He prayed for an assignment to Great Britain, where his father and great-grandfather had served. George even called in a favor with a friend on the Church's missionary committee, who said he would do his best. But when Elder Thomas S. Monson, an apostle in the church, reviewed the list of missionary assignments, he stopped at Romney's name and said, "That's the wrong mission. He's supposed to go to France."

Mitt arrived in the country a few months later, and was assigned to serve in Le Havre, a working-class port city in Normandy that was still recovering from its decimation during the war two decades earlier. The city had a haunted quality to it; according to mission lore, the last missionaries sent to Le Havre were never heard from again.

Romney and three other missionaries took rooms in a hotel across the street from the train station that they would only later learn to be a brothel and went to work. Rising early each morning and mounting their Mobylettes, they scoured the city for people who were willing to listen to young American men share a message about Jesus Christ in broken French. It was a tough sell. Le Havre was predominantly communist, and the residents' default skepticism of religion was compounded by their dislike of Americans, whom they blamed for the bombardment that leveled their city in World War II.

Every day, Romney and his fellow missionaries would pick one of the brutalist concrete towers in town, climb the stairs to the top, and spend hours trudging through the halls, knocking on doors one by one and getting them slammed in their faces: "I don't want any"—BANG—"Get out of Vietnam"—BANG—"*No, no, no*"—BANG.

Entire months would pass like this, without a single person inviting them in to talk. Their shoes wore out; their feet blistered. The Sabbath offered little respite from the rejection—because there were no Mormons in Le Havre, there was no church to attend on Sundays—and their meager budgets meant that they could usually afford to eat just two meals a day.

For Romney, the governor's son, the prep school prankster, this was something altogether new. The day-in-day-out grind, the punishing schedule—it was worse than difficult; it felt pointless. "Why are we doing this?" he repeatedly asked the other missionaries. "We're accomplishing nothing." Back home, he had friends and school and a future and a girlfriend with whom he was madly in love. Here, he just had those concrete towers with their endless flights of stairs and their ever-slamming doors.

Making matters worse, Romney had developed a persistent case of diarrhea shortly after arriving in Le Havre. The condition left him weak and dehydrated, when he wasn't scrambling for a toilet, and no matter what he did, he couldn't seem to find a cure. The low point came one day when he and his companion were talking to a family they'd just met in a courtyard. Suddenly feeling as though he might faint, Romney hobbled out to the street, collapsed into a gutter, and soiled himself.

It was around this time that Elder Romney received a book from his parents in the mail, *The Autobiography of Parley Parker Pratt*. A distant ancestor on his father's side, Pratt was one of Mormonism's legendary early missionaries, having baptized hundreds of people as he preached the gospel throughout North America. Reading the book one night in his run-down room in Le Havre, Romney came across a story about Pratt's own early struggles as a missionary. Pratt had spent months laboring in New York City without converting a single soul. Then, one day, he kneeled to pray with his companions and received a miraculous vision. "The Lord said that He had heard our prayers, beheld our labors, diligence, and long suffering towards that city and that He had seen our tears," Pratt wrote. "Our prayers were heard, and our labors and sacrifices were accepted."

Romney's room did not fill with light when he read the passage; he did not receive a vision. But it struck him with the force of something divine. *Our sacrifices were accepted.* This was the point of his mission, he now realized—doing the hard thing, making the sacrifice. Maybe it would yield fruit, maybe it wouldn't. But the difficulty and deprivation would have their own sanctifying effect, and that was reason enough to keep trying.

Romney's mission didn't necessarily get easier after that. In Nantes, a group of drunk rugby players dragged him into a brawl and he wound up in a police station; in Villemomble, he was arrested again for "impersonating a military official" after he made the mistake of wearing an old army PT jacket he'd picked up at a flea market. He lived in a procession of barely livable apartments—one with fleas, one with contaminated water, one with a hole in the floor for a toilet—and discovered a new appreciation for the amenities of home. In Versailles, he spent a winter in a tenement whose only source of heat was a coal boiler that needed to be stoked through the night. One night, a bleary-eyed missionary accidentally set a can of gasoline on fire and flames engulfed the living room. That Elder Romney experienced these things as character-building misadventures was a sign of his growing fondness for missionary life.

There was, it turned out, something liberating about struggling for a purpose greater than himself. He'd seen his father make sacrifices, but had always assumed they were made in a spirit of grim forbearance. Now Romney was glimpsing the peace of mind that came from setting aside personal striving for the sake of service. In a letter to his parents, he wrote, "Getting up at 6:00—cold, tired, allergic, broke, but without a worry in the world; living for others, dependent only upon God; joy when you hear of others' successes—where would I have ever known these things if it weren't for a mission?" He was beginning to see his time in France as the beginning of a grand future: "If I keep in the same stream, my joy will double, triple, and be multiplied eternally. Eternal wedlock, service to the Church, children, service to the world and my country! The Lord must have loved us to give us all this joy."

As his faith deepened and his French improved, Elder Romney got better at finding new converts. But the most meaningful conversion of his mission took place back in Michigan, where Ann had been attending church every Sunday with his parents. He was surprised by the relief he felt when he received the letter from his girlfriend informing him that she'd decided to join his Church. Romney had never especially cared about this before—he would have happily married an

Episcopalian as long as it was Ann Davies. But his Mormon faith no longer felt to him like just a part of his heritage, an interesting heirloom passed down by his fathers. It was expanding, gaining texture, attaching itself to every part of him.

On an overcast June morning near the end of his mission, Romney climbed into the driver's seat of a Church-owned sedan and headed north toward Bordeaux with a gaggle of mission leaders in tow. He felt good. They'd just completed an eventful visit to a small Mormon branch in the southern city of Pau, where France's mission president, H. Duane Anderson, had been summoned to mediate a feud between two elderly women that was dividing the congregation. After a day of meetings, they'd returned to their car to find it trapped in the middle of an outdoor market, surrounded by vendors' stalls. Anderson feared they were stuck for the day, but Romney took initiative. "*Il nous faut partir!*" he announced to the market—"We must go!"—before forging into the crowd and doling out five-franc coins until the vendors cleared a path. It was an impressive display of initiative, the kind of thing that had gotten Romney assigned in these final months of his mission to serve as an assistant to the mission president, the highest post available to a young Mormon elder. After twenty-one years of hearing endlessly about his "potential," Romney felt like he was starting to live up to it.

Later, he would try to remember those last details of the drive as he wound along the narrow, northbound roads that passed through the village of Bernos-Beaulac. President Anderson and his wife, Leola, sitting next to him; Elder Wood and the Mormon couple from Bordeaux in the back. The contours of the silver Citroën, with its long, animal hood. The viridescent landscape out the window all rolling hills and vineyards. The black Mercedes swerving so fast into his lane that he didn't have time to honk. The crunch of metal. The shattering of glass. The screams. *Were there screams?*

But Romney's only clear memory, the only thing he could be certain wasn't reconstructed from others' accounts, was waking up on the ground and peering up at the gray sky as a light rain fell. Then Elder Wood's hands on his head, and the hurried recitation of a blessing, and the ambulance and the hospital and finally the news: Leola Anderson was dead.

Romney spent several days at a hospital in Bazas after the accident. He'd been in such bad shape when police arrived on the scene that, in their report, they initially wrote he was dead. In fact, Romney was merely unconscious, with a broken arm, a head injury, and some nasty gashes and bruises. While he recovered over the following days, he learned more about what had happened. The driver of the Mercedes was a priest, possibly drunk, and was going about seventy-five miles per hour when he collided with the Citroën at an angle that had pinned Romney's body against the door and sent the steering column into Leola's chest, puncturing her lung. She'd survived for a couple of hours, but the doctors were unable to keep her alive.

Leola was a beloved matriarchal figure in the mission, and her death devastated Romney. He'd gotten to know her well while serving as her husband's assistant. She teased him about Ann, offered relationship advice, served him home-cooked meals. Everybody assured him that the accident wasn't his fault. The other car was moving too fast. There were no brake marks on the road. *There was nothing you could have done.* Some even suggested that he should be grateful, that perhaps he'd been saved by divine intervention, but the thought made him uncomfortable.

No one would have blamed Elder Romney for cutting his mission short, but he refused to go home. When President Anderson returned to the States to bury his wife and heal, Romney effectively ran the mission with his companion—setting ambitious new goals, offering solace to mourning missionaries, and generally staying busy enough to keep the grief and guilt at bay. But he could already feel his brush with death changing him. "Being at a point where the person next to you in an automobile dies," he'd later recall, "and you're in a position where you could have died—it says, 'Okay, this means something.'" Romney had become violently acquainted with the fact of his own mortality. It was time to start taking his life more seriously.

CHAPTER THREE

Hurry

Romney returned from France, just before Christmas in 1968, in a hurry. He proposed to Ann on the ride home from the airport, married her three months later, and immediately transferred from Stanford to Brigham Young University.

He was coming home to America at a moment of enormous social and political upheaval. On college campuses across the country, protests raged and debates over Vietnam and civil rights dominated student life. But on the idyllic, Church-owned campus of BYU, nestled at the foot of Utah's Wasatch Mountains, a Mormon ethos of pragmatism reigned. Clean-cut students were taught to tune out the noise of the late sixties and focus on the essentials: faith, family, and—for the men, at least—preparing for a career.

Romney, who majored in English, considered going into academia. He loved books, saw them as puzzles to be solved, and imagined a life spent poring over Shakespeare, Steinbeck, and Dickens. But his favorite professor talked him out of it. "You can afford to read all the books you'd like," he said. "Why would you get a PhD and starve?" The professor suggested an MBA or a law degree; Romney decided to get both.

By the time he arrived at Harvard, he and Ann already had two kids and plans for more. Unlike the other grad students, who lived in cramped Cambridge apartments, the Romneys settled in suburban Belmont. Mitt mowed the lawn on weekends. Ann cooked dinner and took care of the kids. On Sundays, they attended the local Mormon ward. When classmates visited the Romneys' home, they felt like they were "visiting a friend's parents," one reporter would later note, "not members of their own generation."

As a student in Harvard's newly formed JD/MBA program, Romney put in long hours studying, convinced that he would fall behind if he didn't outwork other students. George W. Bush, who overlapped with him at Harvard Business School, remembered Romney as a "sober guy." "I didn't spend a lot of time with him, nor did I spend a lot of time in the library as he must have done," Bush told me. "At Harvard, there's a lot of people who believe the word 'Harvard' entitles them to think they're smarter than everybody else. Mitt Romney was not that way."

Romney didn't have to struggle for long between pursuing a career in business or law. He spent his first summer interning at a law firm in Detroit, where he was assigned to a case involving the placement of a fountain in a public park. He found the low stakes and legal minutiae maddening. *I cannot do this with my life*, he thought. The next summer, he interned at the Chrysler Corporation, working in a division that oversaw company-owned car dealerships. The work was more interesting, but he was frustrated by his lack of influence as an entry-level cog in a vast corporate machine. "My boss's boss's boss had never met the CEO," he'd later recall. He realized he was too impatient to engage in the slow ladder climbing that his father's generation had accepted without question. He wanted a job where he could make an impact right away.

He found it the next summer. Management consulting was taking off in the 1970s, and his classmates had begun to notice that the blue-chip consulting firms paid even better than the investment banks that typically attracted Harvard's best and brightest. Romney liked that his internship at Boston Consulting Group was coveted by his peers, but he was even more taken with the work itself. As a consultant, you didn't have to wait around for decades of incremental promotions before you were dealing with CEO-level issues; you got to dig in right away. As soon as he graduated, he accepted a job at the firm.

The founder of BCG, Bruce Henderson, had earned his place in the canon of modern management theory with pioneering ideas about competitive advantage, and the environment he fostered at the company was, well, competitive. Inside a closet in BCG's sixteenth-floor offices, the partners kept a list that ranked all the consultants at the firm by the number of billable hours they logged. Romney instantly identified the list as a race that he needed to win. The competition was stiff: his coworkers included several future CEOs as well as Benjamin Netanyahu, the eventual prime minister of Israel. But Romney slogged through enough late nights and weekends to ensure that he was at the top of the list each week.

His hurry manifested at home as well, where Mitt and Ann had five sons in the space of eleven years. Each boy played his own role in the family. "I was the typical oldest child—type A, driven to succeed," Tagg Romney would tell me. "Matt was a little bit younger than I was, and liked to push people's buttons, loved an argument. Josh was a classic middle child, very tender, very much a homebody, would never go sleep at somebody else's house because he missed his mom too much. Ben was very quiet, reserved, living in his own world, really took after my mom's dad, who was an engineer—a deep thinker. And Craig was the baby. Totally spoiled, totally lived by his own rules. Everyone adored him, everyone wanted to hold him as a baby and play with him as a little kid."

The Romney home could be chaotic and loud. Basketballs flew across the living room. Wrestling matches broke out spontaneously. More than once, Ann became so overwhelmed by the boys' misbehavior that she simply got in her car and drove away. But there were also moments of quiet. At night, they had a tradition of gathering in the living room, turning off the lights, and having an uninhibited conversation where the boys were encouraged to share whatever was on their minds. "As a teenager, it's hard to talk openly with your parents," Tagg would recall. "It was a good time to be able to express doubts, share concerns, question things, and be able to not feel like your parents were looking at you and judging you."

As Romney put in long hours at the office, he began to worry that his professional drive was interfering with his responsibilities at home. He was constantly on the road, and routinely missed family dinners. The guilt he felt was as much religious as it was paternal. Families play a central role in Mormon theology. Marriage is considered an eternal bond, and the afterlife is often depicted as a joyful, sprawling tangle of family reunions. David O. McKay, who was president of the Church when Mitt and Ann married, preached about the need to prioritize family life over everything else: "No other success can compensate for failure in the home."

When Bain & Company offered him a job in 1977, Romney told the partners he'd take it, but only if they agreed to a few conditions: he would not work on Sundays, which were reserved for church; he would not work on Wednesday nights, which were reserved for volunteer ministry duties; and with few exceptions, he would be unreachable on weekends so he could spend time with his family.

These were unusual demands for a rising corporate star, but Romney knew he would never live up to his ideals as a husband and father unless he drew bright, uncrossable lines for himself. Decades later, he would look back on his life and conclude with satisfaction that he'd succeeded in honoring those lines when it came to his family. His professional life was a different story.

Romney rose quickly at Bain. He was smart, hardworking, and relentlessly analytical, never allowing emotion or ideology to cloud his judgment. He also had an effortless Harvard-man confidence that impressed the bosses. Bill Bain, one of the firm's founding partners, would recall taking an immediate liking to Romney. "He was very good looking. He was very comfortable in his body. He moved gracefully. He wasn't awkward. He had the appearance of confidence of a guy who was maybe ten years older."

But as talented as he was, Romney realized that he would never be one of Bain's "rainmakers." The consultants who brought in the most money were the ones who put in the extra hours on the golf course; who took out clients for long, luxurious dinners; who schmoozed. Romney did not schmooze. "As soon as I had solved the problem before me, I wanted to be home with my kids," he said.

After a few years, Romney was offered a vice president job at a firm in Chicago. When Romney told Bain he was entertaining the offer, his boss made him a deal: Stick around for a promotion, and if it didn't materialize within the year he could walk away with a $100,000 check. A year later, Romney was placed in charge of the firm's new private equity arm.

Romney presented Bain Capital as an investment firm that understood the intricacies of operating a business better than the typical spreadsheet-obsessed venture capitalists. Rather than simply crunching numbers from the comfort of their offices, Romney's "Bainiacs" would embed inside the companies they were funding and draw on their consulting roots to make each business a success. Romney's early deals suggested a Midas touch—most notably Staples, a local office supply store started by a pair of businessmen in a Boston suburb. With Bain Capital's help, Staples went on to open nearly eight hundred stores in fifteen years, returning 5.75 times Bain's investment. Powered by such high-profile successes, Bain Capital grew from a relatively small $37 million fund to one of the nation's preeminent leveraged buyout firms.

Still, Romney insisted on maintaining an ethic of frugality at the firm. Employees were ordered to fly coach, and told that any meals they expensed while traveling should be "nourishing, but not memorable." He argued that investors would appreciate seeing their money put to good use and not wasted on lavish expense accounts. But the policy was also rooted in how Romney lived his own life. Even as his personal wealth ballooned during his Bain Capital years—growing to more than $200 million by the time he left—he resisted conspicuous spending. His family had no full-time nannies, cooks, or maids, and despite encouragement from his sons to buy a BMW or Mercedes, he insisted on continuing to drive a dented Chevy Caprice Classic that he proudly nicknamed "the gray grunt."

By the time the Romneys finally decided to spend some of their fortune—buying an impressive colonial in their neighborhood, and renovating it to include a pool and a tennis court—Tagg was serving a Mormon mission in France. After seeing photos of his parents' new home, a bewildered Tagg wrote back: "How can you afford that house?"

At the same time Romney's career was taking off, his responsibilities in the lay leadership of The Church of Jesus Christ of Latter-day Saints were expanding. His choice to abstain from work on Sundays had left him time to volunteer extensively in the small Boston-area Mormon community, and the experience was often humbling. He visited families broken by poverty; ministered to men who struggled with addiction. He developed a special relationship with one boy in his early teens who was suffering from cancer. When the young man wanted to become an Eagle Scout, Romney helped him earn the requisite merit badge. When he decided he wanted to write a will, Romney came to the house with a legal pad and diligently recorded which friends and family members would receive his various possessions. Romney spent the boy's final days at his bedside in the hospital. "These are experiences that people in the business world don't normally have," Romney would recall years later.

After a few years as a bishop in the Belmont ward, he was asked to serve as a stake president, overseeing about a dozen congregations in eastern Massachusetts. He stepped into the role at a tense moment.

The Boston suburbs had become the epicenter of a growing Mormon feminist movement that was challenging the Church's male-dominated hierarchy and some of its teachings on gender. They launched a new publication, *Exponent II*, and ran heterodox articles exploring the concept of a "heavenly mother" and agitating for women to receive the priesthood. "Mitt was very anti–*Exponent II*," Barbara Taylor, a former president of the publication, would recall. "He thought we were just a bunch of bored, unhappy housewives trying to stir up trouble."

As the activism attracted national attention, Romney was put in an uncomfortable position. On one side, he faced pressure from the Church's Salt Lake City headquarters, where officials were eager to tamp down the noise. On the other, progressive members of his flock were demanding to be heard. His own views on the matter were fairly traditional, but he was not a zealot—and over time, he found that his natural pragmatism was an advantage.

One evening, after he became stake president, he gathered the most vocal feminists in the stake and leveled with them. "Look, I can't change the doctrine of the Church," he said. "So don't look to me to give women the priesthood." But if they had other ideas to make the Church more equitable, he said, "let's talk about them." Gradually, hands went up and reforms were proposed.

The changes he went on to enact were largely modest and symbolic. He began asking more men to care for children in the Church's Primary, and broke with an old, patriarchal tradition by inviting female leaders of the Church's Relief Society to visit other congregations and offer sermons, as male leaders did. He wrote out a list of proposed reforms to share with the Church's general authorities, including prioritizing women's athletic programs in the Church and requiring men to share more in the "menial tasks" such as serving dinners at ward functions.

Romney knew these measures wouldn't fully satisfy the feminists in his stake. And sure enough, some would remember his handling of their concerns as condescending and dismissive. "He is incredibly entitled," said Judy Dushku, a Mormon political scientist who clashed with Romney in Belmont. He "feels like his story is the most important." But others saw his gestures as ones of goodwill. "Maybe he's made some mistakes, but I think he did have women's best interests at heart," recalled Robin Baker, who helped run *Exponent II.* "Was he a little bit flat-sided? Maybe. But he was also light-years beyond the Church at that time."

A month after the meeting, Romney wrote a letter to the Church's headquarters in Salt Lake City. "In the weeks that have followed," he reported, "the energy which had previously been focused on 'women's issues' has declined precipitously."

In his hurry, he cut corners. Of course he did. No one makes it as a titan of industry by walking the straight and narrow all the time.

Some of Romney's ethical lapses would feel, later on, like gray areas. His decision to start retroactively charging Bain's clients transaction fees that they hadn't agreed to up front might have been questionable, but it was standard industry practice—he was simply bringing Bain in line with his competitors.

Other moves were less defensible. When unionized factories were shut down by Bain-owned companies, executives negotiated the terms of the closure with labor leaders. But the workers at the nonunion plants were often sent packing with a couple weeks' severance and no job prospects in towns where the closures would devastate the local economy. At the Ampad paper plant in Marion, Indiana, more than 250 workers lost their jobs; at the Dade International plant in Puerto Rico, nearly 300 people were laid off.

When Romney put his mind to it, he could rationalize the layoffs. These companies had already been hemorrhaging money when he got there; he had a fiduciary responsibility to his investors to make them profitable; he was just honoring the employment contracts that the workers had signed. But the logical power of these arguments tended to wilt when Romney was faced with the vivid reality: men piling into cars with pink slips, driving home to tell their wives that they weren't sure how they'd cover the mortgage or pay for groceries next month.

Romney discovered, during these episodes, a remarkable ability to justify his choices to himself. It's not that he was without a moral compass; his conscience was well developed and frankly rather pushy. But he found it could sometimes be appeased with sufficient effort. "I have learned through my life experience . . . that it's human to rationalize what's in our best interest," he'd tell me. It was a trait he'd wrestle with for the rest of his life—never more so than when he entered politics.

By 1993, Romney had conquered the world of high finance, and his eye was beginning to wander. When he was young, his father had advised him not to run for office until he was financially independent and his children were grown. Mitt had paid little attention at the time—watching his dad's campaigns had more or less spoiled his appetite. But now that he was richer than he'd ever planned on getting and his youngest son was nearly out of the house, politics seemed like the next logical step.

Romney was not particularly partisan—a registered independent, he'd donated to candidates in both parties—but there was one Democrat he was tempted to take on: Ted Kennedy. Widely known as the "liberal lion of the Senate," Kennedy was a dominant figure in Massachusetts politics, having held his seat since 1962. But people were starting to whisper that he'd lost a step—he'd gained weight and was increasingly prone to verbal stumbles; rumors of day drinking and womanizing abounded.

Romney's own misgivings focused on policy: He believed Kennedy's commitment to expanding the welfare state was more likely to trap people in poverty than help them escape. But a stubborn part of him was also put off by the unearned reverence that surrounded Kennedy in Massachusetts. Romney hadn't forgotten Mary Jo Kopechne, or Chappaquiddick, or all the rumored mistresses and victims of Ted's appetites. And yet, decade after decade, the surviving son of Massachusetts' first family skated to reelection without a serious challenger, largely because of his last name. Romney thought it was time for someone to make him earn it.

In a meeting with Bill Weld, the Republican governor of Massachusetts, Romney shared his interest in running against Kennedy and asked what he thought. Weld replied bluntly: "You can't possibly win." A few weeks later, Romney met with Charley Manning, an experienced GOP consultant, and put the same question to him. Manning said it would be a suicide mission.

The following Sunday, the Romneys fasted and prayed about whether he should run, but Mitt had all but made up his mind against it. Kennedy was unbeatable. The campaign would be a humiliation. Everyone was telling him the same thing—everyone, that is, except Ann.

That night, she told him that she'd had a strange impression while praying: *This will be, for us, like Zion's Camp.* As a convert, Ann was not steeped in Mormon history, and wasn't even sure she knew what the term referred to. Mitt told her the whole story: that "Zion's Camp" was a nineteenth-century expedition led by the early Mormons to reclaim territory that had been seized from them in Missouri; that the expedition was disbanded amid a deadly cholera outbreak before any land was reclaimed; that while the expedition failed, the men involved were strengthened by their trials and prepared for greater things to come.

By the time he finished, Romney knew he was going to run.

The first shock in Romney's education as a Senate candidate came when his advisers told him to grab his Rolodex. To stand any chance of winning, they said, Romney would have to spend much of the next year calling the people in that Rolodex and asking them for money. Friends, family members, coworkers, classmates—everybody would have to pony up. Romney, who had a patrician's distaste for discussing money in polite company, found the experience profoundly uncomfortable. It was a useful harbinger for what was to come.

Everything about running for office, it turned out, was uncomfortable. The reporters rooting through his personal life. The primping and preening before press conferences. The careful calibration of every public utterance. This last requirement was especially difficult for Romney. He'd seen how his dad, a much greater man than him, had been quelled by a gaffe, and so he was careful to rely on the counsel of the political professionals on his staff. But what this meant, in practice, was that he was never quite allowed to say what he actually meant. Early on, when a Republican primary opponent attacked him for having donated to Democrats, Romney wanted to respond, "There are good people in both parties and I give to the ones I believe in." But his advisers vetoed the language: there would be no talk of "good people" on the other side while trying to win the GOP nomination.

Even more fraught was how to articulate his stance on abortion. Before he entered the campaign, Manning had told him flatly, "If you're not pro-choice, you're not going to win." Such were the politics of Massachusetts that the state's Republicans were even more liberal on the issue than the heavily Catholic Democrats. Romney, who took his cues on such matters from his own faith, had long been morally opposed to abortion. Now he wondered if there was any wiggle room in the Church's teachings. As he studied the question, the incentive for rationalization was strong: He found quotes from church leaders who said abortion was "like unto murder"—*but they didn't say it* was *murder.* And while the Church didn't take an official position on when the spirit enters the body, he discovered that a close reading of certain verses could lead one to conclude that it took place sometime after conception. He also seized on the Church's twelfth Article of Faith, which declares a belief in "obeying, honoring, and sustaining the law." He "began to think abortion was a bit like polygamy," he told me later. Before Utah joined the United States, the Church acknowledged the illegality of polygamy and renounced the practice out of respect for the law. Abortion, he reasoned, had been legalized through *Roe v. Wade*—perhaps he had a similar responsibility to honor that?

Eventually, Romney staked out a tortured position on the issue—neither pro-choice nor pro-life, but tepidly supportive of the status quo. If elected, he pledged, he would not vote for any changes to current abortion law.

It didn't feel at the time like selling out. It never really does. "I had convinced myself that I was right," he'd later reflect. "I mean, I could have taken a lie detector test. . . . That's the point of rationalizing. You don't have to live with it."

Of course, taking the stance he did only presented more lines to be crossed. When Planned Parenthood invited him to speak at an event, he dutifully attended—*I can't really say no, can I?* In speeches and interviews, he found himself slipping into pro-choice talking points that he didn't totally believe. A low point came during one of the debates, when Kennedy attacked him for his inconsistency—"I am pro-choice. My opponent is multiple-choice"—and Romney, feeling cornered, launched into a bracingly personal story about a member of his extended family who had died from a botched illegal abortion. The story was true—the woman in question was his brother-in-law's sister—but his weaponization of it was disingenuous. Even worse, he hadn't asked his brother-in-law beforehand if he could share the story in public.

Some of the indignities of campaign life were things he would laugh about later—Kennedy's aides demanding wider podiums at the debates so as to cover the senator's girth; Romney applying antiperspirant to his upper lip to stop from sweating on TV, only to discover just before going onstage that it had created tiny makeup bubbles on his face. But others would sting, even decades later.

As polls tightened in the fall of 1994, Kennedy's campaign ramped up attacks on Romney's record at Bain Capital. They tracked down laid-off workers at the Ampad factory in Indiana and used their testimonials to paint Romney as a ruthless plutocrat who profited from destroying livelihoods. "I'd like him to show me where these 10,000 jobs that he created are," one worker who lost his job said in a commercial. Another said, "I'd like to say to the people of Massachusetts: 'If you think it can't happen to you, think again. We thought it wouldn't happen here [in Indiana], either.'"

Romney was incensed by the attack ads, and instructed his campaign to mount a vigorous defense. But while some of the rhetoric was beyond the pale, it wasn't until later that he'd realize why they bothered him so much: they contained a seed of truth. "There's no attack," he told me, "that hurts like one that's accurate."

Pundits would later point to the anti-Bain ads as the silver bullet that killed Romney's candidacy. But his real problem was that the rumors of Kennedy's decline turned out to be greatly exaggerated. Romney realized it right away during their first debate. They were discussing criminal sentences for minors, and Romney thought he had laid a clever rhetorical trap for his opponent—only to watch Kennedy sidestep the whole thing and begin righteously bellowing, "*Give me a break, Mr. Romney, give me a break!*" Romney could hardly keep from laughing. Here was that Kennedy gene that everybody talked about—the charisma, the audacity, the larger-than-life presence. *That big fella can hunt!* he thought.

There was an irony, of course, to Romney's distaste for Kennedy's dynastic advantage. His own political credibility came largely from his father. George was a constant presence in his son's campaign. He moved into the house shortly after Mitt entered the race, and each morning the Romneys would come downstairs to find him seated at the kitchen table, already awake for several hours, filling legal pads with handwritten campaign memos.

George's involvement was a net advantage, but he could also be a loose cannon. Once, during a debate, Mitt made a comment about

"Iran," and his mother, who thought he meant "Iraq," began whispering a correction from the audience. Mitt managed to ignore the distraction until he heard his father say, in full voice, "Shut up, Lenore!"

Later, when the Kennedy camp began invoking Mormonism in its attacks and Romney called a press conference to respond, a campaign aide had to be tasked with keeping the candidate's infuriated father away from the cameras. The reporters arrived, and Mitt calmly delivered the statement he'd prepared with his advisers. Then George, who'd managed to sneak into the back of the room, stood and began railing against the religious bigotry of the Kennedy campaign. "*It is absolutely wrong,*" he thundered. The cameras swung, and George's outburst led the evening news.

By Election Day, it was clear that Romney was going to lose by double digits, but George still insisted on flying the whole family into Boston. They gathered in a private hotel function room, wearing "Team Romney" T-shirts. As the grim returns trickled in, George was defiant. "This is just the beginning for you," he kept telling his son, to which Mitt kept replying miserably that he would never run for office again. Finally, to illustrate the death of his political career, Mitt grabbed some white lilies from a vase on the table and lay prostrate on the floor with the flowers on his chest. The family laughed, but George was unmoved.

Losing was hard enough for Mitt, but what really bothered him was that after all the speeches and ads and endless campaigning, after dragging his exhausted wife across the state and plowing millions of dollars of their own money into the race, most people could still not answer the question "Why did Mitt Romney run for Senate and what does he stand for?" One longtime Republican would later tell reporters, "His main cause appeared to be himself."

Romney's defeat turned out to be an anomaly in a year that was otherwise defined by historic gains for his party. Across the country that night, Republicans were achieving one of the most sweeping electoral victories in modern American history. They picked up fifty-four seats in the House, seized multiple state legislatures and governorships, and for the first time in forty years took control of both houses of Congress.

The architect of the so-called "Republican Revolution" was an ambitious congressman out of Georgia named Newt Gingrich. A former history professor, Gingrich had pioneered a ruthlessly effective style of politics that fed on conspiracy theories about Bill Clinton and brought strategic obstructionism to Congress. To train a new generation of conservatives in political warcraft, he'd even sent out cassette tapes to candidates throughout the country who wanted to "speak like Newt," providing them with a new vocabulary. In one memo, titled "Language: A Key Mechanism of Control," Gingrich included a list of recommended words to use in describing Democrats: *sick, pathetic, anti-flag, traitors, radical, corrupt.*

Romney had not dealt much with Gingrich, and he was unimpressed with what he saw on TV. "He came across as a smug know-it-all; smarmy and too pleased with himself and not a great face for our party," he remembered thinking. As someone who considered himself a "George Romney Republican," Mitt found Gingrich's approach to politics exotic and undignified (and as a moderate running in Massachusetts, he had little use for it in his own race anyway). What he wouldn't realize until later was that these tactics were about to take over his party—and that the further he rose, the more pressure he'd face to adopt them.

George Romney died eight months after the election, the victim of a heart failure suffered while he was on his treadmill. Lenore discovered his body. She said later that she knew immediately he was gone when she woke up to find no rose on her nightstand.

Emergencies and Catastrophes

The plane was easy enough to spot on the tarmac at LaGuardia. It was the only private jet, Romney noted with some amusement, that had its owner's name stamped across the fuselage. It's not that he was a prude when it came to such things—between his success in the financial sector and his recent Senate run, he'd accumulated his share of rich friends who owned planes. But the financiers and CEOs with whom Romney tended to mingle were respectable types, the kind that knew to indulge their vanity by subtly embedding their initials in the tail numbers of their jets. His host for this weekend was not big on subtlety.

The invitation had come as a surprise: Donald Trump, the celebrity businessman from New York, wanted to fly Romney down to West Palm Beach and put him up at Mar-a-Lago, his sprawling seaside compound. The two men had never crossed paths before, but that came as little surprise to Romney. He'd long placed Trump in a distinct category of rich people that he didn't overlap with much—"the real estate guy." There was nothing wrong, per se, with making one's fortune in real estate. The Marriotts had done it, after all. "But they did it by opening five thousand hotels," Romney would later explain. "That's one way to do it. The other is, hey, you build a big building in New York;

New York gets really hot; and now you're a billionaire. It's a different realm." Trump, to put it bluntly, was not the kind of businessman who got invited to the World Economic Forum in Davos or the Business Roundtable in Washington—he wasn't really a "businessman" at all. He was, to Romney's mind, more of a cartoon character. A few years earlier, George Romney had insisted on hiring a photographer to take a formal portrait of Mitt and Ann. The result was ridiculous—Mitt glowering in a tuxedo, Ann in pearls and a ball gown—and their snickering sons had given the photo a nickname: "The Donald."

And yet, Trump *was* quite famous, and Romney was not above gawking at famous people. So, when the appointed morning arrived in January 1995, he climbed aboard the Boeing 727 with the real-life Donald at his side.

Joining them on the trip was Marla Maples, Trump's most recent wife, and Ted Virtue, a senior executive at Bankers Trust. Virtue was the one who had arranged the trip. Romney assumed the bank was courting Bain Capital's business, and that Virtue had hoped that he could seal the deal by wining and dining him at Donald Trump's house. (Trump, who was deep in debt to several of America's leading banks and in need of a new lender, was in no position to argue.)

After a short flight and a limousine ride, they pulled up to Mar-a-Lago, where a surreal scene awaited them: every member of the service staff—dozens in total—was lined up outside in a white linen uniform, as if posed for a royal reception. Trump grandly exited the limo and strode past the rows of servants, offering a stoic nod to his charges. He looked, Romney thought, like he was impersonating an English lord. *Where on earth are we?* "I had never seen anything like that in America," he'd later recall.

That evening, they dined in a small breakfast nook off the kitchen. Marla and her mother doted over Tiffany, their high chair–bound toddler, while Trump flitted in and out, waiting impatiently for the meal to end so that he could lead his guests on a tour. He'd bought the place a few years earlier from the old-money Posts, and promptly set about remaking it in his own image (much to the consternation of his wealthy neighbors). Gold sinks were installed in the bathrooms, massive Jacuzzis were added to the suites, and baroque furniture was crammed into every inch of the estate. He'd initially envisioned Mar-a-Lago as a private vacation home, but now he was preparing to convert it into an elite social club, where he could charge local swells $75,000 for a membership. Romney wondered if this was primarily a business play or a way to get around the fact that none of the other Palm Beach clubs would take Trump.

At one point during the tour, Trump pulled Romney aside. "You've got to see this," he said. They entered a large walk-in vault, where Trump excitedly opened a drawer to reveal a set of gold-colored silverware. "They didn't know this was here when they sold me the place," Trump boasted. "The silverware is worth more than I paid for the house. I'm gonna make a *fortune* on this place."

Romney, who doubted they were actually looking at solid-gold silverware, chose to smile and play along.

"You know," Trump went on, "the bank has me on $140,000 a month."

Romney was confused. "What do you mean?"

Trump explained that his businesses owed more than a billion dollars to dozens of lenders. "The only chance they have of getting anything back is if we keep up appearances," he said. "So, they loan me $140,000 a month" to maintain the Trump brand. He seemed tickled by this fact, as if he was getting away with something hilarious.

Romney had no idea if Trump was telling the truth, and he didn't especially care. This was the Trump experience he'd been hoping for—memorable, low-stakes, and deeply weird. Trump might not be a serious person, but he was undeniably entertaining. When the weekend ended, Romney thanked his host, departed Mar-a-Lago, and filed the weekend away as a funny story to tell friends. He doubted he'd ever see Trump again.

*   *   *

In the fall of 1998, Ann Romney went to see a neurologist. She'd been experiencing strange symptoms: numbness, loss of balance, and sudden stretches of overwhelming fatigue. Sitting nervously in the waiting room, with Mitt by her side, she took note of the role reversal now occuring in their marriage. She was usually the one who calmed her husband down when he got worked up—within their family, she was known as "the Mitt stabilizer." But now, as they leafed through scary pamphlets about Parkinson's disease and brain tumors, Mitt was the one squeezing her hand.

In truth, he was scared, too. Ann was the focal point of his life. He'd never lost the infatuated thrill he first felt when they met as teenagers—had never really stopped chasing her. Other men in his circle tacked on extra days to their international business trips for sightseeing and extravagant dinners; Romney had no interest unless his wife was with him. When he visited Paris with Ann, they'd stroll endlessly down the boulevards, stopping in at favorite cafés for pain au chocolat. When he traveled to the city for work, he'd eat at McDonald's and turn in early. The life they'd built together didn't make sense without Ann. Losing her would feel like losing everything.

After a series of tests and an MRI, a doctor sat them down and revealed the diagnosis: Ann had relapsing-remitting multiple sclerosis. She didn't know much about the disease in that moment—how it ravages the central nervous system, resulting in neurological, physical, and sometimes psychological deterioration—but she knew immediately that her life would never be the same. When the doctor left the room, she burst into tears.

Mitt cried, too, but he was consoled by one fact: MS wasn't fatal. "Listen to me," he told her. "As long as this isn't terminal we can deal with it. Whatever it is, we're going to deal with it together."

In the years that followed, they'd experiment with a variety of treatments and therapies. One of the more effective ones for Ann turned out to be horseback riding. Though she hadn't ridden since she was a girl, she found that the subtle movements of the sport were ideally suited to maintaining her balance, flexibility, and muscle strength. She became especially enamored of an elite form of riding known as dressage. The sport wasn't cheap—and if Mitt was being honest, he never quite shared his wife's passion for it. But decades later, he'd look back on all the days spent puttering around hotels in equestrian towns, waiting for Ann to get back from the stables, and write in his journal that it was time well spent: "Life with Ann is a lot better than life without, regardless of the environs."

Romney returned to Bain after losing his Senate bid, and the years that followed were some of his most productive and profitable. By the late nineties, his net worth was in the hundreds of millions, and the way things were going, he was poised to become a billionaire in the next decade. But Romney was feeling restless.

The death of his father had made him question how he was spending his time. Those 1,200 people who'd gathered for George Romney's funeral in Michigan had not turned out to mourn a savvy businessman who excelled at outperforming quarterly profit expectations—they were mourning a public servant. And as much as Mitt enjoyed making deals and turning around companies, he worried that he should be doing more with his life.

One day in 1999, Romney received a call at his office. It was Ann. "Don't say no right off the bat," she began. "Just listen to me."

She said she'd just gotten off the phone with Kem Gardner, an old family friend and prominent business leader in Utah. The 2002 Winter Olympics, scheduled to take place in Salt Lake City, were in trouble. The bid committee had been accused of bribing international Olympic officials, and the scandal was threatening to derail the Games. Sponsors were fleeing; fundraising had dried up. Utah, and by extension the state's dominant faith, were at risk of international humiliation. Organizers were searching for a new CEO to turn things around—and Gardner thought Romney should do it.

He'd taken the idea to Ann first because he assumed Mitt would dismiss it out of hand.

Romney's response confirmed his suspicion: "Are you out of your mind?"

Ann went on to lay out all the reasons she thought he should take the job—duty to country, service to their Church—but they all boiled down to an essential argument. "There is more to your life," she told him, "than just making money." Romney agreed to meet with the Salt Lake Organizing Committee.

He'd never cared much before about the Olympics, all the pomp and circumstance around curling and luge and other strange winter sports that no one had heard of. But as he listened to the organizers rhapsodize about the Games as a showcase for humanity's greatest qualities—sacrifice, teamwork, determination—his indifference began to soften. Also compelling to Romney was the chance to help redeem the reputation of a state that his pioneer ancestors had settled.

More than anything, though—and he would never quite figure out what to make of this—he was drawn to the train-wreck quality of the situation. He'd always nursed a certain fascination with crisis. Later, when he wrote his memoir of the Olympics, he would try to cast this as something to be admired—a sense of duty passed down by his forebears. But he knew it was also more visceral than that.

He had a friend once who was free-soloing the face of a cliff when his hand began to cramp. Sixty feet off the ground, thirty feet from the summit, the friend decided to continue his ascent. Romney had no use for rock climbing, but he understood the allure of putting yourself in high-stress situations. The thrill of the challenge, the stakes. "They're exhilarating," he'd admit. "It's probably some part excitement and adrenaline." That his friend wound up falling ninety feet and shattering his jaw hardly mattered to Romney—the probability of failure only made the project more interesting.

On the day Romney assumed his new position in Salt Lake City, Ann, who had long known her husband better than he knew himself, was asked by a reporter in Boston why he took the position. "He loves emergencies and catastrophes," she replied. "He would never have considered doing it if it wasn't a big mess."

It wasn't until Romney settled into the job that he realized the true size of the mess. He'd assumed he was inheriting primarily a public relations problem. His job would be to convince the world that the 2002 Winter Olympics were under new management now, and that all that unseemly bid-rigging business was in the past. But it turned out things were much worse than that.

The finances were a mess. After digging into the books, Romney and his team determined that they had a $400 million budget shortfall, and with sponsors avoiding the radioactive event, there was no obvious way to raise additional funds. Romney also learned that the Justice Department had launched a criminal investigation of the bribery allegations— any indictments, he was warned, would further scare off financing and could even shut down the Games entirely. The situation was so dire that Romney called Ann shortly after moving to Utah and told her he might have made a mistake. "I'm not sure it can be saved," he said.

Making matters worse, Romney's arrival had ruffled some very powerful people in Utah. Mike Leavitt, who was serving as governor of the state, would later recall the bitter carping he heard from some in his circles: *Why are we outsourcing our biggest job to an outsider? Don't we have any homegrown talent?* "There were people who preferred other candidates, and they essentially used that argument to advance their preferences," Leavitt said.

One of those people was the billionaire philanthropist Jon Huntsman Sr. Shortly after Romney took the job, Huntsman gave an incendiary interview accusing Romney of stacking his team with coreligionists and "cronies," and suggested he was giving the Church too much influence over the Olympics. "These are not the Mormon Games," Huntsman seethed.

Romney was mystified by the attack, not least because Huntsman himself was a devout Mormon. When he went to see Huntsman, the hostility was palpable. "Do you think you're the savior of Utah?" the billionaire demanded. "Who do you think you are?"

But once the two men got to talking, the real reason for Huntsman's angst was revealed: He'd been lobbying to install his son Jon Jr. as CEO, and he resented the way Utah's business and political elite had lined up to coronate Romney instead.

Romney was amused by the idea that he'd somehow stolen a job he didn't deserve. He was a blue-chip corporate turnaround artist with political experience and extensive connections in Washington—his resume was tailor-made for the Olympics. As for Huntsman's son? "Jon Jr. has, I'm sure, great skills," Romney would later tell me, diplomatically. "But I don't know that he'd ever run a turnaround, nor had he had the same public experience."

Still, the Huntsmans were Utah royalty, and Romney knew he'd need to be on good terms with the patriarch to do his job. So, Romney responded solicitously. He told Huntsman his son would have performed magnificently in the role, and emphasized the enormous respect the Romneys had for the Huntsman family.

When the meeting ended, the air had been cleared. But it wouldn't be Romney's last run-in with the Huntsmans.

Romney's first task was to close the gaping budget shortfall that he'd inherited. He began, as he did at Bain, by instilling an ethos of austerity inside the Olympic operation. Gone were the elaborate catered lunches for trustees in downtown hotel ballrooms, replaced by no-frills meetings in government buildings where pizza was served for a buck a slice. When the International Olympic Committee summoned Romney to Switzerland for a briefing, he traveled alone—in coach—and checked out of the luxury hotel that had been booked for him in favor of more modest accommodations.

None of these cost-cutting measures meaningfully cut costs, but Romney felt it was important to change the culture of the Salt Lake Organizing Committee. He wanted to preside over a team of penny-pinching scrappers, not bloated bureaucrats enjoying the spoils of their position. Gradually, the symbolic moves helped reshape public perception: when a local newspaper ran a cartoon that portrayed Romney as a pitchman for "MittFrugals"—a low-budget Olympic park—he had it framed and hung it in his office.

Romney also found more substantive ways to close the deficit. Instead of spending millions to decorate Salt Lake City for the Games, he gravitated toward a cheap, novel way to make a visual mark: shrink-wrapping the city's buildings with huge printed images of Olympic athletes. The strategy would save money, but it required the building's owners to consent—and one of the biggest buildings in town was the administrative headquarters of The Church of Jesus Christ of Latter-day Saints.

To get the Church's permission, Romney paid a visit to Elder Robert D. Hales, a member of the Church's Quorum of the Twelve Apostles. Romney laid out his vision and asked Hales if the Church would allow his marketing team to wrap their building with a picture of a figure skater.

"Male or female?" Hales asked.

"Female."

The apostle hesitated for a moment. "What is she going to be wearing?"

Romney assured him that the figure skater would be tastefully dressed, and Hales signed off.

Meanwhile, Romney looked for new sources of revenue. Because he wasn't allowed to line up multiple sponsors in the same marketing category—if Delta had already signed on, United was off the table—Romney created more than twenty new categories. The Salt Lake Olympics, he decided, would have an official furniture supplier (Herman Miller) and an official meat (Certified Angus Beef).

The ongoing Justice Department investigation continued to loom over the Games, but Romney eased sponsors' concerns by pledging full cooperation—and by pinning the blame for the bid-rigging scandal on a pair of former executives, Tom Welch and David Johnson. When the men were eventually indicted on charges of bribery and fraud, Romney reportedly went so far as to urge them to take a plea deal for the good of the Games. They refused, and the charges against them were eventually dropped (an outcome Romney attributed to prosecutorial incompetence).

Five months before the opening ceremonies, Romney traveled to Washington, D.C., to secure the last $13 million in federal funding he needed for the Games. He was feeling good about where things stood—not quite triumphant, not yet, but good. The budget was in decent shape; final logistics were being ironed out. Stories about the miraculous Olympic turnaround in Utah were already appearing in the press, with Romney cast as the hero. There was even some speculation that he might reenter politics when this was all over—the only question was whether he'd run as a Republican in Massachusetts or a Democrat in Utah.

He spent the morning before his meetings working out of an office down the street from the White House. While giving a phone interview to a local radio station in Utah, Romney was interrupted with some startling news: an airplane had just crashed into the World Trade Center. He turned on a TV, and a second plane hit the other tower. Then there were reports of an explosion at the Pentagon, and his aide suggested they get out of D.C. before the entire city was gridlocked.

They drove south on 395 toward Virginia, a strange calm on the empty highway, until they reached the exit for the Pentagon. There, abandoned vehicles blocked the lanes as rubber-necking drivers leaned over guardrails, staring at the flames. Pungent black smoke filled their car, and Romney tried to figure out why the odor was so strange—like nothing he'd ever smelled before, he would later recall. "Like war."

He thought first about Ann, and he called her. He thought about his kids, and called each one of them. He thought about the kids who didn't have parents anymore. He thought about the Olympics—*Will we have to cancel?*—and about the country, how everything would be different now. It wasn't until later that he thought about how he was supposed to be in Manhattan that day. Before the last-minute trip to Washington, he'd planned to announce the names of the Olympic torchbearers at a press conference in Battery Park, at the foot of the World Trade Center.

Romney's job got harder after September 11—he needed more money, much more security, and a new plan to convince the world that the Games could be safely held—but it also felt more urgent. "In the annals of Olympism and the history of Utah," Romney wrote in an email to his staff shortly after the attacks, "this may stand as one of the defining hours."

He coped with the stress and complexity of the moment by maintaining a near-manic focus on every logistical detail—from the mechanics of the glass cauldron that would contain the Olympic flame to the choral arrangement of the national anthem to be performed. A week before the opening ceremonies, he led a small group of Mormon leaders on a tour of the venue. When the walk-through ended, the leaders began filing into an elevator. Perhaps sensing Romney's obsessiveness, Gordon B. Hinckley—the president of the Church, and a man considered by Mormons to be a prophet with a direct line to God—held the door to ask a question.

"What would be the ideal weather for the opening ceremonies?"

"Crispy cold, with just a hint of snow," Romney said.

"Okay," the prophet deadpanned, "I'll take care of it."

On the night of the opening ceremonies, Romney waited in a backstage greenroom with President George W. Bush. Tens of thousands of people were filing into Rice-Eccles Stadium, and the telecast was expected to attract record global ratings as viewers around the world tuned in with morbid curiosity to see if the ceremony would be attacked. As they waited for their cue to go onstage, Romney looked at the stoic president, clad in a long, dark overcoat, and wondered what was going through his mind. When the cue came, Bush turned to Romney and provided the answer. "Do I look fat?" Bush asked.

The ceremony proceeded smoothly as a blizzard that threatened to cancel the fireworks show stalled north of the city, and Olympians from around the world paid tribute to their still-mourning host country. An especially powerful moment occurred when U.S. athletes, accompanied by New York police officers and firefighters, carried in a tattered American flag that had hung in the World Trade Center. Romney expected the crowd to erupt in applause, but instead a reverent silence settled over the stadium. As the Mormon Tabernacle Choir sang the final lines of the national anthem—*O say does that star-spangled banner yet wave*—Romney's eyes filled with tears.

The next seventeen days were exhausting, as Romney scrambled— sometimes in Sisyphean futility—to control every detail that he could. When a traffic jam backed up cars for miles on the highway ahead of the first downhill skiing event, Romney frantically donned a state trooper jacket and went car to car urging people to drive to the next exit. And when he learned that a security guard was refusing to let officials from the International Olympic Committee through a check-point because their bus had the wrong credentials, Romney angrily confronted the rent-a-cop. (Later, when that confrontation made the papers, it was reported that Romney had deployed the F-word during his tirade—a serious allegation for a man who took pride in his G-rated diction. Even decades later, he continued to insist that he restricted himself to *hells* and *damns*—the "biblical swear words.")

If all the fussing and fretting seemed excessive, the results were undeniable. By the time the closing ceremonies arrived, commentators were hailing the 2002 Winter Olympics as an unqualified success—and

Romney as the architect. More than 2 billion people around the world tuned in to the competition; leaders from nearly every nation praised the management of the Games; and the organizing committee ended up with a $50 million budget surplus.

In the years that followed, some people would debate how much credit Romney actually deserved for the turnaround. Most of the organizers insisted publicly that his stewardship was essential. "I have no doubt whatsoever, as the representative of the chief investor of the Salt Lake City Olympics, that Mitt Romney was single-handedly responsible for those Games being the immense success they were," said Dick Ebersol, who was chairman of NBC Sports and Olympics at the time. "The list of people who could have pulled it off began and ended with Mitt Romney." But not everyone was convinced.

A small but vocal contingent of detractors accused Romney of exaggerating the severity of the crisis when he arrived in Utah so that he could play the hero—and set himself up for a return to politics. Ken Bullock, one of Romney's chief antagonists on the organizing committee, would recall him as a self-promoting opportunist. "He tried very hard to build an image of himself as a savior, the great white hope," Bullock told the *Boston Globe*. "He was very good at . . . putting himself on a pedestal." As evidence, Bullock kept a box of collectible Olympic pins that had been approved by Romney bearing his own likeness. (One valentine-themed pin featured Olympic mascots gathered around Romney saying, "Mitt, we love you!") The pins had been cooked up by the Olympic marketing team as a cheeky way to generate revenue, but to Bullock they were proof of Romney's narcissism.

Critics like Bullock tended not to bother Romney too much—their criticism was too blinkered to be taken seriously. But he found them fascinating. Romney considered himself a nice enough guy. He got along with most people. But as he got older, he was forced to acknowledge that something about him inspired a passionate loathing in certain people. "Throughout my life, there's always one person who just can't stand me," he'd reflect.

In any case, the Olympics had given Romney everything he hoped for when he took the job. A sense of purpose, yes, but also a white-knuckled solo up the face of a cliff with the whole world watching. Call it ego or vanity or a commitment to public service: Romney loved feeling like he'd accomplished something both difficult and important.

By the time his plane touched down in Boston, he was already planning his next attempt at a political ascent. This time, he would do what it took to reach the top.

CHAPTER FIVE

What It Took

For one thing, there would be no dithering this time. He would approach his campaign for governor of Massachusetts with the same flinty pragmatism that he'd brought to his business career. Strategy would be rooted in data. Obstacles would be eliminated with unsentimental efficiency.

His first move was to muscle the incumbent governor out of the race. Romney didn't *want* to challenge a sitting Republican for the job—he had said as much publicly a few months earlier. But Jane Swift, the first woman to hold the office, was underwater in the polls and refusing to bow out gracefully. So, Romney gave her a push: he booked a ballroom for a "big announcement," leaked his intention to run, and had his aides circulate poll numbers showing that he'd squash her in a primary. Within two days of his return to Massachusetts, Swift was dropping out in a tearful press conference.

Determined not to repeat the mistakes of his Senate bid, Romney set out to staff his campaign with killers. To run the operation, he approached Mike Murphy, a quick-witted and oft-quoted political consultant who'd made his name leading John McCain's 2000 presidential campaign. Romney was drawn to Murphy's subversive sense of humor—and Murphy liked Romney's drive. But the consultant had a condition before he agreed to sign on. "You can't read any newspaper articles about your campaign," he told Romney. "None." Murphy had seen too many candidates become obsessed with their negative press coverage. "We'll lose every day in the papers," he warned, and "you'll be inclined to respond to some twenty-two-year-old [reporter] who wrote some nasty article that no one actually read." Ignore the *Globe*, Murphy said. "You'll win the race on TV."

One of Murphy's first ideas was to have a camera crew follow Romney around as he performed various blue-collar jobs—selling hot dogs at Fenway, or laying asphalt on a paving crew. Romney did not exactly pull off the regular-Joe schtick. (When he spent a day driving a tractor, he complained about his "severe allergy to hay" and asked for a handkerchief.) But even as the stunts drew scorn in the press—the *Boston Herald* called his costume changes "Village People–esque"— voters seemed to get a kick out of watching him fumble around. "It's not like people believed for a minute that I wasn't some rich patrician," Romney said later. It was just that he seemed like a good sport: "It's like, he cares enough about the job and wants it bad enough that he's willing to do this."

Other efforts to humanize Romney were less successful. Six weeks before the election, his campaign released a TV ad titled "Ann" that featured the Romneys lovingly recounting their youthful courtship and gushing over their children while a cloying soundtrack twinkled in the background. Voters hated the ad. There was something phony and plastic in the way Romney doted on his wife—"Ann is just good to the core," he effused—and he began to sink in the polls. The irony, of course, was that Romney really *did* talk about Ann this way, all the time. But, as he would later reflect, this was one of his failures as a candidate. "I was accused of being inauthentic. But in reality, that's just who I am," he told me. "I'm the authentic person who seems inauthentic."

With Election Day fast approaching, Romney ordered his campaign to pivot. They pulled the "Ann" spot off the air and unleashed a flurry of attack ads aimed at his Democratic opponent, a former state treasurer named Shannon O'Brien. The ads depicted O'Brien as a floppy-eared basset hound who napped on the floor while burglars removed bags of money from the state treasury. It was cartoonish and dumb, but Romney had seen firsthand that elections are not won by the high-minded. "I learned in my race against Senator Kennedy, don't be so naive as to just sit back and say, 'Oh, I'm going to be positive while they're negative,'" he told a TV interviewer at the time. "That doesn't make sense."

On the campaign trail, Romney carefully tailored his views on social issues to match the average Massachusetts voter—pro-choice, in favor of some gun control, and generally supportive of gay rights. He pledged to "preserve and protect a woman's right to choose." His campaign passed out pink flyers at Boston's gay pride parade wishing participants a "Great Pride Weekend!" He presented himself—maybe even *saw* himself—as proudly carrying on his father's venerable civil rights legacy. "At a very young age," he reportedly said in a meeting with gay rights leaders in the state, "my parents taught me important lessons about tolerance and respect. I have carried these lessons with me throughout my life and will bring them with me if I am fortunate enough to be elected governor."

Romney knew his debates with O'Brien would give him his best shot at winning a tight race. But he was still tormented by his humiliating showdowns with Kennedy. He'd thought often in the years since about why he performed so poorly, and had decided it came down to basic psychology: when the cameras blinked on, "major parts of my brain shut down." This time, he insisted on a grueling schedule of debate preparation. O'Brien didn't have Kennedy's raw political talent, but she was smart and tough and he needed to be ready. To serve as his sparring partner, he brought on Beth Myers, a Boston-based GOP strategist, who pored over O'Brien's speeches and interviews, committing each talking point to memory.

Once the mock debates began, it quickly became apparent that Romney's greatest liability would be his temper. He had an almost aristocratic conviction in propriety and good manners, which made him visibly bristle at any criticism he considered unfair. Sensing this, Myers began trying to get under his skin. After each question, she recalled, "I would give my answer and then look at him and say something mean."

The put-downs flustered Romney at first. On one occasion, Romney became so frustrated that he threw his papers onto the floor. "If this is how it's going to go," he'd fume, "I'm just going to lose this election." But with practice, he learned to contain these outbursts. He mastered other tricks, as well. After some advisers worried that his hand motions might come across as patronizing in a debate against a woman, Murphy trained Romney to stick his right hand in his pocket and keep it there while he spoke, thus reducing potentially gendered gesticulation by 50 percent.

By the time the real debates arrived, Romney was so thoroughly prepared that he could anticipate each of his opponent's answers, often word for word. He came across as sharp and confident—every part the capable executive he claimed to be.

O'Brien tried to reprise the attacks on Romney's business record, but they didn't seem to stick this time. The Olympics had given him a surplus of public goodwill, and even a dash of celebrity. (*People* magazine had recently named him one of the fifty Most Beautiful People.) More important, Romney had already suffered through one failed campaign and learned—for better and worse—what it took to win.

Some confidence might have been in order when the night of the election arrived. Still, it came as a surprise to both Mitt and Ann when the race was called for him.

Standing in front of hundreds of supporters at the Park Plaza Hotel in Boston, Romney promised a new approach to politics, untainted by partisanship or special interests. "We took on an entrenched machine," he declared. "And we won."

*   *   *

Governor Romney spent his first year in office doing what he did best: digging the state out of a fiscal crisis. Massachusetts was facing a $650 million deficit when he was sworn in, and a projected shortfall of $3 billion for the following year. As a candidate, Romney had promised not to raise taxes or cut vital services, which meant that balancing the budget would require resourcefulness. He brought in a team of management consultants and together they went line by line through the state's sprawling budget in search of inefficiencies and waste.

He discovered that Massachusetts was spending tens of millions a year on hotel rooms for homeless people. When he inquired about the cost, he was told that whenever someone showed up at a crowded shelter and couldn't get a bed, the state would put them up in a hotel for the night. Romney suspected that this system created bad incentives. "I bet word gets around," he said. So, he tweaked the policy: instead of sending newcomers to hotels, the shelters would make space by booking rooms for the occupants who'd been there longest. The idea was to prioritize care for the chronically homeless. The new policy worked even better than he'd thought: within a year, Massachusetts went from booking around six hundred hotel rooms a night to none.

Romney also ordered $12 million in cuts to the state's public university system. Faculty lounges across the state exploded in outrage, and newspapers filled with mournful stories about the gutting of higher education. But when Romney paid a visit to the University of Massachusetts–Amherst, the chancellor shut his office door behind them and thanked the governor for the mandated cuts. "There are departments here [we've] been trying to get rid of for years," the chancellor said. Tenure and faculty politics had prevented him from cutting classes that students were no longer signing up for. Now he had room to maneuver.

These episodes pleased Romney, but the satisfaction was fleeting. He didn't want his governorship to be remembered for clever cost cutting. He wanted to do big things, like his father had done—to leave a legacy. To help.

Beth Myers, whom Romney hired as his chief of staff, recalled how the governor's thoughts would wander after long days spent slashing the budget. "In the back of his mind, he always had this thought: *I want to be a governor who does something that matters to people*," she said. "Even though we were going through this painful process that helps nobody, that was always there."

He ultimately found his legacy-making project during a conversation with an old friend. Romney had known Thomas Stemberg for sixteen years, ever since Bain Capital first invested in his fledgling office-supply retail chain, and the two men had regularly consulted each other on their latest projects. In a meeting shortly after Romney was elected, Stemberg told the incoming governor he should consider tackling one of the most intractable problems in politics. "Mitt," he said, "if you really want to help the people of Massachusetts, you've got to get everybody health insurance."

Romney was dismissive at first. The quest to provide universal healthcare coverage in the United States had a long and cursed political history, littered with pie-in-the-sky proposals that Romney considered either unworkable or prohibitively expensive. His own secretary of health and human services showed him a study that suggested covering everyone in Massachusetts would cost the state $2 billion per year. His political advisers also pointed out that it was not really a Republican *thing*. "This is going to be a problem for you," one adviser told Romney, warning that many in his party wouldn't like it." But the idea stuck with him.

What Romney found, once he began looking into the issue, was that the wonks and politicians who worked on healthcare policy in America were largely divided into distinct—and often bitterly warring—ideological tribes. There were the Scandinavian-model absolutists and the free-market privatizers and the Canadian-style decentralizers, and none of them ever seemed to talk to each other, let alone share ideas.

Romney was not an ideologue. He prided himself on this fact. Though he was a Republican, he had no patience for Rush Limbaugh and never read the *National Review*. If he adhered to any kind of conservatism at all, it was of the small-*c* variety. He was a believer in fiscal prudence and sober thinking, in well-produced white papers and the *Wall Street Journal*, in spreadsheets and data and running the numbers one more time. He saw himself, proudly, as a partisan of pragmatism. And he decided that was just what the healthcare debate needed.

Romney assembled his policy advisers and told them he wanted to hear the best ideas for achieving universal healthcare coverage in Massachusetts, and that he didn't care where they came from. The state had an estimated 460,000 people without health insurance—but once his team began digging into the data, solving the problem didn't seem quite so daunting. About 40 percent of the uninsured could actually afford basic coverage, but chose not to pay for it—many were young and healthy and figured the risk was minimal. About a quarter were eligible for Medicaid and just needed to be enrolled. The rest—about 150,000 people—would need subsidies to afford private insurance. The trick would be figuring out how to get them covered.

Working with his team, Romney developed a promising framework for his plan, but it hinged on an audacious idea: everybody in the state— poor and rich, young and old, sick and healthy—would be required to have health insurance, or else pay a fine. Romney knew the personal mandate would be unpopular in some circles, but he believed it was essential. When someone without health insurance turned up in an emergency room, they received medical treatment whether they could pay for it or not—so why not simply make sure they could pay for it?

Of course, governors don't get to enact sweeping overhauls of state healthcare systems by themselves. And so there were months of painstaking negotiations—nipping here and tucking there to make the new law attractive to everyone Romney needed to win over. He worked closely with Democrats in the state legislature, and courted the insurers and hospitals, too.

At the same time, he labored to sell the individual mandate to Republicans as a fundamentally conservative idea, rooted in the ideal of personal responsibility. This argument was helped when he found out that the Heritage Foundation, a conservative think tank in Washington, had proposed a similar idea in the 1990s. He made a big deal of the Heritage thing when he spoke to small-government types—this was proof that his plan was founded on timeless conservative principles. But later, he would admit that it was merely a coincidence.

"I don't look and say, 'What's the conservative point of view on this?' and then try to promote it," Romney told me. "I ask, 'What do I think is the right answer to this particular problem?' and then promote that. For instance, my healthcare plan in Massachusetts—that was just, you know, we've got a problem . . . here's a great way to solve it. And then I found out, 'Hey, some people at Heritage agree with you.' *Aha! It's a conservative plan!* But I learned Heritage had proposed something similar well after I proposed my plan."

The hard work paid off, and the state legislature passed the bill on April 4, 2006. At the bill-signing ceremony at Faneuil Hall, Romney was joined by an array of bipartisan allies—from representatives of the Heritage Foundation to Senator Ted Kennedy, his former nemesis. The surrealness of the scene was captured by Kennedy, who joked to reporters, "When Kennedy and Romney support a piece of legislation, usually one of them hasn't read it."

In fact, Kennedy had surprised many when he signed on to Romney's plan. But the senator had been toiling for years to pass healthcare reform in Congress, and was eager to see progress on any front. "We're basically stalemated" in Washington, Kennedy had explained, "so the states are going to have to try to come up with a response." If they did things right, Massachusetts just might offer a blueprint for the rest of the country. Romney was impressed by Kennedy's willingness to partner with him. For all of Kennedy's personal demons, his devotion to public service was real—and, really, what more could one ask of a senator?

The new law was, by virtually any measure, a success. Massachusetts became the first state in the country to achieve universal healthcare coverage—by 2008, 95 percent of adult residents were insured—and mortality rates among non-elderly adults dropped significantly. Romney saw the effects firsthand when a member of his cabinet was diagnosed with brain cancer. "Had I not had Romneycare," she told him, "I would not have been able to have the treatments to save my life."

It was also just the sort of high-profile political accomplishment that propels ambitious governors to higher office. Romney had ignored warnings that the law might backfire if he ran for president; he believed it was the right thing to do. But it was also plausible in 2006 to think that he could run on such an accomplishment. The GOP was still billing itself as "the party of ideas." George W. Bush had been elected not that long ago on a platform of "compassionate conservatism."

Hours after signing the healthcare bill into law, Romney departed for the Ritz-Carlton in downtown Boston, where a gaggle of GOP leaders from Iowa would be waiting for him in a suite. It was time to make his next move.

If he was going to pivot, it would have to be fast. That much was obvious. There was plenty to like on Romney's presidential resume, he was told, but Republican primary voters would have questions. His wealth might be a problem. His position on guns and abortion definitely would be. GOP strategists were straightforward with him: if he was going to overcome the impression that he was just "a rich guy from a liberal state who's got a funny religion," he would have to start now.

The Boston press had already begun to suspect that, despite his insistence to the contrary, their governor was plotting a presidential run. Joan Vennochi, a *Boston Globe* columnist, noted that Romney was "speaking in grandiose slogans that bridge to a national stage, with local facts and figures slipping from instant recall." Romney, she wrote, "has that lean and hungry look."

His national star was, indeed, on the rise. Conservative opinion makers like George Will were singing his praises. Republican power brokers were traveling from early-primary states to size him up. Even Donald Trump, during an appearance on CNN, called Romney an "attractive candidate" and a "very smart guy."

A few years earlier, Romney had run into Trump at a New England Patriots game. Robert Kraft, the team's owner, had invited them both to his box, and Trump spent much of the first half enthusiastically informing Romney about his latest side hustle—a reality TV show called *The Apprentice*. At one point, Trump sidled up to Romney's son Josh and pointed at a leggy brunette across the room. "Have you seen my girlfriend, Melania?" he asked, smirking. "When I drop her, the phone is gonna ring off the hook. Every guy in New York wants to go out with her."

As chairman of the Republican Governors Association in 2006, Romney traveled the country raising money for candidates and road testing his stump speech in front of conservative audiences. His political consultants were telling him that he'd have to change course on a number of hot-button social issues, and Romney understood their rationale. Still, he nursed a quaint notion that he could make his presidential campaign about the things *he* cared about.

But something strange, almost alchemical, happened to Romney when he got in front of those crowds. He would walk into the county fairs and the convention halls with a plan to talk about his unemployment record in Massachusetts only to realize that the people in attendance didn't want to hear it—they wanted to hear about guns and killing terrorists and the evils of abortion. "When you speak to the NRA, you change your tone," he would later tell me. "I admit it. . . . You say the things that make the audience respond positively." The more he gave them what they wanted, the louder their ovations got. A new incentive structure took shape on those stages. A new persona formed.

Before long, he was using his home state as a punch line in speeches. "Being a conservative Republican in Massachusetts is a bit like being a cattle rancher at a vegetarian convention," he told crowds from South Carolina to Missouri. That Romney was now a "conservative

Republican" came as news to the people who knew him back home. But the line was always rewarded with enthusiastic whoops and hollers.

Romney crept up in the national primary polls, while his popularity in Massachusetts plunged. He did not pause to consider whether this political reinvention was more or less authentic to who he truly was. It was a matter of simple math. The polls showed what they showed, the voters were who they were. Another Romney was running for president—and he wasn't going to make the same mistakes that the last one had.

CHAPTER SIX

The Tar Pit

The title of the eighty-eight-page paper was "George Romney in 1968, from Front-Runner to Drop-Out, an Analysis of Cause." Everybody on Mitt's team got a copy. Written four decades earlier by an ex-staffer on the elder Romney's presidential campaign, the BYU master's thesis offered a detailed postmortem for George Romney's candidacy. Organizational dysfunction, financial problems, a candidate unwilling to have friendly drinks with reporters—Mitt carefully studied each weakness, determined to learn from his father's mistakes.

In many ways, his fledgling campaign was defined in contrast to his father's. George had staffed his team with mercenary consultants from Washington who refused to move to Michigan, so Mitt would only hire loyalists—former chief of staff Beth Myers as campaign manager; longtime body man Spencer Zwick as fundraiser. George was known for his fits of off-message candor, so Mitt would choose his words with extreme care—stick to the talking points, no "brainwashing" mistakes. He would be, he'd tell me later, "always watching not to say some word that ends up blowing up my campaign."

But Romney also took a larger lesson from his dad's failed candidacy: Getting elected president required meeting the voters where they were. No quixotic tours of the American ghettos, no righteous crusade to change hearts and minds, no epic, doomed battle for the soul of his party. He would gather the data, follow the polls, stick to the strategy.

Romney officially announced his bid for the presidency at the Henry Ford Museum near Detroit, standing in front of a 1960s-era Rambler—an homage to the father whose unfinished legacy he hoped to fulfill. He spoke of his dad's "humble roots," about his lath and plaster days, about how he'd risen from nothing to become a pioneering auto executive and a transformative governor. "His character and his integrity," Romney said, "left an impression that has lasted through the decades."

What he did not say was that character and integrity only take you so far—political savvy was what got you to the White House. His father had lacked in that department; Romney was confident that he wouldn't.

One afternoon in late 2006, Romney sat in the living room of his Belmont, Massachusetts, home, surrounded by some of the preeminent figures on the religious right. The meeting had been arranged by Mark DeMoss, a power broker in the world of evangelical politics and a key adviser to Romney. The idea had been to gather for a friendly, homemade meal and a productive chat about Romney's presidential aspirations. Instead, he'd later recount, the evangelical leaders were conducting an inquisition.

Several of the men expressed discomfort with Romney's record in Massachusetts, with Franklin Graham homing in specifically on his judicial appointments as governor.

"I cannot in good conscience support you in this campaign," Graham told Romney, "because you named two people who were gay to the court in Massachusetts."

Romney tried to explain the process of judicial appointments—that each one had to pass through a selection committee composed mostly of Democrats, that he'd made more than seventy appointments in his four years as governor, and that he'd been more concerned with their experience and judicial philosophies than their personal lives.

"I didn't inquire about their sexuality," Romney explained.

"Well, you should have," Graham shot back, "and you should not have appointed two people who were gay to the bench." (Graham would later dispute Romney's recollection of the meeting.)

Romney had expected some skepticism along these lines. But as the conversation progressed, it became clear to him that their real problem with him was with his Mormon faith. The tensions between evangelicals and Mormons went back decades, rooted in both profound theological differences and petty cultural divisions. While members of The Church of Jesus Christ of Latter-day Saints considered themselves fully Christian, evangelicals had long viewed them as heretics. Their Book of Mormon was an abomination; their belief in modern prophets made them apostates. And more than a few evangelical ministers had devoted Sunday sermons to preaching against those clean-cut Mormon boys trying to poach their flock. Asking these men now to endorse a Mormon for president was akin to asking David to get in bed with the Philistines.

Richard Land, the head of the Ethics & Religious Liberty Commission, pressed Romney on his church's diversions from the Nicene Creed. Jerry Falwell, meanwhile, led Romney down a conversational rabbit hole on the true nature of God, and the Mormons' rejection of the Trinity. How, he demanded, could Romney possibly call himself a Christian when he didn't believe that Jesus Christ and God the Father were one? Romney explained his belief that Jesus was the literal son of God, a separate and distinct being who nonetheless worked in concert with the Father.

After a prolonged back-and-forth on the finer points of their dueling theologies, Romney finally asked Falwell: "What do the people in your pews believe?"

"Well," Falwell sheepishly admitted, "most people would agree with you."

When the evening ended, Romney shook hands with each man and told him he hoped he would win him over. A few days later, his team sent each man a Windsor-style chair with an engraved plaque on the back that read "There's always room for you at our table."

Romney's advisers thought the meeting had gone well. But Romney—whose life in Mormonism had made him all too sensitive to the wariness with which other Christians approached his religion—was less certain. One thing, however, was sure: neither he nor Ann wanted any of these people anywhere near their table.

But there were political realities to deal with. This was 2006, the second term of the Bush administration, and conservative evangelicals ruled the Republican presidential primaries. To win these contests, he'd need these men—whatever he thought of them—to be in his camp, or at least not actively attacking him. He wasn't going to change his religion, but he could at least take away their other excuses for skepticism. Romney would leave no doubt in their minds that he was a real conservative.

The first debate of the Republican primaries took place on May 3, 2007, at the Ronald Reagan Presidential Library and Museum in Simi Valley, California. A life-size replica of Air Force One hung suspended in the air above the audience, a reminder to the ten men onstage of what was at stake.

Years later, after he had watched most of them breathlessly sell out and suck up to an adulterous casino operator named Donald Trump, Romney would marvel at how seriously he'd once taken these men. But that night, as he looked down the row of candidates from his perch on the far end of the stage, he saw an array of fierce challengers and cutthroat competitors.

There was Rudy Giuliani, "America's mayor," who'd led New York City heroically through 9/11's aftermath, hugging firemen and crying with widows and exuding a public warmth and charisma that Romney could never dream of possessing. But Rudy fit uncomfortably in the national Republican Party. He was unabashedly pro-choice, supportive of embryonic stem cell research, and proud of his city's strict gun-control laws. Voters might be willing to forgive such sins against conservative orthodoxy—Romney himself was counting on their mercy—but Rudy showed no interest in repentance. He seemed to believe, Romney thought, that "by dint of personality he could convince the party to go along with him." Admirable, perhaps, but stupid.

There was Mike Huckabee, the affable governor of Arkansas, who was busy carving out his spot as the field's evangelical standard-bearer. A former Baptist minister, he was quick with a folksy aphorism and skilled at bringing every political discussion back to Jesus. He was also, in Romney's private estimation, a "huckster"—the very "caricature of a for-profit preacher." The two men had first met a few years earlier at a conference for the nation's governors. "Huck," as he liked to be known, had thrown an extravagant, staff-berating, I-demand-to-speak-to-your-manager tantrum upon discovering that Romney got a nicer conference room than he did. The episode had left Romney with an impression that beneath Huck's aw-shucks persona lurked a fragile ego and a petty ruthlessness—two things that could make him a mean competitor.

Then there was John McCain. Romney was primed not to like the long-serving senator from Arizona. He resented how the media fawned over McCain, how the same reporters who'd spent the 2000 primaries throwing back beers with him on his campaign bus—nicknamed the "Straight Talk Express"—now seemed so eager to peddle his spin. His antipathy had hardened when Jon Huntsman Jr., who was now serving as the governor of Utah, endorsed McCain, breaking what Romney believed was a private promise to stay neutral in the race and embarrassing his fellow Mormon and honorary Utahn. (During a heated phone call, Romney—who interpreted this betrayal as a petty act of revenge by Huntsman for losing out on the Olympics job—evoked their families' shared history and hissed, "Your grandfather is rolling over in his grave.") All these factors were compounded by the fact that

Romney and McCain had next to nothing in common. One with his money and Ken-doll looks, his slick lines and nice suits; the other with his war-hero injuries and winking crudity and his abiding affection for the game of politics. Each man rubbed the other the wrong way, and McCain in particular struggled to conceal it. His digs at Romney on the campaign trail always felt more personal than his criticism of the other candidates—more smirky, more mean—a fact that never failed to rile Ann.

The stage was populated by a host of also-rans as well—the Ron Pauls, the Sam Brownbacks, the Duncan Hunters; the guys with no money or name recognition and no real shot at the nomination. Romney found them baffling. He regarded the process of running for office a miserable means to a worthy end: *Why put yourself through it if you're never going to win?* He put this question to everyone he knew, until finally a friend with extensive political experience explained it to him: "Mitt, you don't get it. When you have no chance to win, running for president is actually pretty fun." After that, he envied these men more than he cared to admit.

Setting himself apart from the pack wouldn't be easy. But Romney would begin tonight by introducing America's Republican voters to a new Mitt—still polished and competent and good with numbers, but now a dyed-in-the-wool Reaganite conservative.

Over the next hour and a half, Romney rhapsodized about family values, delivered crisp answers on the economy and Iraq, and deftly diffused questions about the sincerity of his recent lurch to the right on abortion. "I was wrong and changed my mind," he said simply, noting that Ronald Reagan had undergone a similar evolution on the issue. "I'm proud of that, and I won't apologize to anybody for becoming pro-life." He even managed to show flashes of humor: When the moderator asked him what he'd say to Roman Catholic bishops who denied Communion to pro-choice politicians, he replied, "I don't say anything to Roman Catholic bishops. They can do whatever the heck they want," prompting a wave of approving laughter from the audience.

In the post-debate reviews, pundits hailed Romney as "likable" and "articulate" and "good-natured" and even, in the case of one particularly impressed columnist, "statuesque." "He may not be the heir to Reagan, but he looked the most like the former president," the *New York Times* wrote. "The tan, the Brylcreem hair, the straight white teeth and a voice so smooth and friendly it sounds as if he makes his living doing voice-overs for car commercials."

The stage was crowded, and Romney only got to speak for a total of eleven minutes and four seconds. But it was possible that night to squint and see a president on the far end of the stage.

The consensus among Romney's advisers was that his path to the nomination would have to run through Iowa. He was something of a mismatch for the first-in-the-nation caucuses, where right-wing activists and evangelicals typically picked the winner. But McCain and Giuliani—the two ostensible front-runners—had their own struggles with the base, and Romney was confident that he could outhustle them. With a win in Iowa, he'd ride the momentum back to New England and take New Hampshire, after which the field would clear and the party would coalesce around his candidacy by Super Tuesday. The strategy seemed sound—and it would begin in Ames.

The Ames Straw Poll was one of those peculiar local customs that had mysteriously accumulated outsize influence in presidential politics. Every four years, Republican activists gathered in a parking lot outside the Hilton Coliseum at Iowa State University and cast votes for their preferred primary candidates by dropping kernels of corn into jars. Though the event started out modestly in 1979, it had taken on a circus-like atmosphere over the years. The Republican Party of Iowa auctioned off the best swaths of concrete to campaigns for tens of thousands of dollars a pop. Elaborate booths were erected to woo supporters, complete with catered meals, branded swag, and big-screen TVs. The national media descended in hordes to cover the contest and report on the winner once the kernels were counted.

To Romney, the whole thing sounded ridiculous, a clear pay-to-play scheme being run by the Iowa State party. But his advisers assured him it was important. The straw poll was widely treated as a bellwether for the caucuses: In 1999, George W. Bush had placed first in Ames before going on to win Iowa the next year. If Romney could win there, donors and journalists would have no choice but to take his campaign seriously. It took some convincing, but eventually Romney was on board. Maybe it *was* a pay-to-play scheme, but he had cash—why not play?

He had already written his campaign a check for $9 million—a "loan" he'd called it, though he knew he'd never see the money again— and now he had a measurable objective for his team: win him the Ames Straw Poll. In the months that followed, the Romney campaign blanketed Iowa's airwaves with commercials and filled its mailboxes with glossy pamphlets. Dozens of so-called "super volunteers" were paid to talk Romney up among their friends, and an armada of buses was leased to pick up supporters across the state and transport them to Ames on the day of the straw poll.

Romney himself, meanwhile, hit the road, popping up in every Dubuque diner and Sioux City gun show that would have him. But winning hearts and minds proved more difficult than he hoped. Try as he might to say the right things to Iowa's conservative caucus-goers, Romney struggled to shake suspicions that he was a poser, a fraud—a "flip-flopper." This narrative had been seeded a year earlier by McCain's operatives, who spent months compiling meticulous lists of Romney's various policy reversals and emailing them to reporters off the record. The media ran with the story and the label had stuck. Now it seemed to trail him everywhere he went. At the Conservative Political Action Conference in Washington, Romney was shadowed by a man in a Flipper costume. Rivals passed out bright green Romney-branded flip-flops to voters. In TV interviews and town halls, it was impossible for the candidate to escape without fielding skeptical questions about why he'd changed his stance on this issue or that one.

Romney found the attacks maddening. Sure, he'd finessed the language and shifted his emphasis, but he had taken pains to not *technically* change his position on most issues. In many cases, he felt he'd remained constant while the world around him had changed. When he first ran for Senate, for example, he'd opposed gay marriage while supporting domestic partnership rights for same-sex couples. In 1994, that made him fairly progressive; by 2007, articulating the same position made him sound like he was pandering to right-wingers. "The country's changed," Romney would argue. "It's the same position all along."

But the truth, which Romney could never quite articulate, even to himself, was that he simply didn't place much of a premium on unwavering political positions. Foolish consistency was not a virtue. Changing your mind could be good. He didn't see most policy disputes in clearly black-and-white terms—in debates with his staff, he would often wind up arguing against himself, probing each side and usually finding merit in both. If embracing one reasonable position over another got him closer to the White House, well, what was so wrong with that?

And yet, there were moments on the campaign trail when the absurdities of partisanship got to him. During one rally, he'd later recall, the crowd roared with approval after he called for the repeal of the "death tax." This was not a position he felt strongly about, but no one ever lost a Republican primary supporting a tax cut, and the line usually got a good response. "It was one of those things you say because you don't know what you're talking about when you're first running for president," he'd tell me. But at this particular rally, while he watched the crowd cheer, he was struck with an inconvenient moment of clarity: none of these people would ever be subjected to a "death tax." The estate tax, which was designed as a bulwark against entrenched aristocracy by limiting the amount of wealth passed from one generation to the next, only applied to fortunes of $2 million or more. Repealing it probably wouldn't help a single one of the farmers or mechanics or middle-class office workers in the audience. *So why were they all cheering?*

The answer, he realized, was a grim kind of team loyalty—*This is what my side is for, so this is what I support.* It all felt so absurd in that moment, so bleak. He chose not to dwell on the thought for too long.

On August 11, 2007, thousands of Romney supporters were bused into Ames for the all-important straw poll. The Romney campaign had bid top dollar for a massive lot right next to the polling center, and paid a consultant nearly $200,000 to set up a showstopping spread, including a stage, multiple tents, an inflatable slide called "The Screamer," a stadium-style jumbo screen, and free plates of brisket and smoked ribs catered by the most popular barbecue joint in town. Volunteers clad in matching yellow "Team Mitt" T-shirts scoured the premises in golf carts, offering rides to those who promised to vote for Romney. When the kernels were counted at the end of the day, Romney won by a landslide.

Speaking to reporters, he dismissed questions about whether the victory was hollow—both McCain and Giuliani had ended up skipping the straw poll after they saw how much money Romney was spending—and he struck a triumphalist note. "I'm pleased as punch that I won," he crowed.

But by then, Romney was beginning to loathe Iowa and its stranglehold on the presidential race. The straw poll, the state fairs, the endless, myopic focus on local niche issues that mattered a lot to Iowa corn farmers and very little to anyone else. Romney had pictured a campaign for the presidency as a lofty, noble thing—a venue to debate the most pressing issues at the highest level. Instead, he was scarfing down deep-fried Twinkies for the cameras and memorizing trivia about corn-based fuel production and promising state senators that he fully supported federal subsidies for ethanol.

Maybe it wasn't Iowa's fault. Maybe the state was just a stand-in for his broader disappointments in the process. But Romney reserved a special disdain for the Hawkeye State and the way it sucked candidates in with its incessant, petty, dignity-sapping demands. "The Iowa caucus," he grumbled, "is the tar pit of American politics."

By year's end, Romney had climbed into the top tier of the field, gaining a lead in pivotal states like South Carolina and New Hampshire. But as the primaries got closer, one thing was becoming obvious to him: the Mormon problem wasn't going away. As hard as he tried to steer the national conversation about his candidacy away from religion, it continued to define him in the media. When he appeared on the cover of *Newsweek*, the headline read "A Mormon's Journey." When columnists looked for fresh angles on his campaign, they wound up recounting Joseph Smith's visions and parsing the peculiarities of nineteenth-century polygamy.

Some prominent pundits even freely mused that Romney's religious beliefs should be disqualifying. In *Slate*, Jacob Weisberg argued that the presidency could never be trusted to a man who believed in "such a transparent and recent fraud" as Mormonism. In the *New Republic*, Damon Linker wrote that Romney should have to answer questions such as "Would it not be accurate to say that, under a President Romney, The Church of Jesus Christ of Latter-Day Saints would truly be in charge of the country"? These sentiments were not new in politics—John F. Kennedy had faced similar reservations about his Catholicism when he ran in 1960. But while Roman Catholics had eventually gained full initiation into American life, Latter-day Saints never quite had. For all its efforts to project a wholesome, all-American image in its proselytizing, Romney's young church was still widely viewed by its native country as mysterious and strange, even sinister. One 2007 poll found that just 38 percent of Americans thought the country was ready for a Mormon for president.

Most immediately troubling to Romney's prospects was the fact that he had so far failed to alleviate distrust among evangelical voters. He'd tried deflecting theological questions by emphasizing his social conservatism. He'd tried cracking self-deprecating jokes about polygamy. ("I believe marriage is between a man and a woman . . . and a woman and a woman.") He'd tried presenting Mormonism as a mainstream Christian faith. But nothing seemed to work.

The reality of this failure hit home during a private meeting with a small group of faith leaders in South Carolina. Mitt and Ann were making their usual pitch—about their deep belief in God and Jesus Christ, about the values that unite all people of faith—when finally an evangelical minister leveled with them.

"You realize," the minister said, "that if you are elected president, more people will go to Hell." It was simple, he went on: putting a Mormon in the White House would mean that "more people will think being Mormon is normal, more people will become Mormons, and more people will go to Hell."

"My job is to save souls," the minister told the Romneys. "You're gonna have a hard time in our communities here in South Carolina."

Romney's Republican opponents, meanwhile, were eager to capitalize on the electorate's anti-Mormon sentiment. Anonymous robocalls were flying around Iowa with menacing rumors about Romney's church. Huckabee was stoking skepticism of Romney's exotic beliefs in the press, asking one *New York Times* reporter in a tone of faux innocence, "Don't Mormons believe that Jesus and the devil are brothers?" Even McCain's ninety-five-year-old mother got in on the action: during an appearance on MSNBC, Roberta McCain sat next to her visibly uncomfortable son and held forth on how Romney shouldn't be so quick to take credit for rescuing the Olympics since it was "the Mormons" who'd messed them up in the first place. (McCain later called Romney and apologized for his mother's remarks.)

Romney's son Josh experienced the Mormon problem firsthand when he set out on a bus tour of Iowa. His dad had told him that Chuck Grassley, Iowa's long-serving senator, made a point of campaigning in each of the state's ninety-nine counties every time he was up for reelection, and Josh thought it sounded like a fun adventure. So he piled his young family into a Winnebago RV that he bought on eBay and hit the road. As he started talking to voters, he noticed a pattern: They'd often begin by saying they didn't agree with Romney on one issue or another. But when Josh would gently correct them—"No, he actually agrees with you"—their real concerns would surface. Romney didn't have "the right values." He didn't seem "trustworthy." On more than one occasion, Josh was bluntly told, "You don't believe in the same Jesus that I do." The bus tour quickly became a grueling affair. After the third day, Josh's wife, Jen, pointed at the Winnebago and said, "I'm never getting back on that thing again." He spent the next several weeks zigzagging the state alone, his days spent trying to convince evangelicals that his dad believed in Jesus, his nights spent sleeping in sketchy Walmart parking lots with a baseball bat by his side.

Some of Romney's allies encouraged him to publicly angle away from his Mormonism—recast it as a part of his family's heritage, but not central to his personal beliefs. But Romney flatly refused. For all his tortured contortions over policy and politics, this was one part of his life he would not compromise. Maybe it was the *only* part—the part that made everything else feel temporary and pliable by comparison.

Romney's faith had sustained him on the campaign trail. He prayed regularly—kneeling on buses and hotel room floors; rattling off silent petitions for strength backstage before debates—and he spent time every day reading the Scriptures. He instructed his campaign not to schedule events on the Sabbath whenever possible. He even arranged for the Church's Boston temple to hold a special late-night session just for him and his family. Such accommodations were unusual, but the temple president was an old friend—and Romney craved the closeness to God he experienced during those sacred worship ceremonies. Swapping his presidential-candidate costume for the simple white clothing of the temple that night, he felt fully, truly like himself.

With the Iowa caucuses just weeks away, Romney decided it was time to address the questions about his religion head-on. He told his staff to find a venue for a major address, and then locked himself in a hotel room and started writing. Normally he would have relied on a speechwriter for the first draft, but this one was uniquely personal to him. For all his insistence that he wasn't a spokesman for his church, Romney had given a good deal of thought to what his candidacy might mean for Mormonism. He'd been confident that he wouldn't *embarrass* the faith—he had no secret skeletons waiting to be exhumed. But he also knew that by running he'd risk tainting perceptions of Mormonism with partisan politics. "I was going to have about half the country like me and about half the country not like me very much," he reasoned. "But coming from a religion where about 2 percent of the country likes us, you know, that would be an improvement."

He didn't know yet if he would become the Mormon JFK or the Mormon Al Smith or if he'd flame out of politics altogether in a month. But he felt strongly that this would be one of the most important speeches of his life—perhaps the only lasting legacy of his campaign.

On December 6, 2007, Romney appeared at the George H. W. Bush Presidential Library and Museum in College Station, Texas, to deliver an address he'd titled "Faith in America." He spoke of religious freedom as one of the nation's foundational ideas, and invoked Kennedy to argue that no candidate should endure a religious test. He said that while his personal values were deeply rooted in his faith, he didn't see it as his job to answer questions about the Church. Mormon leaders would have no influence on his decisions in the Oval Office, he pledged. If elected, his first duty would be to the Constitution.

But Romney also stressed that he would never disavow his religion. "I believe in my Mormon faith and I endeavor to live by it," he said. "My faith is the faith of my fathers—I will be true to them and to my beliefs. Some believe that such a confession of my faith will sink my candidacy. If they are right, so be it. But I think they underestimate the American people. Americans do not respect believers of convenience. Americans tire of those who would jettison their beliefs, even to gain the world."

On the eve of the Iowa caucuses in January 2008, a *Wall Street Journal*/NBC poll showed Romney at the top of the field nationally among Republican voters. But he couldn't escape the tar pit. On the night of the caucuses, Romney came in a distant second, while Huckabee—*that Mormon-slurring, tantrum-throwing, two-faced conman preacher*—rode a last-minute surge to victory. Adding insult to injury, the Romney campaign had dramatically outspent the other candidates in the state, only to win a paltry 30,021 votes—roughly $300 per vote (much of it from Romney's own personal fortune). He'd staked his campaign on Iowa, and lost miserably.

He took an early flight out of Des Moines the next morning, burdened by the distinct feeling that he'd been fleeced. "We are *never* doing that again," he told his advisers.

The rest of the race went by in a bitter blur. A loss to McCain in New Hampshire. A blowout in South Carolina. Glimmers of hope in Wyoming and Nevada, and a sentimental win in his childhood home state, followed quickly by a succession of campaign-crushing losses on Super Tuesday.

Behind the scenes, Romney's platoon of strategists bickered caustically via email about the reasons for the campaign's foundering. Alex Castellanos faulted Stuart Stevens for failing to position Romney as the true champion of "the Reagan coalition." Stevens countered that "trying too hard to reinvent Romney" had only generated "problems of authenticity." "When we try to put too much emphasis on Mitt Romney as Ronald Reagan's heir," Stevens wrote, "it always stumbles up against the reality that Romney isn't a movement conservative." Other advisers chimed in to pick sides and pile on before Tagg finally forwarded the emails to Myers: "The current consultant situation isn't tenable. We'll need to pick one or the other going forward." On February 7, 2008, Romney officially suspended his campaign.

Romney dutifully endorsed McCain, who asked that he help raise money and campaign for down-ticket Republicans, and Romney dutifully agreed. He was nothing if not dutiful.

When it was time to pick a running mate, McCain vetted him for VP, and Romney thought he had a shot. But the partnership was not to be. The call came from McCain in late August, while Romney was on a shuttle to an airport rental car complex. "Mitt, we've decided to go another direction."

Romney was disappointed, but not shocked that he hadn't been chosen. But when he asked who McCain was selecting, the answer surprised him: Sarah Palin, from Alaska. Romney had gotten to know Palin a little during his tenure as head of the Republican Governors Association, and remembered finding her unimpressive. During their very first phone call, she'd revealed an ignorance of campaign fundraising that was exceeded only by her ignorance of policy. His standard question—"What do you want to accomplish as governor?"—had elicited a slew of platitudes so thin that he forgot them almost instantaneously.

Getting passed over for someone like Palin might have felt like an insult if Romney hadn't already become disillusioned by presidential politics. These campaigns were not, he now realized, about character or leadership or selecting the best statesman for the job. Barack Obama, a freshman senator with less than three years experience in federal government, was on the verge of winning the presidency. McCain had just picked perhaps the least qualified Republican governor in America to join his ticket. All of this was just theater.

And yet, for all his bitterness, Romney couldn't deny that Palin was an extraordinary performer. Watching her on the campaign trail, how the frenzied crowds responded to her, how freely she pushed the boundaries of political norms—Obama wasn't just wrong, he was "pallin' around with terrorists"—he knew that he'd never be able to put on such a show.

"I'd frankly like to just close the door to politics and move on," Romney wrote in an email to Stuart Stevens after McCain selected

Palin as his running mate. "But the faint whisper of perhaps being needed makes that not entirely the right choice. What to do?" Stevens convinced Romney to leave the door open. The Palin pick was a desperation move—all signs pointed to an Obama victory, which meant that he'd have the chance to run again in four years if he chose. In the meantime, Romney would lay low, write a book, and keep tabs on the political news.

OBAMA IS SWORN IN AS THE 44TH PRESIDENT . . . Glenn Beck: "This president, I think, has exposed himself as a guy, over and over and over again, who has a deep-seated hatred for white people or the white culture" . . . *GUN SALES SOAR IN UNITED STATES . . . TEXAS GOVERNOR SAYS SECESSION POSSIBLE* . . . Rush Limbaugh: "When you're dealing with a guy like Obama and the Democrat Party, who are going to impose Nazi-like socialism policies on this country, you've got to say it!" . . . *POLL: PALIN BEST REFLECTS GOP CORE VALUES* . . . Sarah Palin: "My parents or my baby with Down syndrome will have to stand in front of Obama's 'death panel' so his bureaucrats can decide . . . whether they are worthy of healthcare" . . . *THOUSANDS OF ANTI-TAX "TEA PARTY" PROTESTERS TURN OUT IN U.S. CITIES* . . . Newt Gingrich: "What if [Obama] is so outside our comprehension, that only if you understand Kenyan, anti-colonial behavior, can you begin to piece together [his actions]?" . . . *TEA PARTIERS YELL SLURS, SPIT ON CONGRESSMEN* . . . Congressman Trent Franks: "We need to realize that [Obama] is an enemy of humanity" . . . *TEA PARTY MORE POPULAR THAN BOTH POLITICAL PARTIES.*

CHAPTER SEVEN

Heist

They prepared their presentation in PowerPoint, the boss's native language. It was December 2010, and Romney's top political advisers—Beth Myers, Bob White, Spencer Zwick, Matt Rhoades— were gathered in the living room of his beachside mansion in La Jolla, California. It had been an exhausting year. In the past twelve months, they had gotten Romney's new book published, locked down a number of key GOP donors, and begun to build out the political infrastructure for another presidential campaign. And they'd done it all for a demanding, detail-obsessed boss—the kind who dragged them across the country for strategy meetings and fired off dense emails before dawn; who ran on checklists and action items and regularly scheduled conference calls to follow up on said action items. Romney was now at or near the top of every presidential primary poll, and the press was calling him "the closest thing to a Republican front runner" the party had.

But something strange had happened while Romney and his team were busy courting the respectable Republican establishment—a huge swath of their party had radicalized. A recession and a Wall Street bailout and a Black, liberal president in the Oval Office had combined to inflame the white-populist resentments that had always simmered beneath the surface of American conservatism. Tea Party candidates with outlandish ideas and no political experience were toppling long-serving Republicans in primaries. Conservative media was filled with warnings about shadowy socialist plots to take over the country. The institutional power on the right had shifted such that the chairman of the Republican National Committee had less influence than Glenn Beck.

Romney, sensing this shift, was now having second thoughts about running—and his advisers were here to convince him that the nomination was still within reach if he ran. Flipping through their slides, they made the case. Yes, he'd have to contend with some bomb-throwing blowhards, be it Sarah Palin or Mike Huckabee or someone they hadn't thought of yet. And yes, all the attacks from the last campaign—flip-flopper, Mormon, Massachusetts moderate—would likely return in steroidal form. But the country was reeling from a recession, and people were desperate for change. If Romney maintained a ruthless, almost robotic, focus on fixing the economy, he could distract enough conservative voters from his shortcomings to narrowly win the primary.

Stevens put it to him most bluntly. A veteran of Republican presidential campaigns, Stevens was something of an oddity in the political-consulting world. He hated Washington, and spent as little time there as possible, presenting himself as a kind of wisecracking, globe-trotting raconteur. At fifty-seven, he'd hiked across Africa with a former fashion model, skied the North Pole, and traveled Europe in a vintage Mustang—documenting each experience in a series of gritty travel memoirs. Stevens was convinced that the 2012 Republican primary wasn't about ideological differences, not really; it was about identity and grievance and tribal allegiances. Romney, he believed, was by far the most qualified candidate in the field, and also the best man. But he was an utter mismatch for the current GOP. "The base is southern, evangelical, and populist," Stevens told him. "You're a Yankee, Mormon, and wealthy. We're going to have to steal the nomination."

Romney wasn't sure he had the stomach for a heist—and neither was his family. A few weeks after the meeting with his advisers, he gathered his sons and their wives in the same La Jolla living room to survey them on the prospect of another presidential campaign. When they'd held this vote four years earlier, the family was unanimous in its support. This time, the idea was much less popular. As they went around the room, each family member took a turn expressing their dread. There would be more scrutiny of their personal lives, more attacks on their faith, more long, mind-numbing bus rides across hostile primary states. And in the end, even if he got the nomination, he'd have to run against an incumbent who had all the powers of the presidency at his disposal and—how to put this politely—a more *finely honed* political skill set than their beloved dad. When it came time to vote, the tally was 9–2, with only Ann and Tagg supporting another run.

Romney was himself conflicted. He did want the job, and believed he could do it well. Fiscal crises, economic turnarounds—this was the stuff he was good at. There was a part of him, self-aggrandizing perhaps but sincere, that believed he was the only presidential prospect who could deliver the country from widespread unemployment and economic stagnation.

There was also a part of him that wanted to atone for the failures of his last race. With the clarity that comes in between campaigns, he could see the mistakes he'd made in 2008, how he'd lost himself little by little chasing empty applause, how he'd failed to articulate a compelling reason for running beyond "I want to be president."

"If I decide to go for it again," he wrote in an email to some of his advisers in 2010, "it will be with far less concern about what people think or even whether my message is popular or not. Of course, I would want to win, but feeling that I have been true to what I believe is even more important. Reputation is a word I've used but that isn't it really—reputation is what others think; what concerns me is what I think about how true I have been to myself. Integrity is a better word."

As Romney deliberated through the spring of 2011, the climate on the right only seemed to grow more fevered. Glenn Beck was riling up his viewers with predictions of a "Great Depression times 100" and hyperinflation on par with the Weimar Republic. Fox News was running stories suggesting that Obama had deployed the Secret Service to monitor the conservative network. And a bizarre conspiracy theory about the president's birthplace was beginning to gain traction— boosted by an unlikely spokesman.

Donald Trump had begun popping up on political talk shows to muse about whether Barack Obama might perhaps be a secret Muslim born in Kenya who'd defrauded American voters to get elected to the presidency. This theory had been kicking around the fringes of U.S. political discourse for years and had already been debunked, but suddenly it—and Trump—were everywhere. On *The View*: "I want him to show his birth certificate. There's something on that birth certificate that he doesn't like." On Fox News: "He's spent millions of dollars trying to get away from this issue. . . . A lot of facts are emerging and I'm starting to wonder myself whether or not he was born in this country." On *The Laura Ingraham Show*: "He doesn't have a birth certificate, or if he does, there's something on that certificate that is very bad for him. Now, somebody told me—and I have no idea if this is bad for him or not, but perhaps it would be—that where it says 'religion,' it might have 'Muslim.'" On the *Today* show: "If he wasn't born in this country, which is a real possibility . . . then he has pulled one of the great cons in the history of politics."

Romney had not spoken to Trump in years, and he was surprised to see the *Celebrity Apprentice* host so hard up for publicity that he was reduced to pandering to the conservative fever swamps. But he chalked it up to another Trump rebrand, and put it out of his mind—choosing not to dwell on the unsettling fact that Trump was making gains in several hypothetical primary polls, or that half of all Republican voters believed Obama was born outside the U.S. This was a sideshow, Romney told himself, and he refused to pay it any attention.

By April, Romney had made up his mind in favor of running, convinced that he could court Tea Party voters while staying true to himself. The real meat of the movement, he'd decided, was fiscal policy. That's what they were always shouting about, wasn't it? Unchecked government spending and excessive regulations and too-high taxes—this was where he'd win them over. "I didn't see it as a populist movement at that point," he'd later tell me. "I saw it as, these people are really concerned about something I've always been concerned about—the deficit and the debt."

He would cling to this notion for dear life as he plunged into another presidential campaign.

Romney woke up early on the morning of May 12, 2011. He was scheduled to deliver a speech later that day at the University of Michigan, where he'd lay out his plan to reform America's healthcare system. He had labored carefully over every word in the address with his aides, aware of the scrutiny it would draw. His healthcare record in Massachusetts—widely seen in 2008 as a key resume line in his presidential job application—had since curdled in the conservative imagination, after Obama began unhelpfully citing it as a prototype for his own polarizing healthcare overhaul.

Conservative policy wonks were now questioning whether Romney could be counted on to repeal Obamacare if he was elected. GOP donors were withholding contributions. Spencer Zwick, who oversaw the campaign's finances, had privately warned that their fundraising would collapse if they didn't change the perception that Romney was "soft on Obamacare." In one meeting, some of Romney's advisers had even urged him to disavow his Massachusetts record entirely and apologize for it. After hearing them out, Romney made clear that he wouldn't go that far, scribbling in a legal pad, "Mass. healthcare—stick with 100%."

But when he checked his iPad the morning before his speech, he was met with a *Wall Street Journal* editorial that immediately tested his resolve. Titled "Obama's Running Mate," the editorial derided "Romney-care" as a fiscal and philosophical disaster for Massachusetts, and argued that it should disqualify him from the nomination. "The debate over ObamaCare and the larger entitlement state may be the central question of the 2012 election," the editors wrote. "On that question, Mr. Romney is compromised and not credible. If he does not change his message, he might as well try to knock off Joe Biden and get on the Obama ticket."

Romney finished reading and quickly tapped out a panicked email to his top advisers demanding a plan of response. Should he unleash a "Palin like attack" on the paper? Respond "line by line" in his speech? Concede that his healthcare experiment in Massachusetts was a failure? Maybe, he mused, sliding into self-pity, he should consider calling off the campaign altogether. This was not just any critical editorial, after all. It was a devastating takedown from the *Wall Street Journal*—the Rupert Murdoch–owned organ of fiscal conservatism, the paper of record for the GOP donor class. "Is my effort futile?" he wrote to his advisers. "How can I win a Republican nomination with Fox and the WSJ on a Jihad against me?" If he was being "delusional," he needed to know now. "The problem is that the people around me now have a vested interest in me running. I don't."

When half an hour passed without a response, Romney peevishly dashed off another email to his team. "Ok, where is everybody? I don't want you all talking off by yourselves. Call, dang it." It was 6:48 a.m.

Eventually, his advisers did call, and successfully talked him down. Stevens, in particular, was good at dealing with Romney's periodic descents into self-flagellation and despair. Having worked on several presidential campaigns, he understood that the highs and lows of the process could send even the most distinguished candidates careening off into hormonal-teenagerly mood swings. "The dirty little secret about politics is that most things don't matter," Stevens liked to remind him. Romney, for his part, knew he was being handled, and appreciated it all the same, though he did sometimes wonder what Stevens really thought beneath all the sunny spin.

After talking it over with his team, Romney decided he would make known his displeasure with the *Journal* in an old-fashioned letter to the editor, and move forward with his speech as planned. That afternoon, he stood in a campus auditorium and laid out his plan to repeal Obamacare and replace it with a program that empowered states to tailor health coverage to local needs. He would not back away from his own record in Massachusetts, he said, or bow to attacks from the right: "I am not adjusting the plan to reflect the political sentiment." But he also tried to distance himself from Obamacare, clicking methodically through PowerPoint slides for almost an hour as he worked to elucidate the nuanced differences between his plan and the president's.

There is an old campaign adage: When you're explaining, you're losing. Romney's problem was that he loved almost nothing more than explaining things. He believed it was one of his great strengths—his "superpower," as he put it himself—and he held a naive conviction in the idea that logic would prevail if it was stated plainly enough.

Romney's core argument—that the healthcare plan he'd championed as governor worked well in Massachusetts but not as a one-size-fits-all federal solution—was reasonable enough. But *reasonable* didn't play anymore in Republican presidential primaries, and the conservative media panned his speech. He was dismissed as "arrogant," his plan deemed "a liability." On Fox Business, the executive editor of the *Weekly Standard* complained, "He dug himself in deeper." The *Journal* ran another editorial: "These are unbridgeable policy and philosophical differences, though Mr. Romney is nonetheless trying to leap over them like Evel Knievel heading for the Snake River Canyon."

The response demoralized, and embittered, Romney. It wasn't just that so many of his critics had their facts wrong. It was the rank commitment to dogma over practical outcomes. "It was a little ironic," he'd grumble to me years later, "that saving human lives was seen by some as being disqualifying in a Republican primary."

*   *   *

That summer, Romney started keeping a daily journal. The entries began in the clipped, fragmentary style of a travelogue—notes for a future presidential memoir that would never get written. (No one reads memoirs by the losers, he would reason.) But the journal quickly evolved into a kind of running internal dialogue on the race and his various anxieties.

By now, Romney had been effectively running for president for four years, and the process was wearing on him. The endless grip-and-grins with donors who wanted to tell him what he was doing wrong. The distant acquaintances who came out of the woodwork to slander him in the press. The punishing travel. The cheap motel rooms. The candy bars for dinner. He knew nobody wanted to hear these complaints; even his family had limited tolerance for his venting. But there was something therapeutic about tapping them out on his iPad during late-night flights and lonely moments in hotel rooms.

"I feel like that story of the coon hunter in the tree," he wrote in an entry dated September 1, 2011. He had heard the joke from Mississippi governor Haley Barbour: A hunter gets caught in a tree with a rabid raccoon who keeps biting him. His partner on the ground tries firing a warning shot to scare it off, but to no avail. "Shoot up here!" the hunter finally yells. "This pain has got to stop one way or another." For Romney, this roughly approximated what it felt like to run for president. "Looking forward to this being over—a win would be best, but losing would be better than an eternal campaign."

The journal was also where he felt free to record his most candid assessments of his Republican opponents. As his advisers had predicted, the race had attracted a stampede of unqualified cranks and weirdos, from Congresswoman Michele Bachmann ("a nut case") to former Senator Rick Santorum ("sanctimonious, severe and strange") to Newt Gingrich ("Ann says he is a megalomaniac, seriously needing psychiatric attention"). But not all of them were so easy to dismiss.

In August, Texas governor Rick Perry entered the race and shot to the top of the primary polls. Perry was practically a liberal caricature of a GOP presidential candidate—a G-droppin', gun-totin' cowboy who talked about using predator drones on illegal immigrants at the border and insisted that God was calling him to run for president. He was also well-funded and popular with the base. Romney immediately sized him up as both a serious threat for the nomination and, somewhat discouragingly, a dimwit.

In his journal, he complained frequently about Perry's incoherence and paper-thin grasp of policy. "Republicans must realize that we have to have someone who can complete a sentence," he wrote. Romney wasn't alone in holding this view. He'd heard through the grapevine that George W. Bush was similarly unimpressed by Perry, joking, "If they thought I was stupid, wait until they see *him*."

Romney's advisers urged him to ignore Perry and stay on message. So, as summer turned to fall, he stuck rigidly to the stump speech he'd developed with Stevens—a potpourri of talking points about low taxes, small government, and the plight of the small-business owner. He delivered it in creaky, old theaters in Nashua, and fluorescent-lit factories in Reno, and VFWs in Columbia, and airport hangars in Tampa Bay. He had an earnest, old-fashioned style of campaigning, often lacing his speeches with sentimental odes to the beauty of national parks or quotes from "America's patriotic hymns." On more than one occasion, he appeared to choke up while reciting a verse from "America the Beautiful." Once, he actually broke out into song.

The more he traveled, though, the more he sensed that his message wasn't working on those Tea Party voters he'd hoped to win over with policy. They nodded along at his speeches and clapped politely when he finished, but there was no conviction, no animal energy. The lack of enthusiasm perplexed Romney. He was saying all the right things, after all. He had a plan to cut taxes, trim government spending, and gradually bring down the deficit. But when he talked about those plans at town halls or Tea Party rallies, he was met with impatience, sometimes even contempt.

Voters regularly demanded that he commit to balancing the federal budget in his first year as president. When he tried to explain that cutting trillions of dollars in a single year would drive the country into depression, they booed.

At an event in New Hampshire, a man confronted him with an accusatory question. "Are you going to compromise?" the voter asked. "I don't want to vote for anybody who's going to compromise." Romney, unable to restrain himself, replied, "Are you married, sir?"

During a primary debate, a CNN moderator asked how the health-care system should handle an uninsured man in a coma who needed intensive care to survive. Scattered shouts of *Let him die!* rippled through the audience. "So much for 'pro-life'!" Romney wrote in his journal.

Still, Romney refused to give up on the base. He assigned Peter Flaherty, a devout Catholic and former prosecutor he knew from Massachusetts, to serve as a kind of ambassador to the right wing, lining up key endorsements and teaching the candidate which words to use and avoid when discussing abortion and gay rights. At Flaherty's urging, Romney started to read *The Weekly Standard* and *National Review*, and he made time to meet with conservative personalities he would otherwise have blown off. Some of these efforts were more productive than others. On one occasion, a private meeting was arranged for Romney to meet with Glenn Beck, one of the most recognizable voices of the Tea Party movement. Beck was a convert to Mormonism, and he had a habit of intertwining his faith with his paranoid politics. When Romney met with him, Beck was inexplicably carrying a Bible and a Book of Mormon. Before long, Beck had hijacked the friendly meet-and-greet and was offering up tearful prophecies about how conservative patriots would rally to Romney's side, evil would be conquered, and the country would be saved from ruin. As Beck blubbered, Romney turned to a campaign aide who'd accompanied him, and mouthed, "Never again."

It was around this time that Spencer Zwick came to Romney with some unwelcome advice: "You've got to let Donald Trump endorse you."

Trump had, annoyingly, continued to loiter around the conservative political world. After a brief—and very public—flirtation with running for president that ended just in time for the season finale of *The*

Celebrity Apprentice, he had begun to refashion himself into a kind of GOP kingmaker, hosting a parade of endorsement-seeking primary candidates at Trump Tower.

Romney refused to be one of them.

"I really am not going to let that happen," he told Zwick. Soliciting an endorsement from "the Donald" would make him look desperate and ridiculous, Romney argued. Worse yet, Trump was still banging on about that Obama birth certificate nonsense—did he really want to be associated with *that*?

But Zwick was adamant. "If he doesn't endorse you, he's going to endorse someone else," Zwick said. Maybe it would be Perry; maybe he'd breathe life into some other campaign. Matt Rhoades, Romney's campaign manager, concurred. The race was tight, and Trump had a real fan base. The risk of snubbing him was too great.

Romney finally agreed to a meeting with Trump—*just a meeting*—but told his advisers that he wanted as little press coverage as possible when he made his trek to Trump Tower.

"He's going to want to make it very visible," an adviser warned.

"Well, I want to make it almost invisible," Romney said.

So, his team devised a plan. On the appointed day, a campaign aide named Will Ritter was dispatched to stand outside the building's entrance as a decoy. While a gaggle of reporters and cameramen looked on, Ritter pretended to make stressed-out phone calls to his colleagues on a campaign—*Where are you guys? Why are you so late?* Meanwhile, Romney's SUV slipped through the service entrance in the back and rolled into a cargo elevator, ensuring there would be no footage of his arrival. Zwick, who was riding with Romney, thought all the subterfuge was a bit much: "It was like George W. Bush going to Baghdad on Christmas Day. I was like, 'What are we doing?'" But Romney, grasping for any scrap of dignity he could find in this unseemly situation, took what he could get.

Once inside Trump Tower, Romney went through the requisite motions of ring-kissing. He posed for pictures with Trump and his family, and marveled at the various Trump-centric tchotchkes that cluttered every surface of his office. Romney and his host spoke about the economy and Chinese currency manipulation—a rare issue both men felt strongly about—and then Trump turned, inevitably, to his favorite conspiracy theory.

He said he was now convinced that Obama had most definitely not been born in the United States. Trump's people had been looking into it, and they were finding some very nasty things. This was a big deal, he explained, and Romney needed to start talking about it.

Romney began to change the subject, but then he got a better idea: perhaps he could take this opportunity to talk some sense into Donald. As it happened, this was an area of constitutional law in which Romney was fairly well versed. Back when his dad was running for president, some had questioned George's eligibility because he was born in Mexico. Experts were consulted, and a consensus was reached that he qualified as a "natural-born citizen" because his parents were Americans. The question was never taken up by the courts, but most modern scholars agreed. Even if Obama *was* born in another country, his American mother guaranteed that he was constitutionally eligible to hold the office.

Romney spent several minutes walking Trump through all this, searching his face for some glimmer of understanding, a light blinking on in his eyes. But Trump seemed uninterested in constitutional theory, and Romney finally gave up.

"Can we count on your endorsement?" Romney asked, getting to the point.

Trump, suddenly engaged again, flashed a squinty, tight-lipped smirk. He said he wasn't ready to announce yet, but, "I think you'll be very pleased."

That seemed unlikely to Romney.

On October 7, 2011, Romney and several advisers checked into the Omni Shoreham Hotel in Washington, D.C. He was due to speak the next day at the Values Voter Summit, an annual conference for social conservative activists and the politicians who wanted their votes. Romney had been attending the event for years, though he'd never felt entirely comfortable there. It was dominated by religious-right types who tended to smile stiffly when they found out he was Mormon. But this year promised to be especially unpleasant.

Shortly before arriving in town, Romney had been informed that he'd be sharing the stage with a notorious Christian bigot named Bryan Fischer. As a talk radio host for the American Family Association, Fischer had called for the mass deportation of Muslims, argued that the Nazi Party was founded by "homosexual thugs," and railed against welfare recipients, who "rut like rabbits." Most recently, Fischer had devoted an entire segment of his show to explaining why the First Amendment was never meant to apply to non-Christian heretics like the Mormons. Fischer was slated to speak directly after Romney.

Romney knew he would have to distance himself somehow from Fischer, but it would have to be done delicately. Push too hard, and he risked further alienating evangelical voters. Rick Perry, who was still breathing down his neck in the polls, had demonstrated little hesitation in playing the Mormon card. Just that day, he'd been introduced at a rally by a megachurch pastor from Dallas named Robert Jeffress, who urged voters to nominate a "real Christian." When reporters asked him what he meant, Jeffress clarified that he believed Mormonism was a cult. "So now the question is how to address both these guys," Romney wrote in his journal.

He worked on his speech late into the night with his advisers, skipping dinner as he drafted and redrafted various riffs on the spirit of the Constitution and the beauty of religious pluralism. The draft echoed many of the same themes that had informed his 2007 "Faith in America" speech. But by the next morning, he'd decided to scrap most of it. There was no use in arguing with a megachurch pastor about the validity of Mormonism. If Romney had learned anything from his years courting conservative voters, it was that he'd never convince evangelicals he was a real Christian.

Instead, Romney decided he would aim his indignation solely at Fischer—a genuinely loathsome figure whose influence on the GOP he considered an embarrassment.

When he took the stage later that day at the Values Voter Summit, Romney offered a firm denunciation of Fischer's rhetoric.

"We should remember that decency and civility are values, too," Romney said. "One of the speakers who will follow me today has crossed that line. Poisonous language does not advance our cause. It has never softened a single heart nor changed a single mind. The blessings of faith carry the responsibility of civil and respectful debate."

After exiting the stage to tepid applause, Romney confronted Tony Perkins, the organizer of the event. Perkins, an evangelical lobbyist with deep roots in the religious right, defended his decision to give Fischer a speaking slot on "free speech" grounds. Romney found this reasoning unpersuasive—*He didn't invite a commie to speak*, he thought—but he held his tongue.

Perkins went on to explain how he'd asked Fischer to "tone down" his remarks before approving them. As he prattled on in this self-congratulatory mode, Romney could hear Fischer in the background, ranting from the stage about how Muslims could not be trusted with the presidency because they didn't "believe in the same God" as real Americans. Romney couldn't stand to listen to another word.

"I'm out of here, Tony," he snapped, cutting Perkins off and heading for the exit.

When the results of the Values Voters Summit straw poll were announced later that day, Romney drew just four percent of the vote. "This was my 7th year at this event," he wrote in his journal. "Smiling because it is my last."

*   *   *

As the primary race progressed, the pundits took to calling it "whack-a-mole." Every time Romney managed to put down one right-wing primary challenger, a new one popped up and overtook him in the polls.

First, it had been Bachmann, then for several months it was Perry. But after a disastrous debate performance in which he forgot which federal agency he wanted to defund, the Texas governor sank and was replaced by Herman Cain, the former CEO of Godfather's Pizza. Cain was a gregarious political novice whose chief contribution to the campaign season was an oft-mocked proposal to replace the U.S. tax code with a flat tax that he'd enthusiastically branded "the 9-9-9 plan." Romney was personally fond of Cain, but regarded him as a joke. His campaign had no money and virtually no staff, and his understanding of policy was, Romney noted in his journal, "thin as gossamer." In one interview, Cain admitted that he didn't know what neoconservatism was; in another, he said he was unaware that China had nuclear weapons. Party leaders and power brokers privately derided Cain, who was Black, sometimes in barely veiled racial terms. When Romney met with Roger Ailes, the Fox News chief ridiculed Cain's signature fedora, grumbling that he should ditch "the pimp hat."

Cain's reign lasted less than eight weeks before sexual harassment allegations surfaced against him—and by November, Newt Gingrich was surging. Somehow, Gingrich's rise was even more depressing to Romney than the others'. Yes, he was smarter than Perry and more knowledgeable than Cain or Bachmann, but he was also a ridiculous blowhard who babbled about America building colonies on the moon and referred to himself as "the most serious, systematic revolutionary of modern times." What's more, he embodied everything conservative voters—those inscrutable, exotic creatures Romney had spent his adult life studying—were supposed to hate.

"NYT article today describes Newt's business in Washington—no question, he is a lobbyist and influence peddler," Romney seethed in his journal. "So, politician, lobbyist, adulterer times two, and he is soaring."

On November 28, Gingrich scored an endorsement from the *New Hampshire Union Leader*, a newspaper believed to have the power to make or break Republican presidential campaigns in the state. Every candidate had courted publisher Joe McQuaid, and the paper's final decision was as much a rebuke of Romney as it was an endorsement of Gingrich. "We don't back candidates based on popularity polls or big-shot backers," the paper wrote. "We look for conservatives of courage and conviction. . . . We would rather back someone with whom we may sometimes disagree than one who tells us what he thinks we want to hear."

Romney's advisers, sensing a mounting despair in their candidate, rushed to reassure him. Stevens urged calm. "There are some old timers like, apparently, McQuaid, who see Newt the way he sees himself, as some great historical figure instead of a silly windbag," he wrote. "Trust me. That Newt won't last long. Newt can't be the nominee of a serious party." Mike Murphy, who'd been offering Romney informal advice from California, where he now worked as a screenwriter, took the long view: "If [the] primary has indeed gone totally batshit radical this year and they go in all for Newt, he loses in [the] general by a Georgia mile. Party will spend [the] next two decades in tearful apologies to you."

The truth, of course, was that Gingrich—an architect of the modern Republican Party—understood something visceral about Tea Party voters that Romney wouldn't realize until later. Romney kept trying to project a cool rationality onto their behavior and demands, to take their agenda at face value. He continued to nurse a delusion that he could win them over with policy. "I listened to the words they spoke, instead of looking behind it and saying, 'Oh, these are people that are basically angry,'" he'd later tell me. "They weren't interested in policy. They didn't care about the budget or the deficit. They just wanted someone who was . . . going to blow everything up."

Romney had remained the ostensible front-runner almost by default. He had the most money, the most endorsements, and consistently polled as the Republican candidate most likely to beat President

Obama in the general election. But his inability to consolidate the support of his party—especially in the face of such unimpressive opponents—was humiliating. He filled his journal with harsh assessments of his performance on the campaign trail, dwelling on every gaffe and misstep. A single bad news cycle could send him spiraling into self-doubt. "Funny how a campaign can get me to spin up emotions," he mused in one entry. During a debate in Des Moines, Romney disputed one of Perry's attacks by offhandedly challenging him to a $10,000 bet that he was wrong. After Twitter lit up with jokes about the candidate's out-of-touch elitism—*Who makes a $10,000 bet?*—Romney was furious with himself, nearly inconsolable.

"Dad feels really rough and in the dumps about the debate tonight," Josh wrote to his brothers. "Some words of encouragement would go a long way. Mom and I were not much help. . . . Send him some nice, only positive news/encouragement. No advice or strategy."

Amid all the disappointment, there was one source of consolation for Romney: watching the flailing presidential bid of Jon Huntsman Jr. The younger Huntsman had announced his candidacy around the same time as Romney and their campaigns were often linked in the press, held up as proof of a "Mormon Moment" taking place in American politics. But their relationship had never recovered from Huntsman's endorsement of McCain in 2008—and Romney delighted in watching his old foe stumble around on the campaign stage. He meticulously cataloged Huntsman's various failures in his journal—the "smarmy" jokes that no one laughed at in debates, the polls that had him at zero percent. After Huntsman boasted that he would have a motocross track installed at the White House if elected, Romney mocked the phony attempt to seem macho. "Sounds to me like a confused metrosexual," he wrote.

As 2011 drew to a close, with Romney barely clinging to his national lead in the polls, an opportunity presented itself. Romney had all but ignored Iowa this time around, investing virtually no money in the state and refusing to schedule campaign stops there. But somehow, with the caucuses just days away, polls showed a win was within reach. So, a few weeks before Christmas, Romney swallowed his pride and returned to the "tar pit"—flooding the airwaves with ads and barnstorming the state from Cedar Rapids to Sioux City.

The last-minute push paid off. On the night of the caucuses, Romney was declared the winner of Iowa, edging out Rick Santorum by just eight votes and easily beating Gingrich, who placed a distant fourth. The win gave Romney a surge of momentum heading into New Hampshire, where he trounced his opponents a week later. All of a sudden, Romney looked every part the unbeatable front-runner he had longed to be—the consensus standard-bearer, the leader of his party. "Today, for the first time, it actually occurs to me that I may well win the nomination," Romney wrote in his journal. "Previously, I have dismissed the thought of actually winning, perhaps in the Romney way of lowering my own expectations. This realization stuns me a bit." With a win in South Carolina, he would effectively clinch the nomination.

Romney's religion was still a problem in South Carolina—more than half of the state's primary voters were evangelicals who were suspicious of Mormonism, according to polls—but he had reason to believe the voters would look past it this time. His chief rival was now Gingrich, a thrice-married, twice-admitted adulterer who'd left a trail of wounded ex-wives and bitter mistresses. His first wife had accused him of trying to negotiate their divorce while she was in the hospital recovering from cancer; his second wife had recently given interviews claiming he asked her for an open marriage when they were together. Conservative evangelicals might not like the idea of a Mormon president, but surely, Romney thought, they were more uncomfortable with a serial philanderer in the Oval Office.

A few days before the South Carolina primary, the candidates gathered for a debate at the Myrtle Beach Convention Center. There had been over a dozen primary debates by now, and Romney had generally performed well. They were good venues for him, ones where it paid to do your homework and stick to your script. He was sharp and disciplined most nights, keeping his fire trained on Obama's economic policies, and earning high marks from the pundits, which he diligently recorded in his journal ("Post debate grades all give me the win. Chris Cillizza of the *Post* says it is my best. Halperin of *Time* says I got an A.") But it bothered him that, for all the positive reviews, his performances rarely seemed to move the needle.

That night in Myrtle Beach, he saw firsthand what needle-moving looked like in a Republican presidential primary. When the debate began, the CNN moderator asked Gingrich about his ex-wife's recent claims against him. Gingrich took a deep breath, gathered all the righteous indignation he could muster, and let loose one of the most remarkable—and effective—non sequiturs in the history of campaign rhetoric.

"I think the destructive, vicious, negative nature of much of the news media makes it harder to govern this country, harder to attract decent people to run for public office—and I am *appalled* that you would begin a presidential debate on a topic like that."

The moderator sputtered, the audience roared its approval, and a few days later, the voters of South Carolina delivered Gingrich a decisive win in the Republican primary.

On the night of the primary, Romney called Gingrich to formally congratulate him on the win, and gave a brief speech to supporters. "I don't shrink from competition," he told the crowd. "I embrace it."

But when he retreated to the hotel with Ann and Tagg afterward, he was deflated. He'd been ambivalent about this campaign from the start, filling his journal with ruminations about the advantages of losing—the prospect of a quiet life in La Jolla, reading and writing and playing with grandchildren, a place under his own vine and fig tree. "Losing would be such 'sweet sorrow,'" he wrote in one entry. Some of this, of course, was a coping mechanism, a way to preempt the disappointment of defeat. But it also reflected something deeper about Romney.

He did not feel, had never felt, that the fates had aligned to place him at this moment in history. He did not believe destiny demanded his ascent to the White House. "I am not driven for the Presidency like those in history that are written about," he reflected in his journal. Many of his Republican opponents claimed they were answering a divine call to seek the office. Romney found this notion ridiculous and grandiose, even going so far as to write a mock news article about it for the amusement of his staff. ("On the heels of Herman Cain and Rick Perry both affirming that God himself called them to run for president, Mitt Romney today was overheard in a Palm Beach restaurant saying that God did not call him." Ann did.) He was uncomfortable with ascribing political ambitions to God, and doubted whether He cared about elections at all. The question of how much God intercedes in human affairs was, Romney believed, "one of life's great imponderables," and he felt it was best to be humble about such things. When the evangelical broadcaster Pat Robertson called him one day to report that "God told me you are going to be president," Romney politely demurred. "No revelation or promptings have come my way," he wrote in his journal.

He analyzed his motivations regularly in that journal, especially on bad days. In one entry, he wrote:

> We don't *want* this. Of course, no one believes that we are doing this out of a sense of duty. They assume that we are driven to win because of the proverbial fire in the belly. Yes, I am a passionate competitor, and I will fight to win. But the nomination and the presidency are not themselves what drive and invigorate the campaigning—it's the competition that does that. The nomination and the presidency are about the country, God, and the future for our descendants. Of course, because I believe that I am the only candidate that can possibly beat Obama and also fix America, I want to win, but if someone else can do the job, that would be fine with me too. If Jeb [Bush] or Mitch [Daniels] were in this, I'd be inclined to let them have the job.

Traveling the recession-scarred country on the campaign trail, he met people who were barely scraping by—the families on the verge of losing over-mortgaged homes, the small-business owners struggling to make payroll, the laid-off and the looking-for-work who'd gone months, even years, without a regular paycheck and were starting to get scared. Romney was not an I-feel-your-pain politician; nobody would believe him if he tried to emote. But these stories got to him. "Tears at my heart," he wrote after meeting with a group of people who had recently lost homes and jobs. "Really fine people in really stressful situations. . . . Have to help people like this. Soon."

The problem was that when he scanned the field of candidates, he couldn't see a single one who seemed capable of turning things around. Obama was well-intentioned but hopeless. And the idea of allowing someone like *Newt Gingrich* to take the reins of the American economy when so many real people were desperate for help—he couldn't abide it. The only way forward, he told himself—the only right thing to do—was to win. He had to complete the heist.

On February 2, 2012, Romney arrived in Las Vegas for one of the more humiliating chores of his political career: publicly accepting the endorsement of Donald J. Trump. The deed would be done at Trump's eponymous hotel on the Strip—a condition the branding-obsessed billionaire had insisted upon—and a press corps had been summoned to document the occasion. While Trump roamed the gold-hued lobby ahead of the event, plugging his property—"You can see why it's number one in Nevada!"—and boasting to reporters about how extravagantly the campaign had courted him, Romney stayed upstairs, out of view. He didn't want to spend one second longer in front of the cameras than he had to.

There were good reasons to go through with this—supported by data, rooted in sound strategy. Romney knew them all. And yet, when the time came for the photo op, he found himself angling ever so slightly away from the cameras while he shook Trump's hand. He looked sheepish, resigned—"like a guy going to a dentist's office," as one Trump aide later complained. In truth, the absurdity of the moment had simply overwhelmed him. He had entered into a kind of existential shrug.

"There are some things you just can't imagine happening," Romney said once he got to the mic. "This is one of them."

CHAPTER EIGHT

50.1 Percent

Something strange happened once Romney clinched the Republican nomination. Almost overnight, the crowds swelled and became rabidly enthusiastic. The machinery of partisanship had churned into gear, turning Romney into a hero around whom all right-thinking conservatives now had to rally. They showed up with smartphones, snapping pictures and asking for autographs like he was a movie star. He first noticed the change at a rally in Chester County, Pennsylvania. He was giving the same stump speech he'd been giving for months, reciting the exact same lines he'd recited hundreds of times before, only now people were going crazy. It reminded him of the scene in his favorite movie, *O Brother, Where Art Thou?*, when George Clooney's character starts singing "I Am a Man of Constant Sorrow" and is bemused to find the audience going wild and clapping along.

Putting away the nomination had not been easy. Even after he accepted Trump's endorsement and subsequently won Nevada; even after Michigan and Maine and Arizona and cleaning up on Super Tuesday; even after his delegate lead grew virtually insurmountable, a few stubborn right-wing candidates had refused to drop out, and a stubborn contingent of right-wing voters had kept on voting for them.

Getting Rick Santorum out of the race had involved long, pain-staking negotiations with his campaign over what Romney could "offer" him to drop out and make an endorsement. Would Romney help Santorum raise money to retire his campaign debts? Set him up with a lucrative job in the private sector? What about a position in the cabinet, or a spot on the vice presidential short list? The discussions went on for days as Santorum's leverage gradually evaporated. When he was finally ready to suspend his candidacy, in April, Santorum's camp called with one last request: that he get a prime-time speaking slot at the convention. Romney—annoyed by all the demands and repelled by Santorum's apparently bottomless self-interest—flatly refused. Santorum dropped out the next day anyway. "His key consideration," Romney wrote in his journal that night, is "Rick first and foremost. He is driven by ego, not principle."

Convincing Newt Gingrich had been simpler, if not necessarily more pleasant. Over a long breakfast, Romney had listened as Newt grandly held forth, in between bites of pancakes, on his various theories—about how Romney should refine his campaign strategy, about who he should hire for which jobs on his staff, about long-term administration planning and the course of the country over the next eight years.

"I think I've finally figured you out," Gingrich told Romney at one point, looking pleased with himself. He explained that Romney was more of a Dwight Eisenhower than a Ronald Reagan—not an ideological visionary, but skilled at listening to a variety of opinions and synthesizing them before he made a decision. Romney could barely get a word in edgewise, which seemed for the best, because Gingrich left the breakfast in good spirits and dropped out shortly thereafter.

There was plenty to keep Romney busy now that he was the presumptive nominee. He had a convention to plan, and a running mate to pick, and a campaign operation to ramp up for the general. (When the primaries effectively ended in April, Romney wrote in his journal that he had just 72 campaign staffers compared to Obama's 690.) And he had to admit there was a certain thrill to it all. When his campaign hosted a retreat in Park City for top supporters in June, *everybody* in the Republican universe showed up—the high-dollar donors (Ken Langone, Malcolm Pray), the business elite (Brenda LaGrange Johnson, Anthony Scaramucci), the GOP luminaries and elder statesmen (Jim Baker, Condoleezza Rice, Karl Rove). They lined up to shake his hand, and gave rhapsodic remarks about their newly annointed nominee. For Romney, it felt like an initiation.

On good days, he convincingly adopted the posture of a confident partisan warrior. When Obama's chief campaign strategist, David Axelrod, held an outdoor press conference near Romney's campaign headquarters in Boston, he dispatched hecklers to the event—booing and hissing and chanting, "Five more months!"—and then proudly boasted about it to the press. ("Sauce for the goose is sauce for the gander.") He staged a surprise press conference in front of a bankrupt solar panel manufacturer that had taken hundreds of millions of taxpayer dollars under Obama. ("There are a number of people among the president's team who don't want that story to get out. We wanted to make sure it did.")

Somehow, with the mantle of the nomination, one could almost imagine him in the White House. He looked presidential—even Clint Eastwood said so. At an event in Sun Valley, Idaho, the movie star told Romney that he'd seen the campaign ads for his gubernatorial bid back in 2002 when he was filming *Mystic River* in New England. "This guy is too handsome to be governor," Eastwood remembered thinking, "but he does look like he could be president." As spring turned to summer, a growing number of voters agreed. National polls had him dead even with Obama.

But Romney found the life of a presidential nominee suffocating. At nights, he'd lie awake thinking about a gaffe he'd committed, or a strategic question his campaign was mulling, or all the people who were counting on him and the many ways he might let them down. During the day, he felt like he was being watched wherever he went.

He couldn't take a walk without a parade of Secret Service agents trailing him. He couldn't go to the grocery store without reporters following him through the aisles to record what brand of cereal he bought. Once, during some rare downtime at a Florida hotel, he tried to lie out on the terrace of his suite, but his aides hurried him back inside. News helicopters were hovering overhead, they explained, and the photographers had telephoto lenses.

In early June, he was informed that a hacker had gotten into the Dropbox account where he kept his journal and was threatening to give the entire thing to the gossip blog *Gawker*. While the Secret Service worked to track down the hacker, Romney and his campaign manager reread the entries with an eye toward political land mines. The journal was packed with them—the digs at Rick Perry, the venting about conservative voters. "It will be a field day for the media, and it will drive the beast for several days at least," he fretted in his newly secured journal. The Secret Service ultimately caught the hacker before the journal was exposed, but the episode cemented Romney's new reality: any semblance of privacy from here on out was an illusion.

It wasn't just his own inconvenience that bothered him. It was the extravagant security protocols that inconvenienced everyone else for his sake. He hated how the state police would shut down highways in every city he visited, causing massive traffic jams while his motorcade sliced through empty intersections. Sometimes he joked that he wished his SUV had an Obama bumper sticker on it. But those close to him knew it wasn't about politics—he was embarrassed by putting people out. He'd always been hypersensitive to the comfort of those around him, a quality forged by some combination of Waspy manners and Mormon breeding. Once, when his pregnant daughter-in-law, Laurie, was placed on bed rest, he dropped by and was appalled to find her confined to a second-floor bedroom in their townhome with limited entertainment. With Matt working long hours, Romney shifted into concerned-dad mode. He went to the store and returned with magazines, books, and snacks. He lugged a hutch into the bedroom, which he refashioned as an entertainment console with a resourcefully placed piece of plywood, and ran a cable extender up the stairs so she could watch TV. "I felt about an inch tall," Matt recalled, "but it's just who he is."

On June 11, Romney met with his top advisers at the campaign's concrete, fortress-like headquarters on Boston's North End to pick a running mate. His advisers had been debating the subject for months, but no clear consensus had formed. An initial list of two dozen names had been whittled down to five, and some advisers—who had nick-named the vetting operation "Project Goldfish," owing to the team's addiction to late-night snacks—had given each candidate a pescatarian code name: Chris Christie (Pufferfish), Rob Portman (Filet-O-Fish), Tim Pawlenty (Lakefish), Marco Rubio (Pescado), and Paul Ryan (Fishconsin). (Myers, who led the team, would later tell me these nick-names were never used around her and that she disapproved of them.)

Stevens had been lobbying Romney for weeks to pick Christie, the plump, brash governor of New Jersey who'd become famous for viral videos of him shouting down union members and other critics at town hall meetings. "We're in a street fight," Stevens argued, "and Christie is a street fighter." Romney, who was not a street fighter, saw the appeal. But he worried about Christie's prima donna tendencies, and whether he was up to the physical demands of the job. Even more troubling, the campaign's vetting process had turned up dozens of pages worth of barely buried scandals in New Jersey just waiting to be turned into attack ads for the Obama campaign.

Portman and Pawlenty were both solid and smart, but fatally dull. And while pundits and party elders loved the idea of elevating a young, charismatic Latino senator with working-class roots, Rubio had his own vetting issues—not least of which was the surprising revelation that he'd been baptized Mormon as a kid. For several years, Rubio attended a Latter-day Saint congregation with his family before eventually return-ing to Catholicism. It shouldn't have mattered, but evangelical voters were already struggling to stomach a Mormon nominee; a GOP ticket composed of a Mormon-and-a-half might be too much to take.

That left Ryan, the fresh-faced, right-wing fiscal policy wonk from Janesville, Wisconsin. As a youthful devotee of Ayn Rand, "Fishconsin" had formed a staunch belief in small-government conservatism, and as a fast-rising member of Congress he had made a name for himself writing federal budget proposals that cut taxes, slashed government spending, and shrank entitlement programs like Medicare and Social Security. This had made Ryan a polarizing figure in national politics— one Democratic attack ad had depicted Ryan literally pushing an elderly woman in a wheelchair off a cliff—but within Washington's conservative circles, he had a rising reputation as the "intellectual leader of the Republican Party."

Romney had gotten to know Ryan during a campaign swing through Wisconsin in the primaries and took an instant liking to the congressman. He was polished and polite and treated his elders with respect—the very picture of a "client-ready" first-year Bain associate. His well-documented penchant for data and spreadsheets suggested a kindred spirit—"like me on steroids," Romney effused in his journal— and his bland, dark-haired good looks would have blended in comfortably in a Romney family photo. Ryan, for his part, was surprised by how much he liked Romney. He'd expected an "east coast elite, high-finance kind of arrogant guy" but instead found someone who was approachable and funny. "He was a little moderate for my tastes," Ryan would tell me, "so I never thought of him as a great conservative. But when I got to know him riding around with him in a Suburban, I was like, 'This guy's a great *human being.*'"

Stevens warned Romney that picking Ryan was a risk. His austere fiscal policies might be a hit on the conservative think-tank circuit, but they were broadly unpopular in the national electorate. Did Romney really want to saddle himself with all that ideological baggage?

But Romney was unmoved by such warnings. He liked Ryan, he liked his wife and beautiful kids, and he liked the idea of having a guy with experience and relationships on Capitol Hill as his governing partner in the White House. It also helped that Ryan was so beloved by the same conservative media that continued to view Romney with a mix of suspicion and disdain.

Romney announced Ryan as his running mate on August 11, with the USS *Wisconsin* in Norfolk, Virginia as the backdrop. A crowd of two thousand flag-waving Republicans greeted the news with ecstatic approval. "Mitt Romney has finally thrown us a bone," Glenn Beck said on his radio show. The Tea Party Patriots released a statement hailing the pick proof that Romney had embraced the "values of fiscal responsibility."

The base, it seemed, had finally come around to Mitt Romney. After years of chasing his party's right wing, he had won them over. The victory would come with a price.

With the primaries over, some in Romney's circle began encouraging him to distance himself from Donald Trump. In an email, Mike Murphy told Romney the best line available to him in this new stage of the campaign was "Donald, you're fired." During a visit with Nancy Reagan at her home in Bel Air, the former First Lady told Romney over lemonade and cookies that she planned to endorse him that day, but issued a word of warning: stay away from Trump.

Romney was quick to rationalize keeping Trump inside the tent. Alienating a guy with a massive bullhorn and a habit of holding grudges seemed risky. And while, yes, Trump was clearly ridiculous and vapid and filled with outlandish ideas, Obama had accepted endorsements and checks from every dolt and crackpot in Hollywood, from Kanye West to Lena Dunham to Adam Levine—why couldn't Romney have his own silly celebrity surrogate?

But the truth, which surprised even Romney himself, was that he *liked* Trump. Or at least, he liked having him around. Trump was funny and outrageous and talking to him broke up the monotony of the campaign trail. After one entertaining phone call—during which Trump bounced frenetically from a North Carolina real estate deal he'd recently made a killing on to his supposedly huge fan base in China to his latest Twitter row with Cher—a still-chuckling Romney noted that the conversation had lifted his spirits. "This guy is not fake—he says 100% of what he thinks," he wrote in his journal. "No veneer, the real deal. Got to love him. Makes me laugh and makes me feel good, both. They just don't make people like Donald Trump very often."

Still, there was a cost to keeping Trump close. The man was impossible to "handle," in the traditional campaign-surrogate sense. You could not tell him what to say, or hand him a list of topics to avoid. He also tried to make every event he attended about himself. When Trump hosted Romney for a fundraiser at his Las Vegas hotel in May, donors queued up to get their customary photos with the candidates. Trump, assuming the line was for him, elbowed his way to the front and stood next to Romney for every picture. (Afterward, some disappointed donors asked Zwick if they could get a Trumpless photo with Romney.) For the rest of the event, Trump insisted on telling anyone who'd listen about the latest iteration of his Obama conspiracy theory. He was calling on the president to release his college transcripts because he now suspected that Obama may have falsely claimed he was Kenyan to score a foreign-student scholarship. *You can't make this stuff up,* Romney thought as he watched Trump rant to the donors.

Trump's ego was in constant need of care and feeding by the campaign. He called the Boston headquarters so often—offering unsolicited strategy advice, complaining about his lack of visibility on the campaign trail—that some senior staffers simply stopped taking his calls. The task of keeping him happy eventually fell to press secretary Andrea Saul, a natural schmoozer with a disarming Georgia accent and a talent for placating egomaniacs. Her desk became littered with business cards from various Trump associates and Post-it notes reminding her to call them back. The situation was exasperating, Saul would say later, "but we didn't want Trump's ire."

The Obama campaign, meanwhile, took every chance it could to remind voters of the Romney-Trump relationship, presenting it as emblematic of the extreme right-wing figures Romney had indulged to get the nomination. Steve King, the Iowa congressman who'd publicly compared immigrants to dogs, won Romney's endorsement in his reelection bid. Kris Kobach—the Kansas secretary of state who'd gained a reputation as "the dark lord" of the nativist right—was hailed by Romney as a "true leader." Obama's camp cited these unsavory alliances as proof that Romney lacked "moral leadership." "If Mitt Romney lacks the backbone to stand up to a charlatan like Donald Trump because he's so concerned about lining his campaign's pockets, what does that say about the kind of president he would be?" said Stephanie Cutter, Obama's deputy campaign manager. After Romney was captured by a photographer deplaning from his campaign jet in Las Vegas with Trump's plane parked conspicuously in the background, the Obama campaign started jamming the image into attack ads. Their research showed that every time voters saw it, if only for a split second, they connected Romney with the garish celebrity billionaire. "We made a lot of use of [Trump's plane]," David Axelrod would later recall with a laugh. "It was a shorthand way of branding Romney as a corporate Republican."

Romney tried lamely to dismiss the critics who questioned the political company he kept. "You know, I don't agree with all the people who support me, and my guess is they don't agree with everything I believe in," he told reporters. "But I need to get to 50.1 percent or more."

This realpolitik approach to coalition building had been central to the Romney campaign's strategy. Whenever the candidate privately balked at associating with some Republican crank, his advisers would appeal to his pragmatism. "The people who are speaking on your behalf, Mitt, some of them are not your friends," Zwick would recall telling him. "But the whole thing is we're going to have to build support from people who don't live next door to you in Belmont."

Now, though, they were entering a new stage of the race in which they needed the Trump fans *and* the Belmont crowd. The tensions at work in Romney's transition from breathless courter of the base to mainstream presidential nominee were on vivid display in the weeks leading up to the Republican National Convention in Tampa Bay. Presidential nominating conventions are always traffic jams of outsized egos—thousands of delegates and hundreds of politicians converging on an arena, each with their own agenda, bumping into each other and cutting each other off. The 2012 convention was further complicated by a hurricane barreling toward Tampa from the Gulf of Mexico, which forced organizers to cancel the first day's proceedings.

Not everyone was eager to accommodate the last-minute reshuffling of the program. Organizers tried to move New Mexico governor Susana Martinez out of prime time, but her staff went nuts and threatened to have her walk out of the convention "and take the Hispanics with her." Chris Christie, meanwhile, insisted on showing a three-minute hagiographic video about himself before he spoke, and then devoted the lion's share of his address to his own life and accomplishments in New Jersey. Romney, who was recovering from a cold, watched Christie's speech from the VIP box, but his reaction shots played poorly on TV—he looked grumpy and disapproving—and his staff convinced him to stay out of view until his own speech on the last night, lest he offend any of the other speakers.

In the orgy of ego and grievance-airing, none could compare to Trump. The reality TV superstar had expected a top-tier speaking slot. It only made sense to him—who *wouldn't* want Donald Trump in prime time? He was *Mr.* Prime Time! But the Romney campaign was nervous. Even if he let them vet his speech, and even if he stuck to the teleprompter (neither of which were guaranteed), inviting him to wander around the convention hall and blabber about Obama's birth certificate and college transcripts to any reporter who would listen didn't seem like a good idea. It would almost certainly mean ceding an entire day of press coverage to the Donald.

The campaign tried sending an aide to Trump Tower to offer him some media training and talking points, but Trump paid little attention. So, a compromise was proposed: in lieu of a speech, the campaign would produce a short, comic video that revolved around Trump "firing" Obama, *Apprentice*-style. One of Romney's top admen, Russ Schriefer, filmed the bit, spent several days trying to edit it into something usable, and breathed a sigh of relief when the hurricane gave them an excuse to ditch it. Trump was livid—and loud about it: "We don't have to be nice to President Obama," Trump fumed on Fox News the evening of his canceled appearance. "We don't have to say he's a wonderful person, because he's probably not a wonderful person. And, frankly, [Romney's team] cannot be politically correct. They have to say it like it is."

On the final night of the convention, Romney formally accepted his party's nomination and delivered an address intended to frame the election in lofty terms as a choice between two rival visions for America.

"The time has come to turn the page," Romney told the audience of 30 million viewers. "Today, the time has come for us to put the disappointments of the last four years behind us. To put aside the divisiveness and recriminations. To forget about what might have been and to look ahead to what can be. Now is the time to restore the promise of America."

It would end up being remembered as one of the pettiest, most forgettable presidential elections in modern history.

Romney squirmed in his seat, struggling to contain his displeasure with what he saw on the TV in front of him. Stevens and his fellow admen were screening a series of commercials they were ready to launch in swing states across the country. The ads were bleak and melodramatic, interspersing images of Depression-era breadlines with shots of Jimmy Carter while funereal music played in the background.

The idea, Stevens explained, was to give people who had voted for Obama in 2008 "permission" to reject his reelection by reminding them of other past presidents who were unequipped to lead the country through crises.

Romney didn't want to demoralize his team. They seemed proud of their work. But as one ad played after another, he couldn't keep it in any longer.

"This is killing me," Romney blurted.

The ads were all wrong, he told them. For one thing, nobody cared about Jimmy Carter anymore—most voters probably didn't even remember his presidency. For another, invoking breadlines in the current economic moment would come off as disingenuous and hysterical. More to the point, Romney didn't believe swing voters needed "permission" to ditch Obama—it was why the national polls were constantly fluctuating. What people needed was a reason to vote *for* Romney.

Romney sent his team back to the drawing board. In his journal, he fumed, "Obama theme: Forward. Not bad. Good, actually. Opposite of backward. Nice way to box me in. Dang. Why do I have no message yet?!"

It was the same problem that had dogged him since his very first bid for office—the struggle to articulate a big, inspiring reason for his campaign, a grand vision he planned to enact, a future he wanted to create. He seemed to think this was something that could be outsourced to pollsters and ad makers, the type of people who draw up marketing plans for any other product. His mind simply didn't move in sweeping ideological motions. His heart wasn't invested in a distant American utopia. The deepest belief motivating his pursuit of the presidency was in his own power to solve problems, to *fix things*.

But without a compelling vision to rally the country around, his campaign was left to focus voters' attention on Obama. Stevens was committed to the idea that if the election was successfully framed as a referendum on the president—at a moment when unemployment was high, wages were stagnating, and a majority of Americans were telling pollsters the country was on the wrong track—Romney would win. Under Stevens's theory, everything the campaign did should be designed to keep the pressure on Obama.

Even here, though, Romney's natural instinct was toward restraint. When Stevens proposed hijacking attention from the Democratic convention by releasing Romney's college transcripts and a ten-year summary of his taxes, Romney called it a "bad, bad idea" and shut it down. When conservatives urged him to ratchet up the campaign's attacks on Obama's character, Romney resisted.

"We could run ads about Bill Ayers, Rev. Wright, cocaine use," he wrote in his journal, "but that would degrade the office of the President, be inconsistent with the need for an honest debate about the nation's challenges, and maybe not work very well anyway. And it is not in my nature to run a campaign for the presidency on small things."

Romney really did believe this about himself—believed that he wanted the race to be about the big and important. And yet, day after day, small things kept finding their way into the center of the campaign. At a Pittsburgh-area picnic, Romney joked that the cookies looked like they were from a gas station, offending the local baker who had made them and prompting a slew of headlines about "Cookiegate." On a trip to London, Romney was asked about the city's preparations for the upcoming Olympic Games, and he said, "It's hard to know just how well it will turn out," enraging the tabloid press on both sides of the pond, and prompting *The Sun* to dub him "Mitt the Twit."

One prolonged subplot of the campaign had to do with a decades-old anecdote about Romney strapping the family dog, Seamus, to the roof of their station wagon during a road trip. One of Romney's sons had shared the story with a newspaper reporter as a funny demonstration of his dad's organizational skills: when Seamus experienced a bout of diarrhea, Romney moved quickly to find a rest stop, hose down the dog and car, and get back on the road without losing much time. But in the absence of more interesting scandals, *l'affaire Seamus* had been seized on by opponents and pundits as a withering indictment of Romney's character. Seamus showed up in attack ads and think pieces ("Dog Politics: Mitt Romney, Seamus & the Now Infamous Vacation"). Diane Sawyer asked him about it in an interview, as did Sean Hannity. One

New York Times columnist, Gail Collins, made a sport of shoehorning
Seamus references into unrelated columns and by one count ended up
doing so more than eighty times. ("Romney has already ruled out the
payroll tax cap. Also, he once drove to Canada with his dog tied to
the roof of the car," she wrote in one characteristic column.) The story
only receded once bloggers discovered an anecdote in Barack Obama's
memoir about eating dog meat in Indonesia, prompting a proliferation
of jokes on Twitter about the president's taste for German shepherd pie
and how Romney's road trip must have looked like "meals on wheels"
to Obama. Such was the elevated state of American political discourse
in the heat of the 2012 presidential election.

Years later, Collins would revisit this episode and confess that her
fixation on the Seamus story owed largely to boredom. The campaign
felt low-stakes, as far as presidential campaigns go, and Romney, she
wrote, "was a truly sleep-inducing candidate."

The 2012 presidential contest was also the first one in which Twitter
played a central role. Everyone involved in the race—from reporters
to cable news producers to campaign operatives—was addicted to
the platform, with its endless, frenetic stream of news and takes and
tidbits and scooplets and outrage and jokes and pithy insta-punditry.
Of course, they all bemoaned their favorite app's tendency to focus on
the stupidest parts of politics—most days, Twitter felt like a perpetual
distraction machine—but that didn't keep them from logging on. In
fact, the two campaigns could routinely be found on Twitter whack-
ing each other with sardonic quips and half-clever hashtags. By the
summer, even *Politico*—a website founded on cranking out quick-hit
ephemera for political junkies—was complaining that this was "the
smallest campaign ever."

For Romney, the media's fixation on what he called "verbal typos"
only made him more paranoid and prone to error. At a rally in Michigan in August, Romney was playing up his home state roots when
he ventured an offhand joke. "Ann was born at Henry Ford Hospital,
I was born at Harper Hospital. No one's ever asked to see my birth

certificate! They know that this is the place where we were born and raised." The "birth certificate" line immediately exploded on Twitter, and the fallout quickly migrated to the rest of the media as Democrats accused him of pandering to "birthers" and pundits debated the strategic pros and cons of his alliance with Trump. The truth, Romney wrote in his journal that night, was that he'd put no thought into the joke at all—it was simple "boneheaded" free association gone awry.

Romney tried not to sweat these mistakes. He told himself the election would be decided by loftier considerations than Cookiegate and dog-on-roof memes and his own ill-conceived jokes. When his advisers urgently instructed him not to appear in any photos with his wife's Olympic horse for fear of how it might be used against him, he rolled his eyes. He was all for being careful but sometimes he felt it had reached a point of absurdity. "My take—let the truth shine in," he wrote in frustration one day. "If [voters] can't handle the truth, they can have what they've got, a president who is taking America down the road of decline."

Romney's staff was not quite so confident. Their preference was to keep their gaffe-prone boss away from the cameras unless absolutely necessary. When the Supreme Court struck down portions of a controversial Arizona immigration law, and Romney wanted to hold an impromptu press conference about Obama's failure to solve the immigration crisis, his advisers prevailed upon him to settle for a written statement instead. When a Republican Senate candidate in Missouri claimed it was biologically rare for women to be impregnated by "legitimate rape," and Romney wanted to call for him to drop out of the race, his staff talked him down to a more moderate expression of disagreement. (Romney eventually called on the candidate to withdraw after it had become the consensus view in his party.)

The press noticed the campaign's guardedness; one reporter had termed it "the Mittness protection program." Romney hated any suggestion that he was a puppet of his political consultants—as a former consultant himself, he knew the buck always stopped with the principal.

But he did tend to defer to their judgment when all of them were speaking in one voice. And he found himself frustrated in moments like these. *Why are we always on defense? Why are we always so fearful?*

While Romney groped around for a general-election strategy, the Obama camp and its allies suffered from no such confusion. Their goal was clear: convince America that Mitt Romney was a fundamentally villainous character.

The project took various forms. They accused him of waging a "war on women," of flip-flopping and lying and soulless opportunism. There were even some fitful efforts to tag him as a racist: when Romney stated his opposition to Obamacare during a speech to the NAACP, one liberal columnist called him a "race-mongering pyromaniac." (Romney was taken aback by the charge: *Wouldn't it have been pandering to censor my positions for a Black audience?*) And when Joe Biden held a rally in a predominantly Black Virginia neighborhood, he told the crowd that Romney wanted to "put y'all back in chains."

The attacks that proved most effective against Romney were those that presented him as a cold-blooded, out-of-touch plutocrat. "We knew that we probably wouldn't win a race [about] who had the expertise to manage the economy," Axelrod would tell me later. But if the choice was framed as being between a corporate raider and a champion of the middle class, Obama would prevail. "Everything we did was kind of set up to create a contrast with Romney on that matrix."

The Obama campaign carpeted swing states with commercials reviving the old attacks on Romney's private equity career—the plant closures, the outsourcing, the outlandish paydays for Bain's Gekkoesque partners. One especially scathing ad, produced by a pro-Obama political action committee, featured a widower whose wife died of cancer after he lost his job at a plant owned by Bain. "I do not think Mitt Romney realizes what he's done to anyone," the widower said. "And furthermore, I do not think Mitt Romney is concerned."

Democrats made sure midwestern voters were reminded of an op-ed Romney had written for the *New York Times* in 2008 titled "Let Detroit Go Bankrupt." And Obama himself took to describing his opponent's economic agenda as a plot to take from the poor and give to the rich. "It's like Robin Hood in reverse," he would crow in stump speeches. "It's Romney-hood!"

The pugilistic Democratic Senate leader Harry Reid, meanwhile, came up with his own creative line of attack. In interviews and Senate speeches he began claiming that he'd heard from a reliable source that Romney once went a decade without paying any taxes. He offered no evidence, and refused to name his source. But with a push, he was able to insert the rumor into the political discourse. Noting that Romney had failed to release the same extensive tax records that George Romney had in 1967, Reid even feigned disappointment: "His poor father must be so embarrassed about his son."

Not all these attacks stood up to scrutiny. The cancer spot was panned by fact-checkers in the press, and the Obama campaign quietly disavowed the commercial. The headline of the *Times* op-ed, it turned out, had been written by an editor at the paper. (Romney's suggested headline had been "How to Save the Auto Industry.") And Reid himself would later slyly acknowledge that his claim about Romney's taxes was a lie—though he expressed no regret: "Romney didn't win, did he?" he told a reporter with a smirk.

But the veracity of individual claims hardly mattered. Once the fat-cat narrative took hold, every detail of Romney's life became fodder for caricature. Ann's dressage horse was featured in multiple Democratic attack ads. The "car elevator" they planned to install at their La Jolla home was widely ridiculed for its outrageous excess.

Romney was incensed by what he considered, in his more self-pitying moments, a shameless smear campaign against him. But he was less sure of what he could do about it. When his primary opponents had tried to weaponize his wealth against him, he was able to respond with righteous Republican indignation about how *in this country* we don't demonize success, we celebrate it. Now the playbook was less clear.

Some Romney backers argued that he should lean into his wealth and status. In a widely circulated *National Review* cover story that seemed trollish and tongue-in-cheek at the time, and eerily prescient a few years later, the conservative writer Kevin Williamson proposed that Romney abandon the "ordinary schmo" routine and adopt the persona of an "apex alpha executive."

> He should not be afraid of being loaded; instead he should have some fun with it. He will discover something that the Obama campaign has not quite figured out yet: Americans do not hate rich people. Americans love rich people. Americans will sit on their couches and watch billionaire Donald Trump fire people on television—for fun. . . . *Newsweek*, which as of this writing is still in business, recently ran a cover photo of Romney with the headline: "The Wimp Factor: Is He Just Too Insecure to Be President?" Look at his fat stacks. Look at that mess of sons and grandchildren. Look at a picture of Ann Romney on her wedding day and that cocky grin on his face. What exactly has Mitt Romney got to be insecure about?

The consultants on Romney's campaign were skeptical of this analysis—but they also knew that, even if he tried, their boss could never pull off the schtick. He had a decidedly Waspy attitude toward wealth that struck normal people as more remote than aspirational; he believed that flaunting it was gauche and did not behoove a future president of the United States.

Instead, Romney did his best to make voters forget how rich he was. He gave speeches in jeans and rolled-up sleeves, and doled out hot dogs at NASCAR races. He tweeted about his campaign-trail diet of donuts and Subway sandwiches. He flew coach. The frugality was real—Mitt was his father's son—but to many it came off as disingenuous. "In a political environment, it is always difficult for people to show what they're really like," Stevens would later tell me, noting that Romney once arrived late to a meeting with John McCain because he had opted for a cheaper JetBlue ticket over a Delta flight that would have gotten him there on time.

The irony of all the candidates' aesthetic posturing and the media's focus on microscopic minutiae was that there were genuine, important ideological differences between the two men in the race. When Romney had told a group of hecklers at the Iowa State Fair that "corporations are people, my friend"—handing the Obama campaign a golden sound bite for future use—he'd really meant it. For all his complicated feelings about the broader conservative agenda, Romney was a committed capitalist. He believed the things he said in his speeches—that free enterprise was the most successful antidote to poverty in the history of the world, that federal policy should be designed to support existing businesses and help grow new ones, that the best government was one that made the lives of "job creators" as easy as possible. Everybody benefited from what they built.

Critics called these ideas warmed-over trickle-down Reaganism; Romney called them simple common sense. And the more time he spent on the campaign trail, the more reinforcement he found for this worldview. Everywhere he went, his campaign arranged meetings and photo ops with struggling small-business owners—a steel processor in Ohio, a coal pit operator in West Virginia, a furniture seller in Las Vegas, an ice cream shop proprietor in New Hampshire. Romney was innately sympathetic to entrepreneurs—a career in private equity will do that to someone—and as he listened to them talk about their desperate scramble to make ends meet amid a recession and suffocating government regulations, his resolve only hardened. He collected their stories and wedged them into virtually every stump speech he gave.

"When this president attacks businesses for making money," Romney would say in speech after speech, "he is also attacking the very communities he wanted to help. That's how it works in America. Or at least that's how it works when America is working."

Of course, behind closed doors and away from the cameras, Romney was also spending lots of time with a different type of business owner—the type that had Picassos on their walls and Degas sculptures on their credenzas; and job titles that began with "chief" or "chairman"; the type that were capable of hosting a hundred other people like themselves in their multimillion-dollar homes, where everybody came with a checkbook in hand. Romney was just as enamored of this type as he was with the couple that ran the mini-carrot plant. After titans, Romney wrote in his journal, "These guys are heroes."

It wouldn't be until later that Romney realized the fatal flaw in devoting so much of his campaign message to courting and celebrating America's bosses. Most Americans are not bosses, after all—in fact, most don't especially like their bosses. "If I were to go back and do it again, I would not be talking about making America the most attractive place to start businesses," Romney told me. "I'd say, I want to get wages up."

By the end of the summer, the Obama campaign's $85 million ad blitz had done its damage. In a state-of-the-race memo, the Romney campaign's pollster, Neil Newhouse, laid it out plainly: "Their earned media, surrogates and allies were all reading from the same song sheet in going after you. They focused on taxes, Bain, outsourcing, women's issues (contraception, Planned Parenthood and abortion), and out of touch. All of these hits were 'new information' to voters—and that's what they crave. They don't want to be told what they already know. While we hit back, it wasn't with particularly new information or information that they thought was 'fair'—taking Obama's words out of context for example."

Newhouse's internal polling showed Romney trailing by an average of 2 to 3 points in most swing states. In his journal, Romney was stoic and clear-eyed when it came to the likelihood of winning. He knew it would be an uphill climb and continued to tell himself that it might be better for his family if he lost. "Winning would change our lives for the worse—much worse," he wrote. "But losing would also be hard—the country desperately needs leadership. It's win-win or lose-lose—maybe both."

At the same time, he was becoming less charitable when it came to his opponent. In speeches and interviews, Romney had always maintained that he had nothing personal against Obama. He considered the president a "nice guy" who was simply out of his depth—a man who lacked the practical business experience that this crisis called for. But after enduring a blistering, monthslong assault on his character, Romney was cranky and no longer inclined to give Obama the benefit of the doubt. After talking to the president briefly at an event, Romney observed in his journal, "He is not a warm person—friendly but not a friend. Gracious, but without genuine grace." In another entry, he wrote, "I have seen a level of dishonesty I had not imagined in him. He and his team lie time and again. His arrogance is breathtaking. This man should not be the most powerful man in the world."

Years later, Romney would reread this entry and laugh at the irrational hatreds that are forged in the heat of a campaign. He really *had* convinced himself that Obama's reelection would be catastrophic for the country; that his character was unbecoming of the office and his policies would destabilize America's place in the world.

He had no idea how much worse it could get.

The advice was relentless, frequently bad, and came from all quarters. Wherever Romney went—fundraisers, rope lines, celebrity meet and greets—people wanted to tell him why he was losing and how to turn it around.

Often, the advice was contradictory. Mike Murphy told him to slow down when he spoke, but Warren Beatty encouraged him to stick to his natural pace lest he sound unnatural.

During a lunch with Roger Ailes, the head of Fox News told Romney he should work more patriotic themes into his speeches. Romney, surprised, asked Ailes if he'd ever seen his stump speech.

"No," Ailes replied, "but when I watch clips on TV, they always have you talking about policy and process, not American patriotism."

Well, who decides which clips to put on TV, Roger? Romney thought. He bit his tongue.

Biting his tongue turned out to be an important skill in dealing with all the unsolicited advice—especially from donors. As a category, the men and women (but mostly men) who paid top dollar to get in the room with a Republican presidential nominee believed they were entitled to speak their minds. Romney frequently jotted down their pearls of wisdom in his journal: you need to connect with middle Americans; you need to debate like you debated Kennedy in '94; say that Obama is making us like Europe; say that Obama is tearing America apart; use more personal examples; tell the voters how great Big Oil really is; take off the gloves; buck up the troops; you need to be bold; you need to be relatable; you need to give more specifics; you need to be more inspiring—and on and on and on and on.

Romney mostly humored the donors, but sometimes—when a self-appointed expert was acting especially smug—he couldn't quite keep himself from arguing. At one fundraiser, in Chicago, a donor opined that Romney should spend more time publicly litigating the role that Fannie Mae and Freddie Mac played in the financial crisis, and when he demurred, the guy followed him down the hall after the event, shouting that he was doomed to lose the election if he didn't take his advice. At another fundraiser, in Colorado, a donor told him to talk more about turning around the Olympics. Romney explained that the campaign's focus groups hadn't responded strongly to the Olympics story, but the man refused to back down. Exasperated by the arrogance, Romney jumped down his throat.

"The know-it-all advice sometimes gets irritating," he vented later in his journal.

Stevens had implored Romney to simply stop taking questions at these closed-door fundraisers. He didn't like the unpredictability of the entitled-rich-guy crowds, and worried that without cameras around the candidate might wind up saying something imprudent. Romney tried skipping the Q&A portion of the event a few times, but he found it intolerably awkward. These people had written big checks to his campaign—he couldn't just *not* hear them out.

On the afternoon of September 17, Romney received his first classified national security briefing at the FBI building in Los Angeles. It was customary for both major-party nominees to get briefed by the intelligence community in the months leading up to the election to ensure that the next president was up to speed when he took office. Romney savored the high-level rundown on terrorist threats and global hot spots—Afghanistan, Pakistan, Libya, Syria. This is what he'd always thought running for president should feel like: important, substantial—soberly engaging with the most urgent issues of the day.

After the briefing, he slid into the black SUV idling outside. He was feeling good—presidential, even. The motorcade had just begun to roll, when an aide in the back seat said, "Guv, we've got a problem." He handed Romney an iPad with an alarming headline scrawled across the screen: "SECRET VIDEO: Romney Tells Millionaire Donors What He REALLY Thinks of Obama Voters."

The liberal magazine *Mother Jones* had published a grainy recording of a Boca Raton fundraiser Romney had attended back in May. Four months was an eternity in a presidential campaign, and Romney had shuffled through so many high-dollar fundraisers since then that he could barely remember the event at first, let alone what he'd said in the room. But there he was on the screen, his voice metallic and cold, sounding exactly like the plutocratic caricature the Democrats had been painting:

> There are 47 percent of the people who will vote for the president no matter what. All right, there are 47 percent who are with him, who are dependent upon government, who believe that they are victims, who believe the government has a responsibility to care for them, who believe that they are entitled to health care, to food, to housing, to you-name-it. That that's an entitlement. And the government should give

it to them. And they will vote for this president no matter what. . . .
These are people who pay no income tax; 47 percent of Americans
pay no income tax. So our message of low taxes doesn't connect. And
he'll be out there talking about tax cuts for the rich. I mean, that's
what they sell every four years. And so my job is not to worry about
those people. I'll never convince them that they should take personal
responsibility and care for their lives. What I have to do is convince the
5 to 10 percent in the center that are independents, that are thoughtful,
that look at voting one way or the other depending upon in some cases
emotion, whether they like the guy or not.

The clip was rocketing around the internet; the press was in a frenzy.
While the campaign's top lieutenants assembled in Boston to game
out the first stages of damage control, Romney searched his mind for
what had prompted him to say something so idiotic. He remembered
the event now. It had been held in a gaudy mansion with two Ferraris
parked out front. Stevens had later joked that the unusual number of
young, scantily clad women in attendance suggested the presence of
"Russian hookers."

The instigating question had been put to Romney by some faceless,
know-it-all donor: "For the last three years, all everybody's been told
is 'Don't worry, we'll take care of you.' How are you going to do it, in
two months before the elections, to convince everybody you've got to
take care of yourself?"

It was an achingly stupid question—an amateur pundit showing
off for his friends, void of substance or actual thought—and Romney
couldn't believe he had been stupid enough to accept its premise. *I
was just trying to be polite*, he thought to himself miserably, and not
altogether convincingly.

Still, Romney's initial impulse upon watching the video was to
rationalize. He had been making a simple *political* point—that a narrow swath of voters were up for grabs, and those were the ones he was
focused on. Had his phrasing been inartful? Sure, granted. But those

who were trying to turn this into some great controversy were being disingenuous.

At least, that's what he told the hastily convened gaggle of campaign reporters that met him in Orange County. But the half apology did little to quell the growing media excitement. The next day Obama addressed the video on Letterman: "When I won in 2008, 47 percent of the American people voted for John McCain," the president said. "They didn't vote for me. And what I said on election night was, even though you didn't vote for me, I hear your voice and I'm going to work as hard as I can to be your president."

In the days that followed, the pile-on intensified, including from the right. Bill Kristol called the comments "stupid and arrogant." David Brooks suggested that Romney "really doesn't know much about the country he inhabits." In a blistering *Wall Street Journal* column, Peggy Noonan called for an "intervention" with the nominee—shake up the staff, overhaul the strategy, and fire Stuart Stevens. "It's time to admit the Romney campaign is an incompetent one," the columnist wrote. "It's not big, it's not brave, it's not thoughtfully tackling great issues. It's always been too small for the moment."

Romney had no patience for this line of criticism. "Stupid," he wrote in his journal. "The team is excellent—the problem is me, not them!"

"Ninety-nine percent of candidates would have blamed staff for not handling it," Stevens would say later. "He had the exact opposite reaction."

As his polling free fall steepened and the media free-for-all raged on and reports trickled in that the campaign was now begging donors not to bail on his fundraisers, Romney sank into a depression so deep that some in his orbit would wonder if his suffering was clinical.

He could barely eat during the day and struggled to sleep at night, even after popping a Lunesta. He couldn't even bring himself to listen to music in his hotel room—"just too sick at heart," he wrote. When he tried to concentrate on briefing materials, his mind would drift toward the self-inflicted damage he had done to his campaign, and to all the people he had failed. To take his mind off it, he rode the elliptical at a punishing pace.

Night after night, Romney castigated himself in his private diary.

"Stupid, stupid, stupid," he wrote.

"Awful, shameful, sorrowful," he wrote.

"How I will have let so many down," he wrote. "I can't dwell on it— it is overwhelmingly depressing, even agonizing. I am so, so very sorry."

Mike Leavitt, the former governor of Utah and a close friend and adviser, had once told him that political leaders are often defined by the things they least expect. For Leavitt, it had been the Salt Lake City Olympics. For Jimmy Carter, it was a helicopter crash in Iran. Romney now feared that this would be what he was remembered for—a surreptitiously recorded rant that ran directly counter to his true motivations for seeking the presidency.

Because for all his ego and self-regard, for all his visceral love of emergencies and catastrophes, Romney still believed he was running to help the Americans who were in trouble. And yes, that included—*especially* included—those who were poor and wallowing in the federal welfare system. "The rich will do fine with or without me," Romney wrote in his journal. "It's the rest that need my experience and economic direction."

It did not escape Romney that he was now entering the same terminal stage of a campaign that his father once had, and for roughly the same reason. Mitt's diatribe wasn't a perfect parallel to his father's "brainwashing" comment. (In some ways it was worse.) But the spectre of George's gaffe-induced meltdown had haunted his son's entire political career—somehow, it seemed darkly fitting that his own quest for the presidency would end in a similar whimper.

As Romney spiraled, his advisers sought to rally him. A "war council" was convened in Boston, where a retinue of Republican governors and party elders took turns assuring the nominee that he could recover from the 47 percent video. ("I get lower and lower as I think about how I have messed up, with such consequences for everyone who has been counting on me," he wrote. "I leave the session pretty depressed.")

George W. Bush called to buck him up. Don't worry, he said, if Obama is anything like me, he'll screw up before this election is over.

Mike Murphy emailed with a series of ideas to reboot his campaign, and tried to convince him that victory was still within reach: "Obama is [the] country's second choice for POTUS. Today you are third choice, but top slot is still wide open! Jump for it!!"

Ann even made her husband meet privately with Tony Robbins, the famed motivational speaker, one morning at a hotel in San Francisco. Robbins showed Romney tape of himself in public and instructed him on the importance of projecting confidence even when he was feeling the most uncertain—shoulders back, hands and arms out, eyes focused. Striking the right physical pose would inevitably translate to the psyche, Robbins told him. Romney appreciated the counsel—he'd always thought the kind of people who sneered at Robbins were the ones who could most benefit from his counsel—but the session had little lasting effect on his mood.

In the days after the leak of the 47 percent video, Newhouse had decided to temporarily shut down the campaign's polling operation. He knew the numbers would be terrible at first, but with any luck they'd rebound—no use in unnecessarily demoralizing the candidate. Nearly two weeks later, though, the campaign's internal polling was worse than it had ever been. Romney was trailing—in some cases, badly—in every battleground state. Down five in Florida; down eight in Ohio. Virginia, which had been a toss-up, was now looking solidly blue. The race, Romney began to think, was no longer within reach.

Late on the night of September 30, Romney called Stevens with a startling question: "Should I just drop out of the race?"

Romney reasoned that Republicans would have a better chance if they swapped him out for someone who wasn't so easily saddled with claims that he only cared about the rich. He suggested Chris Christie or Rob Portman.

The election was six weeks away, and the Republican presidential nominee was actively discussing resigning his candidacy.

Stevens, who'd continued to play the role of the inexhaustible pep-talker, decided to level with Romney: No, you are not dropping out of this race, he said. I don't really know if you're going to win, but if you lose I can promise you it won't be because of this tape.

It wasn't the most comforting thing Stevens had ever said to him, but it was what Romney needed to hear in that moment. It was enough to snap him out of his funk and return him to the realm of logic and analysis where he thrived. In Romney's estimation, the only chance he had to win now was an apocalyptically bad jobs report from the federal government in the final weeks of the race, or a knockout debate performance. Romney had no control over the former, but he still had the ability to influence the latter. He needed to focus on the things he could control.

The first presidential debate, in Denver, was three days away. Romney swore to himself that he'd be ready.

Romney had devoted an unprecedented amount of time to debate prep, having begun training in earnest for the face-off with Obama almost immediately after clinching the nomination.

The campaign produced reams of detailed briefing material, covering Chrysler's restructuring after the auto bailout and the intricacies of Simpson-Bowles and the Taliban's fighting season in Afghanistan, all of which Romney spent hours poring over. He participated in half a dozen multi-hour mock debates, and after each session Romney assigned his aides to produce yet more briefing material to sharpen his answers. As a matter of strategy, his advisers urged him to spend as little time as possible defending himself—*Don't let Obama bait you*, Stevens repeatedly reminded him—and to focus instead on prosecuting the president. The campaign produced a series of memos anticipating each of Obama's criticisms and laying out how he could "pivot to offense" in fewer than two sentences. Ever the diligent student, Romney studied each bullet point with Talmudic intensity. To play Obama in the mock debates, Romney had recruited Ohio senator Rob Portman, who listened to the president's autobiography on repeat to master his cadence.

During one of the debate sessions, Portman-as-Obama began by wishing the First Lady a happy anniversary: "I love you, sweetie."

Romney looked over at Portman, annoyed. "He's not going to do that."

"Of course he is," Portman replied.

"No," Romney insisted. "Because the debate rules say you can't acknowledge anybody in the audience."

Portman strained not to laugh. "Nobody is going to enforce that," he said. Others in the room agreed, and together they came up with a self-deprecating line for Romney to use just in case Portman was right. ("I'm sure this is the most romantic place you could imagine: here with me.") But Romney remained irritated by the prospect of rule breaking. "He's not supposed to do that," he grumbled to himself.

What made Romney's diligence so impressive was that he *hated* debate prep. He always had, going all the way back to those vexing mock debates with Myers in Massachusetts. But Romney, like many successful people, had an uncommonly high tolerance for doing unpleasant things—and the fruits of his forbearance showed.

By the end of September, Romney and his team felt confident in his answers to every question but one: the 47 percent video. Every response they came up with sounded mealymouthed and insincere, or worse. During one huddle with his staff, an adviser suggested invoking Obama's own sneering, caught-on-mic moment from 2008—the one about "bitter" people in small midwestern towns who "cling to guns or religion." But Romney quickly swatted down the idea.

Finally, Eric Fehrnstrom—a long-serving aide who had been with Romney for more than a decade—came up with a response that everyone liked.

You should be indignant, he told his boss. "I've been a missionary, I've been a bishop in my church, I served the Olympics without pay—how dare you accuse me of not caring about others? How dare you . . . ?" As Fehrnstrom kept going, Romney furiously scribbled in a legal pad. He'd found his answer to "47 percent."

Romney arrived at the University of Denver on October 3 with his family and spent some time relaxing with his grandkids. Minutes before the debate began, Ann pulled him into a backstage shower stall for one last prayer together. As he walked onstage to shake hands with the president, Romney was consumed with a steely calm. He noted to himself, with a measure of surprise, that he was not nervous at all to be confronting the leader of the free world.

When the two men met center stage for perfunctory off-mic pleasantries, Romney leaned in. "The last time we were with each other was at the Gridiron," he told Obama, alluding to the white-tie dinner in Washington where they'd both recently delivered comic speeches. "I hope we can be as entertaining this time."

Presidential campaigns are too often talked about in militaristic metaphors. But what took place over the next hour and a half could only be described as a rout. Romney was sharp, clear, eminently articulate— even funny and human, which were not qualities he often succeeded in showcasing as a candidate. He executed perfectly on his campaign's strategy, landing one rhetorical blow after another—none of which the president seemed interested in parrying. At one point, Romney rattled off a list of unkept campaign promises before telling Obama, "You've been president four years." At another, he accused his opponent of distorting his record: "You're entitled as the president to your own airplane and to your own house, but not your own facts."

It was the strangest thing, but every time Romney glanced over at Obama's podium, he found the president looking down at his notes, his shoulders slumped, his eyes downcast. When Obama did talk, he rambled and meandered, returning repeatedly to pedantic policy points and squabbling with the moderator over how much time he had to answer questions. To Romney's astonishment, he didn't even get to use the answer he'd come up with to counter the 47 percent tape—Obama didn't bring it up.

When the debate ended, Romney returned to his greenroom to find dozens of campaign staffers and family members rhapsodically cheering. The instant polls, the Twitter pundits, even the talking heads on MSNBC—*everyone* was unanimous that Romney had won. Perhaps most gratifyingly, the voices on the right who'd spent the past year and a half steadfastly resisting Romney as their standard-bearer were grudgingly admitting they'd been wrong. Rush Limbaugh, one of his most persistent critics throughout the primaries, had emailed one of Romney's advisers to say the nominee had just pulled off "the best debate performance I have seen in my life"—better, even, than Reagan.

Back at the hotel, while Romney and his family stayed up late replaying the best moments and reading aloud the funniest tweets of the night, someone remarked that this was the best night of the campaign so far. Romney couldn't disagree.

The next two debates weren't quite as triumphant. Obama got off a slew of solid zingers; Romney slipped into highly tweetable gaffes. (When he tried to describe his efforts to promote gender diversity in his gubernatorial administration, the only thing anyone remembered was his awkward phrasing—"binders full of women"—and the days worth of Twitter jokes it generated.) Media coverage of the final debate focused on Obama's withering mockery of Romney for saying that Russia was America's top geopolitical foe.

"The 1980s are now calling to ask for their foreign policy back," the president cracked, prompting laughter to ripple through the press room.

Meanwhile, the gadflies and extremists in Romney's party continued to make life difficult for him. Richard Mourdock, a Republican Senate candidate from Indiana whom Romney had warmly endorsed, publicly mused that "even when life begins in that horrible situation of rape, that's something God intended to happen." Sarah Palin injected some old-fashioned race-baiting into the campaign with a dog-whistling attack on Obama's "shuck and jive schtick." And just as the race reached its final days, Romney's most reckless surrogate tried to turn the cameras back on himself by promising a major announcement that would upend the election.

"I have something very, very big concerning the president of the United States," Trump told Fox News on October 22. "It's very big, bigger than anybody would know."

Romney did not want the election upended, and certainly not by Trump. For a few days, he became obsessed with Trump's gambit, pestering his staffers to find out what this announcement was all about and whether they could stop it. "Heaven only knows what he is planning on doing," he wrote in his journal. When the big "announcement" was finally revealed—Trump said he would write a $5 million check to the charity of Obama's choice if he agreed to release his college transcripts—Romney just sighed and rolled his eyes. There was no use, he now realized, in trying to control people like Trump. This was Romney's party; these were his bedfellows. He had no choice but to sleep with them.

In the frantic final sprint of the campaign, Romney's daily schedule was dizzying—wake up in Florida, fall asleep in New Hampshire, log three flights and five rallies in the nineteen hours in between—but he tried to pause and take in the surreal grandeur of the moment. Politicians were always talking about how "humbled" they were to participate in the grand pageant of democracy that was a presidential campaign. Romney now felt he could relate to the trope. After a long day of campaigning in Virginia and Ohio, he reflected on the experience in his journal:

Gosh, we are in the center of the attention of the nation and the world. There is no other event currently transpiring that is more watched, more debated, or frankly, more important to the future of the world than the race for the presidency of the United States. And Ann and I are in the middle of it. How in the world did this happen?! Who would have ever imagined that we would be where we are doing this? It is simply so far beyond reason that it is hard for us to see it for what it is—we just get up, do our interviews and rallies, and then go to bed, without really contemplating the extraordinary nature of it all, the significance. I see 50 motorcycles in our caravan now, with 15 or so vehicles following, including an assault team, a hazmat team, EMS vehicle, 2 press buses, 5 press vans, and I think nothing about it until I stop and it hits me. As George W. Bush said to Ann when he was in Boston—"This is a big F—ing deal." No kidding.

Beth Myers asked me today what it feels like to have a crowd of 10,000 people cheering for me, pushing to grab my hand, screaming. It just stopped me in my tracks—yeah, it is overwhelming. And it is monumentally humbling. How can I possibly measure up to what is needed so very badly? I'm just Mitt—bird legs, working harder than anyone else in law school so that I don't flunk out, running Cranbrook cross-country until I pass out because I have scant athletic ability, puzzled by my Hampton School first grade teacher's assignment about drawing an apple in four squares, falling down the Park City mountain, getting an F on my poli sci paper at Stanford, stupefied that Ann Davies likes me—Romney!

As eager as he was for it all to be over, Romney knew he would miss this—the rush, the relevance, the sense of urgency. He remembered how badly his father missed public life when his political career was over; how it took him years to emerge from the melancholy feeling of uselessness. Romney had heard once about a rehab hospital for military veterans where they played first-person-shooter video games in a 360-degree IMAX theater. The theory was that the ex-soldiers benefited from weaning themselves off war gradually. Romney privately wondered if he might need something similar if he lost. In his immersive theater, he joked, there would be videos of cheering crowds and motorcades, of course, but also a smug-looking Obama glaring at him on a debate stage, and a health-conscious Stuart Stevens pulling grilled chicken breasts out of his briefcase, and hundreds of identical Marriott hotel rooms.

Romney remained, in the pages of his journal, deeply conflicted about whether he actually wanted to win. "Sometimes, it is hard for me to accurately gauge my true feelings about the election," he wrote a few days before the race's end. "When I read discouraging polls, I note that I too am discouraged—that being the case, I clearly want to win. When I think about the task if I am elected . . . I intellectually think it may not be a job I'd like very much. I may well have to decide whether and how to take military action against Iran's nukes; I will have to reform entitlements, reform the tax code, fix the budget mess, etc. Also, the economy is still under the burden of too much debt—deleveraging is still underway. Some of what I must do to fix the country will be very unpopular, stress-inducing, and miserable to undertake with a Congress that is often dysfunctional."

But as daunting as the challenges of the presidency seemed, the prospect of disappointing so many people with a loss was worse. He wrote long, melodramatic passages in his journal about how he'd be "haunted by the prayers" of millions who'd placed their hopes in him. "It cannot be so easy to lose," he wrote. "I am not certain that I will not feel terribly depressed, having failed so many who counted on me, and having failed the nation."

The election had thrust him into a strange mental place inhabited both by the pace and immediacy of the campaign trail and the existential reflection that such an undertaking inspired. He found himself thinking more and more about his own mortality—in no small part because there were so many people trying to kill him these days. After he got the nomination, the Secret Service had begun briefing him on the credible threats on his life, but Romney asked them to stop unless there were specific precautions he could take. He'd rather not think about all the people who were plotting his death. The Ron Paul wackos, the crazed anti-Mormons, the crazed anti-Romney Mormons, the Muslim jihadists, the Russians, the Chinese, the conspiracy theorists, the union thugs—once he started listing them, it was alarmingly easy to keep going. "I really would prefer not to be killed," he wrote in his journal one day after learning about yet another death threat.

But these weren't the only reminders of life's fragility that he encountered. On the endless fundraising circuit, he was constantly coming across titans of industry, leaders of men, who looked much frailer and sadder than he remembered them—their bodies ravaged by disease, their marriages falling apart. "How the great are brought down, prey to the taxes of infirmity, age, and ego," he wrote.

He remained unsure of whether God had an interest in the outcome of the election—he'd felt at times like he was being guided by Providence, but also knew that such feelings could be deceptive. His dad had felt the same way about his own path to the presidency until it slammed headlong into the reality of defeat. Romney tried to be at peace with not knowing what was on the horizon. He thought about the words of a hymn he sang in church: "Keep thou my feet, I do not ask to see the distant scene, one step enough for me."

In the end, it was an act of God that defined the final days of the election. In late October, a deadly hurricane hit the East Coast, effectively grounding the Republican nominee's campaign, elevating Obama's role as commander-in-chief, and convincing some untold number of swing voters to stick with the devil they knew. Was Hurricane Sandy really the fatal blow to Romney's candidacy? Some of his advisers believed it was, and were especially frustrated with Chris Christie's decision to invite Obama to New Jersey after the hurricane and warmly hug him in full view of the press, giving the incumbent a picture-perfect moment of bipartisan leadership. "Christie is the same in front of a TV camera as he is in front of a refrigerator," Stevens grumbled. "He can't help himself in either case."

Romney didn't know how much effect the hurricane had on the race. What he did know was that, against his better judgment, he had allowed himself to believe in those final days that he would win. Which was how he found himself in a hotel suite in Boston late on the night of the election, surrounded by shell-shocked family members and advisers, asking, "So, what do you think you say in a concession speech?"

He hadn't bothered to write one, so sure he was of victory. Or maybe it was just that he knew it wouldn't be hard to come up with the words in the event of defeat. There was a well-established tradition for presidential losers, not grand exactly, but patriotic in its way—thank his campaign and supporters, congratulate the winner, say a few words about national unity, and then shuffle off the stage as quickly as possible.

Not everybody in Romney's inner circle was ready that night to throw in the towel. The margins were close in several states, and planes filled with election lawyers had been dispatched to wage recount battles. But Romney had no interest in or stomach for an ugly, drawn-out, likely doomed legal battle, and told his staff he didn't want to look like a "nut job" by not conceding. He'd rolled his eyes at bogus conspiracy theories circulating on the left that his son Tagg planned to tamper with the election outcome through an Ohio voting machine company he was supposedly invested in—and Romney didn't want to lower himself to the same level of his most deranged detractors.

Shortly after midnight, he made the call. "It's over," he told his team.

As they talked through his speech, Stevens tried to convince Romney that he might still have a role to play in American politics, but Romney peevishly dismissed him. "My time on the stage is over, guys." His quest for 50.1 percent of the electorate had come up short. (Insult added to injury when the final tally was reached: Romney had won 47 percent of the vote.)

An hour later, Romney stood before a ballroom full of supporters and delivered a short, gracious concession.

"I so wish that I had been able to fulfill your hopes to lead the country in a different direction, but the nation chose another leader," he said. "And so Ann and I join with you to earnestly pray for him and for this great nation."

*   *   *

Somewhere in the sky over the American northeast, Donald Trump sat in the dark of a helicopter, unraveling.

He was supposed to be at a victory party in Boston that night, but something had gone wrong. An election was being stolen. The people had to know.

Just before midnight, the tweets began to appear.

"We can't let this happen. We should march on Washington and stop this travesty. Our nation is totally divided!"

"Let's fight like hell and stop this great and disgusting injustice!"

"This election is a total sham and a travesty. We are not a democracy!"

"Revolution!"

CHAPTER NINE

Just the Beginning

There is a special kind of indignity in losing a presidential race—you are at least momentarily one of the most famous people in America, but half the country hates you, and the rest see you as an object of pity. For Mitt Romney, who retreated to La Jolla after folding up his campaign operation in Boston, the months following his loss were a miserable slog. Venturing into public was a nightmare, of course. Photos of him looking cranky and washed-up spread across the internet in a blur of giddy schadenfreude: Mitt pumping gas in a wrinkled shirt, his hair uncharacteristically mussed; Mitt at the McDonald's counter alone; Mitt looking resigned at Disneyland while gawkers snapped photos from a distance. Even at church, the one place where he expected relief, he was mobbed by admirers requesting selfies and offering condolences. He wasn't "angry" or "despondent," he wrote in his journal. Just "numb."

On TV, ambitious Republicans were lining up to trash the Romney campaign, opportunistically picking apart his failures in order to promote themselves. Bobby Jindal, the governor of Louisiana and a former Rhodes scholar, said it was time for the GOP to "stop being the stupid party." Ted Cruz claimed Romney's "47 percent" comment cost him Hispanic voters. Trump, in an unexpected twist whose dark humor would only become obvious later, glommed onto the pundits' theory du jour and blamed Romney's loss on his "mean-spirited" immigration stance. "He had a crazy policy of self-deportation, which was maniacal," Trump said. "It sounded as bad as it was, and he lost all of the Latino vote. . . . He lost the Asian vote. He lost everybody who is inspired to come into this country." (When Romney called him after the election, Trump shared a different theory for Romney's loss: the campaign needed more Trump. "If you would've had me go to Ohio and Florida, you would have won those states," Trump lectured Romney.)

The truth was that the GOP's problems went deeper than their presidential nominee. As eager as they were to saddle Romney with decades of political and ideological baggage, Republicans had gotten walloped up and down tickets across the country. They lost ground in the Senate and the House, in state legislatures and governor's mansions. In most states, Romney outperformed the Republican Senate candidates on the ballot. The party was in disarray, and the first shots were being fired in a conservative civil war whose outcome nobody could have predicted in the waning days of 2012.

Romney couldn't bring himself to turn on the TV, nor did he have any interest in reading the postmortems in the press. He busied himself calling donors, writing thank-you emails to his staff, and dutifully taking the phone calls he couldn't dodge. His brother-in-law called to share rumors of rampant voter fraud in Philadelphia, which Romney gently brushed off. Bill Clinton called to laud Romney's performance with middle-class voters and offer sympathy for how he'd been treated by the *New York Times*—a great paper on most topics, Clinton told Romney, but one with a very narrow political point of view.

Years later, when Romney looked back on these months, he would insist that he took the loss with a stiff upper lip. "My life is not defined in my own mind by political wins and losses," he'd tell me. But his journal and personal papers told a different story. He agonized over the failed campaign, obsessively wading through exit-poll data and scribbling hypotheses in legal pads.

In his bitterness, he gravitated toward the cathartic analysis of right-wing voices that he'd never taken seriously before. When Rush Limbaugh monologued about Obama buying voters off with big-government giveaways—"It's just very difficult to beat Santa Claus"—Romney found himself nodding along in agreement. The president, Romney decided, had won largely by driving up turnout with policies cynically tailored to key voter blocs—Obamacare for low-income minority voters; student loan interest breaks for millennials; a deferred-deportation executive order for Latinos. This was the only way to explain how Romney had won 59 percent of white voters, 53 percent of people making over $50,000, and still lost the election.

Some in Romney's orbit tried to steer him away from this ungenerous line of thinking. When Romney asked Matt Rhoades to draft a memo for donors, laying out the early data on why they'd lost, his campaign manager left out the material contrasting Romney's support among white voters with Obama's support among minorities. If it leaks, it will look racist, Rhoades tried to explain. Undeterred, Romney floated his theory anyway in a conference call with two hundred donors—the substance of which promptly leaked. "For Romney, Sour Grapes," read the USA Today headline. Eric Fehrnstrom asked Romney if he wanted to put out a statement clarifying his comments, but Romney miserably demurred: commenting now would only keep the story in the news cycle.

With time, Romney was able to shift into management-consultant mode, coolly analyzing the data and attributing his loss to a complex mix of tactical mistakes, personal shortcomings, and unfavorable political conditions. There were things he couldn't have controlled—Hurricane Sandy, the unemployment rate dropping, the death of Osama bin Laden. And there were things Obama had done exceptionally well: connecting with his base, turning out voters, amassing an unprecedented financial war chest. But the things that kept Romney up at night were his own mistakes: framing the campaign as a referendum on Obama, the "47 percent" gaffe, failing to counter perceptions of him as an out-of-touch patrician. "It would be a longer list if I were more honest," he'd later tell me, reviewing the catalog of blunders he'd produced.

The one question Romney would struggle to answer—even a decade later—was whether he had been true to himself in his pursuit of the presidency. By the end of the 2012 campaign, he'd genuinely bought into his own rhetoric—about how the country was at a crossroads, how giving his opponent another term would set the nation on a dangerous course, how he could save America from oblivion, and how this was the most important election of his lifetime. With some distance, he could see that he'd inflated the stakes of the race—and the malevolence of his opponent—in his own mind. Presidents, he would come to believe, had less influence over broad macroeconomic forces than both parties liked to pretend. "I vastly overstated how bad [Obama] was for the country and the economy," he'd reflect. "I think what presidents accomplish by virtue of their personal character is at least as great as what they accomplish by virtue of their policies"—and in that respect, he believed Obama's record would hold up well.

He was proud of the campaign he'd built, the team he'd assembled, and especially the primary he'd won, protecting the nomination from other, less qualified and more extreme candidates. He believed in the economic message at the core of his candidacy, and thought he'd articulated it reasonably well. He was also proud of how he'd represented Mormonism. In a meeting after the election with the top leaders of the Church, Mitt and Ann saw a presentation that showed a significant surge of interest in their religion thanks to his campaign, including referrals to missionaries and an uptick in baptisms. One apostle said that Ann had redefined the public perception of what it means to be a modern Mormon woman. Another told Romney that his campaign had helped bring the Church out of obscurity. This was not why Romney had run for president, but the fact that he and Ann had improved the standing of their faith did bring some consolation. "That's good enough for us," Ann would reflect years later.

Still, Romney couldn't deny that there had been trade-offs. Running for president meant draping your arm around unsavory characters. It meant saying things you wouldn't otherwise say, talking in ways you wouldn't otherwise talk—constantly confronting new ethical lines for that might be crossed for political advantage, and sometimes stumbling over them. To do all that only to lose was hard to take.

On November 29, 2012, Romney went to the White House for lunch with the president. He didn't want to go, and had been noncommittal when Obama first broached the invitation during their brief election-night phone call. He knew it was a publicity stunt, but he also knew that not going would make him look petty and sour.

Romney arrived at the Oval Office—which, he later noted in his journal, looked "far less impressive in browns and tans"—where Obama shook his hand and escorted him into the private presidential dining room. They sat across from each other, eating turkey chili and miniature grilled cheese sandwiches, and made polite conversation about the toll the campaign had taken on their respective wives: *It was harder on Ann than on me . . . I told Michelle not to watch cable news.* It was a strange moment—Romney had spent nearly two years running against the man in front of him, but this was the first time they'd had a proper, one-on-one conversation.

Obama asked Romney about the psychology of American entrepreneurs and innovators: What motivates them? How could he make things easier for them? In the heat of the campaign, Obama could never have conceded Romney's expertise on such matters, but the election was over and national unemployment still hovered around 8 percent—the president could use all the expertise he could get his hands on.

Romney said that some people start innovative businesses to get rich, while others, like the engineer who developed the motorized iBOT wheelchair and the Segway scooter, invent for the thrill of invention. The two men went on to discuss the main impediments to business formation—Romney said he believed it was regulation more than taxes—and Obama lamented the resistance on Capitol Hill to consolidating federal agencies. Each agency is a source of power for one congressman or another, the president explained, and streamlining the federal government would mean diminishing campaign contributions.

The conversation pushed past an hour as they traded views on Pakistan's nuclear threat, the rise of China, and the tug-of-war between modernity and Islamic fundamentalism in the Arab world. Romney observed that some countries, such as Turkey, seemed to be back-sliding toward authoritarianism, but Obama defended Turkish president Tayyip Erdogan's commitment to Western-style capitalism.

When their plates were cleared, Obama asked Romney if he'd be willing to participate in the administration's initiatives related to public infrastructure financing and incentivizing private innovation. Romney, sensing a token invitation, demurred. The lunch had been surprisingly tolerable, and the discussion of high-level world affairs was heady. But the meeting left Romney feeling hollow and grumpy—a painful reminder of the job he'd almost gotten and his sense of aimlessness now that he didn't have it.

The hardest part of losing, it turned out, was having nothing to do. He knew his life with Ann would be nicer now, more pleasant. "But the truth is that I enjoy a challenge a lot more than I enjoy a day at the beach," he wrote in his journal. "Being anxiously engaged in a good cause, particularly when the challenge and the stakes are the greatest— that energizes me most. And with the loss, and given my age, I am pretty certain that there is no great cause left for me to champion."

He found little inspiration when he looked at other recent losers of presidential elections. John McCain and John Kerry both had jobs in the Senate to return to. Good for them, Romney wrote in his journal, "but I am not a senator, and speaking on the Senate floor would not engage me." Al Gore threw himself into climate change activism, "but my passion is focused on decisions and actions that can only happen in the nation's capital." The most dispiriting parallel was Bob Dole, who spent his post-politics career working as a TV pitchman for Dunkin' Donuts and Viagra. In his most famous commercial, a Pepsi ad that debuted during the Oscars, the former Republican presidential nominee was shown leering at Britney Spears while he tells his dog, "Easy, boy." Not exactly an aspirational career path.

Yes, there were boards to serve on, and investments to oversee, and Church projects to aid. "But as a leader," Romney wrote, "I am . . . retired. Terrifying word, but worse reality."

A couple of weeks after his visit to the White House, Mitt and Ann met with Elder Boyd K. Packer, a Latter-day Saint apostle and an old family friend. After visiting for a while, Packer offered to give Romney a priesthood blessing. Laying his hands on the ex-candidate's head, the apostle offered a sacred prayer of comfort and counsel—assuring Romney that generations would be blessed by his service, that his family would benefit from their sacrifice, and that the Lord's will had been done in the election. One line stuck out in the blessing, because Packer said it twice: "This is just the beginning."

When the blessing was over, Packer told the Romneys that he had a strong impression that Mitt's work was not finished in government.

"I guess you don't know much about politics," Ann joked.

Packer was adamant: Maybe you don't know much about prophecy.

Romney made the most of retirement. He skied in Deer Valley and jet-skied in the Bahamas. He fed day-old croissants from his friend's boat to wild pigs on the beaches of Staniel Cay, and took a yacht to Barcelona during Carnival. ("Nudes on the beach, mostly men," he recorded. "Yuck.") He went quail-hunting with Jim Baker, attended the Super Bowl with Woody Johnson, and watched Márquez knock out Pacquiao from ringside seats at the MGM Grand.

Ann wrote a bestselling cookbook. Mitt gave speeches for $100,000 a pop. The couple bulldozed the place in La Jolla and built their eleven-thousand-square-foot dream home, complete with that much-maligned car elevator, which they quite enjoyed, *thank you very much*. Life was good, especially when the kids and grandkids were around. Mitt even had time to join the Marriott board and advise Tagg's private equity firm, Solamere Capital.

But Packer's words continued to ring in Romney's ears. *This is just the beginning.* He doubted a political resurrection was in his future—"I have looked at what happens to anybody in this country who loses as the nominee of their party," he'd told a roomful of supporters early in his first campaign. "They become a loser for life."

And yet, something strange happened when Romney hit the campaign trail in 2014 to stump for Republicans in the midterms. People—real people, *serious* people—kept urging him to run for president again. First it was Senator Joe Lieberman, who lavished him with praise after seeing Romney give a speech at the American Enterprise Institute about America's essential role in the world. Then it was Spencer Zwick, who reported that the donors he talked to weren't ready to give up on the dream of President Romney.

It helped that Romney's public image was in the midst of a somewhat improbable rehabilitation. His famous warnings about Russian aggression—widely mocked when he made them during the campaign—suddenly looked prophetic now that Vladimir Putin was launching military incursions into Ukraine and annexing Crimea. "He was way ahead of the curve," said one Fox News anchor; "Mitt Romney Was Right about Russia," admitted the *New Republic.* Meanwhile, a widely viewed Netflix documentary, *Mitt,* was attracting attention in the media for its intimate depiction of a Romney that most people had never seen—the self-deprecating family man who irons his tuxedo shirt while he's still wearing it, and nervously putters around his hotel room before debates, picking up after his grandkids. In the forgiving light of political irrelevance, Romney's quirks looked, to many, more endearing than alienating, his foreign-policy views more like wisdom than relics.

Romney initially dismissed the notion of another campaign whenever it came up. But Ann was surprisingly supportive, and many of his political advisers insisted that he should consider it. One day in

September of 2014, Romney invited Stuart Stevens to the family lake house in New Hampshire to talk it over. Stevens spent most of the conversation as a neutral sounding board, careful not to nudge his old boss one way or another. But after hours of mulling the pros and cons, he finally offered some obvious advice.

"If you want to be president, you have to run," Stevens told Romney. "Plain and simple."

Romney considered this, and decided he probably did still want to be president. He'd been trying to get the job for nearly a decade now. So, on the night of the 2014 midterm elections, Romney huddled in Boston with key advisers from his last campaign to discuss the logistics of a potential third run. In true Romney fashion, he'd prepared an extensive outline detailing his thoughts on the matter—fundraising prospects, various timelines for an announcement—and invited each adviser to weigh in. He stressed that his goal was to put a Republican in the White House, and that he would not get into the race if another candidate had a better chance of beating Hillary Clinton, the all-but-anointed Democratic nominee. "It's hard to imagine that I would be the strongest the GOP could muster," he told the advisers, in a show of mostly false modesty.

On paper, the emerging crop of Republican presidential contenders looked impressive. There were rising stars, like Marco Rubio, and establishment heavyweights, like Jeb Bush, and an array of interesting voices from across the GOP's ideological spectrum. But the more Romney got to know them, the less impressed he was.

When John Kasich invited Romney to the Ohio governor's mansion, he assumed Kasich wanted to pick his brain about the presidential process. Instead, Kasich prattled for two hours straight, never asking a single question. He bragged about his various gubernatorial accomplishments, then brought in his chief of staff to brag some more on his behalf. At one point, he pulled up one of his campaign ads that Romney simply *had* to see. "Surreal," Romney recorded after the meeting. "I had thought he would be a real possibility for 2016 but I come away very concerned about his lack of thoughtfulness, lack of attentiveness, ego. No wonder he and Chris [Christie] spark."

His meeting with Jeb Bush didn't inspire much confidence, either. When Romney pressed him on whether a candidate with his last name could really win a national election in 2016, he expected a razor-sharp answer. As much as Romney personally respected the Bushes, he knew that the family's Iraq-stained legacy would be a political liability, and Jeb would have to be able to defuse it if he had any chance of winning. But Jeb's response was trite and mealymouthed: "I'm going to make this campaign about the future, not the past." *Easier said than done*, Romney thought.

In his journal, Romney made regular assessments of the aspiring Republican candidates. Bobby Jindal was fine, but a bit of a "twit." Rick Perry was getting some comeback heat, "but his prima donna, low-IQ personality doesn't work for me." The one prospect Romney did fully believe in—his former running mate, Paul Ryan—had all but taken himself out of contention, preferring to continue his work on the House Ways and Means Committee. In an email encouraging Ryan to reconsider, Romney laid out his dim view of the primary field. "A Bush won't beat a Clinton. Chris has become too angry. Kasich is too undisciplined. [Scott] Walker is too opportunistic. Perry is, well, Perry. Marco lacks the stature. I think Rob [Portman] would be good, but I think he is probably too late to the contest. Rand is wrong. And Ted is frightening." Ryan thanked Romney, but decided to stay on the sidelines.

By January 2015 Romney was talking publicly about another bid. He met with twenty of his top donors and told them to get the word out: "Everybody in here can go tell your friends that I'm considering a run." He delivered a high-profile speech aboard the USS *Midway* in San Diego, where he tested new themes for his next campaign: gone were the paeans to "job creators," replaced by a kinder, gentler message about lifting people out of poverty and creating opportunity for all Americans, "regardless of the neighborhood they live in."

These forays were not looked upon kindly by everyone in his party. The conservative media reacted brutally. "Nooooo!" wrote Marc Thiessen in the *Washington Post.* "I thought Romney was a terrible candidate," said Fox News owner Rupert Murdoch. "Don't Do It, Mr. Romney," wrote Peggy Noonan in the *Journal.* The Bush machine, meanwhile, tried to kill Romney's campaign in the cradle by moving aggressively to lock down every worthwhile donor and operative in sight. In the first six months of 2015, Bush raised $100 million.

The resistance sparked a familiar competitive spirit in Romney— "Funny, but the more the print guys attack, the more it makes me interested," he wrote—but in the end what convinced him to bow out was data. A poll, privately commissioned by a former donor in Chicago, showed that Romney was well positioned to win the nomination again, but it seemed he would struggle to beat Clinton in the general. As boring as retirement might be, Romney knew losing another presidential election would be much worse. He wasn't about to put himself or his family through that again. Besides, maybe he was being too harsh on the other candidates—surely one of these young, energetic guys could catch fire like Obama had in 2008.

On January 30, just a few weeks after he began publicly exploring another campaign, Romney announced that he was bowing out. Speaking to donors and former staff, he sounded an optimistic note about his party's future standard-bearer.

"I believe that one of our next generation of Republican leaders— one who may not be as well known as I am today, one who has not yet taken their message across the country, one who is just getting started—may well emerge as being better able to defeat the Democratic nominee," he said. "In fact, I expect and hope that to be the case."

Romney didn't watch Donald Trump descend the escalator that day in June. He didn't listen to Trump announce his candidacy, or read about Trump's new campaign operation, or dig into Trump's policy positions. Like most serious people in politics, Romney's initial reaction to Trump's presidential candidacy was more or less: *Him?*

Their interactions over the years hadn't left Romney with the impression that Trump was serious about—well, anything, but certainly not politics. So, when Trump quickly surged to the front of the primary pack, Romney paid little attention. He assumed the whole thing was a publicity stunt, that he'd fade like all the whack-a-moles back in 2012.

But in the months that followed, Trump demonstrated an unnerving ability to stick around—he stuck around after the rambling announcement speech warning of a Mexican-rapist invasion; he stuck around after mocking John McCain's war record; he stuck around after the calls for a Muslim immigration ban, and the allusion to Megyn Kelly's period, and the debate where he bragged about the size of his manhood.

Trump's staying power defied everything Romney thought he knew about presidential campaigning. Not a day went by without Trump doing something that would have ended Romney's candidacy if he had done it himself. Part of the difference, Romney thought, was the sheer quantity of controversy. As a candidate, Romney had been so disciplined, so relentlessly *on message*, that one verbal stumble could capture a news cycle. With Trump, the media barely had time to react to the latest outrage before he served up a new one, and they all ran after it, like little kids chasing a ball around the soccer field.

But it wasn't just that the scandals and gaffes didn't hurt Trump— they seemed to be central to his allure. This was where Romney's analytical powers failed him. Trump's appeal simply did not compute. Yes, he could be entertaining and brash—Romney himself had gotten a kick out of those qualities just a few years earlier. *But you guys want to elect this buffoon president?* Romney couldn't relate to the subversive thrill certain Republicans felt supporting a candidate who was vulgar and mean to all the right people, who gleefully flouted decorum and decency, all but daring voters to turn on him. Even years later, after studying the Trump phenomenon at length, he would admit that he just didn't get it: "Looking back, I have dramatically underestimated

the number of people who would follow and admire Donald Trump."
He considered this as a weakness on his part—a failure of imagination.
And yet, he clearly also took pride in his natural disgust with Trump.

Watching Trump's rallies on TV, Romney and his wife were mystified. The crowds were somehow even more shocking than the candidate.
They chanted and cheered and booed on command, crescendoing to
a state of near-delirium that bordered on bloodlust. When protesters would try to disrupt his speeches—a not-uncommon occurrence
in presidential campaigns—Trump's fans would surround them and
sometimes attack, shoving and kicking and swinging their fists, while
onlookers shouted, "Shoot him!" and "Kick his ass!" From the stage,
Trump would encourage the violence: "Get him the hell out of here" . . .
"I'd like to punch him in the face" . . . "Knock the crap out of 'em, would
you? . . . I promise you, I will pay for the legal fees."

"Those people weren't at our events," Ann said, watching the crowds.

And in a sense, she was right. The coalition that Trump was building drew heavily from working-class independents, ex-Democrats,
and people who'd never been engaged in politics before. The suburban
Republicans who'd flocked to—and funded—Romney's much-quieter
campaign rallies weren't quite as visible. But Romney suspected that
what he was now witnessing had always existed in the base of his
party—that something visceral, elemental, and long dormant was now
being awakened by an unabashed demagogue.

Romney had hoped to stay above the primary fray, to play the
dispassionate party elder who didn't pick sides. But as 2015 drew to
an end with Trump still leading in the polls, Romney began to get
worried—and restless.

On the night of the Iowa caucuses, he gathered his coterie of aides
and allies in Washington, D.C., and asked them a straightforward
question: I want to stop Trump—what can I do? The answers were all
over the map. Matt Rhoades and Beth Myers wanted him to endorse
Rubio, the only palatable Republican in the field who was polling in
double digits. Stevens and Mike Leavitt disagreed, arguing that Rubio

was untested and could easily flame out in New Hampshire. Spencer Zwick worried that hitching Romney's wagon to any candidate at this stage would diminish his stature in the party. Romney raised the prospect of giving an interview or speech in which he laid out his case against Trump, but there was little enthusiasm for the idea. A head-on attack would most likely backfire, the advisers argued, hurting Romney more than Trump.

Romney left the meeting with little clarity, and a bad feeling in the pit of his stomach. He regarded these as some of the best political minds in the party, and they seemed to have no strategy to keep a manifestly unqualified madman from becoming the nominee.

Trump finished a narrow second that night in Iowa, just behind Ted Cruz, and decamped for New Hampshire with a double-digit lead in the state and a clear path to the nomination.

Five days before the New Hampshire primary, Robert O'Brien, a friend of Romney's who'd served as a foreign policy adviser on his campaign, and Jim Talent, the former Republican senator from Missouri, flew to Salt Lake City with a pitch. The primaries were in chaos, they told Romney. The party was in crisis. An interloping front-runner was on the verge of hijacking the GOP, and the rest of the field had shown they couldn't beat him. If no one else stepped up by March 1, they argued, Romney should enter the race and tap Cruz as his running mate to unite the Republican opposition to Trump. O'Brien and Talent called this the "Robert Kennedy strategy"—get in late to build momentum, win enough delegates to keep the front-runner from clinching the nomination, and then march into the convention girded for a floor fight.

They weren't the only ones privately lobbying for a last-minute Romney bid. Myers had been pushing the idea for months, as had Stevens and Zwick. Mike Leavitt, meanwhile, had proposed skipping the Republican primaries altogether and joining forces with former New York City mayor Michael Bloomberg to form an independent ticket. In January, Romney had run into Bloomberg while vacationing in the Bahamas, and over hors d'oeuvres on his sailboat, they discussed the possibility of an independent bid. In this scenario, the goal would be to deprive both major-party nominees of 270 electoral votes and throw the election to the House of Representatives. Such a move would have been unprecedented, but as far as Romney was concerned, the 2016 election had already blown past "unprecedented." The situation was dangerous and called for dramatic action.

Romney told O'Brien and Talent what he'd told the others. "My number one priority is to stop Trump," he said. The only steps he wanted to take were those he deemed "most likely to damage his candidacy."

Romney was willing to wage a quixotic and humiliating presidential bid if that's what it took. He might even be able to swallow sharing a ticket with Cruz, a man he'd described as "scary" and "a demagogue" in his journal. But Romney didn't think the gambit would actually succeed in taking down Trump. The problem was that no one else in the party seemed to know what to do about Trump, either.

The other candidates had spent most of the primaries scrupulously ignoring the front-runner and clobbering each other instead on the theory that Trump would eventually just . . . *go away* somehow. Romney's old friend Mike Murphy, who was now at the helm of a super PAC supporting Jeb, had burned through much of his $100 million war chest cranking out attack ads aimed at Rubio. In the debates, Christie and Kasich and Cruz and Paul squabbled with each other while a smirking Trump hunched contentedly over his center-stage podium, tossing out occasional insults and laugh lines.

After Trump coasted to a blowout win in New Hampshire, plunging the Republican establishment further into panic mode, Romney emailed his team: What should I do now? Few replies came back. His brain trust, it seemed, was out of ideas.

Over the next four weeks, Trump waltzed to victory in South Carolina, then Nevada, while his rivals dropped like flies—first Christie, then Jeb, then Ben Carson. Romney tried needling Trump on Twitter over his refusal to release his tax returns, but the line of attack got drowned out by the nonstop noise machine that was the Trump campaign. Who could compete with a candidate who would go on Twitter one day to pick a fight with the pope (His Holiness was "disgraceful"), and then speculate the next that his opponent's father might have been involved in the Kennedy assassination?

The more Romney saw, the more he came to despise Trump's schtick and his cancerous effect on the body politic. His opposition was partly rooted in policy. Trump's immigration platform—which advocated for cruel mass deportations and constructing a Mexican-funded wall along nearly two thousand miles of the southern border—was impractical and idiotic (not to mention, Romney would later note, much more barbaric than his own policy that Trump had once called "maniacal"). Trump's proposed Muslim ban also deeply offended Romney as a Mormon whose own ancestors had once faced state-sanctioned persecution, including an effort to block Latter-day Saint immigration from Europe. On foreign policy, Trump's rants about withdrawing from longstanding alliances and his transparent admiration for dictators looked to Romney like the beginnings of a new world order tilted away from American power and Western values.

But more than anything, it was Trump's character that disturbed Romney. He looked at the bullying, the lying, the unrepentant mistreatment of women, and saw a profoundly depraved and broken person whose election would coarsen America's culture. He wanted badly to give a scorched-earth speech denouncing the Republican front-runner, but his team remained ambivalent.

The breaking point came on the morning of Sunday, February 28. Romney was in his bedroom at the house in Deer Valley, when his son Tagg—whose family had been visiting for the weekend—thundered up the stairs. His face was white.

"Can you believe what Donald Trump just said?" he asked.

Romney hadn't seen the interview, so Tagg pulled up a clip. There was Jake Tapper, the CNN moderator of *State of the Union*, asking Trump what he thought of David Duke, the leader of the Ku Klux

Klan, endorsing his candidacy. And there was Trump, looking petulant and annoyed, refusing to disavow Duke's endorsement.

"I don't know anything about David Duke," Trump shrugged. "I don't know what you're even talking about with white supremacy or white supremacist. I don't know. I don't know, did he endorse me, or what's going on?"

Watching the interview finally pushed Romney over the edge. He knew there were risks to tangling with Trump, but surely he could summon the fortitude to denounce a presidential candidate who seemed fine with receiving support from white supremacists. Romney told his team he wanted to give a speech in four days, and asked them to schedule time at the University of Utah.

The words were easy to find once he started writing. He'd been holding them in for months. Soon, he had a draft, which he sent to his advisers for comments and edits. Two days later, Rhoades wrote back asking if he was sure he wanted to go through with it. Trump had just won a slew of southern primaries, further expanding his delegate lead, and there were signs that the party was beginning to coalesce. Christie had recently endorsed Trump. Newt Gingrich and Rudy Giuliani had both called Rhoades to ask if Romney would come on board, too.

But Romney was dug in.

"It is nearly certain that he will be the nominee," Romney wrote in his journal, a dash of drama in his tone, but "I am not tempted in the slightest to retreat. I will fight him on the beaches, I will fight him in the air. . . ."

On March 3, Romney took the stage at the Libby Gardner Concert Hall on the campus of the University of Utah. The room was packed with reporters, many of whom had flown out from D.C. and New York to cover what promised to be a genuinely dramatic political event.

For the next twenty minutes, Romney laid out a detailed indictment of Trump's defective character, his failed businesses, his domestic policies, and his frighteningly weak grasp of foreign affairs.

"Donald Trump is a phony, a fraud," Romney said. "His promises are as worthless as a degree from Trump University. He's playing the members of the American public for suckers. He gets a free ride to the White House and all we get is a lousy hat."

The speech wasn't just a takedown of Trump—it also included an audacious plan to stop him from winning the nomination. Arguing that most primary voters still preferred someone other than the current front-runner, Romney urged Republicans to vote strategically so that the nomination fight could move to an open convention. Anti-Trump Republicans in Florida should cast ballots for Rubio, voters in Ohio should go in for Kasich, and the remaining states should be divvied up among the three non-Trump candidates still running. (In Utah, for example, Romney planned to vote for Cruz, who had a lead in the state.)

"If the other candidates can find some common ground, I believe we can nominate a person who can win the general election and who will represent the values and policies of conservatism," he said.

"I'm convinced America has greatness ahead," Romney concluded. "And this is a time for choosing. God bless us to choose a nominee who will make that vision a reality."

To students of American presidential campaigns, it was a remarkable moment. "There was little precedent for Romney's remarks," the *Washington Post* reported. "Never before in modern political history has the immediate past nominee of a party delivered an entire speech condemning the current front-runner." Historian David Greenberg told the *New York Times*, "There probably hasn't been this level of personal invective by one Republican nominee against another leading candidate, ever."

As Romney's inbox flooded that afternoon with congratulatory emails from fellow Republicans, there was no way to predict that, by the end of the year, the entire GOP would be marching in lockstep behind president-elect Trump—and Romney would be a pariah.

CHAPTER TEN

Vox

T rump threw a tantrum, of course. Within hours of Romney's speech, the candidate was on a stage in Portland, Maine, lashing out at the former Republican nominee in theatrically vulgar and personal terms. Mitt was a "lightweight," a "failed candidate," a "choke artist" who'd blown a race in 2012 that he should have easily won.

"I backed Mitt Romney," Trump snarled at the 1,100 fans gathered at the Westin Portland Harborview hotel. "I backed him! You can see how loyal he is. He was *begging* for my endorsement. I could have said, 'Mitt, drop to your knees,' he would have dropped to his knees."

The crowd laughed and oohed, and the candidate grimaced in a show of faux pity: "It's true."

Romney was delighted to have gotten under his skin, but Trump's point stood: Romney had to account for the fact that, not all that long ago, he had stood next to Trump on a stage and gratefully accepted his endorsement. Some skeptical reporters were already asking questions: Where was this principled stand when Romney was running for president himself? What changed his mind about Trump? Isn't this all a little hypocritical? Romney responded with a Tweet that afternoon: "If Trump had said 4 years ago the things he says today about the KKK, Muslims, Mexicans, disabled, I would NOT have accepted his endorsement."

The truth was that Romney hadn't yet fully reckoned with his own coddling of Trump, and what role he may have played in elevating him. "Obviously if I did anything to help legitimize him, I regretted it," he'd tell me years later. But back in 2012, he didn't think of Trump as a political figure at all, much less a dangerous one. He was a rich blowhard donor—each party had thousands of them. Even Trump's birther crusade had seemed, to Romney, more like evidence of stupidity than a racist effort to delegitimize America's first Black president. "I did not see that as . . . [having] a racial arc to it," he recalled. "And perhaps I'm not as sensitive in that regard as I should be."

What *was* clear now to Romney was that Trump had to be stopped before he won the nomination—and that work would have to be done behind the scenes. To get to an open convention in Cleveland would require an unprecedented level of coordination among Trump's three remaining opponents. Marco Rubio would have to win in Florida, John Kasich would have to carry Ohio, and Ted Cruz would have to siphon delegates away from the front-runner in the more conservative primaries. Most important, they would have to agree to stay out of each other's way—no ads or campaign swings in states that weren't theirs, no money spent splitting the vote while Trump coasted. Romney took it upon himself to act as the intermediary between the candidates.

The plan, while a long shot, was strategically sound and, Romney thought, the best chance any of these candidates had to wrest the nomination from Trump. It was simple math—any rational person could see it. But as Romney would soon be reminded, presidential candidates are not always rational actors.

In the weeks that followed his speech in Salt Lake City, Romney recorded robocalls for Rubio in Florida and Michigan, campaigned with Kasich in Ohio, and urged voters in Utah to support Cruz, who was leading in the state's polls. When the Cruz camp tried to wheedle an unqualified endorsement from Romney, he refused: "I'm with anybody who can stop Trump."

At the same time, he was quietly working to broker a last-ditch anti-Trump unity ticket. On March 6, Romney sent an email asking Rubio to call him. "My topic is getting you and Ted together," he wrote. "Ted would offer you VP, before Florida. I know that idea has to make you ill. But if it is something you'd like to talk about, let's."

Romney had grown to appreciate Rubio as a candidate. In recent weeks, the telegenic young senator had finally started using his talents to take it to Trump, impishly needling the thin-skinned billionaire over his apricot spray tan ("He should sue whoever did that to his face!"), his short fingers ("You know what they say about guys with small hands"), and his dubious self-mythologizing ("If he hadn't inherited $200 million, you know where Donald Trump would be right now? Selling watches in Manhattan"). He'd made his prosecution of Trump the centerpiece of his candidacy: "You all have friends that are thinking about voting for Donald Trump," Rubio said at one rally. "Friends do not let friends vote for con artists." And while it didn't seem to be moving him much in the polls, Romney loved this new, pugnacious Marco.

Still, Cruz had more delegates than Rubio did, which meant that if they were going to join forces, he would have to settle for the VP slot. Romney made it his mission to convince him. He had reason to believe that such an arranged marriage could work. Several people close to the two candidates had encouraged Romney to push for it. Lindsey Graham reported that Rubio had told him he was open to the idea. Andy Puzder, the founder of Carl's Jr. and a Republican mega-donor, said the Cruz people were on board. Texas governor Greg Abbott had even called Romney to talk through strategies for putting together a Cruz-Rubio ticket.

When Romney took the idea to the candidates themselves, both acted like they were amenable. Rubio made supportive noises about sacrificing to stop Trump's ascent; Cruz assured Romney he would do what it took to make it happen. But then days went by, and nothing happened. They were just too self-interested, too unwilling to bend— each of them convinced that they could be *the guy* if only the other one would just drop out. With each passing day of inaction, Trump gained more votes, more delegates, and more momentum.

When the day of the Florida primary arrived, Trump won all ninety-nine delegates with just 45 percent of the primary vote—the rest of the voters were split three ways between Rubio, Cruz, and Kasich.

Rubio, humiliated by his home state loss, suspended his campaign. Two days later, he called Romney. They commiserated about Trump's toxic effect on the party, and the cataclysmic down-ticket consequences they believed his nomination would have. Rubio became especially animated when he got going on the conservative media's support for Trump. "Fox is killing the GOP," Rubio said. He complained that Sean Hannity had effectively turned his prime-time show into an hour-long Trump rally, and speculated that the host was cynically chasing money and ratings. Hannity, he noted, had recently bought his own private plane—"a big nut to cover"—and couldn't afford to see his ratings fall off. But as far as Rubio was concerned, aiding the destruction of the Republican Party wasn't worth a $12 million TV contract. Rubio, who'd chosen to forgo a reelection bid in the Senate, told Romney he was done with politics in the near term, and planned to work in the private sector.

Once Rubio dropped out, Romney turned his attention to trying to usher Kasich out of the race. The moderate Ohio governor had little support outside his own state—as of March 20, he was polling at just 17 percent nationally—and virtually no path to the nomination. But he was so stubborn in his refusal to drop out that many Republicans believed he was deliberately splitting the anti-Trump vote, perhaps with hopes of getting himself on the ticket.

Romney had tried in early March to prevail upon Kasich to drop out for the greater good. But Kasich was unmovable—spouting platitudes about his enthusiastic crowds and his positive message and how once voters in battleground states heard what he had to say, they would propel him to victory.

Romney tried to be blunt: "Your message won't get through. You get no coverage."

But it was to no avail. "Delusion runs deep in politicians' veins," Romney vented in his journal after the conversation.

This time, Romney decided to try a different tack. In a series of increasingly gruff emails throughout March and April, he appealed to Kasich's political interests by cogently laying out the state of play.

> John, I am 100% convinced that . . . the best chance you have to become president is if Cruz prevents Trump from reaching 1237. I have meticulously done the math, checked it with people I respect, and with you and Ted in the race, Trump wins. . . . Cruz has way more delegates than you and leads you in more remaining states. Hence Cruz is the better choice until the convention.
>
> Best thing anyone could do for you to become president is to back Cruz and have you lay low until the convention, working behind the scenes to elect delegates who will vote for you on the second ballot.

Kasich responded a few hours later, with more stump-speech pablum: "I just don't see it the way you do. My effort is to present my record and vision and bring people together not to shame anyone thru the process. . . . I have the best chance to win this fall and I don't know why you can't see this. The other two can't win. This country needs leadership and experience now."

Refusing to believe that Kasich was so obtuse that he couldn't grasp basic math, Romney began to entertain the theory that Kasich was somehow back-channeling with Trump. How else to explain his bullheaded commitment to a nonsensical strategy that only helped the front-runner? What Romney knew for sure was that he didn't trust Kasich, or his campaign manager, John Weaver. On at least one occasion, Romney believed, they'd flatly lied to him by claiming they were coordinating with the Cruz campaign. When Romney asked Cruz about it in an email, the candidate replied that he was open to such an alliance, but that no coordination was taking place: "Not sure why he told you that."

The distrust, apparently, went both ways. Taking questions from reporters in early April, Kasich hinted at his frustration with Romney's meddling. Speculation had been building in the media that a Republican who wasn't currently in the race might swoop in at the eleventh hour and try to win the nomination from the convention floor. "Is Mitt running for president?" Kasich mused when asked about this scenario. "We've been wondering that ourselves."

Romney was incensed by the suggestion that he was doing this all for his own gain. Straining to contain his anger, he emailed Kasich: "I noticed with some humor your query about me running. Very funny. Had I any inclination in that direction whatsoever, I would have gotten in long ago. You'd also have seen me staffing up. And I sure wouldn't have come out attacking Trump. . . . Have you seen what used to be my favorables? I'm smart enough to know that weighing in against him would mean a world of hurt for my voter reputation, but I simply could not sit and watch the train wreck."

In private, Romney was less diplomatic. "Kasich is delusional," he wrote in his journal.

For a brief moment, it looked like all of Romney's lobbying might finally be getting some traction. On April 24, the Cruz and Kasich campaigns put out press releases announcing a strategic alliance. Cruz would focus his time and resources on winning Indiana, while Kasich would compete in Oregon and New Mexico. If they could keep Trump from winning all three states, they had a real path to an open convention.

"Well done," Romney wrote to Kasich that night. "Honorable."

The next morning, Weaver emailed Romney to hit him up for a favor: "Now that Cruz has finally agreed to do this, and we're up to the wall in many states, we could use fundraising help for the upcoming battles."

But before Romney even had a chance to respond, Kasich was publicly backpedaling on the whole thing. "I've never told [Indiana voters] not to vote for me," he told reporters. "They ought to vote for me." The following day, he went further: "I'm not out to stop Donald Trump."

Romney wrote back to Weaver. "From what I saw today, this deal with Cruz is far from a collaboration. As Donald would say: sad."

On May 3, Trump won Indiana, prompting both Cruz and Kasich to drop out of the race. The primaries were over; the battle was lost. Donald Trump was the presumptive Republican nominee for president.

Romney had known from the outset that his plan to stop Trump was a long shot. It had been a long time since presidential nominees were picked by party elders in smoke-filled back rooms, and Romney was prepared for the primary voters to overrule him—*vox populi vox Dei*. What he hadn't anticipated was how feckless and craven and shortsighted his party's supposed leaders would be when faced with a political emergency like Trump's rise.

He hadn't seen anything yet.

Romney spent a few fruitless weeks after the primaries hunting around for a credible third-party candidate. He pitched Ben Sasse, the young conservative senator from Nebraska who had remained an outspoken Trump critic, but he was turned down. He met with Bill Kristol, who was seeking out his own recruits, but was told that James Mattis, Condoleezza Rice, and Mark Cuban had all passed. He even, in a moment of desperation, made a run at Kasich.

"Any chance I could get you to consider an independent run? I mean ANY chance?" Romney wrote to the Ohio governor. "I would raise money, be campaign co-chair, whatever you needed me to do to help."

But Kasich wasn't interested. Nobody was. Instead, as the convention neared, Romney watched miserably as one prominent member of his party after another abandoned principle to line up behind Trump. Every day he looked at the news, it seemed, he learned about a new betrayal. There was Rick Perry, who'd once called Trumpism "a cancer on conservatism," declaring that he'd happily serve as Trump's running mate if asked. There was Bobby Jindal, who'd derided Trump as a "narcissist and an egomaniac," endorsing him in the *Wall Street Journal*.

Even *Marco Rubio*, last seen selling #NEVERTRUMP bumper stickers on his campaign website and warning that Trump could not be trusted with the nuclear launch codes, managed to talk himself into supporting the nominee. (Perhaps not coincidentally, Rubio had decided he wasn't quite ready to walk away from politics after all: he declared his bid for reelection in June.)

It was strange. Watching Trump complete his conquest of the GOP was even more devastating to Romney than losing his own election in 2012. There was something different about the combination of despair and disorientation—a sense that the world was spinning out of control, that he didn't know his place in it anymore, that all he could do was sit back and watch as the disaster unfolded.

Romney's decision to come out against Trump hadn't required much courage back in March—almost everyone in his Republican circles agreed with him at the time. Now he was increasingly isolated.

"Pretty lonely for those of us who aren't backing Trump," Romney wrote to Jeb, with whom he'd struck up a kind of pen pal relationship. "Ann and I have turned off the news until November."

"ESPN is looking mighty fine," Jeb wrote back.

Romney skipped the convention in Cleveland. He couldn't even bring himself to watch it on TV. The few clips he did catch of the nominee's acceptance speech—Trump bellowing like an old-world autocrat with his glowering face stretched across a 1,700-square-foot jumbo screen above him—were exactly as unsettling as Romney had expected. Later, a Republican Congressman would tell him that after Trump's speech ended, House Majority Leader Kevin McCarthy, who was seated in the convention hall, leaned over and whispered, "Benito Mussolini." In public, McCarthy was an avid supporter of Trump, already in the process of turning his sycophancy into an art form. (He would eventually become famous for assigning an aide in his office to sort through packs of Starbursts and fill a jar with just the pinks and reds so that he could present Trump with his favorite flavors.) Romney took little comfort in learning that Trump's purported allies

Mitt Romney grew up idolizing his father, George, the Republican governor of Michigan known for his principled stands against the GOP's right wing. But when George's presidential campaign was derailed by a gaffe, his son took the lesson that caution is key in politics. (*Courtesy of Mitt Romney*)

Mitt met Ann Davies, pretty and reserved, when they were both in high school. Decades later, he'd look back on their life together and credit her high expectations for the person he became. "I want to be as good a person as she thinks I should be." (*Courtesy of Mitt Romney*)

As a Mormon missionary in France, Elder Romney had doors slammed in his face, slept in tenements without indoor plumbing, and was nagged by bouts of illness. For a son of privilege, the experience was an education in hardship and sacrifice. (*Courtesy of Mitt Romney*)

Near the end of his mission, Romney was driving a group of mission leaders through rural France when a black Mercedes slammed into their vehicle, killing the mission president's wife. The brush with death caused Romney to think more seriously about his own mortality. (*Courtesy of Mitt Romney*)

Romney, who started as a management consultant at Bain & Company in 1977, rose quickly through the ranks, eventually leading the company's private equity arm. Bain Capital's record, which included layoffs and plant closures, would come under scrutiny when he ran for office. (*Getty*/Boston Globe)

Even as his career took off, Romney says he was careful to reserve time for family. (*Courtesy of Mitt Romney*)

At top: As a lay leader of Mormon congregations in the Boston area, Romney was known for his pragmatic style in dealing with contentious issues. (*Courtesy of Mitt Romney*)

At left: In 1994, Romney ran against Ted Kennedy for U.S. Senate in Massachusetts. Despite rumors at the time that Kennedy had lost a step, Romney struggled in debates with the "liberal lion of the Senate." (*Getty/Ira Wyman*)

Romney stands with President George W. Bush at the opening ceremonies for the Salt Lake City Winter Olympics in 2002. Romney's mission to turn around the Games was complicated by security concerns stemming from the September 11 terror attacks months earlier. (*Getty/*Newsday *LLC*)

In 2002, Romney was elected governor of Massachusetts, where he became known for digging his state out of a fiscal crisis and signing into law an innovative—and controversial—healthcare overhaul that would later serve as a model for the Affordable Care Act. (*Courtesy of Mitt Romney*)

Romney was widely accused of pandering to the right wing to win the Republican presidential primaries in 2012. The Obama campaign frequently featured this image in ads to remind voters that he'd accepted the endorsement of Donald Trump, who at the time was becoming a conservative political celebrity for his conspiracy theories about Obama. (*Getty/Justin Sullivan*)

Though he campaigned hard, Romney expressed ambivalence in his journal about whether he wanted to win. "I am not driven for the Presidency like those in history that are written about." (*Getty/Justin Sullivan*)

Romney was privately critical of Barack Obama in 2012, calling him "gracious but without genuine grace" and railing against his "arrogance" and "dishonesty." Looking back, he'd conclude that he was overly harsh in his assessment of the president. He had no idea how much worse things could get. (*Getty/John Moore*)

After leading the Republican resistance to Trump in 2016, Romney briefly considered serving as his Secretary of State. This photo of their dinner at Jean-Georges, a three-Michelin-star restaurant at Trump Tower, went viral. (*Getty/Drew Angerer*)

Alarmed by the first year of Trump's presidency, Romney ran for Senate in Utah in hopes of steering his party in another direction. In his private notes, he jotted down a Yeats quote that he believed defined the Trump-era GOP: "The best lack all conviction, while the worst are full of passionate intensity." (*Courtesy of Mitt Romney*)

In November 2019, Oprah Winfrey called Romney with an intriguing proposition. She wanted to keep Trump from another term and worried that Democrats couldn't win. (*Courtesy of Mitt Romney*)

During Trump's first impeachment trial, Romney agonized over which way to vote. He became the first senator in U.S. history to vote to convict a president from his own party. (*Getty/Mandel Ngan*)

As Romney grew more alienated from the Republican base, he felt liberated to emulate his father's civil rights record. In the summer of 2020, he joined a Black Lives Matter march. (*Courtesy of Mitt Romney*)

After the January 6 riot, Romney gave a thundering speech on the Senate floor denouncing Trump for trying to overturn an election and accusing his Republican colleagues of prioritizing rank partisanship over principle. (*C-SPAN*)

With the Trump presidency over, Romney dove headfirst into the work of legislating. He joined a bipartisan group of senators responsible for drafting a $1 trillion infrastructure bill. (*Getty/Samuel Corum*)

Though they rarely talked about it publicly, Romney became friends with President Biden. When some of Romney's family came to town, the president gave them a private White House tour. (*Courtesy of Mitt Romney*)

While most of the Republican caucus opposed Ketanji Brown Jackson's nomination to the Supreme Court, Romney voted to confirm her. "Frankly," he said, "I hoped that I would be able to vote for her." (*Courtesy of Mitt Romney*)

Romney believes that if political leaders thought more about how their decisions will be remembered when they're gone, they'd show more moral courage. His family has helped him think in these terms. "How do I look at my life?" he says. "I look at my relationships with my family, but also my descendants, and what I leave for them." (*Courtesy of Mitt Romney*)

were secretly just as alarmed as he was. It was hard to celebrate an epidemic of cowardice.

Some conservative critics blamed Romney's hurt feelings for his refusal to come around. Trump was still routinely attacking him on the stump. During one extended insult-comedy routine at a rally in Anaheim, California, he'd observed that Romney "walks like a penguin," and demonstrated by performing a little waddle while the crowd laughed uproariously.

But Romney didn't take the taunts personally. They were too silly, too childlike, to cause offense. His resistance to Trump was more simple than that. "It's a matter of personal conscience," he tried to explain in an interview in June. "Presidents have an impact on the nature of our nation," he said in another, "and trickle-down racism and trickle-down bigotry and trickle-down misogyny—all of these things are extraordinarily dangerous to the heart and character of America."

Romney was quick to point out that he hadn't become a Democrat. He considered Bernie Sanders's vilification of Wall Street to be demagogic, and he profoundly disagreed with Hillary Clinton on a range of important policy matters. But that didn't change the fact that Trump was operating well outside the bounds of the American political tradition. "Hillary Clinton is wrong on every issue," Romney said at the Aspen Ideas Festival, paraphrasing the writer P. J. O'Rourke, "but she's wrong within the normal parameters."

As the calamitous campaign season thundered along, many of the Republicans who'd bowed to Trump simply stopped corresponding with Romney. A few tried to warm him up to Trump, but when they did, Romney was defiant to the point of self-righteousness. After Christie became one of the first mainstream Republicans to endorse Trump, Romney sent a curt email saying he was "stunned" by the decision, and then spent several weeks pestering him to retract his endorsement.

"If you ever want to have a rational conversation about all of this, I am always happy to do so," Christie wrote.

Romney's reply was scathing. "He is unquestionably mentally unstable, and he is racist, bigoted, misogynistic, xenophobic, vulgar and prone to violence. There is simply no rational argument that could lead me to vote for someone with those characteristics. I believe your endorsement of him severely diminishes you morally—though probably not politically—and that you must withdraw that support to preserve your integrity and character."

When Reince Priebus called and asked him to consider endorsing the nominee, Romney openly laughed and said, "Trump is nuts." Later, when Priebus tried to reprimand him for his lack of party loyalty, Romney was unsparing in his judgment. "Reince is trying to shame people who won't support Trump, ignoring his greater shame for having done so," he wrote in his journal.

At the same time, Romney was beginning to recognize that beneath all of Trump's clownishness, something real might be shifting in his party. Trump had stood out in the primaries in part by shredding certain GOP orthodoxies on the campaign trail. His success called into question the potency and popularity of those orthodoxies. The Reaganism to which Romney had converted—a platform combining traditional social views with a conservative-libertarian fiscal program and an interventionist foreign policy—could no longer be considered the consensus worldview in the GOP. Trump had won the nomination by calling the war in Iraq "a big, fat mistake," by crusading against free trade, and by promising to protect government entitlement programs. While Romney's campaign had been full of hymns to America's "job creators," Trump's was pitched to job doers—and the results were showing in the polls. Already, there were stories in the press about how the election could be decided by "Obama-Trump" voters or "Romney-Clinton" voters. A once-in-a-generation realignment was taking place in American politics, and Romney wondered if he'd still have a home when it was over.

He wasn't the only one. Across the country, his coreligionists were facing the same dilemma. For decades, Mormons had been the most reliably Republican religious group in America. But unlike white evangelicals, who were rallying around Trump in unprecedented numbers, Latter-day Saints remained skeptical. During the primaries, Trump had finished last in Utah, and consistently underperformed in heavily Mormon districts. In the general election, one poll showed that Mormons were among the voters most dissatisfied with the two major-party nominees. Romney was both a symptom and a supporter of this dissatisfaction—seeing his people resist the pull of partisanship was inspiring to him.

Romney was fairly sure that Trump would lose in the end, and he clung to that certainty throughout the summer. He was sure of it when Trump chose to feud with a gold-star family; he was sure of it when Trump called a federal judge a "hater" because of his "Mexican heritage"; he was sure of it when that notorious video leaked in which Trump could be heard bragging about grabbing random women "by the pussy" because "when you're a star they let you do it." But Trump still had that same eerie staying power that he first demonstrated in the primaries, and Clinton's surprisingly inert campaign struggled to put him away. By the fall, Romney wasn't sure of anything anymore.

Part of the problem, he thought, was Clinton's crippling lack of charisma. He knew she was smart and capable, he'd recall later, but "she had a difficult time connecting with people"—something he could relate to. The ever-present contrast between her and her preternaturally magnetic husband didn't help. Once, during the 2008 presidential primaries, Romney had marched behind the Clintons in a parade. Bill insisted on stopping to interact with everyone he saw, repeatedly grinding the parade to a halt. "He would just talk to people and hug them," Romney told me. "And Hillary was dying—like, *Come on, we gotta get going*."

"Trump frightens me but I'm afraid he will win," Romney wrote to Jeb a few weeks before Election Day. "These debates have to be [a] gift for a reality TV star facing an aging school librarian like Hillary. Heaven help us."

Romney started doing this with all of his friends—predicting victory for Trump. He wasn't sure he actually believed it, but he considered the forecasting a form of psychological "inoculation." It was a lifelong pattern for Romney—predict the worst, and you'll be ready if it happens.

And yet, when the night of the election arrived, Romney found himself unprepared. The electoral map lighting up red, the ashen-faced pundits trying to make sense of what had happened, the stock market crashing, world leaders reacting—it was a black-swan event unfolding in real time. Donald Trump would be the next president of the United States.

Romney was afraid for the country, and the world.

The phone call came while the Romneys were on the back nine at Wailea Golf Club in Hawaii. It was Mike Pence, the newly elected vice president. He told Romney that Trump wanted to meet with him about the secretary of state position. The request was so unexpected that Romney didn't know what to say. He muttered something about needing to talk to Ann, and said he'd let Pence know if he wished to proceed.

But almost immediately after hanging up, he began to worry—had he been too standoffish? Slammed shut a door before it was even open? Surely a meeting with the president-elect would be appropriate, even if he didn't end up taking the job, right? This was *secretary of state* they were talking about—the second most powerful position in the United States government. He called Pence back and said he'd be honored to meet with Mr. Trump.

Romney was wary of the invitation. As tempting as it was to think that Trump was rising to the mantle of his office, that perhaps the shock of winning the presidency had imbued him with a new magnanimity, it seemed just as likely that this whole thing was a trap of some kind. "I was very concerned that it would be a mistake," Romney said. Later that day, he spoke to Reince Priebus, who'd just been tapped to serve as White House chief of staff, and asked him to be frank: Was Trump serious about this?

Priebus assured him the opportunity was real. "He decides things like this based on the reaction of people around him," he told Romney, advising him to ask whatever mutual acquaintances he had with Trump—MSNBC host Joe Scarborough, perhaps, or Jets owner Woody Johnson—to put in a good word.

Romney booked a red-eye to the lower forty-eight, and three days later, he was being escorted down the tree-lined brick road of Trump's private golf club in Bedminster, New Jersey.

Looking back on it later, Romney would acknowledge that his willingness to entertain Trump's offer was propelled by a mix of noble motivations and self-centered ones. Trump clearly needed all the help he could get when it came to foreign affairs. Unlike past presidents-elect who carefully coordinated with the State Department before having any postelection conversations with world leaders, Trump was haphazardly taking calls on an unsecured line without regard for protocol or diplomacy. He spoke to Taiwan before China, Russia and Ireland before Britain, and only connected with the Australian prime minister after the ambassador scored Trump's cell number from the retired pro golfer Greg Norman, who was a Mar-a-Lago regular. None of these faux pas were catastrophic on their own, but they signaled a fundamental unseriousness. "I looked at what was happening in the world, and these were really troubling times," Romney told me. "The emergence of China as the strongest nation on earth. Russia circling the drain, and therefore lashing out, and then ISIS at that point with huge financial resources and a swath of land. Iraq in distress." Somebody had to quell the chaos, Romney thought, or the results could be disastrous.

But there were also more prosaic reasons for playing along: he wanted the job. "I like being involved and being in the middle of things, and having something important to do," he admitted. "It's like, you know, I wanted to be president. If you can't be president, being secretary of state's not a bad spot to come thereafter."

When the time came, Romney was ushered into an office in the Georgian-style clubhouse, where he found Trump and Pence waiting along with Jared Kushner, Steve Bannon, and Priebus. There were pleasantries followed by a pro forma discussion of foreign policy. When Romney was asked what he would do in Syria and Afghanistan, he responded not with doctrinaire recommendations but rather by laying out a series of strategic options and describing what information he would need to make a decision. Trump spoke little.

Once the conversation turned to the possibility of an appointment, Romney decided to be blunt. He told Trump he could accept the job only if the president-elect agreed to four conditions. First, he would need a standing weekly meeting with the president. Second, all foreign policy in the administration would have to emanate from the State Department. Third, Romney would get to select his own subcabinet members—he would have his pick of deputies and assistants without meddling from Trump. And finally, Romney would need veto power over ambassadorial appointments. He knew this last condition would be unprecedented. There was a long and sordid tradition of presidents rewarding political allies and donors with ambassadorships. But Romney also knew that the characters Trump likely wanted to reward were uncommonly seedy, and he dreaded the prospect of overseeing a diplomatic corps polluted by Paul Manaforts and Roger Stones.

Trump raised no objection to the conditions, and after about an hour, he sent everyone else out of the room. Once he was alone with Romney, Trump shifted into a wheedling, schmoozy tone.

"You are right out of central casting," Trump effused. "This is perfect. Just what I need." They shook hands, and Trump said they'd be in touch.

When Romney left the office, he found Trump's entourage lingering in the hallway. Pence asked Romney for a private word.

"You know," Pence said, "it's going to be hard for you to be seen as a credible candidate here with all the negative things you've said about Donald Trump. So, it would be really helpful if you went out to the media after this meeting . . . and just said you were wrong, and that what you've learned has given you much more confidence in him being president."

Romney nearly guffawed. "There's no way I can do that," he said. He tried to be polite about it—maybe Trump *would* prove him wrong as president, Romney told Pence, and if that happened, he would consider retracting his past comments. But there was no way it was happening after a one-hour meeting. Among other things, it would look flatly ridiculous—nobody would believe the praise was sincere. It would not occur to Romney until later that Trump didn't care about the sincerity of the retraction—he wanted a show of subjugation, nothing more.

After making it clear to Pence that he wouldn't change his mind, Romney left the clubhouse and offered a few bland remarks to the press outside before disappearing into an idling SUV. As he rode away, reporters called out after him:

"Do you still think he's a con man?"

"Did you apologize?"

Romney figured that would be the end of it. Trump's other candidates for secretary of state would have fewer conditions and more willingness to dance for him, to do what they were told. He tried to put the job out of his mind.

But in the days that followed, Romney heard from a wide range of prominent people, including several former secretaries of state, who were urging him to take the job. Condoleezza Rice, Colin Powell, even Hillary Clinton—all of them said it was his duty to serve if he had the opportunity. George W. Bush, who had publicly made it known that he didn't vote for Trump, told Romney, "If he actually asks you to be secretary of state, I'll have to rethink what I think about the guy."

In certain elite political circles, where Trump's election was widely regarded as a national emergency, it had become fashionable to argue that the most patriotic thing one could do in this moment was to infiltrate the corridors of power. Take that high-profile administration post. Suck up to the president, develop a rapport. Wedge yourself into his inner circle where you could mitigate against his worst, most erratic impulses. This was a moment when many people still believed in the power of having "adults in the room." And Romney, for all his faults, was undeniably an adult. "At the time, a lot of people were saying, 'It's one way to behave the way [Trump] did on the campaign trail, but the office itself would sand the rough edges off and it was important to get good people around him,'" Bush recalled.

So, when Romney received another call inviting him to dinner with Trump and Priebus ten days later, he decided to accept. They dined at Jean-Georges, a Michelin three-star restaurant at Trump Tower. The conversation was friendly and insubstantial—the place hadn't been cleared of guests, so the most sensitive topics were off-limits. At one point, Trump noticed CNN reporter Jim Acosta staking out the dining room and grumbled, "He is the worst person."

The most memorable document of the evening was a photograph, snapped by Getty's Drew Angerer, of the two men at their table. Trump is smirking impishly at the camera, his face awash in Can-you-believe-I-got-him-to-do-this? glee. Romney's lips are pursed, his eyebrows raised in forlorn defeat. Adding to the effect, they are both underlit by a soft orange glow that looks as if it is emanating from the bowels of hell.

The photo went viral as soon as it hit Twitter, with commenters rushing to point out how it emblematized Trump's humiliation of his erstwhile Republican critics. People took turns writing captions for the picture ("Mitt Romney at the exact moment he realizes he's selling his soul") and imagining the conversation between the two men ("What's for dinner, Donald?" Romney asks. "Your dignity," Trump responds.)

Years later, Romney would insist that his expression in the photo was not humiliation or shame, but simply irritation at being photo-graphed. "It had nothing to do with Donald Trump," he told me. "It had to do with the awkwardness of being in a public restaurant and cameras coming in and taking pictures." But sometimes a photo can convey a truth greater than the actual moment it captures.

After the dinner, Romney spoke to the press outside the restaurant—and this time, he decided to take his shot. He went as far as he could in flattering Trump without retracting what he'd said during the campaign. He told reporters that he had a "wonderful evening" with the president-elect, that their discussion of world affairs had been "enlightening and interesting and engaging."

"What I've seen through these discussions I've had with president-elect Trump, as well as what we've seen in his speech the night of his victory, as well as the people he's selected as part of his transition—all of those things combined give me increasing hope that president-elect Trump is the very man who can lead us to that better future."

This was every plausible compliment Romney could muster without feeling completely foolish. But it wasn't enough.

Shortly after his comments, Romney received a call from Trump. *He loved the idea of making Romney secretary of state,* Trump said, but he was getting a lot of pushback from loyal allies, like Rudy Giuliani and Mike Huckabee.

"You should know that Rudy and Mike really hate you," Trump told Romney. "I don't know what you did to them."

Romney reminded Trump that he had run against both men in Republican presidential primaries, and that there was a simple explanation for their animosity: "I beat them."

Finally, Trump cut to the chase. "You really need to say that you've come to the conclusion that I'm terrific and that I'll be a great president," he told Romney. "We need to clear this up."

But Romney couldn't bring himself to do it. Maybe after so many years of allowing the petty indignities and moral compromises to pile up, he had finally reached his limit. Or maybe some part of him just knew the job would be a disaster, that Trump would never honor Romney's conditions, no matter what he said.

"There's no way it could've worked for me—absolutely no way," he'd later reflect, noting that Trump ended up entrusting a significant swath of foreign policy to his son-in-law, Jared Kushner. Romney's allies agreed: "In retrospect, he dodged a bullet," George W. Bush told me.

After it was all over, critics taunted Romney for trying to get a spot in Trump's administration after opposing his candidacy so vocally. "Mitt Romney is somebody I had respect for. I have none anymore," said Harry Reid. "To go and [pay] homage to this guy he said awful things about, I don't think that shows much character." (Romney, who hadn't forgiven Reid for his dishonest attacks in 2012, shot back, "As for Mr. Reid, I lost respect for him when he repeatedly lied about my taxes and later admitted to it cheerily.")

Trump's various hangers-on, meanwhile, tried to recast the episode as an elaborate prank on Romney. Roger Stone crowed that Trump had just been "toying" with him. Newt Gingrich delighted in Romney's "sucking up."

"Judas Iscariot got 30 pieces of silver; Mitt Romney got a dish of frog legs at Jean-Georges. And even at that, it was an appetizer portion," an anonymous senior White House official told *The Atlantic*. "We've sort of taken out his larynx—how can he criticize [Trump] now?"

Romney wasn't sure what role, if any, he'd eventually play in the Trump era. But he felt certain his larynx was still intact.

CHAPTER ELEVEN

Turning and Turning

R omney watched the first six weeks of the Trump presidency unfold from Utah, in a state of growing alarm. The havoc-wreaking travel ban, the chaos at the airports, the mass resignations at the State Department—each day seemed to bring some new scene of bedlam brought on by the president.

One day in March of 2017, Romney was in Washington, D.C., for a Marriott board meeting, when Senator Orrin Hatch called to ask if they could meet.

"I'll come by and see you," Romney offered.

"No, no, I'll come see you," Hatch replied. He wanted to keep the meeting low-key.

Hatch arrived at Romney's room in the JW Marriott and presented him with a manila folder containing a two-page memo outlining why Romney should run for his Senate seat in Utah. Hatch was up for reelection the following year and was considering retirement, but wanted to make sure his seat would be in good hands before he made the decision.

The two men had known each other for decades. When Romney ran the Olympics, Hatch had been instrumental in helping him navigate the Hill to secure the federal funding he needed. The day after the September 11 terrorist attacks, Romney was in Hatch's Senate office to discuss how to keep the Games alive. During Romney's presidential campaigns, Hatch had been a vocal supporter and a sporadically helpful adviser. Once, during the 2012 race, he emailed Romney a list of proposed jokes to use on the campaign trail, such as *Do you know why Obama's campaign bus keeps getting lost? Because it only turns left!* On another occasion, Hatch encouraged Romney to spice up his language a bit. "You're kind of uptight," Hatch told the candidate. "You need to say 'shit' now and then."

It was no secret that, at age eighty-three, Hatch was past his prime. In recent years, his age had been showing: During a Senate hearing, he was caught on camera reaching toward his face to remove glasses that weren't there. During an interview on healthcare policy, he used a Civil War–era term that referred to firearms, but was now more commonly employed to describe male orgasms. In Utah's political circles, a quiet consensus was forming: Orrin needs to retire.

Still, Romney was surprised by Hatch's proposal. He told the senator he'd give it some thought.

The prospect of having something to do was certainly intriguing to Romney. Four years into his retirement, he was restless and eager for a new project, but none of the opportunities that crossed his radar seemed to grab him. He'd always fancied himself a writer and had kicked around some book ideas, one about careers, another on faith, and another that he described in his journal as a "humor checkout book" tentatively titled *25 Things to Remember When I'm Old.* But the work of writing was too solitary, too quiet to fully absorb him. M. Russell Ballard, a senior apostle in his Church, had asked him to establish a Mormon counterpart to the Jewish Anti-Defamation League. But after looking into it, he concluded that the Church's most pressing challenges in the twenty-first century were not misinformation or discrimination from outsiders—they were retaining young people, promoting faith in a secular world, and addressing prickly issues in the Church's history. "In other words," Romney would later reflect, "we have met the enemy and it was us."

Not even his first love, business, held much allure. In January of 2016, Tagg and Spencer Zwick had approached Romney about taking over a private equity fund in China that they believed would personally net him $500 million over the next several years. Romney was surprised by how little the opportunity tempted him. That kind of money would have effectively doubled his net worth, even after taxes and tithing, but he couldn't imagine how he would spend it. He and Ann had no desire to own a yacht, and his fortune was already large enough to take care of the next several generations of Romneys.

"Money is motivating when you don't have it and when you are young," he wrote in his journal. "A purpose greater than self is what motivates now. . . . Doing nothing is driving me crazy. I help a little at Marriott, help a little at Solamere, make a million a year with paid speeches, help a few campaigns and offer advice that's worthless to my sons—I don't feel like I'm accomplishing much."

Still, Romney wasn't sure a Senate seat was the solution. Hatch actually wasn't the first one to suggest that he run in Utah. Mike Leavitt had floated the possibility a year earlier, but Romney had demurred. Since losing his first race against Ted Kennedy, he'd decided the Senate wasn't for him. Too much speechifying, not enough action.

But the world looked different now that Trump was in office. Giving talks to cardiologist conventions and playing with his grandkids while the world burned simply didn't seem like an option.

In the months that followed, Romney actively explored the prospect of a Senate race. He spoke with Mitch McConnell, who urged him to run if the seat opened up. He spoke with GOP leaders in Utah, who said they'd be thrilled to see him replace Hatch. Determined to bury the blood feud between the Romneys and Huntsmans, he made a point of checking with Jon Huntsman Sr., who he'd heard was privately pushing for his son to run for the seat.

"If Jon Jr. wants to be senator, he can have it," Romney told him.

Huntsman said that Jon Jr. was focused on the diplomatic track—he'd recently been confirmed as Trump's ambassador to Russia—and gave Romney his blessing. Ironically, Romney himself had been offered the Russia post as a consolation prize after being passed over for secretary of state and had declined—a fact that Romney chose not to mention in his conversation with Huntsman.

Romney felt confident that, if he wanted it, the race would be a cakewalk. He was still a hero in the Beehive State—the savior of the Olympics, the Mormon Al Smith. And his fraught relationship with Trump wasn't seen as a political liability the way it would be in other red states. While Trump had carried Utah in 2016, he did so with only 45 percent of the vote, the worst showing for a Republican presidential nominee in a quarter century. (The independent Mormon candidate, Evan McMullin, won 21 percent in the state in 2016.)

Romney began keeping a detailed pros/cons list on his iPad. The arguments against running were mostly obvious: He would only be "1 of 100"; "DC accomplishes very little"; "Time away from Ann, kids!!!!" But one was unique to Romney: "Stress is a silent killer."

The Romney men had a long history of dying from sudden heart failure. His father had died that way; his grandfather, too. And he'd heard stories about a slew of siblings and cousins who supposedly suffered from the same heart condition. In the mental catalog of fatal threats that his preoccupation with death had created, stress-induced heart failure was foremost among them. And it was hard to deny that serving in the U.S. Senate while his party was led by a crazy person would be a stressful undertaking.

Romney's "pros" column was longer: He could draw attention to issues he cared about ("China, debt, climate, protect[ing] religious liberty"). He could keep "an active mind," and "help the people of Utah," a state to which he'd always felt a spiritual bond. And of course there was what he termed the "Romney obligation"—that compulsive need to run toward a crisis.

On August 11, 2017, another reason presented itself when white nationalists marched through the campus of the University of Virginia in Charlottesville, waving torches and chanting Nazi slogans. The scene evoked the darkest chapters of American history and highlighted a disturbing trend of the Trump era—the emboldening of the country's most vile ideologues and bigots. The next day, as counterprotesters clashed with the neo-Nazis, a Trump supporter plowed his car into the crowd, killing a thirty-two-year-old woman named Heather Heyer and maiming several others.

The next week, when Trump was asked at a press conference about the violence, he said there were "very fine people on both sides."

Romney, appalled, wrote on his list, "President's equivocation/incitement of race/bigotry." He couldn't believe how far his party—the party of Abraham Lincoln and Dwight Eisenhower and George Romney—had fallen. In moments like these, he felt strongly that the GOP needed elected officials who would forcefully condemn the president's racism and steer conservatives away from the black hole of white grievance. Instead, all he saw was hedging and dodging and cowardly silence.

At the top of his list—neither a pro nor a con, or possibly both—Romney had typed out a line from Yeats that he couldn't get out of his mind: "The best lack all conviction, while the worst are full of passionate intensity." It captured so much of this political moment, but especially what he saw as "the new GOP."

"The very best among our Senate and House Republicans weren't speaking out and correcting the president. . . . They were silent," Romney later told me. "Whereas there were some people jumping up and down saying, '*This is fantastic!*' and trying to copy it." The few elected Republicans in Washington who *did* seem willing to stand up to Trump were on their way out. Jeff Flake and Bob Corker were mulling retirement from the Senate rather than face Trump-enamored primary voters in 2018. And John McCain, whose proud maverick streak had made him a frequent critic of the president, had recently announced a brain cancer diagnosis. In Romney's view, the Oval Office was occupied by a temperamentally erratic and morally bankrupt president who had a knack for driving both his supporters and opponents insane. He worried about what might happen under these conditions. "If there were to be a constitutional crisis or some other kind of disruption, [I thought] that it would be helpful to have more people of sobriety and stability," he said. "Having been the former nominee, it made me feel that I had a greater responsibility . . . I had the potential to be an alternative voice for Republicans." In the summer of 2017, it still seemed possible that Trump would be remembered as an outlier.

That fall, Romney made up his mind to run, and began preparing his campaign. But while rumors of his reemergence circulated in the political press, the incumbent was having second thoughts. For all his admirable qualities, Hatch was a vain man, and bristled against the perception that he was being pushed off the stage. When reporters asked him about Romney running for his seat, Hatch waffled and wavered and had his office issue ornery statements about how he was still considering his options—*so please back off.* He didn't like how much buzz his chosen successor was getting, didn't like that things weren't happening on his timeline. He believed his legacy deserved more respect: in the latter part of his career, he'd begun privately invoking a rumored Mormon prophecy that one day the Constitution would be "hanging by a thread" and members of the Church would save it. He seemed to believe his work in the Senate represented the fulfillment of the "White Horse prophecy."

He also had Trump in his ear. Hatch was one of the president's most enthusiastic allies in the Senate—and Trump didn't want to lose him. During a visit to Utah in early December, Trump publicly urged Hatch to run for reelection. "You are a true fighter, Orrin, I have to say," Trump said. "We hope you will continue to serve your state and the country and the Senate for a very long time to come." At a bill-signing ceremony at the White House later that month, Hatch declared that Trump's could be "the greatest presidency we've seen not only in generations but maybe ever." After the ceremony, the *New York Times* reported, Trump pulled him aside and once again told him not to retire.

Shortly before Christmas, Romney called Hatch and asked him what was going on.

"Well, you know," Hatch explained, "the president really wants me to stay on. . . ."

"Orrin," Romney said sharply, "you're the one that's been pushing me to do this. This wasn't my idea." He told Hatch that he didn't want to apply undue pressure. "But I've decided I'm going to do this. What are you going to do?"

Hatch must have seen the writing on the wall because within weeks he announced his intention to retire. (It didn't hurt that Zwick, Romney's longtime fundraiser, generously offered to help raise funds to establish an institute in Hatch's name.)

That night, Romney changed the location on his Twitter bio from "Massachusetts" to "Holladay, Utah."

Not long after Romney announced his candidacy, he received a phone call from Trump. Despite the president's best efforts, Romney was now likely headed to Washington, and Trump apparently thought it was worth trying to bring him in line.

Trump did most of the talking, as was his wont, bragging at length about his supposedly fervent support in Romney's state—"I'm loved by the people of Utah"—before explaining the secret to his popularity: "You know, I gave Utah two million square miles of land."

Romney knew what Trump was referring to: the administration had recently rolled back federal protection for two national monuments in Utah, handing a victory to conservative business owners over environmentalists. Romney also knew that Trump had gotten the unit of measurement wrong. He meant acres. ("Two million square miles would be, like, half the country," Romney later noted with some amusement.) But he chose not to say anything. Instead, he and a campaign aide who was listening in stifled their laughter as Trump blustered on, clinging emphatically to his assertion.

"I'm a real estate guy. I know the difference between acres and square miles," Trump volunteered. "This was *square miles*."

By the time the president got around to asking Romney how many followers he had on Twitter (2 million), Romney couldn't help but respond with his own impression of Trumpian embellishment.

"*Five* million!" he replied, just to see what Trump would say.

The president, who did not catch on, seemed grudgingly impressed.

As Romney set out on the campaign trail in Utah, he was determined to dispel the accusations of carpetbaggery. While polls showed him with a huge lead, some of the more Trump-aligned Republicans in the state had been publicly grumbling that Romney had no business representing Utah in the Senate.

"I think he's keeping out candidates that I think would be a better fit for Utah because, let's face it, Mitt Romney doesn't live here, his kids weren't born here, he doesn't shop here," said Rob Anderson, the chairman of the Utah Republican Party and a vocal Trump supporter.

Romney did, in fact, live in Utah, at least most of the time. In addition to their lodge in Deer Valley, he and Ann had built a house outside of Salt Lake City after the 2012 election to be close to their kids and grandkids in the area. Not that it really mattered. He would have been Utah royalty regardless of property records. Still, he told his small campaign team that he wanted to show voters he was taking nothing for granted. He would speak at every Lincoln Day Dinner, show up at every 4-H fair and homecoming parade that would have him. He would make a project of visiting all twenty-nine counties in Utah, and skip interviews with the *Wall Street Journal* in favor of meetings with the publisher of the *Sanpete Messenger*. By the end of his campaign, his staff would claim, he had attended some 470 events.

One thing he wouldn't do was talk about Donald Trump. Romney didn't want his campaign to be a yearlong crusade against the president. He had his own policy agenda to advance, his own vision for the future of the Republican Party. He nurtured a pleasant delusion that he could somehow avoid being defined by his relationship with the president—using his platform to campaign against Trumpism, while largely ignoring Trump himself. He came up with a pat line to deliver anytime he was asked about the president: *I'll support his policies when I agree with them, and I'll continue to speak out when he does something I think is wrong.*

In a video announcing his bid for the Senate, Romney framed his campaign as one that would represent his state's unique brand of politics: "Utah has a lot to teach the politicians in Washington. Utah has balanced its budgets. Washington is buried in debt. . . . Utah welcomes legal immigrants from around the world. Washington sends immigrants a message of exclusion. And on Utah's Capitol Hill, people treat one another with respect."

Once he hit the road, Romney was pleasantly surprised by how much he enjoyed campaigning, an activity he had heretofore rated as only slightly more pleasant than gallbladder surgery. In an email to a friend, he wrote about how much more "enjoyable" this race was than any of his others: "People are Utah nice, places are magnificent and desserts are delicious and everywhere."

He could also be himself. Here, Romney's old-fashioned civic starchiness and golly-gee diction didn't peg him as some relic of a bygone era—a "latter-day Beaver Cleaver," as a *Boston Globe* writer had once put it. To many Mormon voters, Romney evoked a broadly familiar, and largely beloved, type—he was their dad, their grandpa, their bishop.

Unlike in his past campaigns, Romney's advisers adopted a "let Mitt be Mitt" philosophy. They stood back and watched as he hammed it up as emcee at a hot dog–eating contest ("As they say in this business, it's weiner take all!"). They let him riff to reporters about his favorite foods ("My favorite meat is hot dog, by the way. That is my favorite meat. . . . And everyone says, oh don't you prefer steak? It's like, I know steaks are great, but I like hot dog best"). At one point, Romney rewrote the lyrics to Johnny Cash's "I've Been Everywhere" to include various towns and cities he'd visited in Utah, and recorded himself singing it behind the wheel of a pickup truck. The video was deeply dorky, but when he proposed posting it to Twitter, Matt Waldrip, Romney's campaign manager, shrugged: "Sure, let's do it."

Romney found that he enjoyed wading into the minutiae of local issues. It reminded him of Massachusetts, where not every problem to be solved was part of a zero-sum partisan brawl. When he went to Duchesne, he boned up on the planned rail line from the Uintas to Price Canyon; when he went to St. George, he reveled in talking about the proposed pipeline from Lake Powell to Washington County.

But the more he ventured away from the genteel suburbs and into right-wing rural areas, the more signs he encountered that all was not well in Zion.

On February 22, he attended the Iron County Republicans' Lincoln Day Dinner in Cedar City. Right away, he could tell that the event had a strange vibe. The scene was a mix of tie-and-blazer Republicans and libertarians in cowboy hats. At one point, a woman in a pioneer-style dress approached Romney's scheduler and asked if she was interested in joining her family as a "sister wife." The opening prayer was offered by Ammon Bundy, the anti-government activist who'd staged a monthlong armed standoff with federal agents in 2016 over land rights. Bundy's prayer went on for five minutes as he detailed a litany of sins committed by the government and petitioned God to mete out justice. When he finished, he was met not with *Amen*s but a standing ovation.

This was an element of Utah politics that was exotic to Romney—a marginal fringe, he told himself—and he had no desire to be associated with it. Still, he didn't want to be rude. So, when he heard that Bundy was asking for a picture with him, Romney instructed his aides to make sure they never came face-to-face. At one point, they glimpsed Bundy making his way toward them down the hallway and quickly ushered the candidate through the nearest doorway to hide. Only once they were inside did Romney realize he was in a closet.

On April 21, Romney arrived at the Maverik Center for the Utah Republican Convention. The state's unusual nominating system allowed candidates to compete for delegates months before the primary was held: anybody who won support from more than 40 percent of the delegates at the convention would earn a spot on the ballot. Romney knew the state party delegates tended to be more conservative—and lately, more loyal to Trump—than the average Utah voter. But he also knew he was the only serious candidate in the race, and thought he had a good chance of winning the nomination outright at the convention.

The event had all the trappings of a standard partisan circus. American flag–shaped confetti rained from the ceiling. Men wearing lanyards fought bitterly over arcane party rules. An Abraham Lincoln impersonator, who'd filed as "Abe Lincoln Brian Jenkins," roamed the premises trying to gin up support for his Senate candidacy.

But there was an unsettling edge to the proceedings. The delegates in MAGA hats and Trump T-shirts were more numerous than Romney's team had expected, and they seemed enamored of a right-wing state legislator named Mike Kennedy. A Trump-loving family doctor from Alpine, Utah, Kennedy presented himself to the convention as a humble David figure taking on the Goliath-like "Romney machine." To drive the analogy home, he handed out hundreds of small stones to the delegates, and declared them "ready to be flung at the foes of liberty who seek to oppress us." The red-capped delegates roared their approval.

Romney was irritated by his opponent's routine. "First, none of us is David," he said when it was his turn to speak. "David was anointed of God." But the scolding did little to blunt Kennedy's momentum. By the time the voting ended, after eleven long hours, Romney had won just 49 percent of the delegates, while Kennedy had 51 percent. The Utah golden boy had been bested by a no-name state representative.

Both men would advance to the primary in June, where Romney knew he was almost certain to win. He did his best to play the good sport that night: "This is terrific for the people of Utah!" he told delegates. "We're going to have a good primary."

Still, there was something ominous about seeing the most extreme, and unserious, forces in his party stage a successful revolt in his ancestral home state.

*   *   *

Romney won the primary, as expected. But as he entered the fall, his election all but decided, he found himself increasingly conflicted about how the midterms were shaping up. He told friends he was glad that he would likely be serving in the Senate majority, but repulsed by his party's tactics for getting there.

Trump and his allies had been working to whip up public hysteria over a migrant caravan that was reportedly traveling toward the U.S. from Central America. Such caravans were not unusual, but the president made full use of his executive powers to cast it as a crisis. He dispatched thousands of troops to the border, and released a campaign ad that interspersed footage of Hispanic migrants with clips of a convicted cop-killer before issuing an urgent call to action: STOP THE CARAVAN. VOTE REPUBLICAN. His allies in the right-wing media churned out baseless stories claiming the caravan was a vector of dangerous diseases, or a Trojan horse for murderous cartels, or a pawn in a plot by the globalist elite. "Many Gang Members and some very bad people are mixed into the Caravan heading to our Southern Border," Trump tweeted. "This is an invasion of our Country and our Military is waiting for you!"

In an email to Beth Myers and Stuart Stevens on October 22, Romney predicted Republicans would hold the Senate: "The caravan from Honduras is arriving just in time for the bully-in-chief to flex his flabby muscles." But he hardly seemed thrilled. A few days later, after Fox Business host Lou Dobbs featured a guest asserting that the caravan was being funded by the "Soros-occupied State Department," Romney let loose in a flurry of emails to advisers. "Fox is becoming a serious problem," he wrote in one. "Lou is a moron. Fox is an enabler," he wrote in another.

The closer the election got, the more Trump seemed determined to turn up the temperature in an already overheated country. In October, pipe bombs began arriving in the mail at the addresses of prominent critics of Trump, including at the New York headquarters of CNN. At the same time, outrage was growing over the news that *Washington Post* journalist Jamal Khashoggi had been murdered at the direction of the Saudi crown prince, a key ally of the Trump administration.

Trump had made his antipathy toward the press a centerpiece of his campaign speeches. When he was asked by reporters if the recent developments might prompt him to tone down his rhetoric, especially his targeting of journalists, he responded, "I think I've been toned down, if you want to know the truth. I could really tone it up."

Trump made good on his promise in the days that followed, leading his crowds in a ritualistic booing of the reporters who covered his rallies, and egging on his fans as they chanted "CNN sucks!"

The president's crusade put Romney on edge. He'd seen how these undemocratic sentiments were trickling down to the electorate. At a town hall in West Valley, a woman asked Romney if he would "take action to shut down ABC, NBC, CBS, CNN, and the *New York Times* if elected?"

Romney was startled by the question. "Of course not. I will do everything in my power to preserve freedom of speech."

He wasn't used to hearing such authoritarian ideas being casually uttered by everyday voters. "It was a revelation," he'd later tell me, "that people in my party thought so little of some of the protections of the Constitution."

On October 29, Trump posted a pair of tweets blaming the rise in political violence on the press. "There is great anger in our Country caused in part by inaccurate, and even fraudulent, reporting of the news. The Fake News Media, the true Enemy of the People, must stop the open & obvious hostility & report the news accurately & fairly," he wrote.

Trump had begun using this incendiary term—*the enemy of the people*—to describe the press shortly after he was sworn in. Whether he knew its Stalinist roots was unclear, but his strategy behind his demonization of the press was plain. Trump's political project depended on holding his supporters inside a sealed bubble of propaganda—anything that threatened to puncture it had to be destroyed.

"The President's tweet today about the media has me agitated again," Romney wrote to his advisers. "A recurring syndrome."

He told them he was thinking of condemning Trump's anti-press rhetoric. Picking a fight with the president at this late stage of the race was politically fraught, and in his email he laid out the pros and cons. "It will cost me quite a few votes in Utah, though the outcome of the race will probably not change," he wrote. On the other hand, it "establishes where I am about Trump before the election so that I can have more impact after the election." He noted that some had taken his apparent reluctance to talk about the president on the campaign trail as evidence that he was "flipping again" on his view of Trump—an idea that Romney, always sensitive to charges of inconsistency, was eager to dispel.

But the most compelling argument to say something was not political. "What [Trump] is doing is dangerous," he wrote to his advisers, and "the silence from GOP leaders about this is disgusting."

At Beth Myers's suggestion, Romney wrote an essay articulating the vital role of the free press in a functioning democracy, and explicating the dangers of Trump's anti-media rhetoric:

A lesson evidenced by the Arab Spring and by the pseudo-democracies of Venezuela, Russia, and China is democracy and freedom cannot be permanently established in the absence of the basic institutions of freedom, perhaps most notably a free press. . . .

I sometimes become irritated by stories I know are wrong, especially when they are about me. But I cannot conceive of thinking or saying that the media or any responsible news organization is an enemy. The media is essential to our Republic, to our freedom, to the cause of freedom abroad, and to our national security. It is very much our friend.

The conservative backlash to the essay began as soon as it was released by the Romney campaign. Fox News host Mark Levin declared Romney "an empty suit." *Breitbart* played it up on its homepage, reminding readers that Romney was a "failed presidential candidate." Romney's official Facebook page was swarmed by voters who were furious that he'd take the media's side in its war against Trump:

"Washington does not need another globalist as Senator. We need Senators that will support Trump's agenda," wrote one person.

"We have a press that is owned by George Soros and run by democrats," wrote another. "Romney, if you can't speak the truth you are as bad as they are."

"Still trying to win the affection of the very people out to ruin your candidacy," still another chimed in. "W. Bush tried the Wimp approach with the media and by the end of his second term he was a political eunuch. You slap Trump, he slaps you back and calls you a Bi*** in front of your mother."

After a year on the campaign trail, Romney was beginning to reevaluate what he considered the true threat posed by this president. Trump wasn't just erratic or stupid or immoral or mean, all qualities that would be bad enough when possessed by the most powerful man in the world. He was hostile to the very underpinnings of American democracy. And his hostility was contagious.

Election Day arrived with little doubt about whether Romney would win his race. There had been some discussion among his advisers about whether the campaign should organize a big, attention-grabbing victory rally—find a grand venue, fill it with supporters, and invite national media for a speech outlining how he planned to serve as senator—but Romney had nixed it. He had no interest in competing for attention with noisier candidates and tighter races. He wanted his event to be a low-key affair. In an email to his team, he suggested spending the budget on hot dogs and hamburgers for whoever was willing to show up, "not production values."

So, there he was, at a campaign office in Orem with drop ceilings and fluorescent lights, delivering the most benign remarks possible to a small crowd of supporters.

Romney said his victory represented "a call for greater dignity and respect" and "an affirmation that regardless of one's gender or ethnicity or sexual orientation or race or place of birth, that we are equal."

Part of his reluctance to give a more substantive speech stemmed from the fact that Romney was still unsure of how he'd position himself in the Senate. When Mitch McConnell had personally lobbied him to run, he'd assured him that, as an elder statesman in the party, Romney would be given more influence than a typical junior senator. Some in Washington had even speculated that he might be tapped to lead the National Republican Senatorial Committee. Left unsaid was that all that power would surely be conditioned on Romney's ability to get along with Trump. Could he really do that?

The one thing he knew for certain was that his original strategy—to fight Trumpism while ignoring Trump—seemed more untenable by the day.

An elected official in Washington could do many things to the president, but ignoring him was not one of them.

CHAPTER TWELVE

The Punch Bowl

Trump seemed to get more erratic after the 2018 midterm elections. Or maybe it was just that Romney was paying closer attention now. The bewildering stories coming out of Washington no longer felt like some absurd, high-stakes TV show that Romney could simply comment on. They were like dispatches from a foreign capital where the local tin-pot tyrant was growing crazier by the day—a capital to which Romney would soon be moving.

On November 7, the day after the elections, Trump fired his attorney general, Jeff Sessions, whom he despised for appointing a special counsel to investigate Russia's interference in the 2016 election. A few days later, Trump pardoned two army officers who'd been convicted of grisly war crimes in Afghanistan, and reversed the demotion of a third, overruling Pentagon officials who'd pleaded with the president not to interfere in the case.

Meanwhile, as a massive wildfire raged in California, Trump refused to heed expert briefings, choosing instead to hurl recriminations at "radical environmentalists" and Democratic politicians for failing to contain the blaze, and threatening to cut off federal aid to the state if they didn't shape up.

Romney wrote to Stuart Stevens, a frequent recipient of his venting, that the president's recent moves were "mind-numbingly moronic." Still, the senator-elect had resolved to contain his grumbling about Trump to his private email for now. He saw no reason to exacerbate tensions with the White House before he was even sworn in, nor was he eager to start alienating his soon-to-be colleagues in the Republican caucus. Better to keep his options open, to maintain a low profile. He busied himself assembling a staff and scoping out real estate in Washington.

But one longtime adviser refused to let him off the hook. Beth Myers had known Romney for nearly two decades, and was one of his most trusted political confidantes. She knew how he thought, knew his weaknesses and strengths. And she knew that he would be tempted to hide behind a backbencher status when he got to the Senate—rationalizing that he was still getting his sea legs, that he shouldn't rock the boat, that, after all, he was just one senator out of a hundred. Myers wanted to break him out of that pattern of thinking.

Myers's husband had died suddenly in November, causing her to temporarily withdraw from politics while she grieved and made arrangements. But she'd been struck by how many of the mourners and well-wishers who reached out with condolences brought up Senator-elect Romney in their conversations.

On December 12, she wrote to Romney, urging him to keep Trump in check: "He's what you said he would be. There is an opportunity here to put down markers and show that you will be a leading voice. . . . I've been in a fog the last month but the desire for sane leadership from you was expressed by so many of the people who've been in contact with me." She closed with a reminder that was intended as a call to action: "You're the hope for serious-minded conservatives."

The sentiment was flattering, but Romney wasn't sure what to do with it. Any hope of implementing "serious-minded" solutions to America's problems would require leadership from a stable, thoughtful president—the one thing that America had in perilously short supply.

Romney was also frustrated by the constant refrain of the pundit class that principled Republicans must *do something* about Trump.

"The question no one seems to address is exactly what a GOP leader is supposed to do," Romney vented in an email. Trump wasn't like other presidents, whose legislative priorities might be leveraged to rein him in. Trump *had* no legislative priorities apart from his beloved border wall. And Romney wasn't about to start blocking the confirmation of otherwise qualified conservative judges just to make a point about Trump, as some had called for—he saw that as akin to cutting off your nose to spite your face. He told Myers he was "pondering" her suggestion, but planned to keep his powder dry.

On December 16, the president spent the afternoon ranting on Twitter about special counsel Robert Mueller's investigation. The verbal torrent seemed even more splenetic and paranoid than usual. "The Russian Witch Hunt Hoax, started as the 'insurance policy' long before I even got elected, is very bad for our Country," Trump tweeted. "They are Entrapping people for misstatements, lies or unrelated things that took place many years ago. Nothing to do with Collusion. A Democrat Scam!"

The next day, Romney sent an email to Myers, Stevens, and Matt Waldrip, his incoming chief of staff, under the subject "Harder and harder."

"I'm finding it hard to stay silent as T becomes increasingly unhinged," Romney wrote. "I'll hold on for a while longer, don't worry. But gosh!"

Nineteen minutes later, he emailed the same group again with a link to a quote from former FBI director James Comey: "Republicans used to understand that the actions of a president matter, the words of a president matter, the rule of law matters, and the truth matters. Where are those Republicans today?" Romney attached some guttural commentary: "Argh."

On December 19, Trump abruptly announced on Twitter—without consulting advisers or military leaders—that he was withdrawing two thousand U.S. troops from Syria. The move meant ceding crucial territory to Russia, abandoning allies, and imperiling Syria's ethnic Kurds, who'd fought loyally alongside America for years to defeat the Islamic State. The next day, Defense Secretary James Mattis resigned, saying he no longer felt he could implement the president's policies. Mattis, a retired four-star general, had been the quintessential adult in the room—a widely respected figure on whom official Washington had pinned its hopes for staving off an international crisis. Now he was ejecting from the figurative cockpit—and Trump was fully at the controls.

The turbulence wasn't restricted to foreign affairs. The same day Mattis resigned, Trump petulantly declared that he would not sign any bill that continued to fund the federal government unless it included at least $5 billion for a border wall. If Senate Democrats didn't acquiesce, he warned on Twitter, "There will be a shutdown that will last for a very long time."

Two days later, the federal government ran out of money and ground to a halt, sending thousands of workers home without paychecks just before the holiday.

That Christmas Eve, Romney struggled to sleep. He sat up in the great room of his Deer Valley, Utah, ski lodge—his feet resting on the ottoman across from the fireplace, grandkids slumbering down the hall—while he swiped miserably at his iPad, surveying the wreckage of a world on fire and allowing the most apocalyptic scenarios to run through his head.

Just before 10:00 p.m., he sent a cryptic email to Myers, Stevens, and Waldrip about Trump: "His last few weeks have scrambled my thinking about how to proceed."

Stevens was the first to respond. Like Myers, he'd been trying to steer Romney toward a more confrontational approach to Trump. "It's all so bad and will just get worse," Stevens wrote. "Nothing of this era will be remembered except how elected officials reacted to Trump. The tax cuts, the judges, whatever, nothing will matter. Trump is Nixon but worse. He's Vietnam. He's the moral test of the moment."

Language like this would not have worked on the Mitt Romney of a decade earlier, the one still trying to become president. He would have dismissed the appeal as hyperbolic moralizing. But the path to higher office was closed now. Moral tests mattered more than they once did.

Hunched over in an armchair near the Christmas tree, Romney began to type furiously, as though exorcizing a demon. He knew what he was writing was melodramatic—and, sure, more than a little self-aggrandizing—but he didn't care. A very sick man was in the Oval Office, dragging the nation to the brink. And Romney had waited too long to understand the severity of the situation. When he finished writing he clicked send.

From: Mitt Romney
Mon, Dec 24, 2018 at 11:17 p.m.
To: Stuart Stevens, Beth Myers
Subject: I'm no prophet

He was the last person I wanted as the Republican nominee. I made that clear. After he won the nomination, I watched his campaign to see if he might surprise me. He did not. When he won, I hoped he would rise to the occasion. His call for me to potentially serve at State fueled that hope—after all, I had been a very vocal detractor.

Unfortunately, President Trump did not grow to match the office. His smallness has instead diminished it. The American President has long served as a model for the nation; few would imagine holding Donald Trump up for their children to emulate. Around the world, he, and to some degree the nation that elected him, have become a laughing stock. His poverty of character has been exposed so often and in so many ways that many here have become inured to it. Not so for those who watch him from abroad.

I was asked repeatedly to apologize for what I said about Donald Trump, to say that having spent more time with him, I had learned that I was wrong. I demurred. But in truth, I did not imagine that he would

be so tragic as president. The incessant lying, the adulterer payoffs,
the unwillingness to study and deliberate, the weakening of alliances,
the elevation of autocrats, the impetuous decision, the demonizing
of others, the divisiveness, the inability to hire and retain people of
accomplishment—these are as stunning to me as they are to others. I
did not think he would be this bad.

Romney decided he wasn't interested in being cautious anymore. The day after Christmas, he began drafting an op-ed about what he considered to be the president's most dangerous defects. The article, which was published in the *Washington Post* the week he took office, was not as scathing as his Christmas Eve missive. His new staff had steered him toward a more stately, senatorial tone. But it left little doubt about whether Romney was coming to Washington as a friend or foe to Trump.

"The Trump presidency made a deep descent in December," the article began. He argued that the president's abhorrent behavior and reckless foreign policy had caused "dismay around the world," noting that in 2016, 84 percent of people in Germany, Britain, France, Canada, and Sweden believed the American president would "do the right thing in world affairs," and that one year later, that number had fallen to 16 percent.

"On balance," Romney wrote, Trump's "conduct over the past two years, particularly his actions last month, is evidence that the president has not risen to the mantle of the office. . . . With the nation so divided, resentful and angry, presidential leadership in qualities of character is indispensable. And it is in this province where the incumbent's shortfall has been most glaring."

The op-ed provoked a noisy reaction, with the various factions of Trump's Washington dutifully lining up to play their parts. Never-Trump conservatives rejoiced at Romney's gauntlet-throwing, with Bill Kristol declaring him "the leader of the Republican Resistance to Trump." Liberal skeptics rolled their eyes, predicting that Romney would end up voting for the president's agenda when it really mattered.

And the MAGA crowd rushed to cast Romney as a sore loser who was consumed with resentment that he never got to be president.

"I won big, and he didn't," Trump tweeted predictably.

"Jealously [sic] is a drink best served warm and Romney just proved it," Trump's campaign manager, Brad Parscale, tweeted, somewhat more mysteriously.

David Perdue, the Republican senator from Georgia, published his own piece in the *Post* scolding Romney for airing his criticisms on the op-ed page instead of taking his concerns directly to the president. "He ran to the media instead of picking up the phone," Perdue wrote. "That is exactly what is wrong with Washington. Too many career politicians focus on finger-pointing for their own self-interest rather than on getting results." (Romney later noted, with some wry amusement, that he never received a phone call from Perdue on the matter—when they saw each other next, the gentleman from Georgia acted like nothing had happened.)

A few days after Romney was sworn in, *Politico* ran a story about the "chilly reception" he was receiving from his Republican Senate colleagues. The story quoted several senators, on the record and anonymously, griping about his unwillingness to get along with the leader of their party. "Focusing on our political opponents that are trying to annihilate us and embarrass the president is probably a more productive focus, rather than just criticize what the president is, how he does things," said Senator John Cornyn.

Romney emailed the story to his advisers, describing himself as "the turd in the punch bowl."

"Entirely predictable," he wrote. "These guys have got to justify their silence, at least to themselves."

Senate offices are assigned on the basis of seniority, which meant that Romney, who ranked ninety-seventh by that metric, began his legislative career in a cramped, ill-lit subterranean bunker lined with old filing cabinets. Before he saw it for the first time, Waldrip warned his boss not to expect too much—the office was only temporary; he'd get a better one in a few months. But Romney seemed too awed by the hallowed institution he was joining to notice the low ceilings or the worn-out furniture. His father had walked these same halls, spent time in this very same building, when he worked as a junior typist. Eighty years later, his youngest son was serving as a United States senator.

When they arrived at B33 Russell, Waldrip watched as Romney walked reverently to his desk and murmured, almost as if to himself, "My dad would be so proud."

After he was elected, Romney had begun typing out a list on his iPad of all the things he wanted to accomplish in the Senate. By the time he took office, it contained forty-two items and was still growing. The legislative to-do list ranged from complex systemic reforms—overhauling the immigration system, reducing the national deficit, addressing climate change—to narrower issues such as compensating college athletes and regulating the vaping industry. His staff was bemused when he showed it to them—even in less polarized, less chaotic times, the kind of ambitious agenda he had in mind would be unrealistic—but Romney was undeterred. He told his aides he wanted to set up meetings with all ninety-nine of his colleagues in his first six months, and began studying a flip-book of senators' pictures so that he could recognize his potential legislative partners.

Romney began each meeting roughly the same way: "Look, I'm obviously new to this body," he'd say. "I'm happy to share with you the things I would like to accomplish as a senator, but I'm here to understand what things are most important to you." He took notes, asked follow-up questions, and seemed genuinely interested in picking their brains. Many of the senators, who knew Romney primarily from TV, were surprised. "I don't think there was a single senator who assumed that's how Mitt Romney would approach his time in the Senate," Waldrip recalled.

In one early meeting, a colleague leveled with him: "There are about twenty senators here who do all the work, and there are about eighty who go along for the ride." Romney saw himself as a workhorse, and wanted others to see him that way, too. "I wanted to make it clear: I want to do things," he'd later recall.

He quickly became frustrated, though, by how much of the Senate was built around posturing and theatrics. They gave speeches to empty chambers; spent hours debating bills they all knew would never pass. They summoned experts to appear at committee hearings only to make them sit in silence while they blathered some more. The hearings were especially irksome to Romney. "They're not about learning. They're not about fact-finding. They're about performing," Romney complained. "Sometimes I get a little frustrated. . . . If we have someone there who's interesting, why are *we* giving speeches?"

Romney was also jarred by the lack of urgency he encountered among many of his colleagues when it came to confronting potentially cataclysmic threats to the country. A devout institutionalist, Romney had harbored a certain subconscious notion that somewhere in the U.S. government, serious people were sitting in rooms drawing up cohesive plans to address America's long-term challenges. But if those rooms existed, they did not appear to be in the United States Senate. Most of the legislative efforts he learned about were small and scattershot.

Climate change was one issue where this was especially apparent. Like many nationally ambitious Republicans, Romney had downplayed the climate threat for much of his political career. Now freed from the constraints of seeking the presidency, he was ready to roll up his sleeves and get to work on major bipartisan solutions to the problem. But the senators who were working on the issue seemed consumed with what he considered "small-bore measures" that aimed to gradually reduce carbon emissions in the U.S. In Romney's view, delivering the planet from a climate catastrophe would require a massive, well-organized investment in new technologies that prioritized carbon capture and renewable, clean energy. When he tried to ask the logical questions about how to get there—for example, how much lithium, copper, and cobalt would the U.S. need to produce 7.85 billion solar panels and

5 billion batteries, how much would it cost, and where could those materials be sourced?—he was met effectively with shrugs and blank stares. In the business world, Romney had made a career of careful planning and execution. That was not a part of the Senate's ethos. "It concerns me that we don't have long-term, comprehensive plans," he said. "We don't have a five-year plan. We don't have a ten-year plan."

Romney encountered a similar attitude when he sought legislative partners to tackle deficit reduction. This was an issue that had concerned Romney for years. He was convinced that unless federal spending was brought into line with incoming revenues, America would accelerate toward runaway national debt, weakened standing in the world, and a painful fiscal reckoning. Conservatives used to at least pretend they agreed with him. Back when he was running for president, Romney had made the deficit a centerpiece of his campaign, and the crowds always cheered when he railed against the Obama administration's out-of-control spending. But once Republicans took power, the problem only got worse. Even Paul Ryan, whose 2016 surrender to Trump Romney had treated more generously than others', seemed to have given up on the issue to which he'd devoted most of his political career. During Ryan's three years as speaker of the House, the deficit increased by nearly 80 percent—and that included two years in which the GOP held full control of the legislative and executive branches. Their signature piece of legislation during this period was an overhaul of the tax code that dramatically slashed rates for corporations and individuals with few mechanisms to offset the cuts.

In a meeting with Republican senator Ron Johnson in January, Romney asked which of their colleagues he should approach about working with him on the deficit. Johnson replied that, as much as he shared Romney's concerns, there was virtually no appetite in the caucus to meaningfully cut spending. It was too unpopular. The basic laws of political gravity pushed legislators away from the issue.

Romney was already becoming acquainted with these laws himself. One of the first pieces of legislation that came up for a vote when he was senator was a bill authorizing $33 billion in funding for Israel's military. Studying the bill with all the idealistic naivete of a freshman political science student, Romney found that he had some reservations. He considered himself a stalwart supporter of Israel, but what were the fiscal principles at stake? In an email to his policy director, Romney wrote, "It's a challenge to justify borrowing 33 billion from China so we can give it to Israel, particularly when I am under the impression that Israel is sufficiently well financed to provide the funds itself." He proposed an amendment: instead of using the bill's current language of "no less than $33 billion," the text should read "up to $33 billion." The aide responded at great length, summarizing the aims and origins of the bill and then finally laying out the political realities.

"In general, your instinct about the 'up to/no less than' distinction for authorizations is spot on and something we would not recommend you support," he wrote. "In practice, we think an amendment to this particular bill would probably be interpreted as 'anti-Israel' because it would be a step away from precedent." Romney relented.

Life in the Senate could be lonely. Romney didn't have many close friends in Washington, and he spent most evenings at his townhome by himself. He watched TV to pass the time and read books to fall asleep: sci-fi and fantasy for fun (he particularly enjoyed *The Three-Body Problem*, and devoured everything by Brandon Sanderson) and biographies for intellectual stimulation and enlightenment (*American Ulysses*). As the weeks passed, Romney became fascinated by the strange social ecosystem that governed the United States Senate. He spent his mornings in the Senate gym studying his colleagues like he was an anthropologist, jotting down his observations in his journal. Richard Burr walked on the treadmill in his suit pants and loafers; Sherrod Brown and Dick Durbin peddled so slowly on their exercise bikes that Romney couldn't help but peek at their resistance settings: "Durbin was set to 1 and Brown to 8 :) :) My setting is 15—not that I'm bragging," he recorded.

He joked to friends that the Senate was best understood as a "club for old men." There were free meals, on-site barbers, and doctors within a hundred feet at all times. But there was an edge to the observation: The average age in the Senate was sixty-three years old. Several members, Romney included, were well into their seventies and even eighties. And he sensed that many of his colleagues attached an enormous psychic currency to their position—that they would do almost anything to keep it. "Most of us have gone out and tried playing golf for a week, and it was like, *OK, I'm gonna kill myself*," he observed. Job preservation, in this context, became almost existential. Retirement was death. The men and women of the Senate might not need their government salary to survive, but they needed the stimulation, the sense of relevance, the power. "I think for most of us, it's like, 'Well, what am I going to do instead?'" Romney said. One of his new colleagues even told him that the first consideration when voting on any bill should be "Will this help me win reelection?" (The second and third considerations, the colleague continued, should be what effect it would have on his constituents and on his state.) Romney would find out soon just how consequential this mentality could be.

One thing that quickly became evident as Romney spent more time in the Senate was that his disgust with Trump was not unique among his Republican colleagues. "Almost without exception," he said, "they shared my view of the president."

In public, of course, they played their parts as Trump loyalists, often twisting themselves in humiliating rhetorical contortions to defend the president's most indefensible behaviors. But behind closed doors, they ridiculed his ignorance, rolled their eyes at his antics, and made incisive observations about his warped, toddler-like psyche. In one surprising moment of candor, a senior Republican senator privately admitted to Romney, "He has none of the qualities you would want in a president, and all of the qualities you wouldn't."

The senators' reasons for keeping these opinions to themselves were politically obvious: whatever his faults, Trump had unlocked a burning loyalty in Republican voters that hadn't been seen since Reagan. "He has a huge following, which is getting larger and more committed every day," Romney said, summarizing his colleagues' thinking. "So there's no particular upside in attacking him. You just get attacked back. And more importantly, it just weakens our side."

One of Romney's first glimpses at the difference between the caucus's private and public faces came during negotiations to end the government shutdown. By January 24, when Senate Republicans gathered in the Capitol for their weekly caucus luncheon, the shutdown had been in effect for thirty-three days—the longest in U.S. history. Romney thought the whole thing was idiotic. Democrats were never going to agree to fund Trump's border wall without major concessions on immigration; Trump, subject as he was to the whims of Tucker Carlson, was unlikely to acquiesce to such concessions. And while some eight hundred thousand federal workers remained out of work, polls showed an overwhelming majority of Americans disapproved of the GOP's handling of the shutdown. The Democrats had proposed a bill to reopen the government for two weeks while debates continued, but offered no funding for a border wall, and Romney was inclined to support it. His constituents in Utah had made it clear that they wanted the standoff to end, and although the bill was unlikely to pass, Romney wanted to send a strong signal that he supported reopening the government.

His advisers were split. Romney's Senate aides, who had more experience in the ways of Capitol Hill than he did, warned that voting for the Democrats' bill would make him even more of a leper in his new caucus, while tagging him as weak on border security. (Romney was actually in favor of a barrier on portions of the southern border—he'd campaigned for it in 2012—he just didn't think building one was worth indefinitely strangling the federal government.) Myers, meanwhile, told him he should do whatever he thought was right.

Inside the caucus meeting, Vice President Mike Pence urged Republicans to unanimously reject the Democrats' bill. It was essential, he said, to remain a united front. Senator Thom Tillis then stood to pledge his allegiance to the White House's plan, arguing that it would strengthen Trump's negotiating hand.

At this, Romney decided to show his cards: "I can't trade off a negotiating position with a million people out of work," he said.

After the luncheon, Pence brought Romney back to his private office at the Capitol and gave him the hard sell: The president needed Republicans to stick with him on this. Romney needed to be a good soldier.

Romney was not persuaded by good-soldier appeals, especially from the likes of Pence. He found the vice president's brand of sycophancy—which he casually intertwined with Christian moralizing—especially sickening. "No one had been more loyal, more willing to smile when he saw absurdities, more willing to ascribe God's will to things that were ungodly, than Mike Pence," Romney would tell me later.

Unpersuaded, Romney went to the floor and cast his vote for the Democrats' bill. He also voted for a competing Republican bill that would have ended the shutdown while funding the wall. Neither passed.

As he was leaving the chamber, Mitch McConnell asked Romney to sit with him on a bank of chairs next to the Senate well. Romney didn't know McConnell well, but he was familiar with the Senate majority leader's reputation as a ruthless power broker. Unlike many of his predecessors, who cultivated reputations as backslapping dealmakers, McConnell—with his low, cold mumble and inscrutable permafrown—was known as a win-at-all-costs tactician who ruled his caucus with an iron fist. Romney assumed he was about to get rebuked for stepping out of line.

Instead, McConnell leaned in and told Romney that he'd done the right thing, explaining that the vote would help McConnell convince the president to accept a compromise. Of course, he added, he couldn't say any of this when Pence was in the room, "out of respect."

Recounting the episode later in his journal, Romney expressed his surprise. "Lesson for the day: don't take everything people say in our caucus meetings at face value."

*   *   *

While Romney was working to make new friends in the Senate, he got word of an unexpected request from an old enemy. Harry Reid, the former Senate majority leader who'd notoriously accused Romney of tax-dodging during the 2012 campaign, wanted to see him. He'd recently been diagnosed with pancreatic cancer and didn't know how much longer he had left. The acrimony between Reid and Romney had always struck some observers as strange. Yes, they came from different parties, but they also belonged to the same church—one known for producing preternaturally polite, friendly people. *Why were they constantly at each other's throats?* Somehow, their shared faith had added a bitter, personal edge to the partisan sparring.

Romney assumed Reid was ready to make amends and perhaps offer an apology. So, Mitt and Ann agreed to meet with Reid when he was in Salt Lake City.

When they sat down, Reid did apologize—but not for the lie he'd so aggressively spread. Instead, he apologized for the smirking comment he'd made to a reporter years later when asked about the lie. ("Romney didn't win, did he?")

"I want to apologize for being so flip," Reid told Romney.

Mitt could feel Ann next to him getting agitated. Ever protective of her husband, Ann was still upset about that toxic little talking point Reid had unleashed, and couldn't believe he seemed so unrepentant, even now. But when Mitt looked at Reid, bloated from the cancer treatment and dependent on a cane to move around, he couldn't bring himself to argue. He accepted the apology, assured Reid he was forgiven, and the men parted ways.

After the meeting, Ann demanded to know why Mitt so readily accepted Reid's non-apology. "I just decided at this stage in his life, it was not worth getting into a back-and-forth," he explained.

Romney didn't hold a grudge against Reid, who would die in 2021—but he didn't reserve much generosity for him, either. "Harry was a pretty partisan guy," Romney would tell me years later. "I just didn't recognize how extraordinarily partisan he was."

On the afternoon of March 6, 2019, Romney rolled past the east gate of the White House and was deposited near the South Lawn. He was there to have lunch with President Trump—and to break some bad news to him.

Since the shutdown had finally ended a few weeks earlier, Trump had been attempting a new—and even more audacious—strategy to secure funding for his border wall: he'd declared a national state of emergency in a ploy to divert $3.6 billion from military construction projects. The move was virtually without precedent. Only twice before in U.S. history had a president used an emergency declaration to spend federal funds without congressional approval—in the buildup to the Persian Gulf War, and in the aftermath of 9/11.

To Romney, the gambit seemed plainly unconstitutional—a desperate authoritarian lurch by a man who was running out of options to deliver on his signature campaign promise. The White House was whipping votes for the emergency authorization, and Romney was one of several Republicans who was against it.

He would have been fine, of course, quietly casting his vote, but his colleague Lindsey Graham insisted he come to the White House first. Graham was a Senate veteran, having represented South Carolina for nearly two decades, and a quintessential creature of the Washington clubhouse—infatuated with status and at home in a greenroom. Graham, who was moderate on many social issues and hawkish on foreign policy, had been an early critic of Trump's in 2016, calling him a "jackass" and a "kook" who "doesn't represent my party." But he'd pivoted when a pivot became necessary, and now he was one of the president's favorite pets in the Senate. By bringing Romney to the White House, Graham was playing matchmaker—he thought his colleague's vote might go down more easily with Trump if the men talked in person. He suggested Romney lead with his praise for the president's hard-nosed approach to China, a rare area of agreement. Romney considered the rise of China—and its bid to replace America as the world's hegemonic superpower—to be one of those existential threats that few in government seemed to take seriously, and even fewer had a plan to combat. Trump talked about the issue like a demagogue, but his administration was taking substantive steps to counter China's power, and Romney wanted the White House to know that he supported them.

Graham was late for the meeting, so Romney walked with one of Trump's aides into the Oval Office. It was the first time he'd been there since visiting President Obama in early 2013, and he complimented the new decor. Trump had swapped out Obama's scarlet drapes for gold ones, and the walls were ornamented with paintings of Washington, Lincoln, Jefferson, and Jackson. Trump responded by extensively detailing all the changes he and Melania had made to the room, including the restoration of a Winston Churchill bust that Obama had moved to another room. And *yes*, the Martin Luther King Jr. bust *was* still in the office, Trump noted, despite the fake news reporting that it wasn't.

Throughout the small talk, Trump and a number of his aides—including son-in-law Jared Kushner—kept glancing at a sheet of paper on the Resolute desk. When Romney got close enough to make it out, he saw that it contained a list of Republican senators, with each name highlighted in a corresponding color. Green was for those siding with the president on his emergency declaration, orange was for the undecided, and red was for those who planned to vote against him. Trump instructed his hovering aides to start making phone calls to the undecided senators. "Mitt," he said, looking up, "I'm not going to ask you right now in front of everyone how you'll vote on this."

"Fine," Romney said. "Don't ask, don't tell."

The aides left, and then, as if on cue, Ivanka Trump glided into the room, wearing a coral pantsuit and a radiant smile. With a little flourish, she handed her father a jobs report that supposedly contained statistics on how many employees American companies planned to hire. The president grandly praised her "fantastic" work on bringing back jobs to America. The scene had a made-for-TV quality, though Romney didn't see any cameras. He got the feeling that he was the audience.

When Graham arrived, he, Romney, and Trump made their way to the dining room adjacent to the Oval Office, where a table for three was set. Mick Mulvaney, the president's director of the Office of Management and Budget, joined them at the table, but he wasn't served a plate. As the other three ate their Ceasar salad and fried chicken, the conversation turned to China—the president wanted to know Romney's thoughts on his tariff policy, and Romney expressed his support. Trump's trade experts, Peter Navarro and Robert Ligh-thizer, filed in as the lunch continued, and they offered up details of their latest negotiations with Beijing. Romney ably conveyed his hawkishness on the issue, prompting Trump to comment, "He's even tougher on China than I am."

The meal ended, and as they walked back into the Oval Office, Romney knew it was time to come clean. He told Trump that he couldn't support the emergency declaration, because he saw it as a violation of the balance of powers.

"Well, you've got to do what you got to do," the president said, pulling out his color-coded paper. "Mitt moves to the red," he announced. He drew a thick arrow next to ROMNEY—then in the orange section—and moved it to red. "We've lost this one," he said.

After the senators left, Graham seemed delighted that his scheme had worked. Trump had taken the news surprisingly well—perhaps there was still hope for Romney's relationship with the president. But over the next few days, as the White House waged an intense pressure campaign to get Republican senators on board with the emergency declaration, Romney was not spared. Shahira Knight, the White House director of legislative affairs, turned up in Romney's office to lobby him. When the senator refused to change his mind on the merits, the conversation turned argumentative, with Knight warning him that Republican voters wanted the wall and that voting against the president would be bad politics.

"I agree!" he replied, somewhat amused by the argument. "It's just right constitutionally."

When it was finally time to vote, on March 14, Romney announced he would oppose Trump's national emergency declaration. "This is a vote for the Constitution and for the balance of powers that is at its core," he said ahead of the vote. "For the Executive Branch to override a law passed by Congress would make it the ultimate power rather than a balancing power."

Romney was not the only Republican to break ranks—he was joined by eleven others—but when the final votes were recorded, he was stunned by how many of his colleagues had abruptly reversed themselves. Just a few weeks earlier, Thom Tillis had written an entire op-ed explaining that he could not in good conscience abide such a glaring executive overreach, especially having spent years calling out President Obama's abuses of power: "There is no intellectual honesty in now turning around and arguing that there's an imaginary asterisk attached to executive overreach—that it's acceptable for my party but not thy party." And yet, there was Tillis, doing just that. Ben Sasse had similarly talked a big game when Trump first introduced the idea: "If we get used to presidents just declaring an emergency any time they can't get what they want from Congress, it will be almost impossible to go back to a constitutional system of checks and balances." Those concerns were conveniently gone when he cast his vote.

In his journal, Romney spent little time puzzling over the reason for these reversals. "Job preservation above principle preservation," he wrote. Still, he was surprised by the brazenness—the willingness to turn on a dime, right in front of everybody, without evincing even the tiniest flicker of shame. Romney was no stranger to flip-flopping, but even at his most cynical, he'd labored to justify the changes to his position, or to massage his rhetoric so he could argue that he wasn't changing his position at all. Longtime critics had noted this habit of

Romney's: "He's not a natural bullshitter," the liberal columnist Jonathan Chait once wrote about what he called "Romney's endearing lies." "His instinct is to align his position with the facts."

But in the Trump era, that agonizing process no longer seemed to be a requirement. It was pure tribal politics all the way down.

A few weeks after the border-wall episode, Trump paid a visit to the Senate Republicans' caucus lunch. The president was in a buoyant mood—two days earlier, the Justice Department had released a summary of the much-anticipated Mueller report, revealing that the special counsel's twenty-two-month investigation had failed to establish collusion between the Trump campaign and Russia in 2016. Trump was met with a standing ovation fit for a conquering hero, and then he launched into some rambling, stream-of-consciousness remarks. He talked about the so-called Russia hoax and relitigated the midterm elections and swung wildly from border security to China tariffs to the Federal Reserve to the cost of hurricane damage in Puerto Rico. At one point Trump declared, somewhat implausibly, that the GOP would soon become "the party of healthcare." The senators in the room dutifully nodded in agreement.

As soon as the president left, the Republican caucus burst into laughter.

On September 18, 2019, the *Washington Post* published an oddly vague but intriguing story: a whistleblower somewhere in the federal government was raising concerns about an exchange between Trump and a foreign leader. The paper didn't have the details, but apparently the whistleblower's complaint had already caused some consternation in the U.S. intelligence community.

The story was making a minor stir in the media, but Romney wasn't holding his breath for a bombshell. After years of listening to overconfident predictions that some new skeleton would emerge from Trump's closet and end his political career, the senator had learned to be cautious about such things. Months earlier, when the full Mueller report was released, Romney had found the findings sickening. The report showed multiple Trump campaign officials lying, dissembling, even welcoming interference from Russia—and still, the president had emerged unscathed. But as the *Post* unwound the whistleblower story in a steady drip of incremental developments, Romney couldn't help but take notice. The next day, it was revealed that Ukraine was involved; the day after that, it came out that the call was between Trump and Ukrainian president Volodymyr Zelensky. Then, finally, the big revelation: Trump had pressured Zelensky to investigate Hunter Biden, the son of his chief rival in the upcoming presidential election.

As bad as it sounded, Romney remained careful: It was, he tweeted, "critical for the facts to come out."

On the day the full transcript of the call was released, an aide brought him a printout.

"I presume it shows nothing," Romney said without looking at the paper.

"No," the aide replied. "It's actually quite serious."

Romney looked at the transcript and quickly saw that his aide was right. It was all there in black and white: Zelensky, whose country was facing an existential conflict with Russia, pleading with the American president for military aid; Trump responding, "I would like you to do us a favor." According to the transcript, he told Zelensky he wanted Ukraine to announce an investigation of the Biden family's allegedly corrupt business dealings in the country. The whole exchange carried the faint whiff of a Mafia shakedown: *Nice country you've got here, shame if something happened to it.*

If Romney had any doubt as to the seriousness of the situation, it was dispelled when he received an unexpected phone call from Trump's attorney general. Romney had voted to confirm William Barr earlier that year, praising him as an "exceptionally qualified" nominee with a "distinguished record." Since then, Romney had lost a good deal of respect for Barr, who'd taken to behaving like all the other toadies in the Trump administration. Now a nervous-seeming Barr was on the phone assuring Romney that he had no involvement in Trump's call with the Ukrainian leader, and that he never encouraged the president to investigate the Bidens.

Later that day, Romney appeared onstage for a previously scheduled interview at The Atlantic Festival in Washington, D.C. After some discussion of the transcript, which Romney called "deeply troubling," he was asked about his Republican colleagues' reluctance to ever criticize Trump.

"I think it's very natural for people to look at circumstances and see them in the light that's most amenable to their maintaining power and doing things to preserve their power," Romney said.

Afterward, back at the Capitol, McConnell pulled Romney aside and chided him for the first time.

"Don't impugn the conscience and integrity of your colleagues," McConnell advised. It was fine to express disagreement with them on any given issue, but best not to assume you know what's going on inside their heads.

Romney took his point. But he was also becoming increasingly impatient with the cravenness and cowardice that seemed to rule his caucus. For months, he'd had to endure Republican senators smarmily sidling up to him in private to express solidarity with his public criticism of Trump. They'd say things like, "I sure wish I could do what you do" or, "Gosh, I wish I had the constituency you have," and then they'd look at him expectantly, as if waiting for Romney to express profound gratitude that they secretly agreed with him. This happened so often that he started keeping a tally; at one point, he told his staff, he'd had similar exchanges with more than a dozen colleagues. He developed a go-to response for such occasions: "There are worse things than losing an election. Take it from somebody who knows."

Romney was finding it harder to go through the motions of performative respect and party solidarity that membership in the Senate seemed to require.

On October 3, Trump made it clear that the controversy over his Zelensky call had hardly left him chastened. Speaking to reporters at the White House, he said that China should join Ukraine in investigating the Bidens.

Romney went on Twitter to express his displeasure: "By all appearances, the President's brazen and unprecedented appeal to China and to Ukraine to investigate Joe Biden is wrong and appalling."

For some reason that Romney would never fully understand, this was the tweet that finally sent Trump over the edge. Over the course of a Saturday afternoon, the president pounded out an escalating series of wrathful tweets directed at Romney:

@realDonaldTrump: "Somebody please wake up Mitt Romney and tell him that my conversation with the Ukrainian President was a congenial and very appropriate one, and my statement on China pertained to corruption, not politics. If Mitt worked this hard on Obama, he could have won. Sadly, he choked!"

@realDonaldTrump: "Mitt Romney never knew how to win. He is a pompous 'ass' who has been fighting me from the beginning, except when he begged me for my endorsement for his Senate run (I gave it to him), and when he begged me to be Secretary of State (I didn't give it to him). He is so bad for R's!"

@realDonaldTrump: "I'm hearing that the Great People of Utah are considering their vote for their Pompous Senator, Mitt Romney, to be a big mistake. I agree! He is a fool who is playing right into the hands of the Do Nothing Democrats! #IMPEACHMITTROMNEY."

Romney, who was picking pumpkins with his grandkids that afternoon in Utah, didn't pay close attention to the presidential meltdown. But in the weeks that followed, as Democrats convened impeachment hearings in the House, and damning evidence continued to trickle out in the press, and flocks of cameramen swarmed the Capitol to document the possible end of a presidency, Romney began to understand the stakes of what was happening—and the unique position he would be in.

One day in late October, Romney read in the press that McConnell had met privately with Trump and told him to stop publicly attacking members of the Senate. They would, after all, likely soon be serving as his jurors in an impeachment trial.

Romney had grown to respect McConnell's savvy and style of leadership since entering the Senate. Contrary to public perception, he did not rule his caucus through threats or coercion—he was primarily a deft manager of egos. But Romney also knew that McConnell excelled at telling each of his colleagues what they wanted to hear. He wasn't sure anymore which version of McConnell was more authentic: the one who did Trump's bidding in public, or the one who excoriated him in their private conversations.

Later that day, on the Senate floor, Romney thanked McConnell for sticking up for him with Trump.

"It wasn't for you so much as for him," McConnell replied. "He's an idiot. He doesn't think when he says things. How stupid do you have to be to not realize that you shouldn't attack your jurors?"

As they discussed the prospect of an impeachment trial, McConnell was frank in his assessment of the president's behavior with Zelensky: "The facts are pretty clear about what Trump did. I think the only defense that you'll see in the end is that the election is coming so soon that we should let the people decide.

"You're lucky," he continued. "You can say the things that we all think. You're in a position to say things about him that we all agree with but can't say."

CHAPTER THIRTEEN

Conviction

B ack in 2018, around the time Romney announced his Senate run,
John McCain summoned him to his ranch in Sedona. McCain's
cancer had taken a turn for the worse, and he didn't have much time left.
Mitt brought Ann, and the two of them spent time chatting with John
and Cindy. The senator—gaunt and bound to a wheelchair—looked
more frail than Mitt had ever seen him.

Romney and McCain had come a long way since their bitter primary battle in 2008. The two men had always been somewhat unlikely
political rivals. For all their differences, they were cut from the same
Republican cloth—pragmatic, skeptical of ideological dogmas, and
protective of institutional norms and decorum. It was hard to bond
over such things when they were duking it out on a debate stage, but
they'd earned each other's respect. McCain had been surprised by
how hard Romney was willing to work for him in the 2008 general
election, surrogates, hopping on planes, holding rallies and fundraisers,
and generally doing whatever the campaign asked of him without
complaint.

Romney, meanwhile, respected how McCain had tried to push
back on the more radical elements in their party, famously rejecting a
supporter's claim at a town hall that Obama was a secret Arab and not

American. When the 2008 race was over, McCain's mother—who'd made critical comments about Mormons during the campaign—mailed Romney a handwritten letter saying she would be the first supporter of his 2012 campaign. In the years since, the men had done favors for each other—Romney trekking down to Mesa for campaign events, McCain making appearances in Park City for Romney's annual donor summit. In the Trump era, they'd found themselves on the same small and shrinking island of Never-Trumpism (like Romney, McCain did not vote for his party's nominee in 2016). They'd become "friends" in the way that politicians often use the term—officially on good terms, but not especially intimate. Which was why the invitation to Sedona had come as a surprise.

The conversation that afternoon was mostly friendly and banal—the last thing anyone wants to talk about during a deathbed visit is death—but before the Romneys left, McCain did make one request. He asked Romney to serve on the board of the International Republican Institute. The group was founded in 1983, at the height of the Cold War, with the mission to spread democracy throughout the world—a cause that had been uncontroversial at the time, but that now seemed under threat. The Republican Party was becoming more isolationist; more suspicious of democracy both abroad and at home. The president was making friends with dictators and reorienting American foreign policy around those friendships. McCain had been chairman of the group for twenty-five years, and he wanted to ensure that a senator with similar weight—and a similar commitment to global democracy—would take up the cause. Romney agreed. Within six months, McCain was gone.

True to his word, Romney became an active member of the Institute after joining the Senate. On May 7, 2019, he was invited to its annual Freedom Award Dinner at the Capital Hilton. The group had decided to give its Freedom Award to their late chairman's widow, and asked Romney to present it to her. The choice was laden with meaning. With McCain gone, many in Washington had been watching Romney to see if he might fill the "maverick"-shaped void left in the Senate. "With

McCain's Retreat," a *Washington Post* headline read, "Some Turn to Romney to Carry His Torch."

Romney was slightly uncomfortable with these comparisons. He didn't want to be seen as a McCain redux, or to be measured against another man's legacy. At the same time, he thought that legacy was one worth honoring. Speaking that night at the dinner, Romney decided to not only pay tribute to the McCains' personal virtues, but to the cause the couple believed in.

"Today, two of the world's great powers, China and Russia, are not only protecting dictators and autocrats, they are vigorously promoting authoritarianism around the world," Romney said. "The tools that they use—bribery, loan-sharking, intimidation, lies, threats—those aren't new, but in the case of China, the pockets are a lot deeper, and in the case of Russia, the desperation is more intense."

Romney praised Cindy's work, including her extensive travels to war zones in the Middle East and Africa, and her loyal partnership with her husband. "She set her mind to love and partner with one of the most irascible, headstrong, and irresistible men on the entire continent. And she fights to this day to guarantee that his memory, and what he and she together represent—character, honor, duty, compassion, country, freedom—that all of these are preserved in the character of the nation."

When the speeches were over, Cindy tearfully pulled Romney into a long, emotional embrace. The room erupted in a standing ovation. Matt Waldrip, watching the scene from a table near the back, was struck by the intensity of the reaction from the Washington grandees in the room. While he knew Romney didn't see himself as the heir to McCain's legacy, he also knew the senator was trying to send a message to the widow: "It was a little bit of 'Don't worry, there's somebody else here who's going to keep this fight alive,'" Waldrip said.

Around the time the House convened impeachment proceedings, setting up what would become one of the defining political moments of his life, an embarrassing secret about Romney was revealed. In an interview with *The Atlantic*, he casually mentioned that he used an anonymous "lurker" account on Twitter to follow comedians, athletes, and political news. Soon after the interview was published, a *Slate* reporter named Ashley Feinberg found the secret Twitter account, where the senator was using the nom de plume "Pierre Delecto."

He'd created the account years earlier, and come up with the name on a lark, he later told me—"Pierre" because of his mission in France, "Delecto" inspired by a Latin phrase his brother-in-law used, *in flagrante delicto*, to describe being caught in the act of sex. While there was nothing scandalous—or even especially surprising—in the handful of tweets Romney had written as "Pierre," the fact that he had a secret Twitter persona at all was undeniably funny, and the internet had a field day. People shared photoshops of the senator in a beret and a mustache. They spent time debating where Pierre belonged in the pantheon of politicians' online alter egos. "What if Pierre Delecto is the real person and Mitt Romney is just a grift he's been running for the last few decades?" one Twitter user joked. Some commentators even tried to squeeze serious think pieces out of the hubbub, drawing broad conclusions about Romney's character and the state of American politics. One article on CNN's website carried the headline: "What 'Pierre Delecto' Tells Us about the Current Republican Party."

For all the noise, *l'affaire* Pierre was actually revealing in one way. The output of the anonymous account betrayed Romney's anxiety that he wasn't doing enough to hold Trump accountable. Time and again, the tweets that most got under the senator's skin—the ones he felt compelled to respond to in a fit of pique as "Pierre"—were those that pegged him as soft on the president. When *Washington Post* columnist Jennifer Rubin had tweeted that Romney's strategy of dealing with Trump was "verging on spinelessness," Pierre replied that she needed to "take a breath" and recognize that Romney largely agreed with her on Trump's misdeeds. When Soledad O'Brien tweeted that Romney lacked a "moral compass," Pierre responded, "Only Republican to hit

Trump on Mueller report, only one to hit Trump on character time and again, so Soledad, you think he's the one without moral compass?" Under the protection of anonymity, Romney repeatedly defended his own honor against the notion that he was selling out like the rest of his Republican colleagues.

Later, Romney would reflect on why he felt compelled to use the Twitter account. He admitted it was unbecoming, but there was something cathartic about anonymously venting. "It's like yelling at the TV," he'd tell me. "You know they can't hear you, but somehow it feels better to express it. I don't let things that concern me bottle up. I let them out as quickly as I can."

Throughout that fall, while the House conducted its impeachment hearings, Romney had the uneasy feeling that he was being closely watched. He was one of the only Republicans in the Senate who hadn't already dismissed outright the charges against the president, which meant that his reaction to the hearings mattered. Even if Trump wasn't ultimately removed from office, a bipartisan vote to convict him could weigh on his reelection bid. Gaggles of reporters stalked Romney through the halls of the Capitol, pestering him with questions about each incremental impeachment development, and then parsing the wording of his no-comments for clues. (He insisted that as a juror in the coming Senate trial, he was reserving judgment.) One morning over breakfast, Mike Lee, Utah's other senator and a steadfast Trump loyalist, told Romney he was working on a plan to bring a quick end to the impeachment trial once it reached the Senate. Romney was careful not to react, suspecting that Lee would report any read he got back to Trump's team.

On Fox News, meanwhile, prime-time hosts were treating him with mounting hostility. In one especially mean-spirited segment in late October, Sean Hannity accused Romney of "morphing" into a "weak, sanctimonious Washington swamp politician," and suggested the senator was simply "jealous" of Trump's myriad successes. "I don't know what's going on, Mitt, but honestly you're losing it, and to me, it's kind of sad to watch this."

Romney was startled by the venom in Hannity's rant when he saw it the next day. Not that long ago, the host had been an unabashed cheerleader for Romney's presidential campaigns. They'd appeared side by side at rallies; done countless chummy interviews together. Hoping to mend the relationship, Romney decided to give his old buddy a call—but the conversation quickly turned antagonistic. First, the host accused Romney of pandering to the liberal media with his opposition to Trump: "You're just doing this because you want to get praise on MSNBC!" Next, Hannity demanded to know why Romney wasn't more outraged by the Burisma scandal. Romney—who didn't spend enough time in the conservative media bubble to know the shorthand for Hunter Biden's allegedly corrupt dealings with a Ukrainian energy company—responded by asking, "What's Burisma?" Hannity exploded: *"How do you not know what Burisma is?"*

By the time Romney hung up, he knew the relationship was damaged beyond repair. He also couldn't help but wonder what on earth had happened to his erstwhile ally. Perhaps, he reflected, Hannity's fall to second place in Fox's prime-time ratings was causing him to lash out. "I can only imagine that Sean is consumed with Tucker Carlson being ahead of him, and his everyday effort is to find ways to reclaim the throne as the most-watched," Romney would tell me. "He's in the same vein as Tucker. Just not as effective as Tucker—Tucker's smart." But of course there was another possibility: Hannity had always been like this—and Romney was just now noticing.

On November 21, Romney joined several other Republican senators for lunch at the White House. He hadn't seen Trump since the impeachment inquiry began, and when the media caught wind of Romney's visit, speculation swirled that the president had some plan to buy the senator off. *What would he offer Romney to cave?* By the time he returned to the Hill, his office was being inundated with calls urging him to remain strong and friends were sending him concerned emails.

The following day, Romney returned to the White House to discuss antivaping legislation. As he walked toward the West Wing entrance that afternoon, Romney was stopped by Lieutenant Colonel Alexander Vindman. Until recently, Vindman had been an obscure army officer serving on Trump's National Security Council. But his televised testimony in the impeachment hearings, during which the Ukrainian-born Vindman recounted damning details about Trump's call with Zelensky, had turned him into a hero on MSNBC and a villain on Fox News. Conservatives called him a grandstander, a traitor; the president derided him as a "Never Trumper" whom he'd "never heard of." In an instant, his once-promising military career had evaporated.

Now he was standing in front of Romney, visibly out of breath. He explained that he'd spotted the senator from some distance and sprinted to catch him before he disappeared into the White House. He wanted to shake Romney's hand, to thank him for his "character" and "honor."

"Neither of us have many friends around the White House these days," Romney said.

Vindman appeared to tear up. He looked, to Romney, like a man overwhelmed by the moment he was in. Romney assured him he would consider the evidence in the impeachment trial "without bias" and "true to the Constitution."

Perhaps the most surreal moment that fall came one day in November, when Ann received a phone call from Oprah Winfrey. The Romneys had known Winfrey since 2012, when she interviewed them during the campaign. Though she supported Barack Obama, she respected the couple and was especially fond of Ann. In the years since the election, the two women had seen each other a number of times at social events. Now Oprah was calling Ann with a question: Was there any chance Mitt would run for president in 2020 as an independent, with her as his running mate?

Winfrey explained that Michael Bloomberg, the former New York City mayor, was preparing to enter the race and had approached her about joining his ticket. Before she made a decision, she wanted to gauge Romney's interest in running with her. Winfrey was committed to stopping Trump's reelection, but she was also increasingly nervous about the weakness of the Democratic field. She doubted Joe Biden or Pete Buttigieg could beat Trump, and was certain that Elizabeth Warren couldn't. Maybe a Romney-Winfrey ticket could bring together a bipartisan coalition of voters and save America from a second Trump term?

Ann told her there was no way her husband would run in 2020, either as a Republican or an independent. But Winfrey insisted that Romney at least hear her out. Finally, Mitt picked up the phone, heard the pitch, and told her he was flattered, but that he'd have to pass.

The senator had another job to do, and it was about to get very complicated.

As the president's impeachment became more likely by the day, Romney carefully studied his constitutional role in the imminent Senate trial. He read and reread Alexander Hamilton's treatise on impeachment, "Federalist No. 65." He pored over the work of constitutional scholars and reviewed historical definitions of "high crimes and misdemeanors." His understanding was that once the House impeached a president, senators were called upon to set aside their partisan passions and act as impartial jurors, carefully considering the evidence for the articles of impeachment and rendering their verdict without prejudice.

Suffice it to say, not everyone in his caucus was approaching the job with the same level of seriousness. Among Romney's Republican colleagues, rank cynicism reigned. They didn't want to hear from witnesses, they didn't want to learn new facts, they didn't want to hold a trial at all. During an interview with CNN, Lindsey Graham frankly admitted that he was "not going to pretend to be a fair juror here" and predicted the impeachment process would "die quickly" once it reached the Senate. On December 11, McConnell summoned Romney to his office and pitched him on joining the execution. He explained that several vulnerable members of their caucus were up for reelection, and that a prolonged, polarizing Senate trial would force them to take tough votes that risked alienating their constituents. McConnell wanted

Romney to vote to end the trial as soon as the opening arguments were completed.

McConnell didn't bother defending Trump's actions. Instead, he argued that protecting the GOP's Senate majority was a matter of vital national importance. He predicted that Trump would lose reelection, and painted an apocalyptic picture of what would happen if Democrats took control of Congress: they'd turn Puerto Rico and D.C. into states, engineering a permanent Senate majority; they'd ram through left-wing legislation like Medicare for All and the Green New Deal. The leftists would be in control. The nation would be in peril. Romney, unmoved, said he couldn't make any promises about his vote.

A week later, Republican senators met for their regular caucus lunch. Romney had lately come to dread these meetings. They had a certain high-school-cafeteria quality that made him feel ill at ease. "I mean, it's a funny thing," he'd tell me later. "You don't want to be the only one sitting at the table and no one wants to sit with you." Romney had always had plenty of friends growing up, but his faith often made him feel like he didn't quite fit in. At Cranbrook, he was the only Mormon on campus; at Stanford, he would go to bars with his friends and drink soda. "One of the advantages of growing up in my faith outside of Utah is that you are different in ways that are important to you," he'd reflected. Walking into those caucus lunches each week—deciding who to sit with, and whether to speak up—Romney felt his differentness just as acutely as he had in his teens.

With the Senate trial likely to begin after the Christmas break, Romney was hoping the caucus would get some guidance on what to expect from the process. Instead, he was dismayed to learn that their featured guest was Pence, who was there to talk through the White House's defense strategy. "Stunning to me that he would be there," Romney later wrote in his journal. "There is not even an attempt to show impartiality."

The next day, McConnell took to the Senate floor and bitterly denounced the Democrats' impeachment crusade.

"Last night, House Democrats finally did what they decided to do a long time ago: They voted to impeach President Trump," McConnell said. "Over the last twelve weeks, House Democrats have conducted the most rushed, least thorough, and most unfair impeachment inquiry in modern history."

Watching the speech from his office along with his senior staff, Romney shook his head and turned off the TV. "We have good arguments to oppose [Trump's] removal," he told his aides. But it was disingenuous to assert that the entire Democratic Party had been plotting impeachment from the moment Trump took office. "Mitch knows better."

At the next GOP caucus meeting, the senators acted like they were at a partisan pep rally. McConnell once again sneered at the supposed thinness of the House's impeachment articles. Someone else chimed in to say that they should all stop calling themselves "jurors" because they actually had no responsibility to be unbiased.

McConnell told the senators that whether they called themselves "jurors" or not, they should understand that the upcoming trial was not really a *trial* at all. "This is a political process," he told his colleagues— and it was thus appropriate for them to behave like politicians.

Romney, who found himself sitting next to Ted Cruz and Mike Lee, squirmed in his seat, exasperated by his colleagues' glibness. He'd seen nothing in his study of the impeachment process to suggest that the Founders wanted senators to act like partisan hacks during an impeachment trial. The oath they would take at the outset differed from their oath of office—not only were they to support and defend the Constitution, they'd swear to "do impartial justice."

"If impeachment is a partisan political process, then it might as well be removed from the Constitution," Romney muttered grumpily to Cruz and Lee, who politely ignored him.

After the lunch, Romney tried retreating to the less claustrophobic confines of the Senate floor. But he couldn't escape the lobbying. Cory Gardner, a Republican who was up for reelection in Colorado the next year, reminded Romney that it would put him in a very difficult spot if the Utahn insisted on calling witnesses. Arizona Republican Martha McSally had recently made the exact same argument. This time, Romney couldn't keep the revolted grimace from his face. The audacity astounded him. "[Gardner's] request suggests that his reelection is more important to him than finding the truth, than honoring our oath, that I would place politics before truth and oath," Romney wrote in his journal. "Disgusting."

His Senate colleagues weren't the only ones leaning on Romney. In the weeks leading up to the trial, his old friend Robert O'Brien tried to work on him, too. O'Brien, the former adviser who'd tried to recruit Romney to launch a last-minute presidential bid to save the Republican Party from Trump, was now serving in the White House as Trump's national security adviser, having reportedly won the job by lavishing praise on the president and wearing well-tailored suits. Over dinner with Romney one night in December, O'Brien gushed about how warm and friendly Trump was to the servers and staff around him. Romney, dyspeptic and tired of being spun, retorted that the same could be said of Al Capone. Impeachment, thankfully, didn't come up. The next day, however, Matt Waldrip attended a black-tie reception and ran into O'Brien. Pulling Waldrip aside, the national security advisor asked if Romney was going to be with Trump on impeachment. Waldrip said the senator would make his decision based on the evidence at the trial.

"OK," O'Brien said. "Then we're alright, then."

When O'Brien's comment got back to Romney, the senator wasn't sure what to make of it. Was O'Brien simply trying to extract himself from an awkward conversation he knew he shouldn't have started? Or was he suggesting that some evidence existed that would exonerate the president? Romney sincerely hoped it was the latter.

Two articles of impeachment against President Donald J. Trump arrived at the Senate on January 15, 2020, one for abuse of power and the other for obstruction of Congress. Six days later, opening arguments began.

To Romney, the case came down to a few straightforward questions: Did Trump withhold military funding from Ukraine out of concern for investigating corruption, or was it entirely a ploy to damage a domestic political opponent? Was his comment to Zelensky part of a concerted pressure campaign, with figures like Rudy Giuliani twisting arms and greasing palms behind the scenes, or was it just a stupid, impromptu request?

To answer these questions, Romney wanted the Senate to undertake its own extensive investigative process, with the ability to call new witnesses and enter new documents into evidence. But Romney didn't have many allies in this cause. Apart from his two most moderate colleagues—Maine's Susan Collins and Alaska's Lisa Murkowski—nobody in the caucus seemed interested in using the trial to figure out what Trump actually did. The hard-right MAGA types just wanted to deliver a quick victory to the president, and the senators representing purple states wanted the trial over for their own political reasons.

The more Romney pressed, the more he seemed to irritate his colleagues.

At a caucus meeting the day after the trial began, Romney stood to make an earnest case for calling witnesses. "Arguing both sides of an issue is the best way to find the truth," he told them. "If we were on the other side of this, I imagine that we would be coming up with arguments as to [how] we could call witnesses in a timely way."

The room was silent. He later noted in his journal, with a twinge of paranoia, that on his way out he saw one colleague turn to another and shake her head while making "disparaging gestures in my direction."

Without any new evidence to review, Romney found the trial days long, dull, and excruciatingly repetitive. The House impeachment managers replayed the same carefully edited video clips over and over again, recited the same arguments ad nauseam. It didn't help that McConnell, intent on rushing through the process, insisted on scheduling the sessions for twelve or thirteen hours at a time: the first day began at 1:00 p.m. and didn't end until nearly 2:00 a.m.

As the trial progressed, Romney was appalled by the behavior of his colleagues. They muttered dismissive comments while the impeachment managers were presenting their case; they literally cheered for Trump's defense. Maybe his expectations were naive, but he couldn't get over how irresponsible it all seemed. "How unlike a real jury is our caucus!" he wrote after one particularly rambunctious meeting. "Every comment is about how we should oppose any witnesses and how the Dems are just playing politics, and the need to get this finished ASAP. It is an entirely partisan process—our caucus sees its job as defending the president, not determining whether he has committed impeachable offenses."

Romney tried to make productive use out of the idle hours spent listening to the House managers. He took notes, parsed the arguments, and agonized over how he would vote. "Interestingly, sometimes I think I will be voting to convict, and sometimes I think I will vote to exonerate," he wrote in his journal on January 23. "I jot down my reasons for each, but when I finish, I begin to consider the other side of the argument. This is the way it has been going for weeks. I do the same thing—with less analysis of course—in bed. That's probably why I'm not sleeping more than 4 or 5 hours."

One moment early in the trial did rouse Romney from his thoughts. On the second day of opening arguments, a burly protester burst into the Senate gallery screaming, "Dismiss the charges!" Capitol Police rushed to remove him from the chamber, but the man grabbed hold of some railings, commencing an unsightly struggle between the intruder and the officers.

That night, Romney admitted in his journal that the spectacle had startled him—was it really so easy for a deranged person to disrupt the proceedings of a core democratic institution like the Senate? "Amazing that we as a country allow this sort of thing," he wrote. "Good and bad."

By the end of the first week, Romney had come to a preliminary decision that Trump was guilty. A fundamental question of the trial

was whether Trump's pleas to Zelensky were for the sake of the country
(to investigate corruption) or for personal gain (to damage a political
rival). It was becoming clear that Trump's request, if met, would have
had limited benefit to America—at most, it might have resulted in a
private citizen being removed from the board of a Ukrainian company.
Were they really supposed to believe this was a grave matter of national
importance? "At this stage, it is hard to imagine how the Defense might
be able to reverse my conclusion," he wrote in his journal, "but I know
that's always a possibility."

He wasn't the only one who seemed convinced of Trump's guilt.
During a break in the proceedings that day, Romney walked by
McConnell. "They nailed him," the Senate majority leader said.

Romney, taken aback by McConnell's candor, was careful not to
give away too much. "Well, the defense will say that Trump was just
investigating corruption by the Bidens," he said.

"If you believe that," McConnell replied, "I've got a bridge I can
sell you."

Still, Romney hadn't heard the president's full defense yet, and he
was determined to keep an open mind. In his journal, he cited Proverbs:
*He that is first in his own cause seemeth just; but his neighbor cometh and
searcheth him.* "Good advice indeed."

That Saturday, Romney stayed in town and donned a tuxedo for the
Alfalfa Club's annual black-tie banquet. One of Washington's more
unabashedly elitist institutions, the invite-only social club consisted
of roughly two hundred powerful politicians and business leaders who
gathered once a year at the Capital Hilton for an off-the-record night
of drinking, eating, and roasting each other. A year earlier, Romney
had been elected president of the club—a title held over the years
by Ronald Reagan, Sandra Day O'Connor, Michael Bloomberg, and
John Kerry—and, as such, he'd be tasked with delivering the evening's
comic keynote speech.

It was a delicate moment to be cracking topical jokes about politics to a roomful of bipartisan big shots, and Romney's staff cautioned him to go easy. He tried hiring a professional writer, but he was unsatisfied with the material—few of the thousand-dollar lines were as funny as the free stuff he encountered daily on Twitter—so he ended up tapping the funniest people he knew to help him write the speech.

Romney had spoken at the dinner a year earlier when he was a brand-new senator, more idealistic about Washington and wary of making waves. That night, he'd relied on silly zingers and self-deprecation. This time, there was a decided edge to his remarks—and he left little doubt about his favorite target.

He joked: "Speaker Pelosi didn't want to impeach. She fought it off every way she could. But then Trump called Zelensky and asked him for an investigation and she simply had no choice. You see, he's good at getting women to do something they don't want to do."

He joked: "First Lady Melania Trump was all ears when she heard that the WNBA Champion Washington Mystics had declined to go to the White House and meet with President Trump. She asked: 'Is that an option?'"

He joked: "Some people find it hard to understand why so many evangelical Christians support Donald Trump, but let's remember: Donald Trump is the only man who felt so strongly about his marriage vows that he paid $130,000 *not* to have sex with a porn star."

As waves of laughter washed over the ballroom, two unamused guests sat stone-faced and seething: Jared Kushner and Ivanka Trump. As soon as the banquet ended, they beelined for the exit rather than waiting to shake the emcee's hand.

Perhaps they sensed that Romney's "jokes" weren't really jokes at all—that his repulsion for the president was real and getting stronger, that it was spreading in unpredictable directions and pushing Trump further out onto a ledge than he'd ever been before.

*　　　*　　　*

By the time the Senate reconvened the following week, the cordial détente between Romney and the rest of his caucus was beginning to fray.

Kelly Loeffler, a freshman senator from Georgia, went out of her way to attack him on Twitter: "After 2 weeks, it's clear that Democrats have no case for impeachment. Sadly, my colleague @SenatorRomney wants to appease the left by calling witnesses who will slander the @realDonaldTrump during their 15 minutes of fame. The circus is over. It's time to move on!"

The attack surprised Romney. He'd known Loeffler personally for years; she and her husband were supporters of his in 2012. They'd written checks and raised money. Romney had even been to their home. They seemed, by every observable metric, like reasonable, mainstream Republicans—chamber of commerce types. Why was she suddenly picking a fight with him in public? The answer came later that day when news broke that a right-wing Trump loyalist planned to challenge her in the Georgia primary. "Sad to see what happens to people when they want to win at any cost," Romney wrote in his journal that night.

Two days later, at their caucus meeting, Romney's colleagues traded off taking barely veiled swipes at *certain senators* who were aiding and abetting the Democrats by trying to drag out the impeachment trial with calls to hear from witnesses. Romney tried to stay quiet, but after a while he couldn't take the passive-aggressive carping any longer.

"It's clear to everyone in the room that you're only talking about the two of us," Romney seethed, gesturing toward Collins. (Murkowski was not present.) "I haven't been so beaten up since I peed in my father's raspberry garden. But you're wasting your breath, because there is a 100 percent chance I'm going to call for witnesses." He reminded them that hearing from witnesses could actually exculpate the president—but either way, he said, he had no intention of dropping the issue. ("I don't bend to pressure," he noted in his journal. "I get stiffer.")

After Romney sat down, McConnell tried to cut the tension in the room. "I'll put you down as undecided," he joked. But an air of antagonism lingered.

After the meeting ended, a handful of the Senate's most storied right-wing troublemakers—Cruz, Paul, and Lee—approached him privately and told him they knew what it was like to have the entire caucus arrayed against you.

Over the next few days, Romney paid close attention to the defense case presented by Trump's lawyers. The thing about an open mind is that it becomes very easy to talk yourself into the most convenient course of action. Romney was honest with himself on this point: "I'm no fan of the president," he wrote in his journal. "I would rather have almost any other Republican in his office, including Mike Pence. But I do not at all want to vote to convict. The consequences of doing so are too painful to contemplate."

Sure enough, by the time the defense wrapped up its arguments on January 28, Romney was privately leaning toward acquittal. In his journal, he wrote that his reasoning came down to two factors. First, timing: military aid to Ukraine was being withheld weeks before Trump's call with Zelensky, and Trump had spoken out against corruption in Ukraine before the call, too. Second, ambiguities: the House managers never presented clear evidence of Trump explicitly telling Ukraine that aid would be withheld *until* a Biden investigation began, nor was Trump's motive for holding aid fully understood.

Admittedly, it wasn't a perfect argument. And Romney allowed that his analysis might change in the upcoming Q&A sessions, during which senators would be allowed to question the prosecutors and defense. But for the moment, it was good enough for Romney to vote not guilty.

When he informed his senior staff of his thinking the next morning, he detected a palpable sense of relief. Maybe their boss still had a future in Republican politics after all. Romney's wife, though, seemed less elated when he talked to her. Ann didn't argue with him. She didn't render any judgments at all. She just said she was "surprised" to hear he was leaning toward acquittal. Romney, who'd organized much of his life around winning and keeping Ann's respect, couldn't help but wonder if she meant something more.

In preparation for the Q&A session, Romney worked with his staff to craft questions that would help fill in his gaps of knowledge and sharpen his thinking. Most of his colleagues seemed focused on cheap debate-team point scoring, but late in the day on January 30, a question submitted by Lindsey Graham caught Romney's attention: Even if a witness were to confirm the most damning of the evidence heretofore presented against Trump, he asked, "isn't it true that the allegations still would not rise to the level of an impeachable offense?"

The defense concurred.

Romney was stunned. Stunned by the cavalier quality of the defense's argument, and stunned by its implications. Suddenly, his vote seemed more important. "If I were to shrink from doing what I thought was right, the message that would send to future presidents was that so long as they didn't violate a statute, they could do whatever they wanted," he wrote in his journal. "In their second term, they would be even more emboldened than in their first because they would not even face the voters. Trump could become even more unleashed. If no one, no Republican, voted to convict, the whole affair would be written off as a partisan sham; the consequence of doing what I wanted personally and politically to do—just vote not-guilty—could conceivably affect the course of history."

When the Senate recessed, Romney returned to his office to go over the facts of the case again. He reread his copious handwritten notes and dug through the briefs and the testimony from both sides. The gravity of the moment was catching up to him. The stakes seemed somehow higher than before. Finally, Romney knelt on the floor and prayed.

Throughout the trial, he'd returned often to his father's favorite verse of Mormon scripture: *Search diligently, pray always, and be believing, and all things shall work together for your good.* He wasn't sure if God told senators how to vote, but he knew that at the outset of the trial he'd sworn an oath before God. And that was something he took seriously.

A few days earlier, Romney had paid a visit to Senator Joe Manchin's houseboat, *Almost Heaven*—the West Virginian's preferred domicile in

Washington. The impeachment trial had presented a serious political quandary for Manchin, a moderate Democrat whose state Trump had carried with 68 percent of the vote in 2016. While the voters there liked Manchin's independence, they wouldn't be happy with him if he voted to convict. After listening to Manchin describe his predicament, Romney offered his take: "We're both 72. We should probably be thinking about oaths and legacy, not just reelection."

Now it was time for Romney to follow his own advice.

Reviewing the evidence in this new light, Romney was unmoved by his own previous arguments for acquittal. Writing in his journal—because writing was the best way he knew to process his own thinking—he once again laid out the facts of the case as he understood them. Hundreds of words, page after page, he wrote and wrote and wrote, until finally the truth was clear to him:

> Even if the Bidens had done what was alleged by the Defense, there would have been no valid reason for the President to have gone to such lengths to have an investigation announced. The defense presented no evidence that what VP Biden had done was in any way a crime, so the most extreme penalty would be impeachment—if he were actually a sitting VP. Which he is not. And Hunter was doing what kids have long done—taking advantage of his father's good name. Only in his case, it was grossly excessive. So neither father nor son had committed a crime. So why the obsession with [investigating] them by Trump? In fact, the risk that Trump was taking by pushing the investigation was huge if it got out: the public would recoil, the Dems might impeach, he was doing something illegal by withholding appropriated funds, and that he knew all this was clear by the effort he made to hide what he was doing. So why take such a huge personal risk for the tiny national interest of ridding Ukraine of a corrupt corporate director? Solely for political purposes is the inescapable conclusion. Trump takes a huge personal risk to get a huge personal political benefit. That is the only conclusion I can draw.

Romney had made up his mind: He would vote to convict Trump on Article I, abuse of power, and acquit him on Article II, obstruction of Congress. This conclusion came with a stomach-twisting awareness of the potential repercussions. Turning once again to his journal, Romney began to list the consequences he and his family might face:

The Utah Republicans that had nominated me would go crazy with anger. My colleagues in the Senate would have nothing to do with me. It would affect my ability to get any legislation passed. I'd get nothing done through the Administration, of course. The President would attack me mercilessly in his rallies, incentivizing some nut job to shoot me. Fox too would eviscerate me, stoking up the crazies. The President might seek revenge, perhaps by using government in some way to hurt my sons. I would lose some friends who were Trump supporters, though not my few close friends. For the rest of my life, I would be accosted by people who hate what I had done—if I just vote with party, my vote would be expected and people who dislike Trump would just dismiss me as a callous Republican, but voting against party would engender true enmity and vitriol. It would be hard to go anywhere, especially in Utah, without the possibility of encountering some vocally hostile abuse. This would be true to a lesser degree for my sons, particularly Josh; what I was thinking I had to do would exact a real price on the whole family. I might need to move from Utah.

Romney slept fitfully that night in his townhome, finally rising at 4:00 a.m. to review the case once more. Still convinced of the president's guilt, he opened up a laptop at his kitchen table and wrote the first draft of the speech he'd eventually give on the Senate floor.

After that, he made his way to the Russell Building, where he broke the news to his senior staff. Some were surprised but approving; others were distressed. One staffer simply put her head in her hands. She didn't speak or look up again for the rest of the meeting.

*   *   *

The day before the vote, Romney sat for embargoed interviews with a handful of reporters in which he explained how he'd reached his decision to convict. The articles would be published the next day, after he delivered his speech. Conservative critics would later point to the slickly orchestrated press rollout as evidence of the senator's moral vanity. *He doesn't care about right and wrong, he just wants the media to love him.*

And, yes, there was a part of him that was thinking of his legacy—or, more to the point, the *Romney* legacy. He wanted it documented, on the record, that when the nation faced one of its darker political chapters, he'd risen to the occasion, like his dad had before him.

But Romney's interviews were also driven by that unceasing compulsion he had to explain himself. He was convinced that if people would simply hear him out, listen to the painstaking work he'd put in, follow the reasoning step-by-step, they'd understand. "That's just how he's wired," Waldrip would later observe. "He feels the need to logically explain everything."

Shortly before 2:00 p.m., Romney left his office and walked to the Capitol Building, where he waited in his small hideaway for his turn to speak. Minutes before going on, he received an unexpected call on his cell phone. It was Paul Ryan. Romney and his team had kept a tight lid on how he planned to vote, but somehow his former running mate had gotten word that he was about to detonate his political career—and Ryan wanted to talk him out of it.

Romney had been less judgmental of Ryan's acquiescence to Trump than he'd been of most other Republicans'. He'd reasoned that Ryan wasn't just any party hack, he was a policy visionary who saw Trump's presidency as a once-in-a-generation opportunity to turn his big ideas into law. That Ryan had been unable to accomplish nearly as much as he'd hoped was not, in Romney's mind, a strike against his character. The speaker had just tragically miscalculated.

And yet, here was Ryan on the phone, making the same arguments Romney had heard from some of his more calculating colleagues. Ryan told him that voting to convict Trump would make him an outcast in the party, that many of the people who'd worked to elect him president would never speak to him again, and that he'd struggle to pass any meaningful legislation. Ryan said that he respected Romney, and wanted to make absolutely sure he'd thought through the repercussions of his vote. Romney assured him that he had, and said goodbye.

Then he walked onto the Senate floor and read the remarks he'd written at his kitchen table.

"As a Senator-juror," Romney began, "I swore an oath before God to exercise impartial justice. I am profoundly religious. My faith is at the heart of who I am—" His voice broke and he had to pause as emotion overwhelmed him. "I take an oath before God as enormously consequential. I knew from the outset that being tasked with judging the president, the leader of my own party, would be the most difficult decision I have ever faced. I was not wrong."

Romney went on to articulate what he saw as the president's high crimes and misdemeanors. "Corrupting an election to keep oneself in office is perhaps the most abusive and destructive violation of one's oath of office that I can imagine." And while he supported many of the Trump administration's policies, he said, he feared that shirking his constitutional duty to convict would "expose my character to history's rebuke and the censure of my own conscience."

Before he finished, Romney acknowledged that his vote wouldn't change the outcome of the trial. The Senate would fall far short of the sixty-seven votes needed to remove the president from office; he would be the lone Republican to find Trump guilty. "But irrespective of these things," he said, "with my vote, I will tell my children and their children that I did my duty to the best of my ability, believing that my country expected it of me.

"We're all footnotes at best in the annals of history. But in the most powerful nation on earth, the nation conceived in liberty and justice, that distinction is enough for any citizen."

He left the chamber and called Ann, who was in tears. Watching the speech, she said, had been not only an emotional experience, but a spiritual one. Each of his five sons, and their wives, texted him that they were proud. He'd warned them before the vote that the president was a vindictive man and there was no telling how he might try to extract "payback." Tagg expected to lose investors in his private equity firm. Josh worried that the feds might close off his access to federal housing funds for his mortgage business. Matt was bracing for an IRS audit. The fact that none of them had wavered, despite the possible consequences, was an enormous relief to Romney.

In the coming days, as death threats poured in and friends cut him off and the president's allies sought to excommunicate him from their party, Romney would think about his sons, and how they'd remember him when he was gone. He would think about his dad, the one object of little-boy hero worship he still found deserving. He would think again about his ancestors—Gaskell and Miles and Rey—and he would think of that missionary, Parley P. Pratt, kneeling on the floor of a grimy New York tenement after months of grueling, fruitless labor, receiving heavenly assurance that it had not all been in vain—*your sacrifice is accepted.*

"I feel as if a huge weight has been lifted from me," he wrote in his journal. "The anxiety is gone."

"Romney your days are numbered. Every Republican should turn their back on you." . . . "Some Christian, stabbing the President in the back. Pray hard that God will forgive you for teaming up with people on the Devils side." . . . "Had some respect once but no more crawl in a hole and pull the dirt in after you." . . . "Stop referring to God. He has to be much more disgusted by you aligning with people who kill babies and think there are 73 genders. I am sad for the people of Utah." . . . "Your not a trust worthy person and other than your wife no one will ever trust you in the future maybe not even your wife." . . . "Let me be clear about Mr rat face Benedict Arnold Democrat fool @SenatorRomney who has aligned himself with the corrupt treasonous pathological lying Stalinist House managers, his days are done as Senator. We the people will remove his traitor azz." . . . "Judas always kills himself . . . . . . scriptures can not be broken."

CHAPTER FOURTEEN

2020

The backlash to Romney's impeachment vote was swift and savage. "Romney is going to be associated with Judas, Brutus, Benedict Arnold forever," Lou Dobbs raged on Fox. "He's now officially a member of the resistance & should be expelled from the GOP," Donald Trump Jr. declared on Twitter.

Some Republicans reserved special scorn for Romney's invocation of his faith when explaining his vote. Ed Rollins, a high-profile GOP strategist who ran Ronald Reagan's 1984 campaign, snickered that Romney had been led astray by "whoever he is talking to in the Mormon Tabernacle Temple." (In fact, Romney hadn't consulted any Mormon leaders on the impeachment, but Church employees would later report that phone lines at the faith's Salt Lake City headquarters lit up with angry calls from Trump supporters immediately after the senator's speech.) The president himself took a swipe at Romney at the National Prayer Breakfast, traditionally an apolitical affair. "I don't like people who use their faith as justification for doing what they know is wrong," Trump grumbled to the religious leaders in attendance.

Matt Schlapp, the chairman of the annual Conservative Political Action Conference, even went so far as to publicly warn Romney against trying to attend the event: "This year, I would actually be afraid for his physical safety, people are so mad at him."

There was praise, of course, too. Op-eds celebrated Romney's moral courage; pundits on CNN and MSNBC heaped praise on his decision to put country over party. Notes of gratitude poured in from celebrities—George Clooney, Ben Stiller, Susan Sarandon, Oprah. Barack Obama sent Romney a handwritten note.

Romney was gratified by the accolades, but he took the strange new respect with a grain of salt. Most of the people celebrating his vote were partisans who habitually rooted against the GOP—he knew the cheering section would dissolve the second he publicly expressed a conservative opinion again. And a few days of glowing media coverage meant little if the ultimate effect was to be alienated from the party to which he'd dedicated much of his adult life.

The night after his vote, Romney boarded a flight to Salt Lake City so that irate Republicans in his state could yell at him in person. It was time, he told his staff, to "face the music."

Romney's stand against Trump had taken a steep toll on his popularity in Utah. Republicans in the state had largely abandoned their early opposition to Trump, and were reverting to partisan form. Mike Lee, who had called on Trump to drop out a month before the 2016 election, was now one of the president's staunchest allies; Governor Gary Herbert, who'd repeatedly condemned Trump's vulgarity and treatment of refugees, was now supporting him in the upcoming election. Most conservative voters, meanwhile, seemed to view the impeachment trial as an us-versus-them battle for political power—and Romney no longer belonged in the "us" category. In one recent poll, the senator's approval rating had sunk to 36 percent.

Romney's meeting with Republican state legislators at the Utah Capitol Building was predictably tense. One lawmaker had already introduced a bill to censure Romney for his impeachment vote, and another—Representative Mike Schultz—spent the meeting grilling Romney on his lifelong disloyalty to the conservative cause: Why did you change your position on abortion? Why did you say Trump was a good businessman and then take it back? Eventually, Schultz let slip another reason for his ire when he complained that Romney had failed to invite him to a campaign event held in his neighborhood. ("I didn't know who you were." Romney shrugged.)

Later that day, once the Utah struggle session had concluded, Romney received a call from Mitch McConnell. The Senate leader assured Romney he was still welcome in the caucus, but gave him a piece of advice: Don't disparage your Republican colleagues who voted differently than you did.

Romney replied that, on the contrary, he'd bent over backward to publicly give his colleagues the benefit of the doubt.

There was a part of him that wanted to believe he could one day return to good standing in the Republican Party; that the impeachment saga—indeed, the whole Trump era—would pass like a bad dream and things would go back to normal. But while some of Romney's relationships in the party would eventually recover from their post-impeachment nadir, others remained permanently broken. And for all his efforts at congeniality, he would never quite feel comfortable again in those Republican caucus lunches. Even years later, he'd sometimes find himself looking around the room at his colleagues, wondering what they thought of him. "I have to tell you, that goes through my mind," he'd admit. "I don't think they look at me like 'This was our 2012 champion.'" He suspected that many of them would always see him as a traitor.

That same month, Romney began following reports out of China about a mysterious new virus. The initial intel was sketchy but unsettling—in Wuhan, hundreds of people had died from some kind of unknown respiratory disease, and thousands more were suffering from symptoms. It appeared to be spreading fast—first to nearby Asian countries like Malaysia, Singapore, and Japan, then to the Middle East and even

Western Europe. Aside from case counts, little information was being released by from China, but there were whispers of extreme quarantines and lockdown measures.

More alarming still to Romney was the U.S. government's apparent apathy in response to the threat. Even as public health officials warned that it was only a matter of time before the virus started circulating widely in America, the president was downplaying the prospect of an outbreak. On February 28, Trump, standing behind a podium adorned with the presidential seal, told a crowd of supporters in South Carolina to pay no attention to the growing warnings. The media was "in hysteria mode," he said; the Democrats were playing politics. This new coronavirus was much less harmful than the seasonal flu—and anyone who said otherwise was just trying to hurt him politically. "This is their new hoax," the president declared.

On March 11, after attending a briefing on the coronavirus, Romney returned to his office and found Matt Waldrip, his chief of staff. "Send everybody home," he said. Waldrip was startled—none of the other Senate offices had shifted to remote working; the most health-conscious ones were just encouraging staffers to use hand sanitizer and wipe down surfaces. But Romney was adamant.

Later, people who knew Romney would speculate about why he was so quick to take COVID-19 seriously. Some of the conscientiousness could be attributed to his germaphobia. Even before the pandemic, Romney was a man who dutifully washed his hands for the recommended twenty seconds, who adopted best-hygiene practices during flu season. Once, when his staff surprised him with a birthday cake made of Twinkies, he removed each candle one by one and blew them out at a safe distance, so as not to risk covering the confection in his germs. He was also a natural rule follower, a believer in expertise and the institutions that were built on it. If the scientists and public health experts were speaking in one voice, he was going to listen.

More than anything, though, Romney was thinking that afternoon in March about logistics. In every job he'd ever had—in every crisis he'd ever managed—Romney had insisted on digging into details, on drawing up plans and backup plans. And he saw no evidence that the people in charge of the federal government were similarly engaged. He hardly knew anything about this novel coronavirus, but without a national plan of response, he knew it was going to get bad.

After sending home his staff, Romney sat alone in his office, doing the same thing everybody else in America was doing at that moment: reading the internet and getting mad. He emailed his advisers a tweet he wanted to post: "After successfully delaying Covid-19's arrival in the US, what I'm hearing from constituents is puzzling and disturbing: 'Can't buy masks, can't buy sanitizing wipes, can't get a Coronavirus test.'"

Matt Waldrip was the first to respond to Romney's email: "To what end? All this is going to do is freak people out (more)."

Romney grudgingly relented. "I'm just really pissed at the administration for not taking action before, and now. Furious."

That night Trump went on TV to tout his administration's response to the virus—"the best anywhere in the world"—and announced a new ban on travel from Europe. "The virus will not have a chance against us," the president chest-thumped. "No nation is more prepared or more resilient than the United States."

Romney, once again overwhelmed by anger at the ineptitude on display, called Waldrip to vent. If banning travel from Europe was so essential to stopping the spread of COVID-19, why didn't the president do it weeks before when he first restricted travel from China? What was the plan to get Americans home who were stranded on the Continent? And, given that the virus was already circulating in the U.S.—over one thousand cases had been reported already, and the number was growing fast—what would any of this actually accomplish?

As he listened to his boss rant, Waldrip was alarmed by the level of anger. He texted Johnson, "He is freaking out. He thinks the president's ideas were insane . . . wants to blast Trump but I talked him down. He was incredulous about the incompetence."

Romney's incredulity would only grow in the weeks to come as infections exploded and markets crashed and bodies piled up in over-burdened emergency rooms. He did his best to respond to the crisis from his perch in the Senate. He worked the phones at the State Department to get his constituents on planes home from Europe and Asia. His office created a web page to provide Utahns with accurate information about the virus. When, that first night, the Utah Jazz game in Oklahoma City was abruptly canceled after star center Rudy Gobert tested positive for COVID-19, Romney tasked his staff with finding a place for the team to sleep. "I was on the phone with the mayor of Oklahoma City that night well after midnight as he physically drove around town asking hotels to take the Jazz in because the pilots wouldn't fly them back and hotels wouldn't let them stay," Waldrip would later recall. "It was like Armageddon had begun."

Romney also plunged into the legislative process as he advocated for an audacious pandemic policy proposal: direct payments of $1,000 to every adult in America. Some of his colleagues were surprised to see a purported fiscal conservative champion a massive government handout to the tune of $350 billion, but Romney argued that if ever a moment called for dramatic government intervention, this was it. Millions of workers were being forced to stay home; nobody knew when this would end. They'd need money to cover their expenses. Romney's idea quickly attracted bipartisan support, and soon he was thrust into the center of negotiations for the $2.2 trillion relief bill that would become known as the CARES Act.

Watching Romney twist arms and trade favors with his colleagues, Waldrip realized he was seeing a side of his boss that he'd only heard about. The Romney that Waldrip had gone to work for was a sep-tuagenarian elder statesman who cracked corny jokes, not a savvy, hard-nosed negotiator. "I knew Grandpa Mitt," Waldrip would tell me. "Now I was seeing Boardroom Mitt."

Still, Romney struggled with the limited reach of his office. An emergency of this magnitude had to be confronted by a president—and at the moment, the man who held that job was making a spectacular fool of himself. Trump refused to gain mastery of the most basic details about the virus that was killing thousands of citizens. He toggled between tolerating and actively encouraging the right wing's culture war against public-health protocols. He also routinely used his daily White House press briefings to spew nonsensical medical theories and push snake-oil remedies with no scientific basis.

On April 23, Trump mused during one of his briefings that perhaps Americans should inject themselves with bleach as a treatment for COVID-19. Amid the resulting onslaught of media ridicule, Trump tried to claim the comment was sarcastic. But Romney was left shaking his head in bewildered awe. "There's no question he was serious about that," Romney marveled. "It's like, how is that possible for someone over the second or third grade to think that?"

Romney had vacillated on the subject of the president's intelligence. In conversations, he sometimes paid lip service to the idea that Trump was a savant—incapable perhaps of learning new things or reading deeply or thinking through complex problems, but in possession of a certain bestial genius. Jared Kushner, Trump's son-in-law, had once tried to convince Romney that there was a method to the president's madness. Trump, he said, adhered to three ironclad "rules of communication": First, "controversy carries message"; second, "when you are right, fight—even if you are only 51 percent right"; third, "never apologize, ever." According to Kushner, much of Trump's ostensibly imbecilic behavior was actually strategic and savvy. Eventually, though, Romney would come to a simpler conclusion about Trump: "I think he's not smart. I mean, *really* not smart." One tell was that the president had reportedly threatened to sue his various alma maters if they ever leaked his grades. "I don't know a lot of geniuses who would threaten their school, their college, and their graduate school with a lawsuit if their transcript got released."

This had always been a problem, giving the most powerful job in the world to an uncommonly stupid man. But the problem was especially acute now that the country was facing a once-in-a-century crisis. Romney, a man who'd run twice for the presidency and retained a reverence for the institution, thought almost anybody else would be better than Trump.

In a year of untold suffering, one death that summer captured the nation's attention. It began with one of those grim, inescapable realities of modern America: the viral police brutality video. The footage, shot on a bystander's iPhone in Minneapolis, appeared on the internet on May 25: a police officer kneeling on the neck of a Black man, who struggled and gasped for breath and begged for help until eventually his body went limp. Three other officers looked on, ignoring pleas from observers that they help the man.

When Romney first watched the video, he had roughly the same reaction that most Americans had: burning indignation. "The death of George Floyd must not be in vain," he tweeted. "Our shock and outrage must grow into collective determination to extinguish forever such racist abuse."

Then, over the next few days, as protests spread across the country and several of them turned violent, Romney had roughly the same reaction that most Republicans had: a reflexive aversion to the lawlessness on display. "Peaceful protests underscore the urgency of addressing injustices," he tweeted. "But violence drowns the message of the protestors [sic] and mocks the principles of justice."

As May turned to June, the ambivalence that Romney was feeling became more or less the consensus position of America's white moderates—of course Floyd's death was wrong, of course racism in policing was a problem, but these anarchic protests were a problem, too, and they needed to be dealt with at once. That might have been where Romney himself landed, in the comfortable middle space between ally and enemy, where nothing is required or expected. But he felt uneasy about not taking sides.

Trump, of course, was taking every opportunity to demonize the protests in hopes of scaring white suburban voters into reelecting him. He denounced the "anarchy" in the streets, called Black Lives Matter a "symbol of hate," and pledged violent crackdowns on the "domestic terrorists" who were supposedly overtaking America's cities. In one particularly ugly scene, police used tear gas and rubber bullets to clear peaceful protesters outside the White House shortly before Trump went outside for a photo op. The conservative media were striking a similar chord, with Tucker Carlson warning viewers that the rioters would soon "come for you," and Rush Limbaugh describing Black Lives Matter as a "full-fledged anti-American organization."

Watching the fearmongering by Trump and his allies, Romney was overcome with one thought—that he didn't want to be associated with *this*. If America really was in a historic moment of racial reckoning, he wanted to be counted with those who were fighting to make the country fairer and freer for Black people—not with those who were cynically undermining their cause. When the white moderates of his father's day had called for a crackdown on civil rights demonstrators, George had refused to hear it. He chose his side, and joined the marchers in the streets.

On June 6, Romney tweeted a black-and-white photo of his father marching in Grosse Pointe, Michigan. "This is my father, George Romney, participating in a Civil Rights march in the Detroit suburbs during the late 1960s—'Force alone will not eliminate riots,' he said. 'We must eliminate the problems from which they stem.'"

The next day, Romney walked out the door of his Capitol Hill townhome and quietly joined a group of protesters marching toward the White House. It took several minutes before anybody noticed that the man in jeans and a white KN95 mask was the Republican senator from Utah. When a reporter asked him what he was doing there, Romney replied simply, "We need to stand up and say that Black lives matter."

It was a small gesture in the scheme of things, and hardly ranked in the pantheon of heroic civil rights stands by political leaders. Romney would cosponsor a police reform bill after that—one that aimed to improve de-escalation training and reduce racial bias in hiring—but it went nowhere. Democrats were pushing their own, more ambitious bill and the two parties couldn't come to terms. And like many Americans, Romney would largely move on after that summer—to a pandemic and a presidential election and an attempted coup that seemed to demand greater shares of attention and energy. But joining the march was a gut check for Romney, a reminder of the people he wanted to align himself with—and the ones he didn't.

The morning after the march, Trump mocked Romney on Twitter. As the first known Republican senator to join a Black Lives Matter demonstration—and as someone who was already loathed by the party's base—Romney made for an easy target. "Tremendous sincerity, what a guy," Trump tweeted sarcastically. "Hard to believe, with this kind of political talent, his numbers would 'tank' so badly in Utah!"

Romney, who'd spent so much of his political career soliciting the approval of people like Trump, now found that he relished their disdain. It likely helped, of course, that Romney was being cheered on in other quarters. That same day, he received an unexpected text message from George Clooney: "Your father would be so proud of yesterday. I know I was. It won't help you politically but between us I want to say thank you. I promise I won't say it anywhere near your re-election!" The truth was that Romney finally felt free to follow his father's example—the way he'd always wanted to—without worrying about the politics. Trump's ridicule was merely confirmation that he was doing something right.

When it came to the prospect of Trump losing reelection, Romney refused to get his hopes up this time. Even with a pandemic and a recession and widespread racial unrest weighing down the incumbent— even with the polls showing what they did—he'd convinced himself that Trump would pull off a win somehow. Romney still carried the psychic scars of 2016.

He told anyone who would listen that he thought Trump was going to get a second term. It was the same psychological game he'd played with himself in the run-up to the last election—predicting the outcome he most dreaded. He wasn't sure he believed it, but if Trump was reelected, he reasoned, "There's a silver lining to the black cloud, which is, at least I was right." This time, he upped the ante by making a bet with one of his sons: if Trump lost, Romney would give Craig his prized 1985 BMW.

In public, Romney said he wouldn't support either major-party candidate. In 2016 he had cast a write-in vote for his wife, and he planned to do so again. But in private, he made little effort to conceal the fact that he was pulling for Joe Biden. Romney didn't know the former vice president well, and he strongly disagreed with him on a range of policy issues. But he thought of Biden as a return to normalcy in the Oval Office, and as a crucial check against the excesses of the Democratic Party's left wing. Bernie Sanders and Elizabeth Warren scared Romney; Biden seemed like someone he could work with.

In August, Romney was invited to Salt Lake City to brief the fifteen senior leaders of his Church on the upcoming election. Speaking to the men he considered "prophets, seers, and revelators" in a spacious, mahogany-paneled conference room, Romney described the situation bluntly. "The way I look at this choice," he said, "is that you can choose an awful person or awful policies. It's one or the other. And your choice will depend on which you consider more important." After enduring four years of Trump's morally corrosive effect on American culture, Romney knew which quality he prized more in a president.

And yet, despite what his new liberal admirers might have wished, Romney still considered himself a conservative. As bad as Trump was—and as detestable as much of the party had become under his leadership—Romney simply didn't hold the same values as most progressives. He believed in the power of capitalism, in religion's vital place in the public square, and he tended to treat sweeping new government programs with suspicion.

He also favored a conservative Supreme Court—a preference that became newly relevant on September 18, when the long-serving liberal Justice Ruth Bader Ginsburg died. Ginsburg's death, just six weeks before the election, represented a nightmare scenario for Democrats. If Trump succeeded in confirming her replacement before he left office, he would cement a conservative majority on the Court for a generation. Democrats also noted that moving forward with a confirmation before the election would be an act of rank hypocrisy by Republicans. In 2016, Senate Republicans had blocked the confirmation of President Obama's Supreme Court nominee, Merrick Garland, claiming they wanted to wait for voters to choose the next president. But now that they were in a nearly identical situation, Republicans weren't so interested in waiting for the voters to speak. Trump announced that he would move forward with a nomination, and Mitch McConnell said they would work to confirm the justice before Election Day.

Senators Lisa Murkowski and Susan Collins, the two signature moderates in the GOP caucus, quickly announced they would not support Trump's nominee. Democrats only needed one more Republican to buck their party, so naturally they turned to their new ally—pleading with Romney to block the hearings from taking place until after the election. They framed the issue as a matter of principle. In a speech in Wilmington, Delaware, Biden called on Romney to "uphold your Constitutional duty, your conscience." Bret Stephens, the anti-Trump conservative columnist at the *New York Times*, argued that Romney should "show Americans what it means to be courageous by way of sound and independent judgment." But Romney was unpersuaded by these appeals. As far as he was concerned, it didn't matter if the next election was two months away or two years away: the Constitution empowered the sitting president to nominate Supreme Court justices and the Senate to confirm them. Romney hadn't been in the Senate in 2016, but if he had been, he said, he would have met with Garland and given him the same consideration as any other nominee. He believed Trump was owed the same courtesy.

Four days after Ginsburg's death, Romney announced that he would consider the president's nominee. Shortly thereafter he met with Amy Coney Barrett, a Notre Dame law professor and federal judge, and deemed her qualified to serve on the nation's highest court. When Romney informed his staff that he planned to vote for Barrett's confirmation, Waldrip thought he detected some regret in the announcement. The reluctance was strange. The vote seemed like a win-win—Romney's Republican constituents back home would be pleased, and the Court would gain a young, qualified conservative jurist.

But Romney knew the vote would likely mark the end of his short-lived status as every Democrat's favorite Republican.

"Well, I guess that will be it for all my new friends," he told Waldrip, with a comically exaggerated sigh.

As Election Day crept closer, Romney saw signs of yet another crisis on the horizon. Trump—who trailed significantly in the polls—was making it clear that he wouldn't go quietly. In August, the president claimed the only way he would lose was if the election was "rigged." Since then, he'd begun to weave dark rumors of election fraud into his speeches. In a video recruiting volunteers to join the campaign's "election-security operation," his son, Don Jr., asserted that Democrats were planning "to add millions of fraudulent ballots" to the vote: "The radical left are laying the groundwork to steal this election from my father. . . . We need you to help us watch them."

By now, there were few depths to which Trump could sink that would surprise Romney. But he was disturbed by how widely the president's rigged-election narrative was being adopted by his supporters. It didn't take a constitutional scholar to see the threat this posed to democracy.

"If you don't believe in the ballot, then you do believe that someone should be able to assert power without the ballot," Romney would later remember thinking. "And once that happens, you're now in an authoritarian regime."

Late on election night, as votes were still being counted in key battleground states, the president appeared in the East Room of the

White House, "Hail to the Chief" blaring over the speakers. The electoral math was looking bad for Trump, but the networks weren't ready to call the race yet. With the cameras trained on him, the president decided he was.

"This is a fraud on the American public," he declared. "This is an embarrassment to our country. We were getting ready to win this election. Frankly, we *did* win this election."

CHAPTER FIFTEEN

The Cathedral and the Gargoyle

R omney didn't put on his full disguise before heading to the Salt Lake City airport on January 5, 2021—he thought the KN95 mask would suffice. Years earlier, he'd bumped into Zach Braff on a flight and the sitcom actor had given him a useful piece of advice: for most not-quite-A-list celebrities, a simple baseball cap and a pair of reading glasses were usually enough to avoid being spotted in public.

Romney had been a regular target of heckling and harassment by Trump's supporters since voting to convict the president. They shouted "traitor" from car windows and confronted him in restaurants. The situation had only gotten worse in the last two months as Trump whipped his followers into a frenzy with claims that the 2020 election was being stolen from them. Lately, Romney had made a point of donning the Braff-recommended disguise whenever he traveled to Palm Beach—a town crawling with confrontational Trump lackeys, and the place where Ann had somewhat inconveniently chosen to keep her horses. But he didn't think he would need the getup in Utah.

He'd only been sitting at the Delta gate for a few minutes when a man approached him, camera phone set to record, and began taunting the senator.

"Hey, Mitt," the heckler said. "Are you going to object to the electors? No? Come on, now."

The man was referring to the Trump camp's latest ploy, scheduled to take place the next day on Capitol Hill. Dozens of Republican lawmakers planned to vote to reject the certification of the electoral college. Romney knew there was no constitutional mechanism to allow for such a move; what's more, not a single allegation of systemic voter fraud had been substantiated. But while Romney had forcefully condemned the charade, most leading Republicans seemed content to play along with Trump. "What is the downside for humoring him for this little bit of time?" one anonymous GOP official mused to the *Washington Post*. "No one seriously thinks the results will change."

The heckler persisted trying to get a rise out of Romney.

"We're all gonna be there to see you."

"If you're not gonna object to the electors are you prepared to be primaried?"

"When Trump gets reelected, you're getting primaried."

Romney, laboring to ignore the taunts, kept his eyes trained on his iPad. But the spectacle drew attention, and soon another camera-wielding stranger was in his face, loudly demanding answers.

"Why aren't you supporting President Trump?"

"Are you going to support him in the fraudulent votes?"

Straining to keep his cool, Romney tried offering a benign answer. "We have a Constitution, the constitutional process is clear," he said. "I'll follow the Constitution and I'll explain all that when we meet in Congress this week." He gathered his things and left the boarding area, but the jeers followed him.

"Trump is a juggernaut, your legacy is nothing!"

"You're a joke, an absolute joke! It's a disgusting shame."

"You don't belong in Utah!"

"This is gonna be an awkward flight!" one of the hecklers called after him. "You might want to change it."

When Romney took his seat, he realized what the man meant. The plane was packed with right-wing protesters who were on their way to Washington for the Save America Rally. "Big protest on January 6th," Trump had tweeted weeks earlier. "Be there, will be wild!"

Romney was in first class, which meant that every passenger who boarded got a good look at the turncoat Republican seated at the front of their plane. Shouts of "Resign, Mitt!" began echoing through the cabin. An apologetic flight attendant asked Romney if he wanted her to say something to the rowdy passengers, but he demurred—if they knew they were bothering him, they'd only shout louder. Soon, angry chants of *"TRAI-TOR! TRAI-TOR! TRAI-TOR!"* filled the plane.

By the time Romney landed, a video of the heckling had gone viral on Twitter, and two of his aides—worried that he might not be able to escape the D.C. airport safely—were waiting to escort him to his townhouse. Sitting in the passenger seat on the car ride home, he thought about the feral behavior he'd just witnessed. Something bad was going on. The mood in the country—in his party—was running hot. And no one seemed interested in de-escalation.

January 6, 2021: The president gave his incendiary speech. The rally turned into a riot. A violent mob crashed through police barricades and streamed into the Capitol, hunting for traitors. An initial spasm of chaos inside the Senate chamber was followed by confused evacuation orders, and all of a sudden Romney was being rushed down a hallway with several of his colleagues, none of whom had any idea where they were going. The mob was only one level below, so they couldn't take the stairs; instead, the senators piled into elevators, ten at a time, while the rest loitered anxiously in the hallway, hoping the mob didn't discover them. When they reached the basement, Romney asked a pair of police officers for instructions.

"Where are we supposed to go?" he asked.

"The senators know," one of the officers replied.

Chris Marroletti, Romney's exasperated body man, spoke up: "These *are* the senators. They don't know. Where are we supposed to go?"

The officer got on his radio to find out and then instructed the senators to go to a safe room. When they got there, they discovered there were no police to seal off the area. Once the police did show up, a new evacuation plan was announced: all one hundred senators would be loaded onto buses outside the Capitol and driven away from the scene. Romney, incredulous, shouted, "That's insane!" The riot was still raging just outside the building—they'd be sitting ducks. His colleagues concurred and the plan was scrapped. Romney was mystified by the ineptitude. *This is the Keystone Kops,* he thought.

But of course, Romney knew it wasn't the police's fault. He thought about the text message he'd sent to Mitch McConnell a few days earlier explicitly warning of this scenario. How were the political leaders in Washington not ready for this? Even months later, Romney would get angry as he recalled the situation. "They know that we have the potential of being attacked, that there are people talking about storming the Capitol that have guns," he told me. And yet, "they're not properly protecting the building. They haven't drilled us on where to go. They haven't secured a room for us to go to. It's like, this is unbelievable! In the greatest nation on earth, we're so disorganized and unprepared."

It was, in some ways, a perfect metaphor for his party's timorous, shortsighted approach to the Trump era—*What's the harm in humoring him?* As a boy, he'd read *Idylls of the King* with his mother; now he could understand the famous quote from Tennyson's Guinevere as she witnesses the consequences of corruption in Arthur's court: "This madness has come on us for our sins."

There were no chairs in the safe room at first, so the shell-shocked senators simply ambled around murmuring variations of *I can't believe this is happening.* When eventually someone wheeled in a TV and turned on CNN, the senators got their first live look at what was happening—infiltrators ransacking the Senate chamber, rifling through papers, posing triumphantly on the dais with fists in the air as they shouted about how Trump had won the election. A sickened silence fell over the room as anger and outrage were replaced by dread. To Romney, the Senate Chamber was still a sacred place. Watching it transform into a playground for asinine insurrectionists was almost too much to bear.

But Romney had other things on his mind. He was worried about his family back in Utah. The night before, he'd gotten a visceral reminder of what Trump-loving Utahns thought of him. Now he was seeing just how far their hatred could carry them. He put in a call to Utah's newly sworn-in governor, Spencer Cox, who scrambled state troopers to the homes of Ann and Josh. Romney also asked Matt Waldrip, who had stayed back in Utah, to get to Ann's house. When he arrived, she was crying. This was exactly the nightmare she'd envisioned when she begged Mitt not to return to Washington. Waldrip hugged her. "This is our country," she kept repeating through tears. "This is our country."

Shortly after 4:00 p.m., the CNN feed in the Senate safe room switched to president-elect Joe Biden. The room fell silent. "This is not dissent, it's disorder," Biden said. "It's chaos. It borders on sedition, and it must end now. I call on this mob to pull back and allow the work of democracy to go forward." When Biden finished, the senators—Democrats and Republicans alike—stood and applauded.

Trump never called in the National Guard. Reports would later emerge that the president expressed support for the mob that day, that he wanted to get rid of the metal detectors that were keeping his armed supporters from entering the rally, that he believed his vice president deserved the chants of "Hang Mike Pence!" Maybe this was what Trump had in mind all along. In any event, by 6:30 p.m. the crowd had dispersed and the Capitol was clear.

As the Senate prepared to reconvene late that night, Romney took solace at least in assuming that his most extreme colleagues now realized what their ruse had wrought, and would abandon their plan to object to the electors. Romney had written a speech a few days earlier condemning their procedural farce, but now he was thinking of tossing it. Surely the point was moot.

But to Romney's astonishment, the architects of the plan *still* intended to move forward. When Josh Hawley stood to deliver his speech, Romney was positioned just behind the Missourian's right shoulder, allowing the camera to capture his reaction to the rhetoric. Even from behind two face masks, Romney's glare was withering. As Hawley spoke—about the previous summer's violent racial protests, and the so-called election fraud in Pennsylvania, and the vital national importance of using the United States Senate to indulge voters who wrongly believed the election had been rigged—Romney struggled to suppress his running mental commentary: *I can't believe he said that. . . . That's nuts. . . . That doesn't make any sense.*

What bothered Romney most about Hawley's speech was the same thing that had gotten him about Cruz's—the oily disingenuousness. "They know better!" he would later tell me. "Josh Hawley is one of the smartest people in the Senate, if not the smartest, and Ted Cruz could give him a run for his money. They're both really, really smart guys." Too smart, Romney believed, to actually think that Trump won the 2020 election. Hawley and Cruz seemed to be thinking about their own presidential prospects, figuring Republican primary voters would reward this type of behavior. But at what cost? "They were making a calculation," Romney told me, "that put politics above the interests of liberal democracy and the Constitution."

When it was Romney's turn to speak, he wasted little time before laying into his colleagues.

"What happened here today was an insurrection, incited by the president of the United States," Romney said. "Those who choose to continue to support his dangerous gambit by objecting to the results of a legitimate, democratic election will forever be seen as being complicit in an unprecedented attack against our democracy. Fairly or not, they will be remembered for their role in this shameful episode in American history. That will be their legacy."

Romney's voice sharpened when he addressed Hawley's patronizing claim that objecting to the certification was a matter of showing respect for voters who believed the election was stolen. It struck Romney that, for all their alleged populism, Hawley and his allies seemed to take a very dim view of their Republican constituents.

"The best way we can show respect for the voters who are upset is by *telling them the truth*!" Romney said, his voice rising to a shout. Applause rose in the chamber.

Before sitting down, he posed a question to his fellow senators—a question that, whether he realized it or not, he'd been wrestling with himself for nearly his entire political career.

"Do we weigh our own political fortunes more heavily than we weigh the strength of our Republic, the strength of our democracy, and the cause of freedom? What is the weight of personal acclaim compared to the weight of conscience?"

For a blessed moment after January 6, it looked to Romney as if the fever in his party might finally be breaking. GOP leaders, including many Trump loyalists, condemned the president and denounced the rioters. Trump, who was booted from Twitter and Facebook for fear that he might use the platforms in his final days to incite more violence, saw his approval rating plummet. New articles of impeachment were introduced, and this time it looked as if Republicans might join the Democrats in convicting him. McConnell's office leaked to the press that he was considering a vote to convict. While much of the conservative media seemed to turn on Trump, federal law enforcement began sifting through hundreds of hours of amateur footage from January 6 to identify and arrest the people who had stormed the Capitol. Joe Biden was sworn in as the forty-sixth president of the United States, and Trump—who skipped the inauguration—flew off to Florida, where he seemed destined for a descent into political irrelevance and legal trouble.

But the Republicans' flirtation with repentance was short-lived. Within months, Fox News was offering a revisionist history of January 6 and recasting the rioters—many of whom were now being charged with crimes—as martyrs and victims of a vengeful, overreaching Justice Department. House Republican leader Kevin McCarthy, who'd initially blamed Trump for the riot, paid a visit to Mar-a-Lago to mend his relationship with the ex-president.

The House impeached Trump for the second time, but with fewer Republican votes than many had expected, and a conviction in the Senate now looked unlikely. Some of the reluctance to hold Trump accountable was a function of the same old perverse political incentives—elected Republicans feared a political backlash from their base. But after January 6, a new, more existential brand of cowardice emerged. One Republican congressman confided to Romney that he wanted to vote for impeachment, but declined out of fear for his family's safety. The congressman reasoned that Trump would be impeached by House Democrats with or without him—why put his wife and children at risk if it wouldn't change the outcome? Later, during the Senate trial, Romney heard the same calculation while talking to a small group of Republican colleagues. When one senator, a member of leadership, said he was leaning toward voting to convict, the others urgently encouraged him to reconsider. *You can't do that,* one said. *Think of your personal safety,* said another. *Think of your children.* The senator eventually decided they were right. There were too many Trump supporters with guns in his state, he explained to Romney. His wife wouldn't feel safe going out in public.

As dismayed as Romney was by this line of thinking, he understood it. Senators and congressmen don't have security details. Their addresses are publicly available online. Romney himself had been shelling out $5,000 a day since the riot to cover private security for his family—an expense he knew most of his colleagues couldn't afford.

By the time Democrats proposed a bipartisan commission to investigate the events of January 6, the GOP's one-eighty was complete.
Virtually every Republican in Congress came out in full-throated
opposition to the idea. Romney, who'd been consulting with histori-
ans about how best to preserve the memory of the insurrection—he'd
proposed leaving some of the damage to the Capitol unrepaired—was
disappointed by his party's posture, but he was no longer surprised.
He had taken to quoting a favorite scene from *Butch Cassidy and the
Sundance Kid* when he talked about his party's whitewashing of the
insurrection—twisting his face into an exaggerated comic expression
before declaring, "*Morons*, I've got *morons* on my team!"

To Romney, the revisionism of January 6 was almost worse than
the attack itself. If even an attempted coup couldn't wake his party up
to what their complicity had enabled, would anything?

In March, Romney was named the recipient of the John F. Kennedy
Profile in Courage Award for his lonely stand against Trump during
the president's first impeachment trial. Announcing the award, Caro-
line Kennedy praised Romney as a senator who "reminds us that our
democracy depends on the courage, conscience, and character of our
elected officials." The next month, Romney was invited to speak at the
Utah Republican Convention in West Valley City, where he suspected
he'd face a rather different reception. Liz Johnson, whom Romney had
promoted to chief of staff after Waldrip left for a job in the private
sector, told him he should go.

"You've gotta be kidding," Romney replied. "That doesn't make
any sense."

He knew, given his current standing in the party, that he'd get
booed if he stepped foot onstage and that the hostile reception would
make headlines. Why put himself through it? Johnson conceded the
point, but reminded him that some of the delegates were supporters of
his—people his campaign had recruited to join the state party during
his 2018 race. "Show up for those people," she told him. "Remind them
that you're still a Republican."

Romney relented. "Utahns are pretty respectful people," he told himself. "I'll go out there, they'll boo, but that'll be over and then they'll hear my speech." He even came up with a little joke to defuse the tension. As soon as he went onstage, he'd ask the crowd of partisans, "What do you think of President Biden's first one hundred days?" When they booed in response, he'd say, "I hope you got that out of your system!"

But when Romney took the stage on the afternoon of May 1, he quickly realized he'd underestimated the level of vitriol awaiting him. The heckling and booing was so loud and sustained that he could barely get a word out. Romney found himself chuckling at his miscalculation. *Well, this didn't work out like I thought!* His natural instinct when faced with such an overwhelming show of disapproval was to dig in. But as he labored to push through his prepared remarks, he became fixated on a red-faced woman in the front row who was furiously screaming at him while her child stood by her side. He paused his speech.

"Aren't you embarrassed?" he couldn't help but ask her from the stage.

Reflecting on the experience afterward, Romney tried to reframe it as a character-building experience of sorts—a moment in which he got to live up to his father's example. When he was young, Mitt had watched an audience stacked with auto union members vociferously boo his dad during a gubernatorial debate. George had been undeterred. "He was proud to stand for what he believed," Romney told me. "I really do believe if you're not being booed, if people aren't angry at you, you really haven't done anything in public life."

But there was also something unsettling about the episode. As a former presidential candidate, he was well acquainted with heckling. Scruffy Occupy Wall Streeters had shouted down his stump speeches; gay rights activists had "glitter-bombed" him at rallies. But these were Utah Republicans—they were supposed to be *his people*. Model citizens, well-behaved Mormons, respectable patriots and pillars of the community, with kids and church callings and responsibilities at work. Many of them had probably been among his most enthusiastic supporters in 2012. Now they were acting like wild children in public. And if he was being honest with himself, there were moments up on that stage when he was afraid of them.

"There are deranged people among us," he told me. And in Utah, "people carry guns."

"It only takes one really disturbed person."

He let the words hang in the air for a moment, declining to answer the question his confession begged: How long can a democracy last when its elected leaders live in fear of physical violence from their constituents?

CHAPTER SIXTEEN

New Friends

With Trump out of office and the immediate emergency of his presidency passed, Romney decided to dust off the legislative to-do list he'd compiled back when he first entered the Senate. "I came here to do things," he reminded his staff, and himself. There had been little time for lawmaking amid the cascading crises of the past two years. But Joe Biden had been elected in large part by promising to restore an old-fashioned ethic of bipartisan problem-solving to Washington—and Romney was ready to hold him to it. First, though, he'd need to find some like-minded colleagues.

Romney tried to keep an open mind as he sized up potential legislative partners. The left flank of the Democratic Party didn't seem very promising: Bernie Sanders was one of the few senators who'd completely ignored his outreach. "He's a curmudgeon," concluded Romney, who developed a cartoonish impression of Sanders that he used to entertain friends and staffers—hunching his back and scowling as he emitted Scrooge-like grunts. But he found that he could collaborate with almost every other Democrat in the Senate. While he disagreed with Connecticut Democrat Chris Murphy on the vast majority of issues, for example, the two shared an interest in compensating college athletes. So, together they formed a Senate working group to study potential solutions.

Romney had a harder time looking past his differences with the far-right members in his own party—the zealous Trump disciples, the insurrection apologists, the conspiracy theorists. But he drew a mental distinction between those Republican colleagues he viewed as sincerely crazy and those who were faking it for votes. The latter group he found much more contemptible. "I doubt I will work with Josh Hawley on anything," he told me. He simply couldn't stomach associating himself with someone who'd so cynically stoked distrust in democracy for his own selfish political reasons. On the other hand, Romney was open to partnering with Ron Johnson, who seemed to genuinely believe the fevered conspiracy theories he was constantly spouting. Every time Romney talked to "Ron John," as he was known, it seemed like the Wisconsin Republican was suggesting that Nancy Pelosi was somehow responsible for the Capitol riot, or dismissing climate change as "bullshit," or accusing Pfizer of covering up effective COVID treatments (Johnson had suggested mouthwash) to boost profits for its vaccine. Once, after Johnson chastised Romney for not taking a more active interest in Hunter Biden's Ukrainian business dealings, Romney exclaimed in exasperation, "Ron, is there *any* conspiracy you don't believe?" Still, if the opportunity arose to work productively with the sincere conspiracist on border-security issues, Romney was open to it. At least he could expect good faith.

But where Romney really found his crowd was in a group of bipartisan senators that formed shortly after the 2020 election. The "gang of ten," as it was eventually nicknamed in the press, was a motley lot—five Republicans, five Democrats, and an eclectic mix of personalities and styles. Under most circumstances, Jon Tester, a loud, thickset farmer from Montana who'd lost several fingers in a meat grinder, would have little in common with Rob Portman, a buttoned-down budget wonk who spoke in the soporific cadence of a bank teller. But the group was united by an increasingly uncommon trait among America's elected legislators: an interest in legislating. These were people who enjoyed hashing out the language in federal law, who painstakingly pored over numbers from the Congressional Budget Office and dutifully consulted the parliamentarian on the finer Senate procedure.

"A lot of my colleagues would prefer to give speeches and go on cable news and not get their hands dirty with legislation," Portman told me. There was too much political downside in this hyperpolarized era to attaching your name to a bipartisan bill—too much risk of incurring a backlash from the ideologues and activists in your party. Those who joined the gang of ten took pride in not being cowed by partisans.

After successfully passing a $908 million COVID relief package in December 2020, the gang turned its attention to a bill that would fund sweeping updates to America's infrastructure. They also started hanging out more. They took in tennis tournaments together and attended dinner parties on Manchin's houseboat. Romney, who still felt like a reject at the Republican caucus lunches, was thrilled to finally be making friends, though in his eagerness sometimes came on too strong. When the group started a text chain, Romney developed a reputation as its "chattiest" member, prompting Lisa Murkowski to call him out in an interview with *Politico* for his loquaciousness. It was strange for Romney to realize how much more he seemed to have in common with the Democrats in this group than he did with the average Republican these days. Sometimes, to amuse themselves, he and Manchin would debate which of them had to contend with the worst gadflies and extremists in their respective parties. "We'll say, 'Who has the craziest side? I'll trade you one of my crazies for two of your crazies!'" Manchin told me. The West Virginian called this parlor game "playing cards with crazies"—and Romney always left the conversation depressingly convinced that he'd won. One Alexandria Ocasio-Cortez for a Matt Gaetz *and* a Marjorie Taylor Greene? Romney would take that deal every time.

Manchin and Romney fantasized about leaving behind their parties for good and starting something new. "We speak about it every day," Manchin told me. "Spiritually, we probably do belong in the same party. . . . I tell people I'm fiscally responsible and socially compassionate and I can guarantee you Mitt Romney is the same way." But Romney always retreated to pragmatism in these conversations. You can't make a difference outside the two-party system, he reasoned. *Can you?*

One colleague Romney got to know especially well during this period was Kyrsten Sinema, the forty-five-year-old Democrat from Arizona. On the surface, their friendship seemed unlikely. Though both were raised Mormon, Sinema had left the Church after graduating from BYU and later came out as bisexual. She'd begun her political career in the early 2000s as a member of the left-wing Green Party, leading anti-war protests and crusading against the death penalty. When she was eventually elected to the House as a Democrat, she became the only member of Congress to openly identify as religiously unaffiliated, choosing to be sworn into office on a copy of the Constitution instead of a Bible.

The two were elected to the Senate the same year and sat next to each other at the orientation for new members. They made for an odd-looking pair: Romney, cutting a classically senatorial figure in his conservative suits and neat coif, Sinema strutting around the Capitol in zebra-print dresses and funky denim vests, thigh-high boots and pom-pom earrings. But Sinema thought she sensed in Romney a kindred spirit. He didn't seem preoccupied with things like reelection or his status in his caucus. "He's already run for everything, so you know . . . he was not the guy who was worried about being an *important senator*," she'd recall.

Romney, for his part, came to appreciate how Sinema handled herself in the face of intense pressure from Democratic leaders and activists to toe the party line. With the new Senate closely divided in 2021, Democrats had grown impatient with the limits imposed by the filibuster, which effectively required sixty votes for most bills to pass. When Biden called on Senate Democrats to toss the filibuster and jam through a voting-rights bill without any Republican support, Sinema blocked the effort. "I guess some people think it's old-fashioned or whatever, but the Senate . . . was designed to be a slower, more deliberative body," she argued. "It was designed to push senators towards comity, towards compromise, towards solutions." She saw the filibuster as a key mechanism for preserving that ethos.

This stance made her wildly unpopular with the left. Protesters chased her through airports and cornered her in bathrooms. Liberal pundits ridiculed her wardrobe and branded her an enemy of the people. The president of EMILY's List, a progressive group dedicated to electing pro-choice female candidates, disavowed Sinema, declaring, "We believe she undermines the foundations of our democracy." But she refused to back down.

Once, when Romney asked her if she worried about getting reelected, she shrugged matter-of-factly. "I don't care. I can go on any board I want to. I can be a college president. I can do anything," she said. "I saved the Senate filibuster by myself. I saved the Senate by myself. That's good enough for me."

The two senators bonded over their parallel descents into pariah status in their respective parties, and together they relished their self-perceptions as truth tellers and rebels. Sinema affectionately nicknamed Romney "trouble." Romney gleefully followed the left's freak-outs over Sinema on Twitter and congratulated her whenever she went viral. When, one day in February 2021, Sinema presided over a session of the Senate wearing a hot-pink sweater with the words "Dangerous Creature," Romney approached her on the Senate floor and leaned in.

"You're breaking the internet," he told her, in a comment that was picked up by C-SPAN microphones.

"Good," she replied.

Romney wasn't the only Senate Republican who took a liking to Sinema—though in the case of some of his male colleagues, the appreciation seemed to extend beyond politics. Once, while inside the Senate Chamber, Romney remarked to the Republican sitting next to him that Sinema's face was actually "quite pretty."

"My eyes have never gotten that high," the senator responded, leering at her.

Negotiating the Infrastructure Investment and Jobs Act turned out to be one of the most complicated congressional undertakings in a decade. Republicans and Democrats had been talking for years about the need to update America's roads, bridges, railways, and sewage systems—Trump had spent his entire presidency promising, to no avail, that he'd tackle the issue. But the two parties had very different ideas of how much money to spend and on what. Over the course of five months, the gang of ten met more than fifty times to hammer out agreements on a long list of sticking points. Portman, who was appointed lead negotiating partner alongside White House counselor Steve Ricchetti, divided the senators into groups and gave them specific issues to focus on. Romney was assigned to work with New Hampshire senator Jeanne Shaheen on the unglamorous issue of lead pipe removal. Romney jumped in enthusiastically, teaching himself everything he could about the subject, consulting experts on best practices, and then presenting his detailed findings to the group. Sinema teased him about his zeal, often quoting an old Mormon hymn: *We all have work, let no one shirk, put your shoulder to the wheel.*

Portman would later admit he was surprised by Romney's can-do attitude. "I told him privately [before he ran] that I thought he'd be frustrated in the Senate because he's a natural executive," Portman said. He figured Romney would balk at having to navigate the bureaucratic morass of Capitol Hill and build consensus gradually rather than simply making a decision. "I just thought he wouldn't like it."

But Romney thought this reflected a misunderstanding of his business career. "I think people forget I worked for ten years as a management consultant," he told me. "Which meant I was able to make no decisions, I was able to get nothing done, and I had to try and convince people through a long process." In retrospect, it seems, he was destined for the United States Senate.

Romney's colleagues would later describe his negotiation style as a peculiar give-and-take. He was "often the most conservative voice in the room" on fiscal issues, Portman said, arguing strenuously that each item in the bill had to be paid for somehow, either with new revenues or offsetting budget cuts. When Democrats proposed allocating an inordinate sum to cleaning up pollution in abandoned urban areas and federal construction sites, Romney looked into it and made a vigorous case that such a large sum couldn't possibly be spent effectively within the relevant time frame. After extensive back-and-forth, the Democrats agreed to reduce the number. "He was very frank with people," Portman said.

But what made Romney unusual was how he reacted when he lost one of these battles, which happened more often than not. "Mitt would say, 'That's stupid, we shouldn't be doing that. . . . But if it's better than what we have, I'll vote for it," Manchin recalled. "His feeling was 'Take what you can get and build off it.'" Once upon a time this comfort with incrementalism was the prevailing sentiment in the Senate; today, Manchin said, "that's a rare quality."

The final infrastructure bill passed the Senate, 69–30, on August 10 and was signed into law three months later. The $1.2 trillion bill represented the largest investment in American roads and bridges in seventy years, and the largest-ever investment in public transit.

To celebrate, the senators went out for a lavish dinner. When the check came, the waiter was instructed to hand it to Romney. This was one area where the group had a clear consensus. "We're all very strong capitalists," Susan Collins would later tell me. "But on this, we're very Marxist: 'From each according to his ability, to each according to his needs.'"

While Romney spent much of 2021 making new friends across the aisle, one Democrat remained puzzlingly absent: Joe Biden.

The Utah senator had assumed, perhaps a bit egotistically, that the new president would want to cultivate a relationship with him. Washington wasn't exactly suffering from a surplus of Republican lawmakers eager to work with the White House, after all. But aside

from a couple token gestures early on, he almost never heard from the
president or his advisers. Where was the charm offensive? Where were
the after-hours phone calls? Where was the schmoozy, old-school D.C.
operator he'd heard so much about? Romney was just sitting there,
waiting to be schmoozed.

The truth was that Biden's presidency had not gotten off to a stellar
start. Inflation was accelerating; everything cost too much. Americans
were angry and blaming the president. His order to withdraw all troops
from Afghanistan—officially bringing an end to the longest war in
U.S. history—led to weeks of chaos and bloodshed, with Kabul quickly
falling to the Taliban while hundreds of American citizens and visa
holders were left stranded there. As his first year in office neared its end,
Biden's approval rating had fallen nearly fifteen points and was hovering in the low forties. To Romney, it seemed obvious that Biden's best
chance at turning things around was to pivot back to the themes that
resonated during his campaign—competency, sanity, uniting America.
But Romney saw little evidence that the White House was interested
in that message.

The dynamic was best illustrated at the signing ceremony for the
infrastructure bill in November 2021. The event could have been used
to highlight Biden's bipartisan bona fides, but nothing about the cho-
reography of the photo op suggested he wanted to send that message.
"They didn't have any of the Republicans who wrote the bill speak,"
Romney huffed to me shortly afterward. The president had signed
the bill into law surrounded by congressional Democrats and cabinet
secretaries. "And the ten of us who actually drafted it, put the whole
thing together, negotiated it? Not there. It's like, wow.

"Frankly," Romney hastened to add, trying not to sound wounded,
"I didn't really want to get photographed with Biden."

Instead of using the infrastructure bill to take a much-needed
victory lap, Biden immediately lurched into another messy, divisive
fight in Congress as he lobbied for passage of the Build Back Better
Act—a $3.5 trillion spending package designed to fund a laundry list

of Democratic policy priorities. Then, in January 2022, Biden went to Atlanta to stump for the Democrats' voting-rights bill and delivered a provocative speech condemning every Republican opponent of the legislation as an heir to segregationists and confederates.

"The goal of the former president and his allies is to disenfranchise anyone who votes against them," Biden said. "Simple as that."

"I ask every elected official in America: How do you want to be remembered?" he went on. "Do you want to be on the side of Dr. King or George Wallace? Do you want to be on the side of John Lewis or Bull Connor? Do you want to be on the side of Abraham Lincoln or Jefferson Davis?"

Romney, who felt he'd proven his commitment to democracy during the Trump years, resented the implication that he was no different than the most sinister figures in his party because he opposed a single bill. If anyone in the White House had asked for his input, he fumed—*if they'd reached out even once*—he would have explained his position. He disagreed with the bill's requirement that all states allow recently released felons to vote; he also disagreed with its changes to federal campaign finance policy. But the biggest problem, in his opinion, was that it didn't address the most urgent threat of disenfranchisement facing the country. The crisis wasn't a lack of access to voting—he'd seen little evidence that supposedly racist voter ID laws actually reduced Black turnout—but in how the ballots were counted. An effective voting-rights bill would start with safeguarding against corrupt election administrators willing to toss out votes they didn't like.

Speaking from the Senate floor the following week, Romney accused Biden of recklessly framing the voting-rights bill as a make-or-break moment for American democracy. "Political overstatement and hyperbole may be relatively common, and they are often excused," he said, "but the president and some of my Democratic colleagues have ventured deep into hysteria."

In private, Romney expressed bafflement at the White House's strategy. Why give a speech vilifying the entire GOP instead of simply working behind the scenes to win over a few Senate Republicans? And why try to pass a multitrillion-dollar funding bill without even taking the temperature of Romney, Collins, and Murkowski, who'd already demonstrated their willingness to negotiate in good faith? Romney didn't know Ron Klain but he was beginning to doubt the wisdom of Biden's chief of staff. "If you had a strategy to get some Republican votes, and you were the chief of staff, you might say, 'Is there anything in this you like, Mitt?'" Romney mused to me. "President Biden is an old horse trader. He might say, 'Oh, well, how about that expansion of Interstate 15 in Utah?' But we've never heard from him."

Romney's only conclusion: "The team around him is not so inclined."

In early 2022, something changed. A few days after Supreme Court associate justice Stephen Breyer announced his retirement, Biden cold-called Romney to ask his opinion on potential replacements. Romney said he hoped Biden would tap a judge in the same mold as Breyer— smart, respectable, and someone whose views were within the normal bounds of political and constitutional thought.

Romney was under no illusions that Biden would pick a conservative. "I understand that elections have consequences," he told the president. But as long as he picked a capable jurist, he could count on Romney's vote. A few days later, after Biden honed his short list, Steve Ricchetti—the White House aide whom Romney had gotten to know while working on infrastructure—called with an update. The president was leaning toward picking Ketanji Brown Jackson, a Harvard-educated judge on the D.C. circuit who, if confirmed, would become the first Black woman to serve on the Supreme Court.

Romney winced.

"Judge Jackson is someone who would be very hard for me to get to," Romney told Ricchetti. "I've already voted no on her once."

A year earlier, when Jackson was first nominated to the federal bench, Romney had joined the majority of his caucus in opposing her, citing a ruling she'd made in 2019. The case, *Make the Road New York, et al. v. McAleenan*, challenged a Trump administration policy that allowed for the expedited removal of undocumented immigrants. Jackson ruled that the Department of Homeland Security erred when it implemented the rule. Some of Romney's Republican colleagues who'd followed the case argued that Jackson's ruling was blatantly illegal. Decisions like these made by DHS administrators were not allowed to be reviewed, they said, but Jackson had ignored that rule to pursue an activist agenda in favor of illegal immigrants. Romney chose to believe his caucus—a decision he'd later acknowledge was hasty. "I never met with her, and never really dug into it much."

Ricchetti asked Romney to keep an open mind. He agreed. When it came to presidential appointees, especially to the highest court, Romney believed a senator's job was to "advise and consent"—not to block anybody he disagreed with. "If she is a mainstream Democrat, in the mold of Justice Breyer, I'd be inclined to vote for her," Romney said. "If she's more extreme than Justice Breyer, I won't."

On February 25, Biden announced Jackson as his nominee. In his speech, the president noted that Jackson had been "enthusiastically" endorsed by Judge Thomas Griffith, a retired member of the D.C. Circuit Court and the former general counsel of Brigham Young University. Biden's invocation of a prominent Mormon judge was an unsubtle bit of outreach to Romney. (Ironically, Romney missed the reference, and wouldn't notice it until months later.)

In late March, Romney invited Jackson to his Senate office. They sat across from each other in lacquered wood chairs by the fireplace. "Let's talk about that case," Romney said. He articulated the argument as best he could that he'd heard from his GOP colleagues, explaining that the Administrative Procedure Act prevented decisions by Homeland Security administrators from being reviewed.

"Well, yes," Jackson responded. "It can't be reviewed." But, she argued, the law's language only applied to other parts of the executive branch, not the Courts. She went on to make a compelling argument that her decision was rooted in constitutional norms. "You can't have Congress write laws saying, 'This can't be reviewed by the Court,'" Jackson said. It would undermine the basic principle of checks and balances.

Romney wasn't wholly persuaded by her interpretation, but he found her argument reasonable. She was clearly not the fire-breathing extremist some of his colleagues had made her out to be. And as he weighed his vote, Romney couldn't help but take another consideration into account.

As a lifelong Mormon who'd grown up at a time when his church was still barring Black men from the priesthood, Romney was sensitive to how his vote would reflect on his faith. He still remembered sitting in the Salt Lake Mission Home in 1966 as a young missionary-in-training while Elder Bruce R. McConkie instructed them not to preach the gospel to "negroes." A missionary seated near Romney, a gasbaggy fellow with a southern accent, seemed a bit too enthusiastic about this policy. So, when the time for questions came, Romney righteously raised his hand.

"We believe that all people are equal, right?" he asked.

McConkie glared down at him from the podium. "Do you think you're equal to Jesus Christ?" he demanded. "Do you think you're equal to Joseph Smith?"

Young Elder Romney had sunken quietly into his seat that day, unprepared to spar over theology with an apostle. But in the decades since, he'd thought often about that exchange. It bothered him that he didn't give a better answer. "I wish I would have said, 'Yes, yes, we *are* all equal,'" he reflected. "'We can all achieve the highest level of glory.'" Romney's father—who faced sharp criticism at times from Mormon leaders for his support of civil rights—had always been adamant that the Church would one day lift its priesthood ban. When it finally happened in 1978, Mitt heard the news on a car radio. He pulled over and cried.

Given all this history, Romney was wary of opposing the first Black woman to be nominated to the Supreme Court. "Frankly, I hoped that I would be able to vote for her," he'd later tell me. "I know I'm going to be criticized every time she makes a decision that I disagree with. But I felt that was the right thing to do for a lot of reasons."

On April 7, Jackson was confirmed to the Supreme Court. Romney was one of three Republican Senators to vote in her favor. As Justice Jackson was introduced on the Senate floor, and as Republicans ducked their heads and darted for the exits, Romney stood and proudly applauded.

In the months that followed, an unexpected bromance blossomed between the president and the Utah senator. Biden called Romney frequently, sometimes with an agenda, sometimes just to chat.

They commiserated about the indignities of aging, and on one occasion Romney gave Biden some advice for appearing more vigorous in public. "You look old when you shuffle," Romney informed the president. "You've got to take longer strides." Later, Biden called him back and reported excitedly, "I tried it!" He'd made a point of lengthening his paces as he exited the stage after a speech, and the First Lady had taken notice. "What's gotten into *you*?" she asked him.

Eventually, Biden began identifying himself on their phone calls with a casual "This is Joe." The first time this happened, Romney, who didn't realize the two were now on a first-name basis, spent the first few seconds of the conversation assuming he was talking to Joe Manchin.

Around Easter Romney's son Craig brought his family to Washington and the senator arranged for a tour of the White House. After a few minutes with a tour guide, they turned a corner to find the president waiting to greet them with the First Lady and their German shepherd. Biden dismissed the guide and took over the tour himself, gregariously leading the Romney family around the rest of the West Wing, from the swimming pool to the bowling alley to the Grand Hall. He encouraged Romney's grandson to play the Steinway piano and posed for pictures with each child. After the tour, the youngest grandson shrugged when he was asked what he thought of Biden: "I thought he would be less old." Romney was moved by the gesture.

Neither Biden nor Romney had much interest in advertising the extent of their friendship, and few of their private interactions ever made it into the press. The president had endured a constant thrum of complaints from progressives that he wasn't doing enough to advance their agenda or hold on to Democratic control of the Senate—news of him palling around with Mitt Romney would not be received warmly by the base. Romney, meanwhile, was still considering a run for reelection in Utah, where the president's approval rating stood at around 35 percent.

Still, their relationship was an interesting window into the political moment they were living through. It was tempting to interpret the alliance as a return to a lost, halcyon era of Washington, when Ronald Reagan and Tip O'Neill could end a day of political combat with a friendly drink together. Romney liked to make self-deprecating jokes along these lines. "You got a couple of guys in their late seventies to get along that are a throwback to an earlier age. I can't imagine why." But perhaps it was more emblematic of how the stakes were changing in American politics. At a moment of rising authoritarianism at home and abroad, when the country's founding ideas of democracy and self-governance were suddenly up for debate, Romney and Biden seemed to recognize in each other a shared set of values that transcended normal politics. "He puts his principles and the good of the country over partisan politics and extremism," Biden told me. "And that matters more than ever."

One Sunday morning, Romney was sitting in church when the number for the White House appeared on his phone. He climbed over the grandkids who were sitting next to him in the pew and took the call in the foyer. It was the president.

"I just wanted to call and tell you that I admire your character and your personal honor," Biden said. "We disagree on a lot of things, but I think highly of you as a person."

Romney, taken aback by the out-of-nowhere compliment, responded in kind. "I feel the same way."

CHAPTER SEVENTEEN

"What We Used to Be"

E arly on the morning of February 24, 2022, Russian troops crossed the eastern border into Ukraine's Luhansk Oblast region for a "special military operation" that would soon mushroom into the largest armed conflict in Europe since World War II. The Western world exploded in outrage. Presidents and prime ministers condemned the invasion. Superpowers promised crippling sanctions. Major companies announced plans to pull out of Russia. As America and its allies scrambled to send missiles, guns, and ammunition to Ukraine, the international community turned its attention to the man responsible for all this upheaval: Russian president Vladimir Putin.

The question of how to deal with Putin's growing recklessness on the world stage had long been a subject of heated debate—something Romney knew better than most. For years, he'd been calling for the U.S. to take a more clear-eyed view of Putin, a former KGB agent who first rose to power in 1999, and his agenda. But Romney's warnings had failed to gain traction: during the 2012 campaign, when he identified Russia as America's number-one geopolitical foe, he'd been met with withering scorn from Democrats and pundits. In the ensuing decade, Romney had watched as one administration after another coddled, enabled, and underestimated the Russian leader. When Putin annexed

Crimea in 2014, brazenly violating international law, Obama responded with economic sanctions and a shrugging acknowledgment that the invasion was inevitable. When Putin orchestrated an operation to swing the 2016 U.S. presidential election, Trump responded by inviting the Russian ambassador to the Oval Office after he was elected. "We had not sufficiently responded to [Putin's] villainy in the past," Romney reflected. "We've downplayed those things and somehow pretended . . . everything would be fine." Now, Romney believed, Ukraine was reaping the consequences of Western inaction.

As Russia's aggression dominated headlines, Romney's 2012 comments circulated widely in the U.S. press and on social media. Former critics took turns offering mea culpas and acknowledging the senator's vindication. "There's no other way to look at it: Romney had a point," David Axelrod said on CNN, adding that Obama's debate quip about the 1980s wanting their foreign policy back had aged "obviously not well." Some noted that Romney's credibility on the issue extended beyond old campaign rhetoric: his vote to impeach Trump had famously rested on the case that the president tried to withhold military aid from Ukraine amid Russian saber rattling—all to extract political favors.

Romney struck a modest pose in media interviews: "I don't think that by any means I was the only person who saw Russia's intent." But he couldn't help but be pleased by the belated credit.

Still, there was an irony in this outpouring of validation: just as liberals were coming around to Romney's view of Russia, his own party seemed to be moving in the opposite direction. Polls showed that Republicans were significantly less likely than Democrats to support the U.S. arming Ukraine, and an array of influential conservatives was lending voice to this sentiment. The dynamic was partly a reflection of GOP voters' shifting attitudes on foreign policy. In the aftermath of 9/11, neoconservatives had enjoyed broad support for their agenda of foreign intervention and nation-building abroad, and Americans initially rallied around George W. Bush as a wartime president. But nearly two decades of bloody, futile wars in Iraq and Afghanistan had soured Americans on foreign adventurism—something Trump had masterfully exploited in 2016 when he campaigned on ending the "forever wars" and pursuing a policy of "America First."

The ascent of Trump's worldview had left old-guard Republicans with traditional views of American power feeling estranged. Bush would describe the frustration of watching his former supporters get taken in by the animating ideas of "populist rage"—first anti-trade protectionism, then anti-immigrant nativism. "Then the Republican Party lurches isolationist, and guys like me and Mitt are out on our own," he told me.

Romney strongly disagreed with those who argued that America should focus on its own problems and leave Ukraine to fend for itself. He saw America's role in the world as part of a global struggle between liberal democracy and authoritarianism. The more the U.S. withdrew, the more space was left for illiberal nations like China and Russia to exert influence.

But Romney at least understood the political arguments for isolationism. What worried him was too many Republicans were really just enthralled by Putin's authoritarianism. Mike Pompeo, Trump's former secretary of state, had spent the run-up to the invasion publicly expressing his "enormous respect" for the "very savvy" Russian leader: "He knows how to use power. We should respect that." Trump himself was extolling Putin's genius: "He's taking over a country for two dollars' worth of sanctions. I'd say that's pretty smart."

Just days before the invasion, Tucker Carlson had dedicated the lead segment of his highly rated Fox News show to an unabashed defense of Russia. "Why do Democrats want you to hate Putin?" he asked in his signature cadence of faux-curiosity. "Has he shipped every middle-class job in my town to Russia? Did he manufacture a worldwide pandemic that wrecked my business and kept me indoors for two years? Is he teaching my kids to embrace racial discrimination? Is he making fentanyl? Is he trying to snuff out Christianity? Does he eat dogs? These are fair questions and the answer to all of them is no. Vladimir Putin didn't do any of that. So why does permanent Washington hate him so much?"

To Romney, the answer was obvious: Putin was a poisoner of dissidents, a murderer of journalists, a committer of war crimes—the very archetype of an autocratic thug. But Romney suspected Carlson knew this—and that he also knew his audience. For many of his viewers, these traits were not sins, but signs of strength. According to a January 2022 poll, 62 percent of Republicans believed Putin was a stronger leader than Biden.

And Putin wasn't the only one. The growing allure of the strongman could be seen in the American right's infatuation with Viktor Orbán, the Hungarian prime minister working to transform his country into what he called an illiberal "Christian democracy." Orbán's project involved exerting political control over schools and universities, weakening judicial independence, and chipping away at press freedoms. Watchdogs and political scientists around the world had condemned Hungary's democratic backsliding. But in the U.S., conservatives— including several of Romney's Senate colleagues—celebrated Orbán for his skill at wielding state power against cultural progressives. "I recognize the liberal left doesn't like Hungary," Ron Johnson effused, "but there are so many positive things about what they're doing in that country." In 2021, Carlson had broadcast his Fox News show for an entire week from Budapest, where he interviewed Orbán and lavished his regime with glowing coverage.

Romney understood that Republican voters had been drawn to Trump's authoritarian personality. But he'd only recently begun to grasp how far his party's taste for illiberalism had spread. After four years of watching Trump mimic and cozy up to the world's most shameless dictators, many conservatives had not only been desensitized to autocracy—they'd come to value it.

"It's hard to imagine," Romney would tell me, but Carlson and his cohorts are effectively turning the GOP into "the pro-Russian, pro-authoritarian party. And that's not what we used to be."

The same month Russia invaded Ukraine, the Republican National Committee passed a resolution censuring two Republican members of Congress—Adam Kinzinger and Liz Cheney—for "participating in a Democrat-led persecution of ordinary citizens engaged in legitimate political discourse." Their sin? Joining the House committee tasked with investigating the January 6 insurrection.

Romney was astonished when he read the statement. He'd come to think of January 6 as a global inflection point. "Have you noticed how in every election around the world, the losing party now says it's rigged?" Romney told me. "We're in this competition with authoritarianism, and it's winning." For one of America's two major political parties to call a deadly riot at the Capitol "legitimate political discourse" aided the cause of the authoritarians.

Romney, indignant, decided to place a rare call to his niece, Ronna McDaniel, the daughter of Romney's brother, who was Trump's hand-picked chairwoman of the RNC. They'd maintained a cordial relationship over the years largely by never discussing politics. On this occasion, Romney asked her why she'd allowed the resolution to go forward. She assured him the statement was being misinterpreted. Romney chose to take her at her word, and the party did eventually issue a "clarification." But he suspected the people at the RNC knew the fire they were playing with. And on some level, he could sympathize—he was all too familiar with the incentive system in which they were operating.

"This is a great challenge that I've faced, and that every Republican faces," Romney would tell me. "You say, 'Okay, I better get closer to this line, or maybe step a little bit over it. If I don't, it's going to be much worse, because this other [candidate] is *really* nuts. So in order to save our party and to save our country, I've got to go a little further over the line.' And the problem is that line just keeps on getting moved, and moved, and moved."

* * *

Even as he grew more isolated from his party, Romney didn't shy away from criticizing the Biden administration's agenda. When the president announced plans to forgive student loan debt of up to $10,000—at an estimated cost of $400 billion to taxpayers—Romney pilloried the move. "Sad to see what's being done to bribe the voters," he wrote on Twitter. "Biden's student loan forgiveness plan may win Democrats some votes, but it fuels inflation, foots taxpayers with other people's financial obligations, is unfair to those who paid their own way & creates irresponsible expectations." Similarly, when Democrats passed the Inflation Reduction Act—a retooled version of the multitrillion-dollar Build Back Better bill that had been languishing in the House for a year—Romney posted a video mocking the rebranding effort. "This is not about inflation reduction," he said. "This is all about Democrats spending on things they want to spend money on."

Romney said he posted tweets like these because he knew they were read closely by a handful of senior officials in the White House. As one of the only high-profile Republicans who didn't constantly look for excuses to attack Biden, he believed they listened when he spoke.

But people close to Romney could tell he also enjoyed these moments. There was something familiar, even comforting, about squabbling with Democrats over federal spending. It was nice sometimes to just feel like a Republican again, a member of the team. Some commentators saw these moments of partisan relapse as evidence that Romney had forgotten the stakes of the moment America was facing. "After [the Trump] crisis passed, he returned to the narrow thinking of a party man," *The Atlantic*'s George Packer wrote. "It seems Romney can't bring himself to imagine that democracy is threatened not just by Trump, but by his own party." Alas, that cozy sense of partisan belonging only seemed to last so long for the senator these days before something snapped him out of it.

In early May, fourteen Senate Republicans—including Ted Cruz, Josh Hawley, Rand Paul, and Ron Johnson—introduced a bill aimed at overturning the military's vaccine mandate for service members. If passed, the law would allow troops who chose not to get the COVID vaccine to remain in service. The bill's authors gave it a gimmicky, forced-acronym title—the "Allowing Military Exemptions, Recognizing Individual Concerns About New Shots (AMERICANS) Act"— and sent it to a committee, where it looked destined for a mercifully quiet death.

But in the months that followed, Cruz and Johnson refused to let it go. When the opportunity arose to attach their proposal as an amendment to the National Defense Authorization Act—a must-pass bill that approved the military's annual budget—the senators seized it, even adding language that would reinstate, with back pay, servicemembers who'd been dishonorably discharged for refusing to follow the order.

They pitched their amendment during caucus lunches. Cruz argued the true purpose of the vaccine mandate was to purge the military of conservatives and turn it "woke." Mike Lee claimed the military was unjustly forcing religious service members to violate their beliefs by forcing them to get vaccinated. At one point, Ron Johnson began trotting out his go-to Big Pharma conspiracy theories, and Romney was relieved to see several of his colleagues roll their eyes.

Romney found their arguments wholly unpersuasive. Once, over dinner, he'd asked General Mark Milley about the military's vaccine policy, and Milley had offered a simple explanation: "We don't want soldiers in the hospital. We need them on the battlefield." That was good enough for the senator—was it really his place to overrule a general?

During one of the last meetings before the vote, Romney stood to ask a question. "I've not been in the military," he said. "So, I'd like to know what the implications would be of overturning a decision by the generals like this." Wouldn't reinstating thousands of dishonorably discharged service members through legislation risk undermining the chain of command?

A spirited discussion followed. One senator, who'd served in the Iraq War, seconded Romney's concern: "I don't like the vaccine mandate, but we can't have members of the military feel like they don't have to obey a direct order." Others chimed in with their own skepticism of the amendment.

By the time they walked onto the Senate floor to vote, Romney was hopeful that most of his colleagues had come to their senses. But when the final tally was in, only three Republicans had joined him in opposing the amendment, along with every Democrat—enough to assure its defeat, but an embarrassing indictment of his caucus, Romney thought. How could Republicans claim to be the party of "law and order," or the party of the troops, when they were willing to so casually overrule military leaders?

Seeing him seethe, one of his GOP colleagues tried feebly to explain his vote. "These people legitimately felt like getting the vaccine would hurt their health," the colleague said.

"So would charging a machine gun nest," Romney replied. "What happens when service members feel they can disobey that order, too?"

For reasons Romney couldn't quite figure out, this little episode continued to gnaw at him. Days later he was still stewing. He tried to put himself in the position of his normal, non-crazy Republican colleagues— the ones that had rolled their eyes at Johnson's conspiracizing—to figure out how they'd justify such a stupid vote. "My guess is," he speculated, "there's some who'd say, 'This thing's not going to pass anyway.'" They could vote to signal solidarity with anti-vax voters while knowing there was no actual risk of overturning the vaccine mandate. *What's the harm in humoring them?*

Romney, of all people, knew the power of such rationalizations. But he also knew the pandering came with a cost. The elected leaders of his party had forgotten how to say no to their base. They'd forgotten how to do unpopular things simply because they were right. That muscle had atrophied—and Romney believed voters would notice sooner or later.

"If you keep on doing things that you know are wrong but politically expedient," Romney predicted, "you can expect over time that, instead of people rushing to support all the wonderful things they agreed with that you did, they'll turn away from you. Because they know you have no character."

On May 24, 2002, an eighteen-year-old man entered Robb Elementary School in Uvalde, Texas, with an AR-15 rifle and fatally shot nineteen children and two teachers. He was inside the school for an hour before police finally killed him. It was the deadliest school shooting the U.S. had seen in a decade. Most of the victims were fourth-graders.

Romney was coming out of a meeting that day when his chief of staff, Liz Johnson, shoved her phone into his hands. The images on the screen were grimly familiar—flashing police sirens, haphazard caution tape, sobbing parents. The national discourse was entering into the same bitter cycle it always went through after a mass shooting—shock, then sorrow, then recriminations and pleas that elected officials do *something* to stop this.

Like most Americans, Romney had lived through many—far too many—of these news cycles. But he was surprised by how different it felt this time. "When you're not in the Senate, you say to yourself, *Someone ought to do something about that.* When you're in the Senate, it's like *Okay, one of us ought to do something about that.*"

Listening to his fellow Republicans trot out all the usual attempts to deflect blame from guns, Romney was unmoved. "The old arguments ring a little hollow," he'd tell me. *We have a mental health crisis.* "Well, every country has mental health issues, and we're not going to eliminate all the crazy people and all the angry people." *We should beef up security in schools.* "A good idea, but not sufficient"—elementary schools weren't going to become prisons, and former students would always be able to find a way in.

In the days after the shooting, a bipartisan group of senators began working on a framework for a bill that would restrict access to assault-style weapons by expanding background checks and increasing wait periods for people under twenty-one. Thom Tillis and John Cornyn were leading the effort on the Republican side, with Chris Murphy and Kyrsten Sinema representing the Democrats. Romney told them he supported their effort, but decided not to join the group at first, feeling he had little to offer in terms of bringing along NRA Republicans.

Romney had never had much credibility with conservatives when it came to the Second Amendment. As governor of Massachusetts, he'd signed an assault-weapons ban into law. And despite his widely mocked claim as a presidential candidate that he liked to hunt "small varmints," the truth was that he didn't much care for the pastime. (The last time he hunted was in 2015, when he joined a friend on an elk-hunting trip. After two days of standing around in the cold without firing a single shot, Romney returned home and wrote in his journal, "Why do people do this?")

All of this made it especially surreal when, in the days after the Uvalde shooting, some gun-control activists tried to cast Romney as an NRA stooge. In a series viral tweets citing the Brady Campaign to Prevent Gun Violence, Romney was identified as the senator who'd received the most donations from the NRA: $13 million. The accusation was misleading; Romney had not taken any money from the NRA when he ran for Senate. The figure came from 2012, when the organization spent millions to defeat Barack Obama's reelection. Still, his office was flooded with phone calls from angry people demanding that he stop acting as a puppet for the gun lobby. (Romney, incensed by the slander, briefly entertained suing the Brady Campaign, before thinking better of it.)

When Romney did finally join the bipartisan group, he was impressed by what Murphy and the others had come up with. "Chris was very realistic," Romney said. "He wasn't trying to get a bill that wouldn't pass." On more than one occasion, after a horrific shooting, Senate Democrats had put forward partisan "messaging bills" that proposed dramatically overhauling gun laws in a way they knew no Republican would support. This time, both sides had come to the table in good faith. In addition to notching up background checks for young people, the bill made it illegal for anyone convicted of domestic abuse to own a gun, and incentivized states to enact "red flag laws" designed to prevent individuals who were deemed dangerous from purchasing firearms. Romney knew the bill wouldn't solve the whole problem, but he sincerely believed it would save lives without infringing on the Second Amendment.

In early June, Cornyn introduced the bill to his Republican colleagues at a caucus meeting and opened the floor for discussion. Over the next hour, the senators took turns grumbling about the fact that they were being forced to vote on such a divisive bill in an election year. Ron Johnson protested that it was a "lose-lose" for his campaign. Mike Lee complained that he was in a tight race and would rather not be made to take a "bad vote." As the conversation continued in this vein, Romney's agitation mounted. Afterward, he reported to his staff that every single point raised by his colleagues focused on the bill's implications on the midterm elections—not on its substance, or whether it would prevent future gun deaths.

"I have come to recognize that the overwhelming consideration in how people vote is whether it will help or hurt their reelection prospects," he'd tell me later. "Amazing that a democracy can function like this."

As the 2022 midterms approached, Romney paid close attention to the Senate races, searching for signs of how his caucus might change in the coming years. The field did not make him optimistic. Trump, determined to maintain his stranglehold on the GOP, had waded into races across the country to endorse a sordid cast of kooks and con men made in his own image. In Georgia, the Republicans had put forward Herschel Walker, a former NFL star whose ex-wife had accused him of stalking and violent threats. ("Pointing a gun at [your] wife's head . . . would have normally been disqualifying," Romney noted. "I find it strange that our voters don't seem to be bothered by it.") In New

Hampshire, the nominee was Don Bolduc, a retired army brigadier general who'd once claimed the COVID-19 vaccine was part of a plot by Bill Gates to inject people with microchips. ("He's said some very unusual things," Romney deadpanned.)

Perhaps most disconcerting was J. D. Vance, the thirty-seven-year-old Republican candidate for Senate in Ohio. "I don't know that I can disrespect someone more than J. D. Vance," Romney told me. They'd first met years earlier after he read Vance's bestselling memoir, *Hillbilly Elegy*. Romney was so impressed with the book that he hosted the author at his annual Park City summit in 2018. Vance, who grew up in a poor, dysfunctional family in Appalachia and went on to graduate from Yale Law School, had seemed bright and thoughtful, with interesting ideas about how Republicans could court the white working class without indulging in toxic Trumpism. Then, in 2021, Vance decided he wanted to run for Senate, and reinvented his entire persona overnight. Suddenly, he was railing against the "childless left" and denouncing Indigenous Peoples' Day as "a fake holiday" and accusing Biden of manufacturing the opioid crisis "to punish people who didn't vote for him." The speed of the MAGA makeover was jarring.

"I do wonder, how do you make that decision?" Romney mused as he watched Vance degrade himself on the campaign trail that summer. "How can you go over a line so stark as that—and for what?" Romney wished he could grab Vance by the shoulders and scream: *This is not worth it!* "It's not like you're going to be famous and powerful because you became a United States senator. It's like, really? You sell yourself so cheap?" The prospect of having Vance hang around the caucus made Romney uncomfortable. "How do you sit next to him at lunch?"

There was one race, however, that Romney was following more closely than any other. His fellow Utah senator, Mike Lee, was up for reelection, facing off against Evan McMullin, a moderate independent. Normally, an incumbent Republican would barely have to open his mouth to win in Utah. But Lee was unusually unpopular. A former constitutional lawyer, he had ridden the 2010 Tea Party wave into the

Senate, where he made a name for himself as a rabble-rousing wing-man to Ted Cruz. Within the local Utah establishment, many viewed Lee as a showboating obstructionist whose penchant for provocation routinely embarrassed his home state (and its dominant religion). But the Trump years were especially bad for his reputation.

After initially opposing Trump in 2016, the senator pivoted abruptly, distinguishing himself as one of Trump's most loyal lackeys. During the 2020 campaign, he gave a notorious speech comparing Trump to Captain Moroni, a beloved hero in the Book of Mormon, and had to apologize amid a backlash from Latter-day Saints who found the comparison blasphemous. Then, in the aftermath of January 6, more than sixty leaked text messages between Lee and White House chief of staff Mark Meadows showed the senator enthusiastically assisting Trump's plot to overturn the results of the election. In one text, Lee claimed to be spending "14 hours a day" on the effort.

By 2022, anti-Lee voters in Utah were fed up enough to attempt an unprecedented experiment. Utah Democrats, who hadn't won a state-wide race since 1996, chose not to field a candidate of their own and instead endorsed McMullin's independent bid. Early polls suggested McMullin had an outside shot at unseating Lee if he could unite a coalition of Democrats, independents, and Trump-averse Republicans.

Romney thought it was a long shot—in private, he frequently predicted that Lee would win by ten points—but he had no interest in wading into the race. He knew he'd be expected to endorse the Republican incumbent, but he couldn't bring himself to do it. In March, he told *Politico* that he planned to stay neutral because both candidates were "friends." It was a bit of a stretch. Romney had only met McMullin a handful of times, and while he knew Lee better, their relationship was little more than cordial. But it was a tidy way for him to stay on the sidelines, and he figured Lee would let it go.

He figured wrong. As Election Day neared, and the polls stayed too close for comfort, the National Republican Senatorial Committee was forced to spend its scarce resources protecting a seat that was supposed to be in the bag. Party leaders began lobbying Romney behind the scenes to endorse Lee and bring an end to the race. Romney refused.

Then, a few weeks before the election, Lee appeared on Tucker Carlson's show to call out Romney's lack of support. The host and the senator worked as a tag team, with the former ridiculing Romney and the latter begging for his endorsement.

"This is a guy, Pierre Delecto, who marched with Black Lives Matter, which hates the nuclear family and endorsed riots—I think he's gone insane!" Carlson said.

"It's noteworthy here that all forty-eight of my other Republican colleagues are on board with me," Lee said.

At one point, Lee looked straight at the camera to address Romney directly. "Please get on board," he pleaded. "Help me win reelection. Help us do that. You can get your entire family to donate to me, through LeeForSenate-dot-com."

Romney was confused by the desperate spectacle. *Why would Mike want to draw attention to this?* More than that, though, he was galled by the presumption that he should automatically support Lee, no questions asked. Romney had tried to be civilized and discreet about his reasons for withholding support, but now he was annoyed. When people in their overlapping circles would bring it up with Romney, he'd pointedly remind them that his colleague, a supposedly strict constitutionalist, had spent months trying to help a president remain in power despite losing his election. Perhaps, Romney speculated, Lee had foolishly convinced himself that his fealty would be rewarded by Trump with an appointment to the Supreme Court. In any case, Romney would insist, it should hardly come as a shock that he's wary of lending his support to Lee.

Lee had not only refused to work with Romney on any of the major bills he helped draft—he routinely went out of his way to attack them. When Romney helped negotiate a bill designed to make the U.S. tech sector more competitive with China, Lee called the final product "foolish." When Romney backed the bipartisan post-Uvalde gun control bill, Lee called it "the legislative equivalent of running through a congested intersection with our eyes closed."

To Romney, the contrast in their approaches was best illustrated during the infrastructure negotiations. In August, when it seemed the bill was finally done, Romney discovered that funding for a water project in Utah had been omitted at the last minute. Determined to deliver the project for his state, Romney insisted on reopening negotiations so they could put the language back into the bill. While he and his colleagues scrambled to fix the problem before the Senate's August recess, Mike Lee was nowhere to be found. But he reappeared on Sunday night when the final text of it was revealed to deliver an hour-long speech condemning the bill as an "orgiastic convulsion of federal spending."

When Election Day arrived, Lee won by about ten points—just as Romney had predicted. But the episode did lasting damage to their relationship. Romney chafed at how Lee had used him as a punching bag to rile up his right-wing base. And in ungenerous moments, Romney wondered aloud if his colleague had simply acted out of resentment. Though Lee was technically Utah's senior senator, few in the state—or the Senate—thought of him that way. As a former presidential nominee, Romney had all the name recognition and the gravitas. He was Mitch McConnell's first call on any Utah-related issue, and everything he said seemed to attract national media coverage. At six foot two, he even physically towered over his colleague. "Maybe," Romney mused to one confidant, "he just can't stand being in my shadow."

Republicans severely underperformed in the 2022 midterms, with many of Trump's hand-picked candidates blowing winnable races. And Romney realized quickly that he wouldn't be getting much done in the 118th Congress. The House of Representatives, now narrowly under GOP control, appeared ungovernable. It took Kevin McCarthy five days of frantic negotiations with various right-wing factions of his conference just to get himself confirmed speaker—and by the time they finally handed him the gavel, there was little question as to who was leading whom. "You know, Nancy Pelosi was far from my hero, but boy, she knew how to whip her caucus into voting for what she wanted," Romney said, a bit wistfully, as the episode unfolded. In the Senate, meanwhile, many of the centrist dealmakers with whom Romney had bonded were gone or on their way out. His days of working on big, important bipartisan bills were likely over—and the prospect of another Senate term looked much less attractive.

By the spring of 2023, Romney had privately made it known to his inner circle that he very likely wouldn't run again. He'd been leaning this way for at least a year but had kept it to himself. There were practical reasons for the coyness: He didn't want to start hemorrhaging staffers or descend into lame-duck irrelevance. But some close to Romney wondered if he was simply being stubborn. Several prominent Republicans in Utah were already lining up to run for his seat—some more publicly than others—and the talk in political circles was that he'd struggle to win another Republican primary. Romney couldn't stand the idea that he might have to be put out to pasture. He wanted to retire on his own terms and was adamant that the only barrier to his reelection was a lack of desire. "I've invested a lot of money already in my political fortunes," he told me, "and if I needed to do so again to win the primary, I would."

Romney was proud of his service in the Senate. When he looked at the to-do list he'd written for himself when he first got into office, he was heartened to see that he'd made progress on most of the issues he identified. But he was now at an age when he had to ruthlessly guard his time—and there were opportunity costs to spending another term in the Senate. His father had lived longer than any Romney man on record, passing away at eighty-eight. Mitt had turned seventy-six in March. The way he saw it, he had twelve more years at most. "Do I want to spend eight of the twelve years I have left sitting here and not getting anything done?" he mused. He still had books he wanted to write; still dreamed of teaching. Most important, he wanted to spend time with Ann while they were both still healthy.

Still, Romney wasn't ready to walk away from politics completely, not yet. Trump was running for president again, after all. The crisis wasn't over. And as Romney watched the 2024 race take shape, he was alarmed to see many of the same dynamics that had enabled Trump's rise to power in 2016. A vast and fractured GOP primary field threatened to split the anti-Trump vote, and the prospective candidates all seemed unwilling or unequipped to prosecute the former president.

Nikki Haley, the former governor of South Carolina and ambassador to the United Nations, had always impressed Romney. But since throwing her hat in the ring, she'd been reluctant to criticize the ex-president, which Romney felt boded poorly: "I listened to Nikki Haley on one of the Sunday shows that [asked], 'Is there anything you'd do differently than Donald Trump?' [She] was like, *Oh, he's marvelous! He's wonderful!* I mean, how do you run against him?" Mike Pence was exploring a bid, but Romney was skeptical that Trump-weary voters would get behind a guy who'd served as "a lap dog to Trump for four years." He liked Tim Scott, a Black Republican senator from South Carolina with a talent for soaring, optimistic rhetoric, and he thought it would be a hoot to watch another bridge-and-tunnel loudmouth like Chris Christie tangle with Trump on the debate stage. But he wasn't sure any of them were serious threats to take down the front-runner.

Then there was Ron DeSantis. The Florida governor had become Fox News–famous for his theatrical resistance to facemasks and vaccine mandates during the pandemic, and for his war on what he called "woke indoctrination." Romney had never met DeSantis, but he often spent weekends with Ann in Palm Beach, where the governor was a fixture on the local news. Romney noted that DeSantis's schtick was harder to take in large doses than in the short, viral clips that circulated on social media. "There's just no warmth at all," Romney observed. "It's very stark." When photos of DeSantis posing for selfies in Iowa hit the internet, Romney observed, "He looks like he's got a toothache."

Romney wanted to like the governor, as he seemed like the GOP's best shot at keeping Trump from the nomination. DeSantis's military service suggested genuine patriotism, and his marriage and personal life appeared to be without scandal. When it came to one quality Romney especially valued—intelligence—there was no comparison: "He's much smarter than Trump." And yet, Romney couldn't escape the sense that DeSantis possessed many of the same "odious qualities" that defined the former president. The governor's penchant for culture-war stunts—such as rounding up illegal immigrants and flying them to Martha's Vineyard—was repellant. And his crusade to punish the Walt Disney Corporation for its liberal stance on LGBTQ issues reeked of government overreach. Romney also acknowledged that DeSantis's intelligence could be a double-edged sword. "You might point out, 'Mitt, DeSantis is real smart—do you want an authoritarian who's smart or one who's not smart?'" he told me. "I realize there's a peril to having someone who's smart and pulling in a direction that's danger-ous." When it came down to it, though, Romney still saw Trump as a unique threat to America—and if keeping him out of the White House meant helping someone like DeSantis, the choice was a no-brainer. "I don't think he would be as damaging to the Republic."

Of course, there was one more potential candidate who could shake up the 2024 presidential race: Mitt Romney. For months, people in his orbit—most vocally, his son Josh—had been urging him to embark on one last run for president, this time as an independent. The goal wouldn't be to win—Romney knew that was impossible—but to mount a kind of protest against the terrible options offered by the two-party system. He also wanted to ensure that someone on the stage was effectively holding Trump to account. "I was afraid that Biden, in his advanced years, would be incapable of making the argument," he told me.

The prospect was tempting. Romney relished the idea of running a presidential campaign in which he simply said whatever he thought, without regard to political consequences. "I must admit, I'd love being on the stage with Donald Trump . . . and just saying, 'That's stupid. Why are you saying that?'" He nursed a particular fantasy in which he devoted an entire debate to asking Trump to explain why, in the early weeks of the pandemic, he'd suggested that Americans inject bleach as a treatment for COVID-19. To Romney, this comment represented the apotheosis of the former president's idiocy, and it still bothered him that the country had simply laughed at it and moved on. "Every time Donald Trump makes a strong argument, I'd say, 'Remind me again about the Clorox," Romney told me. "Every now and then, I would cough and go *Clorox*."

One afternoon in late January, during a lull in between meetings, Romney sat down in his Senate office and started typing out the planks of his dream campaign platform. Within twenty minutes, he had seventeen bullet points. The list was an idiosyncratic mix of traditionally conservative ideas (implementing work requirements for federal welfare recipients), traditionally liberal ones (raising the minimum wage and linking it to inflation), and a smattering of proposals that neither party would touch. The fourth bullet point read simply, "Stop the bribes," followed by a list of government expenditures to eliminate, including farm subsidies, ethanol subsidies, and student loan forgiveness.

For a few weeks that winter, Romney seemed determined to go through with it, this maximally disruptive, personally cathartic primal scream of a presidential campaign. He riffed about ideal running mates (Kyrsten Sinema was high on the list) and thought about which donor friends he might ask to back him.

But when Romney presented the idea to his old friend and adviser Stuart Stevens, it was not well received. Stevens argued that Romney would mostly end up siphoning off votes from the Democratic nominee and ensuring a Trump victory. Another adviser concurred: "The only way you could weaken Donald Trump is if you had David Duke or someone like him as an independent."

So, Romney shelved the kamikaze campaign and went back to the drawing board. Whatever his next move, he wouldn't be bound by party loyalty. Romney had never felt more distant from the GOP's base than he did now. None of his five sons identified as Republicans anymore, according to Ann, and he worried that the party was "shedding thoughtful people, considerate people, people who love others" at an unsustainable rate. What remained was a core of "angry, resentful individuals" and a collection of institutions intent on keeping them that way. He could no longer stomach most of the conservative media. The fights they picked, the targets they chose—all of it seemed so alien. One day the bogeyman would be a U.S. Olympian struggling with mental health, the next an evangelical writer who'd defended pluralism as an American value. "It's almost like you take what is praiseworthy and of good report and you say, 'Let's attack that!'" Romney said. "I don't recognize my party in some respects," he added later. "The things that people say in my party—it's like, how can I even associate myself with a party that's doing some of those things and saying some of those things?"

Maybe he wouldn't need to for long. In April, Romney privately approached Joe Manchin with his latest idea: building a new political party. They'd talked about the prospect before, but it was always hypothetical. Now, Romney wanted to make it real. The goal of the yet-unnamed party (working slogan: "Stop the Stupid") would be to promote the kind of centrist policies their Senate gang had championed. Manchin was himself thinking of running for president as an independent, and Romney tried to convince him this was the better play. Instead of putting forward their own doomed candidate in 2024, their party would gather a contingent of like-minded donors and pledge their support to the candidate who came closest to aligning with their agenda. "We'd say, 'This party's going to endorse whichever party's nominee isn't stupid,'" Romney said.

He acknowledged that attracting a critical mass of voters to a new party would be a long-term project. But in the meantime, Romney argued, it could serve as a countervailing force to the polarization he believed was pulling the Republican and Democratic leaders toward their respective fringes. "Right now, you've got Bernie and Elizabeth (Warren) saying, 'We got you elected!' So [Biden] has to do their bidding to a certain degree." But if Biden were reelected with the support of a Romney-Manchin coalition, the president would feel pressure to make good on his promises to them as well. Romney hoped he could win Manchin over to this vision, but if he didn't, he planned to take the idea himself to No Labels, a nonpartisan organization that promotes centrist policies and candidates.

There was something strange about all this restless plotting, a manic quality that seemed out of character for the measured management consultant. As a rule, septuagenarian senators on the verge of retirement don't spend their spare time earnestly game-planning long-shot schemes to save democracy. But Romney couldn't just stop. He felt, as ever, that he had something unique to offer—that if he didn't solve this problem himself, well, who would? This meld of moral obligation and personal hubris was, in some ways, Romney's defining trait. It was why, when so many fellow Republican statesmen were content to fade into the background of American life as their party left them behind, Romney insisted on clawing his way back into the fray. It was why he spent years running for president despite finding almost everything about the process unpleasant, and why he left Bain at the height of its success, with hundreds of millions of dollars still on the table, to take over the Olympics. When he was feeling sentimental, he attributed this impulse to the "Romney obligation," and talked about the sense of duty and public service he'd inherited from his father. When he was in a more introspective mood, he talked about the surge of adrenaline he felt when he rushed toward emergencies and catastrophes. Both, of course, were true.

The new-party plan was far from foolproof, and even Romney acknowledged that he might ultimately be talked out of it. "Maybe someone's going to tell me, 'That's the stupidest thing in the world,' and I'm going to be convinced they're right," he said. "But this is an idea."

If it didn't pan out, he'd come up with another. He always did.

Epilogue

Every summer, Mitt Romney gathers his entire family at their Edenic compound on the shores of New Hampshire's Lake Winnipesaukee. His sons are middle-aged now and spread across the country—Massachusetts, Utah, California—and even many of the grandkids are grown. When Romney first tried retirement, after losing his second presidential bid, he imagined spending his days with his family, teaching, mentoring, passing along wisdom to the next generations. He quickly realized this was a fantasy. They had their own lives; no one wanted him incessantly hovering. Still, Romney has made it understood that the family reunion at "Winnie" is mandatory. Craig, his youngest, calls it "inheritance week."

I arrive on a summer afternoon. After winding down a private driveway marked with a faux street sign that says "Romney Way," I'm greeted by Mitt, in swim trunks, and Ann, in a tank top. As they lead me on a tour of the twelve-acre grounds, Mitt insists that they didn't *set out* to build a Kennedyesque compound. It started with a six-bedroom summer "cottage," purchased in 1997, that they planned to use for family getaways. But as their progeny multiplied, the house started to feel cramped. After a brutal stomach bug in the summer of 2014 tore through the family, they decided it was time to spread out.

And so, the expansion began: in 2016 Tagg built his own ten-bedroom, ten-bath house just up the hill from his parents, which Mitt took to calling the "Tagg Mahal," and shortly thereafter, a spacious guesthouse was added to the property. Complete with a tennis court, a volleyball pit, and a boathouse containing (by my count) seven boats, the spread is estimated to be worth at least $14 million.

Romney, who never saw the point of private jets or yachts, who buys his suits off the rack and still comparison shops for vacuum cleaners, tells me these are the luxuries he likes to spend his money on—the things he can enjoy with his family.

Romney is an "easy grandparent," his son Matt tells me. The boys like to joke about how the same man who used to drag them out of bed on Saturday mornings to do yard work now tells the grandkids not to bother with the dishes and slips them money for sodas when their parents aren't looking. "I'm like, oh, that's pretty rich coming from you!" Matt says. The grandkids, who call him "Papa," respond by messing with him relentlessly. At one point, Romney takes a gaggle of grandkids out wakeboarding and becomes so engrossed in telling me about the John D. Rockefeller biography he's been reading that he doesn't realize two of his grandkids have pushed a third off the back of the boat. By the time Romney notices, the marooned kid is bobbing in the water several hundred yards off.

"*Guys*," Romney grumbles, turning the boat around as the perpetrators double over in laughter.

Watching Romney in this setting, I can't help but think of a certain former president, cocooned in his Palm Beach Xanadu with his third wife, fuming over something he saw on cable news, walking into ballrooms to bask in the applause of strangers. Researchers who study the effects of power on the brain have found that it can be enormously damaging. Powerful people tend to become more impulsive and less empathetic; the neural process that enables them to simulate others' experiences ceases to function. To mitigate these effects, experts say, it's essential to have a "toe-holder" in your life—someone to keep you grounded and admonish you when necessary. Romney has built a life full of toe-holders, chief among them Ann—the girl he fell in love with sixty years ago, the woman whose approval he still desperately courts. "She's his biggest supporter, but she'll also challenge him," says Bob White, an old friend of Mitt's.

After a dinner of sweet potato burritos and strawberry pie under the pergola—all forty Romneys sitting shoulder to shoulder at a collection of long picnic tables—the adults start to clean up, and I join Mitt and Ann on a nearby patio overlooking the glistening lake. The sun is beginning to set, giving everything a soft, orange hew.

Romney tells me he's been thinking about a question I asked him when we first started meeting. I wanted to know if he thought there were any lessons in his story that future political leaders might take. Romney is uncomfortable—or at least feigns discomfort—with the idea of himself as a moral exemplar. He knows all too well that no one emerges from a life in politics free of regret. These days, when he speaks to student groups, his most frequent piece of advice is to not sacrifice their integrity at the altar of ambition. "It's not worth it," he tells them. "Believe me."

It occurs to me that in a setting like this, the stakes of life might seem a little lower than they do for regular people. Idealistically risking one's political career might not feel like quite such a big deal when you get to keep all of *this*. At the same time, I can also imagine how easy it would be to look out the window each morning and feel like Providence is shining down on you regardless of what choices you make. The breathtaking views, the beautiful family—*Can these really be the fruits of a poorly lived life?* That Romney was able to resist the temptation of complacency inherent in such trappings and make a late-in-life attempt at political repentance seems like a minor miracle.

Still, the reckoning hasn't always been smooth. In our two years of interviews, Romney's efforts to process his party's evolution—and his own—were halting and messy. He'd seem to confess complicity in one meeting, then walk it back in the next. He'd get angry and then cool off. Some days he worried he was being too harsh to certain fellow Republicans, who weren't entirely bad after all—no one ever is. Later, after reading a draft of this book, he will complain that I made too much of his transformation in the Trump years, and that I dwelled too much on the self-serving rationalizations he employed earlier in his career. Those lapses, he argued, have been the exceptions in his life, not the rule, and they're hardly unique to him. Fair enough. Romney is the ultimate authority on how often he's deferred to his better angels. I wouldn't presume to know better than him.

But his rationalizations fascinate me *because* they're so common in Washington. The path to this fraught moment in American history is paved with compromises made for political advantage that didn't seem like compromises at the time. What makes Romney unusual as a political figure is not his capacity for self-justification but the fact that he recognized it in himself and worked to guard against it. I once asked him if he would have taken the same lonely, principled vote to convict Trump if he'd been put in the same position thirty years earlier. "I don't know the answer to that," he reflected. "I think I recognize now my capacity to rationalize decisions that are in my self-interest. And I don't know that I recognized that to the same degree back then."

At a moment when courage is in vanishingly short supply in politics, it's worth considering what made Romney finally choose to do the right thing instead of the convenient one—and whether the phenomenon can be replicated.

Romney tells me he thinks the key is getting political leaders to think more deeply—and more often—about how they'll be remembered when they're gone. You can rationalize anything when the only thought is how it will play in the next election. Start thinking about how it will look in your obituary, and the calculation changes.

This gets easier with age, of course. Mortality has a way of concentrating the mind. The trick is compelling politicians to think in these terms when they're still young and feel immortal.

For Romney, family has made the difference. "How do I look at my life?" he says. "I look at my relationships with my family, but also my descendants, and what I leave for them." This idea is rooted deep in the doctrines of his faith. He thinks seriously about what he owes to his ancestors and posterity; feels a duty to do well by their shared name. He mentions a Republican colleague who spent the Trump years conspicuously cozying up to the president to the severe detriment of his once-sterling reputation. "He isn't married. He doesn't have any kids," Romney says. "I don't know that he spends a lot of time thinking about legacy."

One Christmas, years ago, his daughter-in-law Andelynne gave him a copy of *The New York Times Book of the Dead*, a collection of obituaries that had run in the newspaper throughout its history. "She knows I'm fascinated with this stuff," he says. Among the hundreds of obituaries—covering celebrities, presidents, entrepreneurs, and civil rights leaders—he looked for his dad's. To Mitt, no man loomed larger in history than George Romney. He was an icon, a legend, the embodiment of integrity in public service. But George's entry was nowhere to be found.

It bothered him at first. But eventually he made peace with it.

"Even if history only writes one line about you," he tells me, "you'd like it to be a good line."

Author's Note

This book is based on more than forty-five interviews that I conducted with Mitt Romney between March 2021 and May 2023, as well as hundreds of pages of his personal journals and thousands of emails and text messages from his private correspondence. This level of access and disclosure is virtually unprecedented from a high-profile political leader who's still in office, and I will always be grateful to Romney for choosing to be so forthcoming. But he's not the only source for this book. Whenever possible, I worked to corroborate his memories with contemporaneous notes, press accounts, and video footage. I also interviewed his wife and sons, friends, colleagues, current and former advisers, and people who have known and worked with him throughout his life, many of whom shared with me their own correspondence and notes. In some sections involving his Senate colleagues, Romney shared stories without naming his interlocutors, and I went on to identify them through my own independent reporting. A detailed list of sources can be found in the endnotes.

I owe a debt of gratitude to many people who made this book possible. First, the team at Scribner: Rick Horgan, whose wisdom and insight sharpened my thinking and prose; Sophie Guimares, who expertly guided me through the publishing process; Paul Samuelson, Victor Hendrickson, Laura Wise, Stu Smith, and of course Nan Graham and Colin Harrison all contributed their considerable talents and support.

Samuel Benson, my tireless and exceptionally talented research assistant, transcribed interviews, tracked down sources, helped me outline each chapter, and substantially improved the book with his research and reporting. He'll be a star. From March to May 2023, Sam worked with Ena Alvarado to fact-check this book; any remaining errors are my fault.

My agents, Matt Latimer and Keith Urbahn, not only saw my vision for this book and got it sold, they also read drafts, offered notes, and strategized to get the final product in front of the widest possible audience of readers. Sheri Dew encouraged this project at a crucial moment and offered valuable advice on how to proceed. Katherine Miller, my old editor and friend, reprised both roles as she read the still-in-progress manuscript and helped me figure out what I was trying to say (and what I wasn't). My brilliant bosses at *The Atlantic*—Jeffrey Goldberg, Denise Wills, Yoni Applebaum, Adrienne LaFrance, Margy Slattery, and Peter Lattman—were patient and supportive throughout the entire process, and I'm grateful to them, as well as Laurene Powell Jobs and David Bradley, for making America's best magazine and holding a spot for me there. My reporting and writing for *The Atlantic* informs sections of this book.

Many people agreed to be interviewed for this book, in some cases repeatedly and at great length. There are too many to list them all here, but I want to acknowledge a few—Matt Waldrip, Beth Myers, Spencer Zwick, Stuart Stevens, Paul Ryan, Bob White, Joe Manchin, Kyrsten Sinema, Susan Collins, Rob Portman, George W. Bush, and Joe Biden. Liz Johnson dedicated an enormous amount of time and energy to this project, and Chris Marroletti and Meagan Shepherd made sure I had the time with Romney I needed.

I want to thank the many diligent journalists who've covered Romney over the years, in Massachusetts, Utah, Washington, and on the campaign trail. I should also acknowledge Michael Kranish and Scott Helman, whose 2012 biography *The Real Romney* was an important resource for me as I wrote this one. And I have to thank Ben Smith for teaching me how to cover a campaign.

I would not have become a writer without the relentless encouragement of my incredible parents, David and Carol. I hope my own kids feel as loved and supported as I did growing up. I'm also grateful to my in-laws, Kevin and Sue, for blessing their daughter's marriage to an aspiring reporter in 2009, a year when prospects for aspiring reporters were in short supply.

Like every other good thing in my life, my wife Annie deserves most of the credit for this book. Her early enthusiasm for the idea gave me the confidence to pursue it, and her inexhaustible support gave me the time and space to finish it. She read pages, gave feedback, imposed deadlines, and spent countless hours listening to me talk through various questions related to my writing. In the midst of it all, she oversaw a home renovation, kept our finances organized, ran the ward Primary program, raised our three kids, and prepared to give birth to a fourth. Nothing makes me happier than spending time with her, Ellis, Alden, Margot, and Hewitt.

Finally, I want to express my gratitude to the Romney family—to Ann for her thoughtfulness and hospitality; to Tagg, Josh, Matt, Craig, and Ben for allowing me a glimpse into their lives; to their spouses and kids for their grace when a biographer crashed their family reunion; and finally, to Mitt, who entered this process in a spirit of honesty, good faith, and openness that's rare to find in politics. I first started covering Romney in 2012, when he was running for president and I was the lone Mormon reporter on the campaign press bus. Our shared faith didn't make me many friends among his consultants, who were wary of my stories probing his religious life, nor did it win me any access to the candidate. He never gave me an interview that year. But when, nearly a decade later, I approached him about writing this book, he said that, upon reflection, he considered it an advantage that I "get the Mormon thing." (The Church of Jesus Christ of Latter-day Saints has in recent years asked that people stop using "Mormon" as a nickname for its teachings and members. I use the term in this book because Romney uses it.) Romney and I don't agree on everything, including some of the contents of this book. But I've worked hard to understand him. I hope he feels I've done his story justice.

Notes

PROLOGUE

Unless otherwise indicated, Mitt Romney's account of January 6 (and the preceding days)—as well as all firsthand quotes—come from an interview with the author conducted on May 18, 2021. (Romney is hereafter referred to as "MR.")

1   *"So much is"*: MR, interview, June 21, 2021.

2   *"Could you give me"*: Angus King, text message to MR, January 2, 2021.

2   *Romney sends his text*: MR, text message to Mitch McConnell, January 2, 2021.

4   *Trump is tweeting*: "Tweets of January 6, 2021," American Presidency Project, January 6, 2021, https://www.presidency.ucsb.edu/documents/tweets-january-6-2021.

5   *When Romney encounters*: Jordan Carney, "Romney on Georgia: Trump Calling Election Rigged 'Not a Great Way to Turn out Your Voters,'" *The Hill*, January 6, 2021.

5   *"Nearly half the country"*: "Challenge to the Electoral College," *Congressional Record* 167, no. 4 (January 6, 2021): S14.

5   *"Protestors* [sic] *getting closer"*: Chris Marroletti, text message to MR, January 6, 2021.

5   *"They're on the west front"*: Chris Marroletti, text message to MR, January 6, 2021.

6   *A man in a neon sash*: Nicholas Fandos, Erin Schaff, and Emily Cochrane, "'Senate Being Locked Down': Inside a Harrowing Day at the Capitol," *New York Times*, January 7, 2021.

6   *At least one reporter*: Fandos, Schaff, and Cochrane, "'Senate Being Locked Down.'"

7   *When he was first elected*: Jeff Flake, email message to MR, November 9, 2018; Rob Portman, email message to MR, November 9, 2018; Beth Myers, email message to MR, November 9, 2018.

8   *"I can't be objective"*: MR, interview, May 11, 2021.

9   *"A very large portion"*: MR, interview, May 26, 2021.

10   *He showed the map*: Grace Panetta, "Mitt Romney Keeps in His Senate Office a Chart Displaying 4,000 Years of World History That He Says Shows the Fragility of Democracy," *Insider*, March 15, 2022.

10   *"A man gets some people"*: MR, interview, May 26, 2021.

CHAPTER ONE   The Body Upstream

Unless otherwise noted, all firsthand quotes from Mitt Romney are taken from an interview with the author conducted on September 22, 2021.

11   *When George was five*: Tom Mahoney, *The Story of George Romney: Builder, Salesman, Crusader* (New York: Harper & Brothers, 1960), 62–65.

11   *Life was not easy*: Benjamin Wallace-Wells, "George Romney for President, 1968," *New York*, May 18, 2012.

11   *By the time he hit puberty*: Mahoney, *The Story of George Romney*, 66–68.

12   *Upon visiting one*: Wallace-Wells, "George Romney for President."

12   *When he was old*: Mahoney, *The Story of George Romney*, 80.

12   *After his mission*: Mahoney, *The Story of George Romney*, 80–95.

12   *"I'll build you"*: T. George Harris, *Romney's Way: A Man and an Idea* (Englewood Cliffs, NJ: Prentice-Hall, 1968), 52.

13   *"When a Romney drowns"*: Harris, *Romney's Way*, 17.

13   *Gaskell, who sued*: Michael Kranish and Scott Helman, *The Real Romney* (New York: Harper, 2012), 49.

13   *George's other uncle, Vernon*: Harris, *Romney's Way*, 18.

13   *Miles became fixated*: MR, interview, June 21, 2021.

14   *a "miracle baby"*: Neil Swidey and Michael Paulson, "The Making of Mitt Romney, Part 2: Privilege, Tragedy, and a Young Leader," *Boston Globe*, June 24, 2007.

14   *"I don't see how"*: Swidey and Paulson, "The Making of Mitt Romney, Part 2."

14   *One day, when he was*: MR, interview, September 22, 2021.

15   *"twin evils"*: David D. Kirkpatrick, "For Romney, a Course Set Long Ago," *New York Times*, December 18, 2007.

15   *When the journalist*: Theodore H. White, *The Making of the President, 1968* (New York: Atheneum, 1969), 36.

15   *causing one labor leader*: Brock Brower, "Puzzling Front Runner," *Life*, May 5, 1967.

16 *"Michigan's most urgent"*: "Michigan Civil Rights Commission Honors the Life and Work of George Romney," Department of Civil Rights, State of Michigan, July 24, 2015.

16 *He established*: "Michigan Civil Rights Commission Honors the Life and Work of George Romney."

16 *They were, in his estimation*: Jake Miller, "George Romney Decries 'Extremism' at 1964 GOP Convention," CBS News, July 15, 2016; Jonathan Cohn, "Parent Trap," *New Republic*, July 1, 2007.

17 *"extremism and lily-white Protestantism"*: Miller, "George Romney Decries 'Extremism.'"

18 *"We must rouse ourselves"*: "Michigan Civil Rights Commission Honors the Life and Work of George Romney."

18 *"Some are already saying"*: Nikole Hannah-Jones, "Living Apart: How the Government Betrayed a Landmark Civil Rights Law," ProPublica, June 25, 2015.

18 *George had visited Vietnam*: "10 Governors Plan to Visit Vietnam in October," *New York Times*, August 3, 1965.

18 *"morally right"*: Andrew L. Johns, "Achilles' Heel: The Vietnam War and George Romney's Bid for the Presidency, 1967 to 1968," *Michigan Historical Review* 26, no. 1 (Spring 2000): 10.

18 *"When I came back"*: "Republicans: The Brainwashed Candidate," *Time*, September 15, 1967.

CHAPTER TWO "This Means Something"

Unless otherwise noted, all firsthand quotes and accounts of Romney's early life are taken from interviews with the author conducted on September 27 and October 4, 2021.

21 *When double-breasted suits*: MR, interview, April 27, 2022.

23 *When the episode*: Jason Horowitz, "Mitt Romney's Prep School Classmates Recall Pranks, but Also Troubling Incidents," *Washington Post*, May 11, 2012.

23 *He gave a vague apology*: David Greene and Ari Shapiro, "Romney Apologizes for High School Bullying Incident," NPR, May 11, 2012.

27 *"The Lord said"*: Parley P. Pratt, *The Autobiography of Parley Parker Pratt* (Chicago: Law, King & Law, 1888), 185.

28 *In a letter*: Willard Mitt Romney, "Without a Worry in the World," *Improvement Era* 72, no. 1 (January 1969): 75.

29 *On an overcast June morning*: Michael Kranish and Scott Helman, *The Real Romney* (New York: Harper, 2012), 79.

30 *The driver of the Mercedes*: Michael Paulson, "Survivors Recall Tragic Car Crash in France with Romney," *New York Times*, June 24, 2007.

CHAPTER THREE Hurry

Unless otherwise noted, all firsthand quotes—as well as accounts of Romney's early career and 1994 Senate run—are taken from interviews with the author conducted on November 2 and 15, 2021.

33 *He proposed to Ann*: MR, interview, October 4, 2021.

33 *But the chairman*: MR, email message to author, March 2, 2022.

34 *By the time he arrived*: Jodi Kantor, "At Harvard, a Master's in Problem Solving," *New York Times*, December 24, 2011.

34 *Ann cooked dinner*: Jodi Kantor, "The Stay-at-Home Woman Travels Well," *New York Times*, December 16, 2007.

34 *they attended the local Mormon ward*: Jodi Kantor, "Romney's Faith, Silent but Deep," *New York Times*, May 19, 2012.

34 *When classmates visited*: Kantor, "At Harvard, a Master's in Problem Solving."

34 *a "sober guy"*: George W. Bush, interview, October 12, 2022.

35 *"I was the typical oldest child"*: Tagg Romney, interview, May 11, 2022.

36 *"As a teenager"*: Tagg Romney, interview.

36 *"No other success"*: Mark D. Ogletree, *No Other Success: The Parenting Practices of David O. McKay* (Provo, UT: BYU Religious Studies Center, 2017): 1.

37 *"He was very good-looking"*: David D. Kirkpatrick, "Romney's Fortunes Tied to Business Riches," *New York Times*, June 4, 2007.

37 *"nourishing, but not memorable"*: Robert Gavin and Sacha Pfeiffer, "The Making of Mitt Romney, Part 3: Reaping Profit in Study, Sweat," *Boston Globe*, June 26, 2007.

38 *growing to more than $200 million*: "Bain Capital: Judging How Romney Got Rich," *This Week with George Stephanopoulos*, January 8, 2015.

38 *His family had no full-time nannies*: Neil Swidey and Stephanie Ebbert, "The Making of Mitt Romney, Part 4: Journeys of a Shared Life," *Boston Globe*, June 27, 2007.

38 *buying an impressive colonial*: Swidey and Ebbert, "The Making of Mitt Romney, Part 4."

39 *Tagg wrote back*: Swidey and Ebbert, "The Making of Mitt Romney, Part 4."

39 *"Mitt was very anti–Exponent II"*: Jason Horowitz, "In Boston, Mitt Romney 'Evolved' in Mormon Leadership, Some Churchwomen Say," *Washington Post*, November 21, 2011.

39 *He began asking*: Helen Claire Sievers, handwritten notes, April 18, 1993.

39 *"He is incredibly entitled"*: Joanna Brooks, "Mitt Romney's Best-Known Mormon Critic Tells All. One Last Time," Religion Dispatches, September 11, 2012.

40 *"Maybe he's made some mistakes"*: Robin Baker, interview, September 20, 2022.

40 *A month after the meeting*: MR, letter to Elder Cree-L Kofford, May 11, 1993.

40 *At the Ampad paper plant*: Alexander Burns, "Bain in the States, Indiana Edition," *Politico*, May 21, 2012.

40 *at the Dade International plant*: Michael Barbaro, "After a Romney Deal, Profits and Then Layoffs," *New York Times*, November 12, 2011.

40   *"One of the lessons I've learned"*: MR, interview, August 4, 2021

41   *"liberal lion of the Senate"*: Andrew Glass, "Ted Kennedy, 'Liberal Lion of the Senate,' Dies at 77," *Politico*, August 25, 2017.

44   *"I am pro-choice"*: Emily Schultheis, "Ted Kennedy Tribute Video Features Romney in '94 Debate Footage," *Politico*, September 4, 2012.

44   *a bracingly personal story*: Justin Elliott, "The Abortion That Mitt Doesn't Talk About Anymore," *Salon*, August 8, 2011.

44   *As polls tightened*: Peter T. Kilborn, "The 1994 Campaign: Labor; Bitter Strike in Indiana Echoes in Massachusetts," *New York Times*, October 10, 1994.

45   *"Give me a break"*: R. W. Apple Jr., "The 1994 Campaign: Massachusetts; Kennedy and Romney Meet, and the Rancor Flows Freely," *New York Times*, October 26, 1994.

46   "It is absolutely wrong": Matt Canham and Thomas Burr, "'Mormon Rivals'—Mitt Romney Modeled His Life after His Father and Idol, George Romney," *Salt Lake Tribune*, June 29, 2015.

46   *"His main cause"*: Kranish and Helman, *The Real Romney*, 195.

46   *They picked up fifty-four seats*: Stephanie Schragger, "Do the Midterm Elections Matter?" *PBS NewsHour*, n.d.

47   *for the first time in forty years*: "The Republican Revolution," History.com, January 11, 2023.

47   *To train a new generation*: Andrew Kaczynski, "The GOPAC Tapes," BuzzFeed News, January 28, 2012.

47   *In one memo*: Newt Gingrich, "Language: A Key Mechanism of Control," 1990.

47   *George Romney died*: David E. Rosenbaum, "George Romney Dies at 88; A Leading G.O.P. Figure," *New York Times*, July 27, 1995.

47   *woke up to find no rose on her nightstand*: "Special Programming—Romney: Dad Gave Mom a Rose Every Night," CNN video, YouTube, August 30, 2012, https://www.youtube.com/watch?v=qk-csvXMvFw.

CHAPTER FOUR Emergencies and Catastrophes

Unless otherwise noted, all firsthand quotes—as well as Romney's accounts of his Mar-a-Lago trip and the 2002 Olympics—are taken from interviews with the author, conducted on June 7 and December 8, 2021.

52   *Eventually an MRI*: Ann Romney, *In This Together: My Story* (New York: Thomas Dunne Books, 2015), 15.

53   *The most effective for Ann*: Ned Martel, "For Ann Romney, Horses Are a Lifeline," *Washington Post*, March 11, 2012.

53   *"Life with Ann is a lot better"*: MR, personal diary, February 6, 2016.

53   *Those 1,200 people*: Malcolm Johnson, "Romney Eulogized as Devout Family Man," Associated Press, August 1, 1995.

53   *The bid committee*: Duncan Mackay, "Bribes Scandal Forces Olympics Shake-Up," *The Guardian*, January 25, 1999.

53   *On the day Romney*: John Powers, "Golden Opportunity," *Boston Globe Magazine*, February 3, 2002.

54   *$400 million budget shortfall*: Peter Henderson, "Mitt Romney's Thrill of Victory at the Olympics," Reuters, November 22, 2011.

54   *Romney also learned*: Irvin Molotsky, "Olympics; Justice Department Begins Investigation of Salt Lake Bid," *New York Times*, December 24, 1998.

54   *"There were people"*: Mike Leavitt, interview, September 26, 2022.

54   *"These are not the Mormon Games"*: Felicia Sonmez, "Jon Huntsman, Mitt Romney Faced Off over 2002 Salt Lake City Olympics," *Washington Post*, January 16, 2012.

56   *"Do you think you're the savior"*: MR, interview, June 21, 2021.

57   *when a local newspaper*: Powers, "Golden Opportunity."

58   *Romney reportedly went so far*: "Not Guilty Pleas in Olympic Bribery Case," CBS News, August 7, 2020.

58   *an outcome that Romney attributed*: Mitt Romney, *Turnaround* (Washington, DC: Regnery, 2004), 22.

58   *Five months before*: Romney, *Turnaround*, 301.

58   *He spent the morning*: Romney, *Turnaround*, 302.

58   *"Like war"*: Romney, *Turnaround*, 302.

59   *"In the annals"*: Romney, *Turnaround*, 305.

60   *As the Mormon Tabernacle Choir*: Mitt Romney, "The Most Touching Moment Involved a Flag, a Choir and an Anthem," *Deseret News*, September 7, 2021.

60   *And when he learned*: Mike Gorrell, "Standoff Led to Romney's 'Un-Mormon-Like' Anger," *Salt Lake Tribune*, February 13, 2012.

61   *More than 2 billion people*: "Salt Lake 2002 Olympic Winter Games: Global Television Report," Olympic Television Research Centre, Sports Marketing Surveys LTD, 2002.

61   *"I have no doubt whatsoever"*: Bob Hohler, "The Making of Mitt Romney, Part 5: In Games, a Showcase for Future Races," *Boston Globe*, June 28, 2007.

61   *"He tried very hard"*: Hohler, "The Making of Mitt Romney, Part 5."

CHAPTER FIVE What It Took

Unless otherwise noted, all firsthand quotes—as well as Romney's accounts of his gubernatorial campaign and tenure—are taken from interviews conducted on December 14, 2021, and February 1, 2022.

63   *"You can't read any newspaper"*: MR, interview, December 14, 2021.

63   *Romney didn't want to challenge*: Bob Bernick Jr. and Lisa Riley Roche, "Boston GOP Beseeching Mitt," *Deseret News*, February 22, 2002.

63 *So, Romney gave her a push*: Dan Collins, "Mass. Gov Out, Olympics Chief In," CBS News, March 19, 2002.

63 *Mike Murphy, a quick-witted*: Howard Kurtz, "Along for the Ride," *Washington Post*, March 12, 2000.

64 *When he spent a day*: Jason Cherkis, "Mitt Romney Blue-Collar Work Days: Candidate Once Pretended to Be Mechanic, Farmer, Butcher," *HuffPost*, August 24, 2012.

64 *"Ann is just good"*: "Mitt Romney Ad 'Ann,'" Andrew Kaczynski video, YouTube, October 27, 2011, https://www.youtube.com/watch?v=5sIpMmgj5oo.

64 *he began to sink*: Matt Viser, "Romney Overcame Similar Deficit in '02 Race," *Boston Globe*, October 2, 2012.

64 *"I was accused of being inauthentic"*: MR, interview, March 8, 2022.

64 *With Election Day fast approaching*: Andrew Kaczynski, "Where Mitt Romney Learned How to Go Negative, and Win," BuzzFeed News, June 4, 2012.

65 *"I learned in my race"*: Michael Kranish and Scott Helman, *The Real Romney* (New York: Harper, 2012), 226.

65 *He pledged to "preserve"*: "Romney on Abortion—2002," OpenSourcePolitics video, YouTube, February 16, 2007, https://www.youtube.com/watch?v=P_w9pquznG4.

65 *His campaign passed out*: Andrew Kaczynsky, "Mitt Romney 2002 Pride Weekend Flier," BuzzFeed News, January 8, 2012.

65 *"At a very young age"*: Igor Volsky, "In Private Meeting with Gay Leaders, Romney Compared LGBT Equality to Father's Fight for 'Civil Rights,'" ThinkProgress, January 17, 2012.

66 *"I would give my answer"*: Beth Myers, interview, April 18, 2022.

66 *"If this is how it's going"*: Beth Myers, interview, April 18, 2022.

66 People *magazine had recently*: Stephen M. Silverman, "*People*'s 50 Most Beautiful: Okay, Who?" *People*, May 1, 2002.

66 *"We took on"*: Fox Butterfield, "The 2002 Elections: Massachusetts; Ex-Steward of Olympics Wins Governor," *New York Times*, November 6, 2002.

67 *Massachusetts was facing*: "2003 Budget: Major Spending Cuts Still Required," Massachusetts Taxpayers Foundation, June 1, 2002.

67 *projected shortfall of $3 billion*: Scott Brooks, "Mass. Budget Troubles Consistent with National Trend," *New Bedford Standard Times*, February 4, 2003.

67 *He discovered that Massachusetts*: McKay Coppins, "Romney Says He Fixed Mass.'s Homeless Problem. Did He?" BuzzFeed News, January 9, 2012.

67 *within a year*: Coppins, "Romney Says He Fixed Mass.'s Homeless Problem."

68 *"Even though we were going"*: Beth Myers, interview, April 18, 2022.

68 *In a meeting shortly after*: Beth Myers, interview, April 18, 2022.

68 *His own secretary*: Kranish and Helman, *The Real Romney*, 265.

68 *"Republicans won't like this"*: MR, interview, February 1, 2022.

69 *The state had an estimated*: Scott S. Greenberger, "Romney Eyes Penalties for Those Lacking Insurance," *Boston Globe*, June 22, 2005.

70 *This argument was helped*: Stuart M. Butler, "Assuring Affordable Health Care for All Americans," *Journal of Health Care for the Poor and Undeserved* 1, no. 1 (February 1990): 63–73.

70 *"I don't look and say"*: MR, interview, May 11, 2021.

70 *The hard work paid off*: Pam Belluck, "Massachusetts Set to Offer Universal Health Insurance," *New York Times*, April 4, 2006.

70 *"When Kennedy and Romney support"*: Brian C. Mooney, "Romney and Health Care: In the Thick of History," *Boston Globe*, May 30, 2011.

70 *"We're basically stalemated"*: Brian C. Mooney, Stephanie Ebbert, and Scott Helman, "The Making of Mitt Romney, Part 1: Ambitious Goals; Shifting Stances," *Boston Globe*, June 30, 2007.

71 *by 2008, 95 percent*: Nancy Reardon, "Study: 95 Percent of State Residents Are Insured," *Patriot Ledger*, June 3, 2008.

71 *mortality rates among non-elderly adults*: Benjamin D. Sommers, Sharon K. Long, and Katherine Baicker, "Changes in Mortality after Massachusetts Health Care Reform," *Annals of Internal Medicine* 160, no. 9 (May 6, 2014): 585–93.

71 *hours after signing*: Kranish and Helman, *The Real Romney*, 281.

71 *"a rich guy from a liberal state"*: Harvard Institute of Politics, *Campaign for President: The Managers Look at 2008* (Lanham, MD: Rowman & Littlefield, 2009), 17.

71 *"speaking in grandiose slogans"*: Joan Vennochi, "See Mitt Run," *Boston Globe*, January 4, 2005.

72 *Even Donald Trump*: Donald Trump, interview with Wolf Blitzer, *The Situation Room*, CNN, March 16, 2007.

72 *A few years earlier*: MR, interview, June 7, 2021.

73 *"Being a conservative Republican"*: Adrian Walker, "Home to Roost," *Boston Globe*, February 1, 2008.

CHAPTER SIX The Tar Pit

Unless otherwise noted, all firsthand quotes from Romney are taken from interviews conducted on February 1, 2022.

75 *The title of the eighty-nine-page*: Richard M. Eyre, "George Romney in 1968, from Front-Runner to Drop-Out, an Analysis of Cause," master's thesis, Brigham Young University, 1969.

76 *The meeting had been arranged*: Mark DeMoss, interview, August 29, 2022.

76 *Several of the men*: MR, interview, February 1, 2022.

76 *he'd made more than seventy appointments*: Jerry Markon and Alice Crites, "As Governor, Mitt Romney Backtracked on Promised Reforms in Appointing Judges," *Washington Post*, May 30, 2012.

77   *A few days later*: Mark DeMoss, interview, August 29, 2022.

79   *"Mitt, you don't get it"*: MR, interview, March 8, 2022.

79   *He was unabashedly pro-choice*: "Religion and Politics '08: Rudolph Giuliani," Pew Research Center, November 4, 2008.

79   *proud of his city's strict*: Michael Daly, "How Rudy Giuliani Went from Gun Scourge to Gun Nut," *Daily Beast*, August 7, 2018.

79   *He seemed to believe*: MR, interview, April 27, 2022.

79   *a "huckster"*: MR, interview, May 5, 2022.

79   *The two men had first met*: MR, interview, June 15, 2021.

80   *the "Straight Talk Express"*: Dan Balz, "McCain Rides 'The Straight Talk Express,'" *Washington Post*, September 2, 1999.

80   *His antipathy had hardened*: Frank Pignanelli and LaVarr Webb, "Huntsman's McCain Endorsement Raises Questions," *Deseret News*, August 13, 2006.

80   *"Your grandfather is rolling"*: MR, interview, December 8, 2021.

81   *"likable"*: Alessandra Stanley, "A Show Where Candidates Are More Prop Than Player," *New York Times*, May 4, 2007.

81   *"articulate"*: "Reagan Night," *National Review*, May 4, 2007.

81   *"good-natured"*: Peggy Noonan, "An Incomplete Field," *Wall Street Journal*, May 4, 2007.

81   *"statuesque"*: Noonan, "An Incomplete Field."

81   *"He may not be the heir"*: Stanley, "A Show Where Candidates Are More Prop Than Player."

82   *In 1999, George W. Bush*: Janine Yagielski and Kathleen Hayden, "Bush Wins Iowa GOP Straw Poll," CNN, August 15, 1999.

82   *a check for $9 million*: "Romney's Edge over McCain Proves Money Matters," Associated Press, July 8, 2007.

82   *Dozens of so-called "super volunteers"*: Jonathan Martin, "Does Romney Have Iowa Locked Down?" *Politico*, July 8, 2007.

82   *Romney struggled to shake*: "Romney Deflects the 'Flip-Flop' Tag," Associated Press, December 16, 2007.

82   *Romney was shadowed*: "'Flip Romney' at CPAC 2007," NYSunPolitics video, YouTube, https://www.youtube.com/watch?v=jUeJYBkvVqU.

82   *Rivals passed out*: Michael Scherer, "The Republican Candidates—and Ann Coulter—Try Out Their Acts," Salon, March 3, 2007.

83   *When he first ran for Senate*: Adam Nagourney and David D. Kirkpatrick, "Romney's Mixed Views on Gay Rights and Marriage Rile Conservatives," *New York Times*, December 9, 2006.

83   *"It was one of those things you say"*: MR, interview, December 14, 2021.

83   *The estate tax*: Brian Raub and Joseph Newcomb, "Federal Estate Tax Returns Filed for 2007 Decedents," in *Compendium of Federal Estate Tax and Personal Wealth Studies*, Statistics of Income Bulletin, Summer 2011.

84   *On August 11, 2007*: John Whitesides, "Romney Wins Iowa Republican Straw Poll," Reuters, August 11, 2007.

84   *paid a consultant nearly $200,000*: "Romney Rolls Out Dough in Iowa," *Tampa Bay Times*, August 10, 2007.

84   *an inflatable slide*: Todd Dorman, "Romney's the Big Ames Straw Poll Winner," *Globe Gazette*, August 12, 2007.

84   *free plates of brisket*: "Romney Rolls Out Dough in Iowa."

84   *"I'm pleased as punch"*: Adam Nagourney and Jeff Zeleny, "Romney Wins Iowa Straw Poll by a Sizable Margin," *New York Times*, August 12, 2007.

85   *When he appeared on the cover*: Jonathan Darman, "A Mormon's Journey: The Making of Mitt Romney," *Newsweek*, October 8, 2007.

85   *"such a transparent and recent fraud"*: Jacob Weisberg, "Romney's Religion," *Slate*, December 20, 2006.

85   *"Would it not be accurate"*: Damon Linker, "The Big Test," *New Republic*, January 14, 2007.

85   *One 2007 poll*: Peter Hart and Bill McInturff, "Study #6077," NBC News/*Wall Street Journal*, November 2007.

85   *"In my faith"*: "Polygamy Was Prominent in Romney's Family Tree," Associated Press, February 25, 2007.

86   *The reality of this failure*: MR, interview, February 1, 2022.

86   *Anonymous robocalls*: Michael Levenson, "Romney Cries Foul on Pro-Huckabee Calls," *Boston Globe*, December 5, 2007.

86   *Huckabee was stoking skepticism*: Zev Chafets, "Magazine Preview: The Huckabee Factor," *New York Times*, December 12, 2007.

86   *Even McCain's ninety-five-year-old mother*: Thomas Burr, "McCain's Mom Slams Romney," *Salt Lake Tribune*, November 10, 2007.

86   *McCain later called*: Beth Myers, interview, May 2, 2022.

86   *Romney's son Josh*: Josh Romney, interview, June 1, 2022.

89   *"trying too hard to reinvent"*: Stuart Stevens, email message, February 2, 2008.

89   *Alex Castellanos faulted Stuart Stevens*: Alex Castellanos, email message to Beth Myers, Bob White, Tagg Romney, Russ Schriefer, Stuart Stevens, Curt Anderson, Brad Todd, Larry McCarthy, Cindy Gillespie, Ron Kaufman, Eric Fehrnstrom, Matt Rhoades, and Kevin Madden, February 2, 2008.

89   *Stevens countered*: Stuart Stevens, email message to Beth Myers, Bob White, Tagg Romney, Russ Schriefer, Alex Castellanos, Curt Anderson, Brad Todd, Larry McCarthy, Cindy Gillespie, Ron Kaufman, Eric Fehrnstrom, Matt Rhoades, and Kevin Madden, February 2, 2008.

89   *"The current consultant situation"*: Tagg Romney, email message to Beth Myers, February 3, 2008.

90   *"Mitt, we've decided to go"*: MR, interview, February 1, 2022.

THE POLITICAL NEWS, 2009–2010

93 *OBAMA IS SWORN IN*: Carl Hulse, "Obama Is Sworn In as the 44th President," *New York Times*, January 20, 2009.

93 *"This president, I think"*: Glenn Beck interviewed on *Fox & Friends*, Fox News, July 28, 2009.

93 *GUN SALES SOAR*: Lauren Kirby, "Gun Sales Soar in United States," VOA News, November 2, 2009.

93 *TEXAS GOVERNOR SAYS*: Alexander Mooney, "Texas Governor Says Secession Possible," CNN, April 16, 2009.

93 *"When you're dealing with a guy"*: Rush Limbaugh, *The Rush Limbaugh Show*, WJNO, August 19, 2009.

93 *POLL: PALIN BEST REFLECTS*: Paul Steinhauser, "Poll: Palin Best Reflects GOP Core Values," CNN, November 30, 2009.

93 *"My parents or my baby"*: Andy Barr, "Palin Doubles Down on 'Death Panels,'" *Politico*, August 13, 2009.

93 *THOUSANDS OF ANTI-TAX*: "Thousands of Anti-Tax 'Tea Party' Protesters Turn Out in U.S. Cities," Fox News, April 16, 2009.

93 *"What if [Obama]"*: Chris Good, "Biden 'Stunned' by Gingrich's 'Kenyan Anti-Colonialist' Talk," *The Atlantic*, September 15, 2010.

93 *TEA PARTIERS YELL*: Adam K. Raymond, "Tea Partiers Yell Slurs, Spit on Congressmen," *New York*, March 21, 2010.

93 *"We need to realize that"*: Brian Montopoli, "Rep. Trent Franks: Obama Is 'Enemy of Humanity,'" CBS News, September 29, 2009.

93 *TEA PARTY MORE POPULAR*: Chris Good, "Tea Party More Popular Than Both Political Parties," *The Atlantic*, May 13, 2010.

CHAPTER SEVEN Heist

95 *It was December 2010*: Michael Barbaro, "Defeat, Introspection, Reinvention, Nomination," *New York Times*, August 29, 2012.

95 *"the closest thing"*: Michael Scherer, "Election 2012: Mitt Romney Readies a Different Kind of Campaign," *Time*, January 24, 2011.

96 *Tea Party candidates with outlandish*: Ewen MacAskill, "Tea Party Rocks Republicans with Sweeping Primary Victories," *The Guardian*, September 15, 2010.

96 *"The base is southern"*: Greg Whiteley, dir., *Mitt*, Los Gatos, CA: Netflix Originals, 2014.

97 *A few weeks after*: Barbaro, "Defeat, Introspection, Reinvention, Nomination."

98 *"Great Depression times 100"*: Glenn Beck, *Glenn Beck*, Fox News, January 5, 2010.

98 *"I want him to show"*: Donald Trump interviewed on *The View*, ABC, March 23, 2011.

98   *"He's spent millions of dollars"*: Donald Trump interviewed on *Fox & Friends*, Fox News, March 28, 2011.

98   *"He doesn't have a birth certificate"*: Donald Trump interviewed by Laura Ingraham, *The Laura Ingraham Show*, Talk Radio Network, March 30, 2011.

98   *"If he wasn't born in this country"*: Donald Trump interviewed on the *Today* show, NBC, April 7, 2011.

98   *Trump was now making gains*: "CNN Poll: Trump at 10 Percent in Hypothetical GOP Battle," CNN, March 23, 2011.

98   *half of all Republican voters*: Frank James, "Half of GOP Primary Voters Wrongly Say Obama Non-U.S. Born: Poll," NPR, February 15, 2011.

99   *"I didn't see it as a populist movement"*: MR, interview, February 15, 2022.

99   *In one meeting, some of Romney's advisers*: MR, interview, March 1, 2022.

100 *"The debate over Obamacare"*: "Obama's Running Mate," *Wall Street Journal*, May 12, 2011.

100 *a panicked email*: MR, email message to Beth Myers, Stuart Stevens, Eric Fehrnstrom, and Russ Schreifer, May 12, 2011.

100 *"The dirty little secret"*: Stuart Stevens, interview, October 3, 2022.

101 *an old-fashioned letter to the editor*: Mitt Romney, "Romney Responds to Health-Care Criticism," *Wall Street Journal*, May 13, 2011.

101 *"I am not adjusting the plan"*: Kasie Hunt, "Romney: No Apologies for Mass. Plan," *Politico*, May 13, 2011.

101 *his "superpower"*: MR, interview, May 11, 2021.

101 *dismissed as "arrogant"*: Adam Martin, "Reactions from the Right to Romney's Health Care Speech," *The Atlantic*, May 12, 2011.

101 *deemed "a liability"*: Paul West, "Mitt Romney Acknowledges His Healthcare Dilemma," *Los Angeles Times*, May 12, 2011.

101 *"He dug himself in deeper"*: Fred Barnes, interviewed on *Lou Dobbs Tonight*, Fox Business, May 12, 2011.

101 *"These are unbridgeable policy"*: "Romney's Daredevil Act," *Wall Street Journal*, May 13, 2011.

101 *"It was a little ironic"*: MR, interview, December 14, 2021.

102 *"I feel like that story"*: MR, personal journal, September 1, 2011.

102 *He had heard the joke*: MR, interview, March 8, 2022.

102 *"a nutcase"*: MR, personal journal, September 2, 2011.

102 *"sanctimonious, severe, and strange"*: MR, personal journal, February 10, 2012.

102 *"Ann says he is"*: MR, personal journal, March 17, 2012.

103 *"Republicans must realize"*: MR, personal journal, September 22, 2011.

103 *"If they thought I was stupid"*: MR, personal journal, July 22, 2011.

103 *Once, he actually broke out*: Phillip Rucker, "Mitt Romney Sings 'America the Beautiful' (VIDEO)," *Washington Post*, January 30, 2012.

104 *At an event in New Hampshire*: MR, interview, February 1, 2022.

104 *"So much for pro-life"*: MR, personal journal, September 12, 2011.

104   *At Flaherty's urging*: Michael Barbaro, "Aide to Romney Leans to the Right with a Soft Touch," *New York Times*, February 17, 2012.

104   *On one occasion*: Spencer Zwick, interview, September 28, 2022.

104   *"You've got to let Donald Trump"*: MR, interview, June 7, 2021.

105   *"It was like George W. Bush"*: Spencer Zwick, interview, September 28, 2022.

105   *Once inside Trump Tower*: MR, personal journal, September 26, 2011.

106   *Romney began to change the subject*: MR, interview, June 7, 2021; interviews with multiple individuals with knowledge of the meeting, n.d.

107   *had called for the mass deportation*: Tim Murphy, "Mitt Romney Slams One Anti-Muslim Activist, Praises Another," *Mother Jones*, October 8, 2011.

107   *"homosexual thugs"*: Tim Murphey, "What the *New York Times* Got Wrong about Gay Nazis," *Mother Jones*, August 5, 2011.

107   *"rut like rabbits"*: Bryan Fischer, "Jesus Groomed His Apostles for Political Office," *Rightly Concerned* blog, April 5, 2011.

107   *Fischer had devoted an entire segment*: Kyle Mantyla, "Fischer: First Amendment Does Not Apply to Mormons," Right Wing Watch, September 29, 2011.

107   *a "real Christian"*: "Conservative Pastor on Romney: Don't Vote for a Mormon," CNN, October 7, 2011.

107   *He worked on his speech*: MR, personal journal, October 7, 2011.

108   *"We should remember"*: Murphy, "Mitt Romney Slams One Anti-Muslim Activist."

108   *After exiting the stage*: MR, personal journal, October 7, 2011.

CHAPTER EIGHT 50.1 Percent

117   *He first noticed the change*: MR, personal journal, April 10, 2012.

118   *Getting Santorum out*: MR, personal journal, March 30, 2012.

118   *"His key consideration"*: MR, personal journal, April 10, 2012.

118   *Over a long breakfast*: MR, personal journal, March 23, 2012.

118   *When the primaries effectively ended*: MR, personal journal, April 12, 2012.

119   *the high-dollar donors*: Michael Barbaro, "For Wealthy Romney Donors, Up Close and Personal Access," *New York Times*, June 23, 2012; Philip Rucker, "Romney Mixes and Mingles at Rarefied Retreat as Top Donors Taste Victory," *Washington Post*, June 23, 2012.

119   *the business elite*: Barbaro, "For Wealthy Romney Donors."

119   *the GOP luminaries*: Barbaro, "For Wealthy Romney Donors."

119   *he dispatched hecklers*: Byron Tau, "Axelrod Heckled in Boston," *Politico*, May 31, 2012.

119   *"sauce for the goose"*: McKay Coppins, "Mitt Romney Wins Over the Right by Confronting Obama," BuzzFeed News, May 31, 2012.

119   *He staged a surprise*: Reid J. Epstein, "Romney Taunts Obama from Solyndra," *Politico*, May 31, 2012.

119   *even Clint Eastwood said*: Maggie Haberman, "Clint Eastwood Endorses Mitt Romney," *Politico*, August 3, 2012.

120   *Once, during some rare downtime*: MR, personal journal, August 28, 2012.

120   *In early June*: MR, personal journal, June 5, 2012.

120   *He hated how the state police*: MR, personal journal, June 25, 2012.

120   *Once, when his pregnant*: Matt Romney, interview, August 5, 2022.

121   *On June 11, Romney met with*: MR, personal journal, June 11, 2012.

121   *An initial list of two dozen names*: Mark Halperin and John Heilemann, *Double Down: Game Change 2012* (New York: Penguin, 2013), 345.

121   *"We're in a street fight"*: Halperin and Heilemann, *Double Down*, 350.

121   *Romney, who was not*: MR, personal journal, March 31, 2012.

121   *Even more troubling*: Halperin and Heilemann, *Double Down*, 354–55.

121   *Portman and Pawlenty*: MR, personal journal, March 31, 2012.

121   *he'd been baptized Mormon*: McKay Coppins, "Exclusive: Marco Rubio's Mormon Roots," *BuzzFeed News*, February 23, 2012.

122   *a youthful devotee*: Rachel Weiner, "Paul Ryan and Ayn Rand," *Washington Post*, August 13, 2012.

122   *writing federal budget*: "Paul Ryan Unveils FY 2012 Budget," Committee for a Responsible Federal Budget, April 5, 2011.

122   *one Democratic attack ad*: Kenneth Rapoza, "In Attack Ad, Paul Ryan Kills Grandma in Wheelchair," *Forbes*, August 12, 2012.

122   *the "intellectual leader"*: Seema Mehta, "Romney Declares Paul Ryan the 'Intellectual Leader' of the GOP," *Los Angeles Times*, August 11, 2012.

122   *a "client-ready" first-year*: Halperin and Heilemann, *Double Down*, 356.

122   *His well-documented penchant*: MR, personal journal, March 31, 2012.

122   *Stevens warned Romney*: Halperin and Heilemann, *Double Down*, 353.

123   *Romney announced*: Jeff Zeleny and Jim Rutenberg, "Romney Chooses Ryan, Pushing Fiscal Issues to the Forefront," *New York Times*, August 11, 2012.

123   *"Mitt Romney has finally thrown"*: "Glenn Beck: Mitt Romney's Paul Ryan VP Pick Is 'Tremendous News,'" *HuffPost*, August 13, 2012.

123   *The Tea Party Patriots*: "Reaction to Romney's Choice of Ryan as Running Mate," Reuters, August 11, 2012.

123   *"Donald, you're fired"*: Halperin and Heilemann, *Double Down*, 250.

123   *During a visit with Nancy Reagan*: MR, personal journal, May 31, 2012.

123   *After one entertaining phone call*: MR, personal journal, May 17, 2012.

124   *When Trump hosted Romney*: Spencer Zwick, interview, September 28, 2022.

124   *For the rest of the event*: MR, personal journal, May 29–June 11, 2012.

124   *"We didn't want"*: Andrea Saul, interview, February 10, 2023.

125   *Steve King, the Iowa congressman*: Chis Godburn, "Romney Endorses Rep. Steve King," MSNBC, September 7, 2012.

125 *the Kansas secretary of state*: Alan Greenblatt, "Will Backing of Anti-Immigration Movement's 'Dark Lord' Haunt Romney?" NPR, January 25, 2012.

125 *a "true leader"*: "Press Release—Mitt Romney Announces Support of Kansas Secretary of State Kris Kobach," American Presidency Project, January 11, 2012.

125 *"If Mitt Romney lacks the backbone"*: Jonathan Easley, "Obama Campaign Says Romney Lacks 'Backbone' and 'Moral Leadership,'" *The Hill*, May 29, 2012.

125 *After Romney was captured*: Kathleen Hennessey, "Obama Camp Takes Aim at Romney's Ties to Trump," *Los Angeles Times*, May 29, 2012.

125 *"We made a lot of use"*: David Axelrod, interview, February 23, 2023.

125 *"You know, I don't agree"*: Maggie Haberman and Reid J. Epstein, "Romney Won't Dump Trump," *Politico*, May 29, 2012.

125 *"The people who are speaking"*: Spencer Zwick, interview, September 28, 2022.

126 *which forced organizers to cancel*: Michael D. Shear, "First Day Canceled, but Republican Show Goes On," *New York Times*, August 26, 2012.

126 *Organizers tried to move*: MR, personal journal, August 29, 2012.

126 *his staff convinced him*: MR, personal journal, August 28, 2012.

126 *in lieu of a speech*: Erica Orden, "In Tell-All Book, Michael Cohen Says Trump Hired a 'Faux-Bama' Before White House Run," CNN, September 6, 2020.

127 *One of Romney's top ad men*: Spencer Zwick, interview, September 28, 2022.

127 *"We don't have to be nice"*: Donald Trump interviewed by Griff Jenkins, *On the Record*, Fox News, August 27, 2012.

127 *the audience of 30 million*: Carl Marcucci, "Final Night of RNC Draws 30.3 Million Viewers," *Radio & Television Business Report*, September 1, 2012.

127 *Romney squirmed in his seat*: MR, personal journal, May 6, 2012.

128 *"Obama theme"*: MR, personal journal, April 30, 2012.

128 *a majority of Americans*: Gary Langer, "55% 'Wrong Track' Matches 2004; a Difficulty for Obama, but Survivable," ABC News, November 2, 2012.

129 *When Stevens proposed hijacking*: MR, personal journal, September 1, 2012.

129 *"We could run ads"*: MR, personal journal, August 15, 2012.

129 *At a Pittsburgh-area picnic*: Erik Hayden, "Mitt Romney's Newest Mini-Headache: 'Cookiegate,'" *Time*, April 19, 2012.

129 *"It's hard to know"*: Steve Holland, "Romney's adventure abroad begins with stumbles," *Reuters*, July 26, 2012.

129 *"Mitt the Twit"*: Elspeth Reeve, "Look How Mad the British Press Is at Mitt Romney," *The Atlantic,* July 27, 2012.

129 *One of Romney's sons had shared*: Neil Swidey and Stephanie Ebbert, "The Making of Mitt Romney, Part 4: Journeys of a Shared Life," *Boston Globe,* June 27, 2007.

129 *"Dog politics"*: Sue Kottwitz, "Dog Politics: Mitt Romney, Seamus & the Now Infamous Vacation," Zimbio, January 8, 2012.

129   *Diane Sawyer asked him*: Tim Mak, "Ann Romney: Seamus 'Loved' Car Roof," *Politico*, April 17, 2012.

129   *as did Sean Hannity*: Tim Mak, "McCain Snarls at Obama," *Politico*, April 19, 2012.

130   *more than eighty times*: Matthew Aldrige, "An Attempt to Compile a Complete List of Every Time Gail Collins Has Mentioned That Mitt Romney Once Drove to Canada with the Family Dog Strapped to the Roof of the Car," Tumblr, February 15, 2012.

130   *"Romney has already ruled out"*: Gail Collins, "Romney Has Already Ruled Out," *New York Times*, February 29, 2012.

130   *an anecdote in Barack Obama's memoir*: Jake Tapper, "Romney Campaign Notes That Obama as a Boy Ate Dog Meat," ABC News, April 18, 2012.

130   *Collins would revisit*: Gail Collins, "I Was Wrong about Mitt Romney (and His Dog)," *New York Times*, July 21, 2022.

130   *By the summer, even* Politico: Maggie Haberman and Alexander Burns, "The Smallest Campaign Ever," *Politico*, June 20, 2012.

130   *what he called "verbal typos"*: MR, personal journal, August 7, 2012.

131   *Romney wrote in his journal that night*: MR, personal journal, August 24, 2012.

131   *"My take—let the truth shine"*: MR, personal journal, August 4, 2012.

131   *When the Supreme Court struck down*: Eyder Peralta, "Supreme Court Strikes Down Key Provisions of Arizona Immigration Law," NPR, June 25, 2012.

131   *"legitimate rape"*: John Eligon and Michael Schwirtz, "Senate Candidate Provokes Ire with 'Legitimate Rape' Comment," *New York Times*, August 19, 2012.

131   *Romney wanted to call for him*: MR, personal journal, August 22, 2012.

131   *"the Mittness protection program"*: Ben Smith, "Romney's Low-Profile Strategy," *Politico*, August 1, 2011.

132   *a "war on women"*: Rachel Weiner, "Mitt Romney Stumbles Over 'War on Women,'" *Washington Post*, April 11, 2012.

132   *a "race-mongering pyromaniac"*: Michael Tomasky, "Michael Tomasky on Mitt Romney the Race Baiter at the NAACP," *Daily Beast*, July 13, 2017.

132   *"put y'all back in chains"*: Jake Tapper, "VP Biden Says Republicans Are 'Going to Put Y'all Back in Chains,'" ABC News, August 14, 2012.

132   *"We knew that we probably"*: David Axelrod, interview, February 23, 2023.

132   *"I do not think Mitt Romney realizes"*: Olivier Knox, "Pro-Obama Ad Ties Romney to Woman's Death from Cancer," ABC News, August 7, 2012.

133   *an op-ed Romney had written*: Mitt Romney, "Let Detroit Go Bankrupt," *New York Times*, November 18, 2008.

133   *"It's like Robin Hood"*: Margaret Chadbourn, "Obama: Romney Tax Plan Is 'Robin Hood in Reverse,'" Reuters, August 6, 2012.

133   *In interviews and Senate speeches*: Sam Stein and Ryan Grim, "Harry Reid: Bain Investor Told Me That Mitt Romney 'Didn't Pay Any Taxes for 10 Years,'"

HuffPost, July 31, 2012; "Tax Planning," *Congressional Record* 158, no. 117 (August 2, 2012).

133 *The cancer spot was panned*: Robert Farley, "Is Romney to Blame for Cancer Death?" FactCheck.org, August 8, 2012.

133 *the Obama campaign quietly disavowed*: Olivier Knox, "Obama Campaign: Don't Blame Us for Ad Blaming Romney for Cancer Death," ABC News, August 8, 2012.

133 *The headline of the* Times: Charles Brown, "Let Detroit Go Bankrupt: The Famous Line Romney Never Said," Michigan Radio, July 18, 2012.

133 *Romney's suggested headline*: MR, personal journal, November 12, 2012.

133 *"Romney didn't win"*: Chris Cillizza, "Harry Reid's Appalling Defense of His Attack on Mitt Romney's Tax Record," *Washington Post*, March 31, 2015.

133 *Ann's dressage horse was featured*: Jonathan Karl, "DNC Regrets Offending Ann Romney, No More Horse Videos," ABC News, July 19, 2012.

133 *The "car elevator"*: Devin Dwyer, "Mitt Romney Ordered $55,000 'Phantom Park' Car Elevator, Designer Says," ABC News, May 25, 2012.

134 National Review *cover story*: Kevin D. Williamson, "Like a Boss," *National Review*, August 22, 2012.

134 *"In a political environment"*: Stuart Stevens, interview, October 3, 2022.

135 *"corporations are people, my friend"*: Philip Rucker, "Mitt Romney Says 'Corporations Are People,'" *Washington Post*, August 11, 2011.

136 *"These guys are heroes"*: MR, personal journal, March 15, 2012.

136 *"If I were to go back"*: MR, interview, February 15, 2022.

136 *$85 million ad blitz*: "Mad Money: TV Ads in the 2012 Presidential Campaign," *Washington Post*, November 14, 2012.

136 *"Their earned media"*: MR, personal journal, August 16, 2012.

136 *"Winning would change our lives"*: MR, personal journal, June 25, 2012.

137 *He considered the president a "nice guy"*: Ashley Parker, "Critics from Base See Romney Pulling Punches on 'Nice Guy' Obama," *New York Times*, June 1, 2012.

137 *After talking to the president*: MR, personal journal, October 18, 2012.

137 *In another entry, he wrote*: MR, personal journal, October 17, 2012.

137 *He really* had *convinced himself*: MR, interview, March 1, 2022.

137 *Mike murphy told him*: MR, personal journal, September 12, 2012.

137 *Warren Beatty encouraged*: MR, personal journal, March 14, 2012.

138 *Romney frequently jotted down*: MR, personal journal, June 1, 2012; September 18, 2012; September 22, 2012.

138 *At one fundraiser, in Chicago*: MR, personal journal, June 14, 2012.

138 *At another fundraiser, in Colorado*: MR, personal journal, August 2, 2012.

138 *Stevens had implored Romney*: MR, interview, July 14, 2021.

139 *On the afternoon*: MR, personal journal, September 17, 2012.

140 *Stevens had later joked*: Stuart Stevens, interview, October 3, 2022.

140 I was trying to be polite: Romney, interview, September 13, 2022.

141 *At least, that's what he told*: Seema Mehta, "Romney Defends 'Off the Cuff' Remarks on Obama Backers as Victims," *Los Angeles Times*, September 17, 2012.

141 *"When I won in 2008"*: Barack Obama interviewed by David Letterman, *Late Show with David Letterman*, CBS, September 18, 2012.

141 *"stupid and arrogant"*: William Kristol, "A Note on Romney's Arrogant and Stupid Remarks," *Weekly Standard*, September 18, 2012.

141 *Romney "really doesn't know much"*: David Brooks, "Thurston Howell Romney," *New York Times*, September 17, 2012.

141 *Peggy Noonan called for an "intervention"*: Peggy Noonan, "Time for an Intervention," *Wall Street Journal*, September 18, 2012.

141 *Romney had no patience*: MR, personal journal, September 20, 2012.

141 *"Ninety-nine percent"*: Stuart Stevens, interview, October 3, 2022.

141 *He could barely eat*: MR, personal journal, September 30, 2012.

142 *Night after night*: MR, personal journal, September 20, 2012; September 30, 2012.

142 *political leaders are often defined*: MR, interview, November 15, 2021.

142 *"The rich will do fine"*: MR, personal journal, September 20, 2012.

142 *A "war council" was convened*: MR, personal journal, September 30, 2012.

143 *Mike Murphy emailed*: MR, personal journal, September 22, 2012.

143 *Ann even made her husband*: MR, personal journal, September 22, 2012.

143 *Late on the night of September 30*: MR, personal journal, September 30, 2012.

144 *In Romney's estimation, the only chance*: MR, personal journal, September 21, 2012.

144 *The campaign produced*: Memos produced by the Romney 2012 campaign, n.d.

144 *To play Obama in the mock debates*: Brett Smiley, "Romney's Debate Prep Stand-in Mastered Obama's Voice with Audiobooks," *New York*, August 28, 2012.

145 *During one of the debate sessions*: Rob Portman, interview, January 25, 2023.

145 *During one huddle*: MR, interview, September 13, 2022.

145 *"I've been a missionary"*: Halperin and Heilemann, *Double Down*, 407.

146 *Minutes before the debate began*: MR, personal journal, October 3, 2012.

146 *"The last time we were with each other"*: MR, personal journal, October 3, 2012.

147 *"the best debate performance"*: MR, personal journal, October 3, 2012.

147 *"binders full of women"*: Maura Judkis and Michael Cavna, "'Binders Full of Women' Quip Goes Viral," *Washington Post*, October 17, 2012.

147 *"even when life begins"*: Annie Groer, "Indiana GOP Senate Hopeful Richard Mourdock Says God 'Intended' Rape Pregnancies," *Washington Post*, October 24, 2012.

148 *"shuck and jive schtick"*: Kevin Cirilli, "Palin Defends 'Shuck and Jive,'" *Politico*, October 25, 2012.

148 *"I have something very, very big"*: Donald Trump interviewed on *Fox & Friends*, Fox News, October 22, 2012.

148 *"Heaven only knows"*: MR, personal journal, October 23, 2012.

148 *Trump said he would write*: "Trump to Give $5 Million to Charity if Obama Releases Records," Reuters, October 24, 2012.

148 *"Gosh, we are in the center"*: MR, personal journal, October 12, 2012.

149 *Romney had heard once*: MR, personal journal, October 17, 2012.

150 *"Sometimes, it is hard for me"*: MR, personal journal, October 30, 2012.

150 *"It cannot be so easy to lose"*: MR, personal journal, October 7, 2012.

150 *Romney asked them to stop*: MR, personal journal, April 5, 2012.

151 *"I really would prefer not to be killed"*: MR, personal journal, May 11, 2012.

151 *in late October, a deadly hurricane*: Andy Sullivan, "Hurricane Sandy Blows U.S. Election Off Course," Reuters, October 28, 2012.

151 *"Christie is the same"*: MR, personal journal, November 1, 2012.

152 *"So, what do you think you say"*: Greg Whiteley, dir., *Mitt*, Los Gatos, CA: Netflix Originals, 2014.

152 *he didn't want to look like a "nut job"*: MR, personal journal, November 6, 2012.

152 *As they talked through his speech*: Whiteley, dir., *Mitt*.

153 *Somewhere in the sky*: McKay Coppins, "The Donald Problem," BuzzFeed News, November 7, 2012.

153 *Just before midnight*: Gregory King, "Sound Familiar? Trump Called 2012 Vote a 'Total Sham,'" CNN, October 20, 2016.

CHAPTER NINE Just the Beginning

155 *Mitt pumping gas*: Dashiell Bennett, "Mitt Romney Is Back to Pumping His Own Gas," *The Atlantic*, November 20, 2012.

155 *Mitt at the McDonald's counter*: Kim Bhasin, "Here's Mitt Romney at McDonald's," Insider, November 29, 2012.

155 *Mitt looking resigned*: Walt Hickey, "Mitt Romney Goes to Disneyland," Insider, November 21, 2012.

155 *Even at church*: MR, personal journal, November 11, 2012.

155 *He wasn't "angry"*: MR, personal journal, November 16, 2012.

155 *"stop being the stupid party"*: "Jindal: GOP Mufst 'Stop Being the Stupid Party,'" CBS News video, YouTube, https://www.youtube.com/watch?v=z8kwxlHfocE.

155 *Ted Cruz claimed*: Rachel Weiner, "Ted Cruz: '47 Percent' Cost Us Hispanics," *Washington Post*, November 30, 2012.

156 *"He had a crazy policy"*: Ronald Kessler, "Donald Trump: Mean-Spirited GOP Won't Win Elections," Newsmax, November 26, 2012.

156 *When Romney called him*: MR, personal journal, November 12, 2012.

156 *His brother-in-law called*: MR, interview, September 13, 2022.

156 *Bill Clinton called*: MR, personal journal, November 12, 2012.

156 *"My life is not defined"*: McKay Coppins, "The Liberation of Mitt Romney," *The Atlantic*, October 20, 2019.

157   *"It's just very difficult to beat"*: Kevin Cirilli, "Rush: You Can't Beat 'Santa,'" *Politico*, November 7, 2012.

157   *Romney found himself nodding*: MR, personal journal, November 8, 2012.

157   *Romney had won 59 percent*: "President Exit Polls," *New York Times*, November 2012.

157   *When Romney asked his campaign manager*: MR, personal journal, November 9, 2012.

157   *"For Romney, Sour Grapes"*: "Your Say: For Romney, Sour Grapes," *USA Today*, November 18, 2012.

157   *Eric Fehrnstrom asked Romney*: MR, personal journal, November 15, 2012.

157   *With time, Romney was able*: MR, interview, March 1, 2022.

158   *"I vastly overstated"*: MR, interview, March 1, 2022.

158   *"I think what presidents accomplish"*: MR, interview, June 13, 2022.

158   *In a meeting after the election*: MR, personal journal, November 2013.

159   *On November 29, 2012*: MR, personal journal, November 29, 2012.

160   *"But the truth is"*: MR, personal journal, November 16, 2012.

161   *"But as a leader"*: MR, personal journal, November 16, 2012.

161   *A couple of weeks after*: MR, personal journal, December 16, 2012.

161   *"I guess you don't know much"*: Ann Romney, interview, April 20, 2022.

161   *He skied in Deer Valley*: MR, personal journal, January 17–18, 2014.

161   *jet-skied in the Bahamas*: MR, personal journal, January 6–13, 2013.

161   *"Nudes on the beach"*: MR, personal journal, September 10–22, 2014.

161   *He went quail-hunting*: MR, personal journal, January 6–13, 2013.

161   *attended the Super Bowl*: MR, personal journal, February 2014.

161   *watched Marquez knock out*: MR, personal journal, December 10, 2012.

161   *their eleven-thousand-square-foot dream home*: San Diego City Site Development Permit, No. 73791.

162   *"I have looked at what happens"*: Greg Whiteley, dir., *Mitt*, Los Gatos, CA: Netflix Originals, 2014.

162   *First it was Senator Joe Lieberman*: MR, personal journal, March 9, 2014.

162   *Then it was Spencer Zwick*: MR, personal journal, January 2015.

162   *"He was way ahead"*: Neil Cavuto on *Your World*, Fox News, May 6, 2014.

162   *"Mitt Romney Was Right"*: Isaac Chotiner, "Mitt Romney Was Right about Russia," *New Republic*, March 3, 2014.

162   *a widely viewed Netflix documentary*: Whiteley, dir., *Mitt*.

162   *Romney initially dismissed*: MR, personal journal, September 10–22, 2014.

162   *One day in September of 2014*: MR, personal journal, early fall 2014.

163   *on the night of the 2014 midterm*: MR, personal journal, November 4, 2014.

163   *When John Kasich invited Romney*: MR, personal journal, October 28, 2014.

164   *His meeting with Jeb Bush*: MR, personal journal, January 23, 2015.

164   *Bobby Jindal was fine*: MR, personal journal, April 21, 2015.

164 *Rick Perry was getting*: MR, personal journal, April 21, 2015.

164 *In an email*: MR, email message to Paul Ryan, November 7, 2014.

164 *"Everybody in here can go"*: Patrick O'Connor and Beth Reinhard, "Romney Tells Donors He Is Considering 2016 White House Bid," *Wall Street Journal*, January 9, 2015.

165 *"Nooooo!"*: Marc A. Thiessen, "Romney 2016? Nooooo!" *Washington Post*, September 1, 2014.

165 *"I thought Romney was"*: Dylan Beyers, "Rupert Murdoch Weighs In on 2016, Calls Romney 'A Terrible Candidate,'" *Politico*, January 1, 2015.

165 *"Don't Do It"*: Peggy Noonan, "Don't Do It, Mr. Romney," *Wall Street Journal*, January 16, 2015.

165 *The Bush machine*: Matt Viser, "Jeb Bush Pressing to Lock in Mitt Romney's Donors," *Boston Globe*, February 13, 2015.

165 *"Funny, but the more"*: MR, personal journal, January 9, 2015.

165 *A poll, privately commissioned*: Dan Balz, Philip Rucker, Robert Costa, and Matea Gold, "One Year, Two Races: Inside the Republican Party's Bizarre, Tumultuous 2015," *Washington Post*, January 3, 2016.

165 *"I believe that one"*: Philip Rucker and Dan Balz, "Mitt Romney Decides against Running for President Again in 2016," *Washington Post*, January 30, 2015.

166 *a Mexican-rapist invasion*: "Full Text: Donald Trump Announces a Presidential Bid," *Washington Post*, June 16, 2015.

166 *mocking John McCain's war record*: Erik Ortiz, "'He's Not a War Hero': Donald Trump Mocks John McCain's Service," NBC News, July 18, 2015.

166 *the Muslim immigration ban*: Eli Stokols and Daniel Strauss, "Donald Trump Calls for 'Total and Complete Shutdown of Muslims' Coming to U.S.," *Politico*, December 7, 2015.

166 *musing about Megyn Kelly's period*: Holly Yan, "Donald Trump's 'Blood' Comment about Megyn Kelly Draws Outrage," CNN, August 8, 2015.

166 *discussing the size of his manhood*: Gregory Krieg, "Donald Trump Defends Size of His Penis," CNN, March 4, 2016.

166 *Part of the difference*: MR, interview, December 14, 2021.

166 *"Looking back, I have dramatically"*: MR, interview, June 7, 2021.

167 *Trump's fans would surround them*: McKay Coppins, "Trump Campaign Rally Erupts in Chaos and Ugly Confrontation," BuzzFeed News, December 15, 2015.

167 *"Get him the hell out of here"*: "Trump to Protester: 'Get Him the Hell out of Here,'" Reuters, November 22, 2015.

167 *"I'd like to punch him"*: Michael E. Miller, "Donald Trump on a Protester: 'I'd Like to Punch Him in the Face,'" *Washington Post*, February 23, 2016.

167 *"Those people weren't"*: Ann Romney, interview, July 7, 2022.

167   *The coalition that Trump was building*: Nicholas Confessore and Nate Cohn, "Donald Trump's Victory Was Built on Unique Coalition of White Voters," *New York Times*, November 9, 2016.

167   *But Romney suspected*: MR, interview, February 15, 2022.

167   *On the night of the Iowa caucuses*: MR, personal journal, January 2016.

168   *A head-on attack would*: Matt Viser, "Mitt Romney Spoke Out against Donald Trump after Months of Rising Frustration," *Boston Globe*, March 12, 2016.

168   *Trump finished a narrow second*: Steven Shepard, "Insiders: Trump Will Rebound in New Hampshire," *Politico*, February 4, 2016.

168   *Five days before the New Hampshire*: MR, personal journal, February 4, 2016.

168   *Myers had been pushing*: MR, personal journal, October 2015.

168   *as had Stevens and Zwick*: MR, personal journal, October 2015; February 9, 2016.

168   *Mike Leavitt, meanwhile*: MR, personal journal, January 2016.

169   *Romney told O'Brien*: MR, personal journal, February 4, 2016.

169   *"scary" and "a demagogue"*: MR, personal journal, April 21, 2015; May 20, 2015.

169   *Romney's old friend Mike Murphy*: Maggie Haberman and Michael Barbaro, "Jeb Bush Allies Threaten Wave of Harsh Attacks on Marco Rubio, an Ex-Mentee," *New York Times*, November 9, 2015.

169   *Romney emailed his team*: MR, personal journal, February 9, 2016.

169   *Romney tried needling Trump*: Mitt Romney, ".@realDonaldTrump taxes for last 4+ years are still being audited. There are more #bombshells or he would release them," @MittRomney, Twitter, February 25, 2016, 10:28 p.m.

170   *His Holiness was "disgraceful"*: Alan Rappeport, "Donald Trump Calls Pope's Criticism 'Disgraceful,'" *New York Times*, February 18, 2016.

170   *involved in the Kennedy assassination?*: Donald Trump interviewed on *Fox & Friends*, Fox News, May 3, 2016.

170   *Romney would later note, much more barbaric*: MR, interview, February 15, 2022.

170   *The breaking point came*: Matt Viser, "Mitt Romney Explains His Decision to Criticize Donald Trump," *Boston Globe*, March 12, 2016.

171   *"I don't know anything about"*: Donald Trump interviewed by Jake Tapper, *State of the Union*, CNN, February 28, 2016.

171   *Watching the interview finally pushed*: MR, personal journal, March 2, 2016.

171   *Christie had recently endorsed*: Jeremy Diamond, Jake Tapper, Phil Mattingly, and Stephen Collinson, "Chris Christie Endorses Donald Trump," CNN, February 26, 2016.

171   *Newt Gingrich and Rudy Giuliani*: MR, personal journal, March 2, 2016.

172   *"There was little precedent"*: Ed O'Keefe, "Mitt Romney Slams 'Phony' Trump: He's Playing 'the American Public for Suckers,'" *Washington Post*, March 3, 2016.

172   *"There probably hasn't been"*: Alexander Burns and Michael Barbaro, "Mitt Romney and John McCain Denounce Donald Trump as a Danger to Democracy," *New York Times*, March 3, 2016.

CHAPTER TEN Vox

Unless otherwise noted, Mitt Romney's account of the secretary of state interview process—as well as all firsthand quotes—come from an interview conducted by the author on June 15, 2021.

173 *Romney responded with a Tweet*: Mitt Romney, "If Trump had said 4 years ago the things he says today about the KKK, Muslims, Mexicans, disabled, I would NOT have accepted his endorsement," @MittRomney, Twitter, March 3, 2016, 2:13 p.m.

174 *"Obviously if I did anything"*: MR, interview, June 7, 2021.

174 *"I did not see that"*: MR, interview, June 7, 2021.

174 *"I'm with anybody"*: MR, personal journal, March 2, 2016.

175 *"My topic is getting you"*: MR, email message to Marco Rubio, March 6, 2016.

175 *"He should sue"*: Alexandra Jaffe, "Donald Trump Has 'Small Hands,' Marco Rubio Says," NBC News, February 29, 2016.

175 *"If he hadn't inherited"*: Nick Gass, "Rubio: Trump Would Be 'Selling Watches,'" *Politico*, February 25, 2016.

175 *Lindsey Graham reported*: MR, personal journal, March 6, 2016.

175 *Andy Puzder, the founder*: MR, personal journal, March 2, 2016.

175 *When Romney took the idea*: MR, interview, June 15, 2021.

176 *Two days later, he called*: MR, personal journal, March 17, 2016.

176 *Romney turned his attention*: MR, personal journal, March 14–17, 2016.

176 *But he was so stubborn*: Dana Bash, "Kasich Responds to Anti-Trump 'Split the Map' Strategy," CNN, March 20, 2016.

176 *Romney had tried in early March*: MR, personal journal, March 2, 2016.

177 *"John, I am 100% convinced"*: MR, email message to John Kasich, March 19, 2016.

177 *"I just don't see it the way"*: John Kasich, email message to MR, March 19, 2016.

177 *On at least one occasion*: MR, personal journal, March 14, 2016.

177 *"Not sure why he told"*: Ted Cruz, email message to MR, March 17, 2016.

178 *"Is Mitt running"*: John Kasich, video on *Meet the Press*, NBC News, April 3, 2016.

178 *"I noticed with some humor"*: MR, email message to John Kasich, April 2, 2016.

178 *"Kasich is delusional"*: MR, personal journal, April 15, 2016.

178 *On April 24*: "Press Release—Cruz Campaign Releases Statement on Upcoming Primaries," American Presidency Project, April 24, 2016.

178 *"Well done"*: MR, email message to John Kasich, April 24, 2016.

178 *"Now that Cruz has finally"*: John Weaver, email message to Mitt Romney, April 25, 2016.

178 *"I've never told"*: Mark Hensch, "Kasich Wants Ind. Votes Despite Cruz Pact," *The Hill*, April 25, 2016.

178 *"I'm not out to stop"*: John Kasich interviewed on the *Today* show, NBC, April 26, 2016.

179 *"From what I saw today"*: MR, email message to John Weaver, April 25, 2016.

179 *He pitched Ben Sasse*: Philip Rucker and Robert Costa, "Inside the GOP Effort to Draft an Independent Candidate to Derail Trump," *Washington Post*, May 14, 2016.

179 *He met with Bill Kristol*: MR, personal journal, August 30, 2016.

179 *"Any chance I could get you"*: MR, personal journal, May 6, 2016.

179 *There was Rick Perry*: Dana Bash, "First on CNN: Rick Perry Endorses Donald Trump for President," CNN, May 6, 2016.

179 *There was Bobby Jindal*: Gregory Krieg, "Eventually Trump? The GOP's Most Vocal Critics Are Falling in Line," CNN, May 27, 2016.

180 *Even Marco Rubio*: Max Boot, "Marco Rubio's Humiliating Transformation into a Trump Fan-Boy Is Complete," *Washington Post*, June 20, 2019.

180 *"Pretty lonely for those of us"*: MR, email message to Jeb Bush, June 2, 2016.

180 *"ESPN is looking"*: Jeb Bush, email message to MR, June 2, 2016.

180 *Romney skipped the convention*: MR, personal journal, August 30, 2016.

180 *sort through packs of Starbursts*: Josh Dawset and Robert Costa, "Kevin McCarthy Relishes Role as Trump's Fixer, Friend and Candy Man," *Washington Post*, January 15, 2018.

180 *Romney took little comfort*: MR, interview, June 15, 2021.

181 *"It's a matter of personal conscience"*: Jake Miller, "Mitt Romney: No Donald Trump, no Hillary Clinton, no independent bid," *CBS News*, June 29, 2016.

181 *"Presidents have an impact"*: Mitt Romney interviewed by Wolf Blitzer, *The Situation Room*, CNN, June 10, 2016.

181 *"Hillary Clinton is wrong"*: Jake Miller, "Mitt Romney: No Donald Trump, No Hillary Clinton, No Independent Bid," CBS News, June 29, 2016.

181 *Romney sent a curt email*: MR, email message to Chris Christie, February 26, 2016.

181 *"If you ever want to have"*: Chris Christie, email message to MR, March 24, 2016.

182 *"He is unquestionably"*: MR, email message to Chris Christie, March 24, 2016.

182 *When Reince Priebus called*: MR, personal journal, August 30, 2016.

182 *"Reince is trying to shame"*: MR, personal journal, September 19, 2016.

182 *crusading against free trade*: Nick Corasaniti, Alexander Burns, and Binyamin Appelbaum, "Donald Trump Vows to Rip Up Trade Deals and Confront China," *New York Times*, June 28, 2016.

182 *protect government entitlement programs*: Yoni Appelbaum, "Trump Wants to Make Government Huge Again," *The Atlantic*, March 13, 2016.

182 *"Obama-Trump" voters*: Yamiche Alcindor, "Some Who Saw Change in Obama Find It Now in Donald Trump," *New York Times*, November 2, 2016.

183 *one poll showed that Mormons*: Robert Gehrke, "Trump Leads (Barely) in Utah, Where Voters Are Repulsed by Major-Party Choices," *Salt Lake Tribune*, October 31, 2016.

183 *feud with a gold-star family*: F. Brinley Bruton, "Gold Star Families Attack Trump over Comments about Ghazala Khan," NBC News, August 1, 2016.

183 *called a federal judge*: Donald Trump, interviewed by Jake Tapper, *The Lead*, CNN, June 3, 2016.

183 *Trump could be heard bragging*: Jonathan Lemire, "Trump Caught on Video Making Lewd, Crude Remarks about Women," Associated Press, October 7, 2016.

183 *"Once, during the 2008 presidential primaries"*: MR, interview, June 8, 2023.

183 *"Trump frightens me"*: Mitt Romney, email message to Jeb Bush, September 26, 2016.

184 *Romney started doing this*: MR, personal journal, September 19, 2016.

184 *The phone call came*: MR, personal journal, November 17, 2016.

184 *Later that day, he spoke*: MR, personal journal, November 17, 2016.

185 *He spoke to Taiwan before China*: Anne Gearan, "Trump Speaks with Taiwanese President, a Major Break with Decades of U.S. Policy on China," *Washington Post*, December 3, 2016.

185 *only connected with the Australian*: Lauren Said-Moorhouse, "Golf Legend Greg Norman Hooks Up Australian PM's Call with Donald Trump," CNN, November 17, 2016.

187 *As he rode away, reporters called out*: Michael C. Bender, "Mitt Romney Under 'Active and Serious Consideration' as Secretary of State," *Wall Street Journal*, November 20, 2016.

187 *Romney heard from a wide range*: Michelle L. Price, "Romney: Clinton Told Me to Take Trump Secretary of State Job," Associated Press, June 9, 2017.

187 *"If he actually asks you"*: MR, interview, November 3, 2022.

188 *"Mitt Romney at the exact moment"*: Dr. Bucky Isotope, Professional Pizza Critic, "PICTURED: Mitt Romney at the exact moment he realizes he's selling his soul," @BuckyIsotope, Twitter, November 29, 2016, 9:44 p.m.

188 *"What's for dinner, Donald?"*: Marc Caputo, "'What's for dinner, Donald?' 'Your dignity,'" @MarcACaputo, Twitter, November 29, 2016, 8:54 p.m.

189 *He told reporters that he had*: "Mitt Romney: 'Wonderful' Evening with Donald Trump | NBC News," NBC News video, YouTube, November 30, 2016, https://www.youtube.com/watch?v=Ct8PxX7YKlw.

189 *"In retrospect, he dodged"*: George W. Bush, interview, October 12, 2022.

190 *"Mitt Romney is someone I had"*: Sam Stein and Ryan Grim, "The Humbling of Mitt Romney, By Donald J. Trump," *HuffPost*, December 13, 2016.

190 *"As for Mr. Reid"*: Mark Hensch, "Reid on respect for Romney: 'I have none'," *The Hill*, December 13, 2016.

190 *Roger Stone crowed*: Brooke Seipel, "Roger Stone: Trump Interviewed Romney to 'Torture' Him," *The Hill*, December 12, 2016.

190 *"Judas Iscariot got 30 pieces"*: Molly Ball, "Kellyanne's Alternate Universe," *The Atlantic*, April 2017.

CHAPTER ELEVEN Turning and Turning

Unless otherwise noted, all firsthand quotes come from an interview with Mitt Romney conducted by the author on June 21, 2021.

191 *One day in March of 2017*: MR, interview, June 21, 2021.
191 *The two men had known each other*: MR, interview, June 21, 2021.
192 *During Romney's presidential campaigns*: MR, interview, November 3, 2022.
192 *"You're kind of uptight"*: MR, interview, April 27, 2022.
192 *During a Senate hearing*: Emily Tillett, "Orrin Hatch Draws Twitter Reaction for Removing Imaginary Glasses during Hearing," CBS News, January 17, 2018.
192 *During an interview on healthcare*: Liz Stark, "Hatch Defends Colorful Comment with a Lesson on Civil War Jargon," CNN, August 7, 2017.
192 *He'd always fancied himself a writer*: MR, personal journal, January 2016.
192 *M. Russell Ballard, a senior apostle*: MR, personal journal, August 30, 2016.
192 *"In other words"*: MR, email message to Stephen Studdert, November 18, 2018.
193 *"Money is motivating"*: MR, personal journal, January 2016.
193 *Mike Leavitt had floated the possibility*: MR, personal journal, January 2016.
193 *He spoke with Mitch McConnell*: MR, interview, June 21, 2021.
193 *"If Jon Jr. wants to be senator"*: MR, interview, June 21, 2021.
194 *Ironically, Romney himself had been offered*: MR, interview, June 8, 2023.
194 *Romney began keeping a detailed*: MR, personal document, "Senate pros/cons, Fall 2017."
195 *"very fine people"*: Donald Trump news conference, Trump Tower, New York City, August 15, 2017.
195 *recently announced a brain cancer diagnosis*: Susan Scutti, "Sen. John McCain Has Brain Cancer, Aggressive Tumor Surgically Removed," CNN, July 20, 2017.
196 *When reporters asked him about Romney*: McKay Coppins, "Orrin Hatch Tells Friends He Plans to Retire," *The Atlantic*, October 27, 2017.
196 *In the latter part of his career*: Orrin Hatch, interview, 2010.
196 *"You are a true fighter"*: Louis Nelson, "Trump Says He Wants Hatch to Seek 8th Senate Term," *Politico*, December 4, 2017.
196 *"the greatest presidency we've seen"*: Thomas Burr, "'You Are One Heckuva Leader': After Tax Vote, Sen. Orrin Hatch Says Trump May Become the Best President Ever," *Salt Lake Tribune*, December 20, 2017.
196 *After the ceremony*: Jonathan Martin, "Orrin Hatch, Utah Senator, to Retire, Opening Path for Mitt Romney," *New York Times*, January 2, 2018.
197 *Shortly before Christmas, Romney called*: MR, interview, July 19, 2021.
197 *It didn't hurt that Zwick*: Coppins, "Orrin Hatch Tells Friends."
197 *That night, Romney changed*: Erica Pandey, "Mitt Romney Changes Twitter Location to Utah," Axios, January 2, 2018.
197 *Not long after Romney*: MR, interview, July 14, 2021.

197 *"Two million square miles"*: MR, interview, May 11, 2021.

198 *"I think he's keeping out candidates"*: Courtney Tanner, "Utah GOP Chief Slams Mitt Romney's Expected Senate Run; Romney Delays Announcement, Citing Florida Shooting," *Salt Lake Tribune*, February 14, 2018.

198 *he and Ann had built a house*: Matt Canham and Thomas Burr, "The Hidden Room inside Mitt Romney's New Utah House," *Salt Lake Tribune*, October 24, 2013.

198 *By the end of his campaign*: Matt Waldrip, interview, July 12, 2021.

199 *In a video announcing his bid*: Mitt Romney, "I am running for United States Senate to serve the people of Utah and bring Utah's values to Washington," @MittRomney, Twitter, February 16, 2018, 8:18 a.m.

199 *"People are Utah nice"*: MR, email message to Bill Ryan, October 25, 2018.

199 *A "latter-day Beaver Cleaver"*: Alex Beam, "A big win for the Mormon Church," *Boston Globe*, November 14, 2012.

199 *"As they say in this business"*: "Hot Dog Eating Contest Feat. Mitt Romney (Utah County Fair) | August 18, 2018," uploaded by Spanish Fork 17, YouTube, August 27, 2018, https://www.youtube.com/watch?v=eJ3Nw5S3Bzw.

199 *"My favorite meat is hot dog"*: David M. Drucker, "Mitt Romney: Insurgent and Insider," *Washington Examiner*, May 1, 2018.

199 *Romney rewrote the lyrics*: Herb Scribner, "Video: Mitt Romney Sings Utah Version of 'I've Been Everywhere,'" *Deseret News*, November 8, 2018.

200 *"Sure, let's do it"*: Matt Waldrip, interview, July 12, 2021.

200 *On February 22, he attended*: MR, interview, July 14, 2021.

200 *Bundy's prayer went on*: Paul Rolly, "Rolly: Romney Gets an Introduction into the Wild and Wacky World of Rural Utah Politics," *Salt Lake Tribune*, May 11, 2018.

201 *The event had all the trappings*: Lee Davidson and Courtney Tanner, "Utah Republican Delegates Force Mitt Romney into a Primary Election with State Lawmaker Mike Kennedy in the Race for the U.S. Senate," *Salt Lake Tribune*, April 21, 2018.

201 *"ready to be flung at the foes"*: Maeve Reston, "Mitt Romney Fails to Secure Utah GOP Nomination, Will Face Primary," CNN, April 22, 2018.

201 *"First, none of us is David"*: Davidson and Tanner, "Utah Republican Delegates Force Mitt Romney."

201 *"This is terrific"*: Reston, "Mitt Romney Fails to Secure."

202 *Trump and his allies*: Christopher Cadelago and Ted Hesson, "Why Trump Is Talking Nonstop about the Migrant Caravan," *Politico*, October 23, 2018.

202 *He dispatched thousands of troops*: Michael D. Shear and Thomas Gibbons-Neff, "Trump Sending 5,200 Troops to the Border in an Election-Season Response to Migrants," *New York Times*, October 29, 2018.

202 *"STOP THE CARAVAN"*: David Martosko, "Video: POTUS Says He Knows 'Nothing' about News Networks Banning 'Racist' Pro-Trump Campaign Ad That Stoked Fear over Caravan Migrants—after Fox Joins CNN and NBC in Pulling It from the Air," *Daily Mail*, November 5, 2018.

202   *a vector of dangerous diseases*: Jason Le Miere, "Fox News Guest Claims Migrant Caravan Carries 'Leprosy,' Will 'Infect Our People,' Offers No Evidence," *Newsweek*, October 29, 2018.

202   *a Trojan horse for murderous cartels*: Stephen Dinan, "Kirstjen Nielsen Warns of Cartels' Role in Migrant Caravan," *Washington Times*, October 21, 2018.

202   *a pawn in a plot*: John Wagner, "Trump Says He 'Wouldn't Be Surprised' If Unfounded Conspiracy Theory about George Soros Funding Caravan Is True," *Washington Post*, November 1, 2018.

202   *"Many Gang Members"*: Donald J. Trump, "Many Gang Members and some very bad people are mixed into the Caravan heading to our Southern Border. Please go back, you will not be admitted into the United States unless you go through the legal process. This is an invasion of our Country and our Military is waiting for you!," @realDonaldTrump, Twitter, October 29, 2018, 10:41 a.m.

202   *"The caravan from Honduras"*: MR, email message to Beth Myers and Stuart Stevens, October 22, 2018.

202   *the "Soros-occupied State Department"*: Chris Farrell interviewed by Lou Dobbs, *Lou Dobbs Tonight*, Fox Business, October 25, 2018.

202   *"Fox is becoming"*: MR, email message to Beth Myers, Stuart Stevens, and Matt Waldrip, October 28, 2018.

202   *"Lou is a moron"*: MR, email message to Stuart Stevens, October 29, 2018.

202   *In October, pipe bombs began*: Kari de Vries, Evan Perez, and Shimon Prokupecz, "'Act of Terror': Bombs Sent to CNN, Clintons, Obamas, Holder," CNN, October 26, 2018.

203   *Jamal Khashoggi had been murdered*: Kareem Fahim, "Turkey Concludes Saudi Journalist Jamal Khashoggi Killed by 'Murder' Team, Sources Say," *Washington Post*, October 6, 2016.

203   *"I think I've been toned down"*: "President Trump: 'I Think I've Been Toned Down . . . I Could Really Tone It Up . . . ,'" uploaded by C-SPAN, video, YouTube, https://www.youtube.com/watch?v=fSfDlMBtQzA.

203   *at a town hall*: Mitt Romney, "As I See It: The Free Press, a Pillar of Democracy," RomneyForUtah.com, November 1, 2018.

203   *"It was a revelation"*: MR, interview, June 21, 2021.

203   *"There is great anger"*: Donald J. Trump, "There is great anger in our Country caused in part by inaccurate, and even fraudulent, reporting of the news. The Fake News Media, the true Enemy of the People, must stop the open & obvious hostility & report the news accurately & fairly. That will do much to put out the flame . . ." @realDonaldTrump, Twitter, October 29, 2018, 8:03 a.m.; Donald J. Trump, ". . . of Anger and Outrage and we will then be able to bring all sides together in Peace and Harmony. Fake News Must End!" @realDonaldTrump, Twitter, October 29, 2018, 8:07 a.m.

204   *"The President's tweet today"*: MR, email message to Beth Myers, Stuart Stevens, and Matt Waldrip, October 29, 2018.

204 *"A lesson evidenced by the Arab Spring"*: Romney, "As I See It."

205 *"an empty suit"*: Mark R. Levin, "Romney is an empty suit," @marklevinshow, Twitter, November 3, 2018, 12:25 p.m.

205 a *"failed presidential candidate"*: Joshua Caplan, "Mitt Romney: Donald Trump's Vilification of the Media Is Unprecedented," *Breitbart*, November 4, 2018.

205 *There had been some discussion*: Matt Waldrip, email message to MR, Beth Myers, and Stuart Stevens, October 29, 2018.

205 *"not production values"*: MR, email message to Beth Myers, Stuart Stevens, and Matt Waldrip, October 29, 2018.

206 *"a call for greater dignity"*: Dennis Romboy, "Mitt Romney Is Headed to Washington After All—as U.S. Senator for Utah," *Deseret News*, November 6, 2018.

CHAPTER TWELVE The Punch Bowl

Unless otherwise noted, all firsthand quotes—as well as Romney's accounts of his first year in the U.S. Senate—are taken from an interview conducted on July 19, 2021.

207 *Trump fired his attorney general*: Peter Baker, Katie Benner, and Michael D. Shear, "Jeff Sessions Is Forced Out as Attorney General as Trump Installs Loyalist," *New York Times*, November 7, 2018.

207 *Trump pardoned two army officers*: Idrees Ali, "Trump Pardons Army Officers, Restores Navy SEAL's Rank in War Crimes Cases," Reuters, November 15, 2019.

207 *"radical environmentalists"*: Alejandra Reyes-Velarde and Joseph Serna, "California Fires: Trump Administration Now Blames Devastation on 'Radical Environmentalists,'" *Los Angeles Times*, November 19, 2018.

208 *"mind-numbingly moronic"*: MR, email message to Stuart Stevens, November 19, 2018.

208 *"He's what you said"*: Beth Myers, email message to MR, December 12, 2018.

209 *"The question no one seems to address"*: MR, email message to Beth Myers, December 23, 2018.

209 *"The Russian Witch Hunt Hoax"*: Donald J. Trump, "The Russian Witch Hunt Hoax, started as the 'insurance policy' long before I even got elected, is very bad for our Country. They are Entrapping people for misstatements, lies or unrelated things that took place many years ago. Nothing to do with Collusion. A Democrat Scam!" @realDonaldTrump, Twitter, December 16, 2018, 3:56 p.m.

209 *"I'm finding it hard"*: MR, email message to Beth Myers, Stuart Stevens, and Matt Waldrip, December 17, 2018.

209 *"Republicans used to understand"*: MR, email message to Beth Myers, Stuart Stevens, and Matt Waldrip, December 17, 2018.

209 *Trump abruptly announced on Twitter*: Mark Landler, Helene Cooper, and Eric Schmitt, "Trump to Withdraw U.S. Forces from Syria, Declaring 'We Have Won against ISIS'," *New York Times*, December 19, 2018.

210   *The next day, Defense Secretary James Mattis*: Paul Sonne, Josh Dawsey, and Missy Ryan, "Mattis Resigns after Clash with Trump over Troop Withdrawal from Syria and Afghanistan," *Washington Post*, December 20, 2018.

210   *Trump petulantly declared*: Julie Hirschfeld Davis and Emily Cochrane, "Demanding Wall Funding, Trump Balks at Bill to Avert Shutdown," *New York Times*, December 20, 2018.

210   *"There will be a shutdown"*: Donald J. Trump, "The Democrats, whose votes we need in the Senate, will probably vote against Border Security and the Wall even though they know it is DESPERATELY NEEDED. If the Dems vote no, there will be a shutdown that will last for a very long time. People don't want Open Borders and Crime!" @realDonaldTrump, Twitter, December 21, 2018, 7:24 a.m.

210   *That Christmas Eve, Romney*: MR, interview, November 3, 2022.

210   *"His last few weeks"*: MR, email message to Beth Myers, Stuart Stevens, and Matt Waldrip, December 24, 2018.

210   *"It's all so bad"*: Stuart Stevens, email message to MR, Beth Myers, and Matt Waldrip, December 24, 2018.

211   *"He was the last person I wanted"*: MR, email message to Beth Myers and Stuart Stevens, December 24, 2018.

212   *"The Trump presidency made"*: MR, "The President Shapes the Public Character of the Nation. Trump's Character Falls Short," *Washington Post*, January 1, 2019.

212   *"the leader of the Republican resistance"*: Bill Kristol, "For now at least Mitt Romney has become the leader of the Republican Resistance to Trump," @BillKristol, Twitter, January 1, 2019, 9:49 a.m.

213   *"I won big, and he didn't"*: Donald J. Trump, "Here we go with Mitt Romney, but so fast! Question will be, is he a Flake? I hope not. Would much prefer that Mitt focus on Border Security and so many other things where he can be helpful. I won big, and he didn't. He should be happy for all Republicans. Be a TEAM player & WIN!" @realDonaldTrump, Twitter, January 2, 2019, 7:53 a.m.

213   *"Jealously is a drink"*: Brad Parscale, "The truth is @MittRomney lacked the ability to save this nation. @realDonaldTrump has saved it. Jealously is a drink best served warm and Romney just proved it. So sad, I wish everyone had the courage @realDonaldTrump had," @parscale, Twitter, January 1, 2019, 8:31 p.m.

213   *"He ran to the media"*: David Perdue, "Mitt Romney Makes the Same Mistake That Cost Him the White House," *Washington Post*, January 4, 2019.

213   the *"chilly reception"*: Burgess Everett and James Arkin, "Romney Gets Chilly Reception from GOP Senators after Trump Attack," *Politico*, January 8, 2019.

213   *"the turd in the punch bowl"*: MR, email message to Beth Myers, Stuart Steven, and Matt Waldrip, January 8, 2019.

214   *His father had walked*: MR, interview, July 27, 2021.

214 *When they arrived at B33 Russell*: Matt Waldrip, interview, July 12, 2021.

214 *He told his aides he wanted*: Matt Waldrip, interview, September 19, 2022.

214 *began studying a flip-book*: Thomas Burr, "Mitt Romney Sworn In as Utah's Newest Senator amid Shutdown, Trump Criticism," *Salt Lake Tribune*, January 3, 2019.

214 *"Look, I'm obviously new"*: Matt Waldrip, interview, September 19, 2022.

214 *Many of the senators*: Susan Collins, interview, January 27, 2023.

215 *"small-bore measures"*: MR, interview, May 11, 2021.

216 *He was convinced that unless*: MR, interview, February 15, 2022.

216 *the problem only got worse*: Allan Sloan and Cezary Podkul: "Trump's Most Enduring Legacy Could Be the Historic Rise in the National Debt," *Washington Post*, January 14, 2021.

217 *"It's a challenge to justify"*: MR, email message to Chris Barkley, January 7, 2019.

217 *"In general, your instinct about"*: Chris Barkley, email message to MR, January 7, 2019.

217 *He spent his mornings*: MR, personal journal, March 14, 2019.

218 *In one surprising moment of candor*: MR, interview, August 4, 2021.

219 *polls showed an overwhelming*: Anthony Salvanto, Jennifer De Pinto, Fred Backus, and Kabir Khanna, "Pelosi Has Edge over Trump on Budget Negotiations, CBS News Poll Shows," CBS News, January 23, 2019.

219 *Romney was inclined to support it*: MR, personal journal, January 24, 2019.

220 *"I can't trade off a negotiating position"*: MR, personal journal, January 24, 2019.

220 *"No one had been more loyal"*: MR, interview, May 26, 2021.

220 *As he was leaving the chamber*: MR, personal journal, January 24, 2019.

222 *On the afternoon of March 6*: MR, personal journal, March 6, 2019.

222 *Only twice before in U.S. history*: Peter Baker, "Trump Declares a National Emergency, and Provokes a Constitutional Clash," *New York Times*, February 15, 2019.

222 *a "jackass" and a "kook"*: Lindsey Graham, interviewed by Erin Burnett, *Erin Burnett OutFront*, CNN, July 20, 2015; Tom Namako, "Lindsey Graham in 2016: Trump's a 'Kook,'" BuzzFeed News, December 1, 2017.

222 *"doesn't represent my party"*: Lindsey Graham, interviewed by Alisyn Camerota, *New Day*, CNN, December 8, 2015.

222 *one of the president's favorite*: Burgess Everett and Josh Dawsey, "Once a 'Jackass' and 'Idiot,' Trump and Graham Now Pals," *Politico*, October 23, 2017.

224 *Romney was not spared*: MR, personal journal, March 14, 2019.

225 *"This is a vote for the Constitution"*: "Romney Announces Vote to Disapprove of National Emergency Declaration," Romney.Senate.gov, March 14, 2019.

225 *"There is no intellectual honesty"*: Thom Tillis, "I Support Trump's Vision on Border Security. But I Would Vote against the Emergency," *Washington Post*, February 25, 2019.

225   *"If we get used to presidents"*: Alexander Bolton and Jordain Carney, "Trump Faces Growing Senate GOP Backlash on Emergency Declaration," *The Hill*, March 14, 2019.

225   *"Job preservation above"*: MR, personal journal, March 14, 2019.

226   *"He's not a natural bullshitter"*: Jonathan Chait, "Romney's Endearing Lies," *New Republic*, June 30, 2011.

226   *A few weeks after the border-wall*: MR, personal journal, March 26, 2019.

226   *the Justice Department had released*: "Read Attorney General William Barr's Summary of the Mueller Report," *New York Times*, March 24, 2019.

227   *When the full Mueller report*: "Read and Search the Full Mueller Report," CNN, July 21, 2019.

226   *On September 18, 2019*: Greg Miller, Ellen Nakashima, and Shane Harris, "Trump's Communications with Foreign Leader Are Part of Whistleblower Complaint That Spurred Standoff between Spy Chief and Congress, Former Officials Say," *Washington Post*, September 18, 2019.

227   *Romney had found the findings sickening*: "Senator Romney's Statement on Mueller Report," Romney.Senate.gov, April 19, 2019.

227   *The next day, it was revealed*: Ellen Nakashima, Shane Harris, Greg Miller, and Carol D. Leonnig, "Whistleblower Complaint about President Trump Involves Ukraine, According to Two People Familiar with the Matter," *Washington Post*, September 19, 2019.

227   *the day after that, it came out*: Matt Zapotosky, Greg Miller, Ellen Nakashima, and Carol D. Leonnig, "Trump Pressed Ukrainian Leader to Investigate Biden's Son, According to People Familiar with the Matter," *Washington Post*, September 20, 2019.

227   *"critical for the facts"*: Mitt Romney, "If the President asked or pressured Ukraine's president to investigate his political rival, either directly or through his personal attorney, it would be troubling in the extreme. Critical for the facts to come out," @MittRomney, Twitter, September 22, 2019, 2:34 p.m.

227   *an aide brought him*: MR, personal journal, September 25, 2019.

227   *"I would like you to do"*: "Full Document: Trump's Call with the Ukrainian President," *New York Times*, October 30, 2019.

227   *If Romney had any doubt*: MR, personal journal, September 25, 2019.

227   *"exceptionally qualified"*: "Senator Romney Announces Support for William Barr," Romney.Senate.gov, February 7, 2019.

228   *Later that day, Romney appeared*: "Mitt Romney," uploaded by the Atlantic Festival, video, YouTube, September 25, 2019, https://www.youtube.com/watch?v=2no3lLz_XNQ.

228   *McConnell pulled Romney aside*: MR, interview, May 18, 2021.

228   *For months, he'd had to endure*: Matt Waldrip, interview, March 20, 2023.

229   *China should join Ukraine*: Zeke Miller and Jill Colvin, "Not Just Ukraine: Trump Now Calls for China to Probe Bidens," Associated Press, October 3, 2019.

229 *"By all appearances"*: Mitt Romney, "By all appearances, the President's brazen and unprecedented appeal to China and to Ukraine to investigate Joe Biden is wrong and appalling," @MittRomney, Twitter, October 4, 2019, 12:02 p.m.

229 *"Somebody please wake up"*: Donald J. Trump, "Somebody please wake up Mitt Romney and tell him that my conversation with the Ukrainian President was a congenial and very appropriate one, and my statement on China pertained to corruption, not politics. If Mitt worked this hard on Obama, he could have won. Sadly, he choked!" @realDonaldTrump, Twitter, October 5, 2019, 10:06 a.m.

229 *"Mitt Romney never knew how"*: Donald J. Trump, "Mitt Romney never knew how to win. He is a pompous 'ass' who has been fighting me from the beginning, except when he begged me for my endorsement for his Senate run (I gave it to him), and when he begged me to be Secretary of State (I didn't give it to him). He is so bad for R's!" @realDonaldTrump, Twitter, October 5, 2019, 10:17 a.m.

229 *"I'm hearing that the Great People"*: Donald J. Trump, "I'm hearing that the Great People of Utah are considering their vote for their Pompous Senator, Mitt Romney, to be a big mistake. I agree! He is a fool who is playing right into the hands of the Do Nothing Democrats! #IMPEACHMITTROMNEY," @realDonaldTrump, Twitter, October 5, 2019, 3:06 p.m.

229 *Romney, who was picking apples*: McKay Coppins, "The Liberation of Mitt Romney," *The Atlantic*, October 20, 2019.

230 *McConnell had met privately*: Burgess Everett and Nancy Cook, "After McConnell Advice, Trump Lays Off GOP Senators on Impeachment," *Politico*, October 30, 2019.

230 *"It wasn't for you so much as for him"*: Matt Waldrip, interview, March 20, 2023; an individual with knowledge of the conversation, interview, n.d.

230 *"You're lucky"*: Matt Waldrip, interview, March 20, 2023; an individual with knowledge of the conversation, interview, n.d.

CHAPTER THIRTEEN Conviction

231 *John McCain summoned him*: MR, interview, February 1, 2022.

231 *McCain had been surprised*: Beth Myers, interview, May 2, 2022.

231 *famously rejecting a supporter's claim*: Jonathan Martin and Amie Parnes, "McCain: Obama Not an Arab, Crowd Boos," *Politico*, October 10, 2008.

232 *who'd made critical comments*: Roberta McCain, interviewed by Chris Matthews, *Hardball with Chris Matthews*, MSNBC, November 9, 2007.

232 *mailed Romney a handwritten letter*: Beth Myers, interview, May 2, 2022.

232 *"With McCain's retreat"*: Paul Kane, "With McCain's Retreat, Some Turn to Romney to Carry His Torch," *Washington Post*, February 15, 2018.

233   *"Today, two of the world's great powers"*: "IRI Board Member Senator Mitt Romney Presents Cindy McCain with the 2019 Freedom Award," uploaded by International Republican Institute, video, YouTube, May 14, 2019, https://www.youtube.com/watch?v=c7ptnU2VQlk.

233   *Cindy tearfully pulled*: Matt Waldrip, interview, September 19, 2022.

233   *"It was a little bit of"*: Waldrip, interview, September 19, 2022.

234   *In an interview with* The Atlantic: McKay Coppins, "The Liberation of Mitt Romney," *The Atlantic*, October 20, 2019.

234   *Within twenty-four hours, a reporter*: Ashley Feinberg, "This Sure Looks Like Mitt Romney's Secret Twitter Account (Update: It Is)," *Slate*, October 20, 2019.

234   *"He'd created the account"*: MR, interview, June 8, 2023.

234   *the internet had a field day*: Herb Scribner, "Is Mitt Romney Also Pierre Delecto? Social Media Goes Wild with Speculation," *Deseret News*, October 20, 2019.

234   *"What if Pierre Delecto is the real"*: flglmn, "what if pierre delecto is the real person and mitt romney is just a grift he's been running for the last few decades," @flglmn, Twitter, October 20, 2019, 7:36 p.m.

234   *One article on CNN's website*: Chris Cillizza, "What 'Pierre Delecto' Tells Us about the Current Republican Party," CNN, October 21, 2019.

234   *When* Washington Post *columnist*: Mihir Zaveri, "Mitt Romney Admits to Having a Secret Twitter Account, 'Pierre Delecto,'" *New York Times*, October 21, 2019.

234   *When Soledad O'Brien tweeted*: Thomas Burr, "Meet Pierre Delecto: Mitt Romney's Alter-Twitter-Ego," *Salt Lake Tribune*, October 21, 2019.

235   *"It's like yelling at the TV"*: MR, interview, November 3, 2022.

235   *He insisted that as a juror*: Lindsay Whitehurst, "Romney Undecided on Impeachment, Stands by Trump Criticism," Associated Press, October 10, 2019.

235   *One morning over breakfast*: MR, personal journal, November 21, 2019.

235   *"I don't know what's going on"*: Sean Hannity, *Hannity*, Fox News, October 22, 2019.

236   *They'd appeared side by side*: MR, interview, May 23, 2022.

236   *Hoping to mend the relationship*: MR, interview, August 4, 2021.

236   *"I can only imagine that Sean is consumed"*: MR, interview, August 14, 2021.

236   *Romney joined several other*: MR, personal journal, November 21, 2019.

236   *As he walked toward*: MR, personal journal, November 22, 2019.

237   *the president derided him*: Donald J. Trump, "Supposedly, according to the Corrupt Media, the Ukraine call 'concerned' today's Never Trumper witness. Was he on the same call that I was? Can't be possible! Please ask him to read the Transcript of the call. Witch Hunt!" @realDonaldTrump, Twitter, October 29, 2019, 9:09 a.m.; David Jackson and Michael Collins, "'I Never Heard of Him': Donald Trump Says He Doesn't Know Lt. Col. Alexander Vindman," *USA Today*, November 19, 2019.

237   *Ann received a phone call*: MR, personal journal, November 10, 2019.

237   *In the years since*: MR, interview, August 4, 2021.

238 *Romney carefully studied*: MR, personal journal, December 19, 2019.

238 *"not going to pretend"*: Veronica Stracqualursi, "'I'm Not Trying to Pretend to Be a Fair Juror Here': Graham Predicts Trump Impeachment Will 'Die Quickly' in Senate," CNN, December 15, 2019.

238 *On December 11*: An individual with knowledge of the conversation, interview, n.d.

239 *They had a certain high-school-cafeteria*: MR, interview, August 4, 2021.

239 *he was the only Mormon*: MR, interview, May 5, 2023.

239 *at Stanford, he would go*: MR, interview, September 27, 2021.

239 *"One of the advantages"*: McKay Coppins, "The Most American Religion," *The Atlantic*, December 16, 2020.

239 *"Stunning to me"*: MR, personal journal, December 18, 2019.

240 *"We have good arguments"*: An individual with knowledge of the conversation, interview, n.d.

240 *Predictably, the next Republican caucus meeting*: An individual with knowledge of the caucus meeting, interview, n.d.

241 *"[Gardner's] request suggests"*: MR, personal journal, December 18, 2019.

241 *In the weeks leading up to the trial*: MR, personal journal, December 10, 2019.

241 *lavishing praise on the president*: Aaron Blake, "Trump hires another top official with a history of pro-Trump hyperbole," *The Washington Post*, September 18, 2019.

241 *Wearing well-tailored suits*: Michael Crowley, Peter Bajer and Maggie Haberman, "Robert O'Brien 'Looks the Part,' but Has Spent Little Time Playing It," *The New York Times*, September 18, 2019.

241 *Pulling Waldrip aside*: MR, personal journal, December 11, 2019.

242 *To Romney, the case came down*: MR, personal journal, January 21, 2020.

242 *"Arguing both sides of an issue"*: MR, personal journal, January 22, 2020.

243 *"How unlike a real jury"*: MR, personal journal, January 23, 2020.

243 *"Interestingly, sometimes I think"*: MR, personal journal, January 23, 2020.

243 *"Amazing that we as a country"*: MR, personal journal, January 22, 2020.

243 *By the end of the first week*: MR, personal journal, January 23, 2020.

244 *"They nailed him"*: Matt Waldrip, interview, March 20, 2023; an individual with knowledge of the conversation, interview, n.d.

244 *A year earlier, Romney had been elected*: Thomas Burr, "Utah Sen. Mitt Romney Elected President of Secret Washington Group of Politicians, Business Leaders," *Salt Lake Tribune*, January 28, 2019.

245 *He tried hiring a pair of writers*: MR, interview, July 27, 2021.

245 *This time, there was a decided edge*: MR, interview, July 27, 2021.

245 *As waves of laughter washed*: Matt Waldrip, interview, September 19, 2022.

246 *"After 2 weeks, it's clear"*: Kelly Loeffler, "After 2 weeks, it's clear that Democrats have no case for impeachment. Sadly, my colleague @SenatorRomney wants to appease the left by calling witnesses who will slander the @realDonaldTrump during their 15 minutes of fame. The circus is over. It's time to move on! #gapol," @SenatorLoeffler, Twitter, January 27, 2020, 12:42 p.m.

246   *she and her husband were supporters*: Danny Hakim, Jo Becker, and Astead W. Herndon, "Kelly Loeffler, a Wall Street Senator with a Hardscrabble Pitch," *New York Times*, December 21, 2020.

246   *The answer came later that day*: Rachel Bade, "Rep. Collins to Challenge Appointed Sen. Loeffler in GOP Clash in Georgia," *Washington Post*, January 27, 2020.

246   *"Sad to see what happens"*: MR, personal journal, January 27, 2020.

246   *"It's clear to everyone in the room"*: MR, personal journal, January 29, 2020.

247   *"I'm no fan of the president"*: MR, personal journal, January 28, 2020.

247   *When he informed his senior staff*: MR, personal journal, January 29, 2020.

248   *"If I were to shrink"*: MR, personal journal, January 30, 2020.

248   Search diligently, pray always: McKay Coppins, "How Mitt Romney Decided Trump Is Guilty," *The Atlantic*, February 5, 2020.

248   *Romney had paid a visit*: MR, personal journal, January 26, 2020.

249   *they wouldn't be happy with him*: Alexander Bolton, "Poll: West Virginia Voters Would View Manchin Negatively If He Votes to Convict Trump," *The Hill*, January 15, 2020.

249   *"We're both 72"*: MR, personal journal, February 4, 2020; Joe Manchin, interview, January 24, 2023.

249   *"Even if the Bidens had done"*: MR, personal journal, January 30, 2020.

250   *"The Utah Republicans that had nominated"*: MR, personal journal, January 30, 2020.

250   *Romney slept fitfully that night*: MR, personal journal, January 31, 2020.

251   *Minutes before going on*: Matt Waldrip, interview, March 30, 2023.

251   *That Ryan had been unable*: MR, interview, June 15, 2021.

253   *He left the chamber and called Ann*: MR, personal journal, February 5, 2020.

253   *"I feel as if a huge weight"*: MR, personal journal, February 5, 2020.

CHAPTER FOURTEEN 2020

Unless otherwise indicated, all firsthand quotes from Mitt Romney come from an interview with the author conducted on August 4, 2021.

257   *"Romney is going to be associated"*: Lou Dobbs, *Lou Dobbs Tonight*, Fox Business, February 5, 2020.

257   *"He's now officially a member"*: Donald Trump Jr., "Mitt Romney is forever bitter that he will never be POTUS. He was too weak to beat the Democrats then so he's joining them now. He's now officially a member of the resistance & should be expelled from the @GOP," @DonaldJTrumpJr, Twitter, February 5, 2020, 2:32 p.m.

257   *"whoever he is talking to"*: Ed Rollins, interviewed by Lou Dobbs, *Lou Dobbs Tonight*, Fox Business, February 5, 2020.

257 *In fact, Romney hadn't consulted*: Employee of The Church of Jesus Christ of Latter-day Saints, interview, February 5, 2020.

257 *"I don't like people who use"*: Quint Forgey, "Trump Attacks Impeachment Foes at National Prayer Breakfast for Invoking Faith," *Politico*, February 6, 2020.

258 *"This year, I would actually be afraid"*: Fadel Allassan, "CPAC Chair Says He Would Fear for Romney's 'Physical Safety' If He Attended," Axios, February 10, 2020.

258 *Notes of gratitude poured in*: Matt Waldrip, interview, September 19, 2022.

258 *In one recent poll*: Bryan Schott, "Romney's Job Approval from Utah Voters Drops Significantly During Impeachment," Utah Policy, February 7, 2020.

258 *Romney's meeting with Republican state legislators*: MR, personal journal, February 6, 2020.

258 *One lawmaker had already introduced*: Benjamin Wood and Bethany Rogers, "Utah Lawmaker Files Bill to Censure Mitt Romney over Trump Impeachment Vote," *Salt Lake Tribune*, February 6, 2020.

258 *Mike Schultz—spent the meeting*: Matt Waldrip, interview, March 30, 2023.

259 *Later that day, once the Utah*: MR, personal journal, February 6, 2020.

260 *"This is their new hoax"*: Lauren Egan, "Trump Calls Coronavirus Democrats' 'New Hoax,'" NBC News, February 28, 2020.

260 *Romney returned to his office*: MR, journal, March 11, 2020.

260 *Once, when his staff surprised him*: William Cummings, "On His Birthday, Twitter Mocks Mitt Romney for the Way He Blows Out His Candles," *USA Today*, March 12, 2019.

261 *"After successfully delaying"*: MR, email message to Liz Johnson, Beth Myers, and Matt Waldrip, March 11, 2020.

261 *"To what end?"*: Matt Waldrip, email message to Liz Johnson, Beth Myers, and MR, March 11, 2020.

261 *"I'm just really pissed"*: MR, email message to Liz Johnson, Beth Myers, and Matt Waldrip, March 11, 2020.

261 *Romney, once again overwhelmed*: Matt Waldrip, interview, March 30, 2023.

262 *"I was on the phone"*: Matt Waldrip, interview, March 30 2023.

262 *direct payments of $1,000*: Jordan Carney, "Romney Proposes Giving $1K to Every US Adult amid Coronavirus," *The Hill*, March 16, 2020.

262 *"I knew Grandpa Mitt"*: Matt Waldrip, interview, March 30, 2023.

263 *Trump mused during one of his briefings*: Allyson Chiu, Katie Shepherd, Brittany Shammas, and Colby Itkowitz, "Trump Claims Controversial Comment about Injecting Disinfectants Was 'Sarcastic,'" *Washington Post*, April 24, 2020.

263 *"There's no question he was serious"*: MR, interview, June 21, 2021.

263 *Jared Kushner, Trump's son-in-law*: Matt Waldrip, handwritten notes taken in a meeting between MR and Jared Kushner, May 15, 2019.

263 *"I think he's not smart"*: MR, interview, April 27, 2022.

264 *"Our shock and outrage"*: Mitt Romney, "No Americans should fear enmity and harm from those sworn to protect us. The death of George Floyd must not be in vain: Our shock and outrage must grow into collective determination to extinguish forever such racist abuse," @MittRomney, Twitter, May 28, 2020, 9:01 a.m.

264 *"Peaceful protests underscore"*: Mitt Romney, "The George Floyd murder is abhorrent. Peaceful protests underscore the urgency of addressing injustices. But violence drowns the message of the protestors [*sic*] and mocks the principles of justice," @MittRomney, Twitter, May 30, 2020, 9:56 p.m.

265 *the "anarchy" in the streets*: Krishnadev Calamur, Ayesha Rascoe, and Alana Wise, "Trump Says He Spoke with Floyd's Family, Understands Hurt and Pain of Community," NPR, May 29, 2020.

265 *a "symbol of hate"*: Max Cohen, "Trump: Black Lives Matter Is a 'Symbol of Hate,'" *Politico*, July 1, 2020.

265 *on the "domestic terrorists"*: Oliver Milman, "Trump Complains about 'Ugly Anarchists' as Police Continue Aggression on US Protesters," *The Guardian*, June 11, 2020.

265 *In one particularly ugly scene*: Tom Gjelten, "Peaceful Protesters Tear-Gassed to Clear Way for Trump Church Photo-Op," NPR, June 1, 2020.

265 *soon "come for you"*: Allyson Chiu, "Tucker Carlson Says Protests Are 'Definitely Not about Black Lives,' Prompting Backlash," *Washington Post*, June 9, 2020.

265 *a "full-fledged anti-American organization"*: Rush Limbaugh, *The Rush Limbaugh Show*, Premiere Radio, July 27, 2020.

265 *"This is my father"*: Mitt Romney, "This is my father, George Romney, participating in a Civil Rights march in the Detroit suburbs during the late 1960s—'Force alone will not eliminate riots,' he said. 'We must eliminate the problems from which they stem,'" @MittRomney, Twitter, June 6, 2020, 10:35 a.m.

265 *"We need to stand up"*: "Sen. Mitt Romney Joins Black Lives Matter Protest in DC," Associated Press, June 7, 2020.

265 *Romney would cosponsor*: "Romney Cosponsors Bill to Reform Policing Practices," Romney.Senate.gov, June 17, 2020.

266 *"Tremendous sincerity"*: Donald Trump, "Tremendous sincerity, what a guy. Hard to believe, with this kind of political talent, his numbers would 'tank' so badly in Utah!" @realDonaldTrump, Twitter, June 8, 2020, 8:30 a.m.

267 *"There's a silver lining"*: MR, interview, November 3, 2022.

267 *"The way I look at this choice"*: MR, interview, May 26, 2021.

268 *Senators Lisa Murkowski and Susan Collins*: Allan Smith, "Lisa Murkowski Becomes 2nd GOP Senator to Oppose Pre-Election Supreme Court Vote," NBC News, September 20, 2020.

268 *"show Americans what it means"*: Bret Stephens, "An Open Letter to Mitt Romney," *New York Times*, September 21, 2020.

269 *Four days after Ginsburg's death*: "Romney Statement on Supreme Court Vacancy," Romney.Senate.gov, September 22, 2020.

269   *"Well, I guess that will be it"*: Matt Waldrip, interview, March 30, 2023.

269   *if the election was "rigged"*: Morgan Chalfant, "Trump: 'The Only Way We're Going to Lose This Election Is If the Election Is Rigged,'" *The Hill*, August 17, 2020.

269   *"The radical left are laying"*: Donie O'Sullivan and Daniel Dale, "Fact Check: Trump Jr. Touts Baseless Rigged-Election Claims to Recruit 'Army' for His Dad," CNN, September 23, 2020.

269   *"If you don't believe in the ballot"*: MR, interview, September 13, 2022.

CHAPTER FIFTEEN   The Cathedral and the Gargoyle

Unless otherwise indicated, Mitt Romney's account of January 6—as well as all firsthand quotes—come from an interview with the author conducted on May 18, 2021.

271   *Years earlier, he'd bumped into*: MR, interview, May 5, 2022.

271   *Lately, Romney had made a point*: Jonathan Martin and Alexander Burns, *This Will Not Pass: Trump, Biden, and the Battle for America's Future* (New York: Simon & Schuster, 2022), 336.

271   *He'd only been sitting at the Delta gate*: "Sen. Mitt Romney Mocked by Trump Supporters at Airport," uploaded by the *New York Post*, video, YouTube, January 6, 2021, https://www.youtube.com/watch?v=SyoNqJNRSNA.

272   *Dozens of Republican lawmakers*: Jake Tapper, "At Least 140 House Republicans to Vote against Counting Electoral Votes, Two GOP Lawmakers Say," CNN, December 31, 2020.

272   *"What is the downside"*: Amy Gardner, Ashley Parker, Josh Dawsey, and Emma Brown, "Top Republicans Back Trump's Efforts to Challenge Election Results," *Washington Post*, November 9, 2020.

273   *"Big protest on January 6th"*: Donald J. Trump, "Peter Navarro releases 36-page report alleging election fraud 'more than sufficient' to swing victory to Trump: https://washex.am/3nwaBCe. A great report by Peter. Statistically impossible to have lost the 2020 Election. Big protest in D.C. on January 6th. Be there, will be wild!" @realDonaldTrump, Twitter, December 19, 2020, 1:42 a.m.

273   *Shouts of "Resign, Mitt!"*: "Romney Heckled by Trump Supporters While Flying from Utah to D.C.," *Politico*, January 6, 2021.

273   *The mob was only one level below*: Paul Kane, "Inside the Assault on the Capitol: Evacuating the Senate," *Washington Post*, January 6, 2021.

275   *He put in a call*: MR, interview, May 26, 2021.

275   *"This is our country"*: Matt Waldrip, interview, March 30, 2023.

275   *Trump never called in*: Ellen Mitchell, "DC National Guard Deployment Wasn't Purposefully Delayed on Jan. 6, Final Report Finds," *The Hill*, December 23, 2022.

275   *he wanted to get rid of the metal detectors*: "Witness: Trump Wanted Metal Detectors Taken Away for Jan. 6 Rally, Said Armed Rallygoers Were 'Not Here to Hurt Me,'" Associated Press, June 28, 2022.

275   *he believed his vice president deserved*: Betsy Woodruff Swan and Kyle Cheney, "Trump Expressed Support for Hanging Pence during Capitol Riot, Jan. 6 Panel Told," *Politico*, May 25, 2022.

276   *Romney had written a speech*: MR, interview, May 26, 2021.

277   *saw his approval rating plummet*: Scott Keeter, "How We Know the Drop in Trump's Approval Rating in January Reflected a Real Shift in Public Opinion," Pew Research Center, January 20, 2021.

277   *McConnell's office leaked to the press*: Seung Min Kim and Paul Kane, "McConnell Breaks with Trump, Says He'll Consider Convicting Him in Senate Trial," *Washington Post*, January 13, 2021.

278   *Within months, Fox News was offering*: Jeremy W. Peters, "Fox News Gives Its Viewers a Revisionist History Lesson of Jan. 6," *New York Times*, June 9, 2022.

278   *paid a visit to Mar-a-Lago*: Maggie Haberman, "McCarthy to Meet Trump after Rift over His Assertion That the Former President 'Bears Responsibility' for the Capitol Attack," *New York Times*, January 27, 2021.

278   *When one senator*: MR, interview, May 11, 2021; Matt Waldrip, interview, March 20, 2023.

278   *Romney himself had been shelling*: MR, interview, May 26, 2021.

279   *he'd proposed leaving some of the damage*: Graig Graziosi, "Mitt Romney Wants Some of the Damage at the US Capitol Left as a Reminder of the Attack," *The Independent*, January 26, 2021.

279   *"You've gotta be kidding"*: MR, interview, May 11, 2021.

280   *"Utahns are pretty respectful people"*: MR, interview, May 11, 2021.

280   *"He was proud to stand"*: MR, interview, May 11, 2021.

280   *Scruffy Occupy Wall Streeters*: Nia-Malika Henderson, "Occupy Wall Street Protesters Move to the Campaign Trail," *Washington Post*, November 22, 2011.

280   *gay rights activists had "glitter-bombed"*: Keith Coffman, "Colorado Student Charged in 'Glitter Bomb' of Romney," Reuters, February 8, 2012.

281   *"There are deranged people among us"*: MR, interview, May 11, 2021.

CHAPTER SIXTEEN New Friends

283   *"I came here to do things"*: MR, interview, June 13, 2022.

283   *"He's a curmudgeon"*: McKay Coppins, "The Liberation of Mitt Romney," *The Atlantic*, October 20, 2019.

284   *"I doubt I will work with Josh Hawley"*: MR, interview, May 18, 2021.

284   *suggesting that Nancy Pelosi*: Tom Porter, "GOP Senator Attempts to Blame Nancy Pelosi, Not Trump, for the Capitol Riot as Impeachment Trial Looms," *Insider*, February 8, 2021.

284 *dismissing climate change*: Em Steck, Andrew Kczynski, and Drew Myers, "GOP Sen. Ron Johnson Mouths to GOP Luncheon That Climate Change Is 'Bullsh*t,'" CNN, July 7, 2021.

284 *accusing Pfizer of covering up*: Aaron Blake, "Ron Johnson Takes 2 Covid Conspiracy Theories from Fever Swamps to Fox News Prime Time," *Washington Post*, October 5, 2021.

284 *Johnson had suggested mouthwash*: Andrew Jeong, "A GOP Senator Suggested Gargling Mouthwash to Kill the Coronavirus. Doctors and Listerine Are Skeptical," *Washington Post*, December 9, 2021.

284 *"Ron, is there any conspiracy"*: MR, interview, May 18, 2021.

285 *"A lot of my colleagues"*: Rob Portman, interview, January 25, 2023.

285 *its "chattiest" member*: Burgess Everett and Marianne Levine, "The Power of 10: Inside the 'Unlikely Partnership' That Sealed an Infrastructure Win," *Politico*, August 10, 2021.

285 *he and Manchin would debate*: Joe Manchin, interview, January 24, 2023.

285 *"We speak about it every day"*: Manchin, interview, January 24, 2023.

286 *leading anti-war protests*: Andrew Kaczynki and Christopher Massie, "Arizona Senate: Kyrsten Sinema's Anti-War Group Blasted 'U.S. Terror,' Depicted Soldier as Skeleton in 2003 Flyers," CNN, September 15, 2018.

286 *crusading against the death penalty*: Jonathan Martin, "A Senate Candidate's Image Shifted. Did Her Life Story?" *New York Times*, September 24, 2018.

286 *a copy of the Constitution*: Stephanie Northwood, "Kyrsten Sinema Uses Constitution, Not Bible, to Take Oath of Office," MIC, January 9, 2013.

286 *"He's already run for everything"*: Kyrsten Sinema, interview, February 1, 2023.

287 *"I guess some people think"*: Sinema, interview, February 1, 2023.

287 *cornered her in bathrooms*: Julie Luchetta, "Activists Ambush Sen. Kyrsten Sinema in Public Bathroom over Immigration, Infrastructure," *Arizona Republic*, October 4, 2021.

287 *"We believe she undermines"*: Felicia Sonmez, "Emily's List Says It Will No Longer Endorse Sen. Sinema as She Holds Firm on Filibuster," *Washington Post*, January 18, 2022.

287 *"I don't care"*: MR, interview, May 5, 2022.

287 *Once, while inside the Senate Chamber*: MR, personal journal, March 14, 2019.

288 *Trump had spent his entire presidency*: Jeff Stein, "Trump's 2016 Campaign Pledges on Infrastructure Have Fallen Short, Creating Opening for Biden," *Washington Post*, October 18, 2020.

288 *the gang of ten met more than fifty times*: Everett and Levine, "The Power of 10."

288 *"I told him privately"*: Portman, interview, January 25, 2023.

288 *"I think people forget"*: Coppins, "The Liberation of Mitt Romney."

289 *"often the most conservative voice"*: Portman, interview, January 25, 2023.

289 *"Mitt would say, 'That's stupid'"*: Manchin, interview, January 24, 2023.

289 *went out for a lavish dinner*: Susan Collins, interview, January 27, 2023.

290 *Biden's approval rating had fallen*: Jeffrey M. Jones, "Biden Year One Approval Ratings Subpar, Extremely Polarized," Gallup, January 18, 2022.

290 *"They didn't have any"*: MR, interview, November 15, 2021.

292 *"If you had a strategy"*: MR, interview, February 9, 2022.

292 *Biden cold-called Romney*: MR, interview, February 9, 2022.

292 *A few days later, after Biden honed*: MR, interview, April 27, 2022.

293 *"I never met with her"*: MR, interview, April 27, 2022.

293 *"If she is a mainstream Democrat"*: MR, interview, March 1, 2022.

293 *In late March*: MR, interview, April 27, 2022.

294 *He still remembered sitting*: MR, interview, October 4, 2021.

294 *When it finally happened in 1978*: MR, interview, November 2, 2021.

294 *"Franky, I hoped"*: MR, interview, April 27, 2022.

295 *Romney stood and proudly applauded*: Dennis Romboy, "Video: Mitt Romney Stands and Applauds Historic Confirmation of Ketanji Brown Jackson to Supreme Court," *Deseret News*, April 7, 2022.

295 *"You look old when you shuffle"*: Matt Waldrip, interview, August 25, 2022.

295 *"This is Joe"*: MR, interview, April 27, 2022.

295 *Romney's son Craig*: MR, interview, April 27, 2022.

295 *"I thought he would be less old"*: Mary Romney, interview, July 7, 2022.

296 *stood at around 35 percent*: Dennis Romboy, "What a Grocery Store Commercial and President Joe Biden's Approval Ratings Have in Common," *Deseret News*, July 7, 2022.

296 *"You got a couple of guys"*: MR, interview, September 13, 2022.

296 *"He puts his principles"*: Joe Biden, written statement, June 2, 2023.

296 *Romney was sitting in church*: March 1, 2022.

CHAPTER SEVENTEEN "What We Used to Be"

297 *Russia as America's number-one*: Mitt Romney, interviewed by Wolf Blitzer, *The Situation Room with Wolf Blitzer*, CNN, March 26, 2012.

298 *a shrugging acknowledgment*: Jeffrey Goldberg, "The Obama Doctrine," *The Atlantic*, April 2016.

298 *When Putin orchestrated*: Jeremy Diamond, "Intel Report: Putin Directly Ordered Effort to Influence Election," CNN, January 6, 2017.

298 *inviting the Russian ambassador*: Julie Vitkovskaya and Amanda Erickson, "The Strange Oval Office Meeting Between Trump, Lavrov and Kislyak," *Washington Post*, May 10, 2017.

298 *"We had not sufficiently responded"*: McKay Coppins, "Romney Was Right about Putin," *The Atlantic*, February 27, 2022.

298 *"There's no other way"*: David Axelrod, interviewed by Brianna Keilar and John Berman, *New Day*, CNN, February 15, 2022.

298 *"I don't think that by any means"*: Coppins, "Romney Was Right."

298 *Polls showed that Republicans*: William Saletan, "Republican Voters Are Now America's Foreign Policy Doves," The Bulwark, March 21, 2022.

299 *"Then the Republican Party lurches"*: George W. Bush, interview, October 12, 2022.

299 *the "very savvy" Russian leader*: "A Discussion with Mike Pompeo: The Future of US Nuclear Strategy and Deterrence," uploaded by CFTNI, video, YouTube, February 18, 2022, https://www.youtube.com/watch?v=Xwu2ZqdWQFM.

299 *"Why do Democrats"*: Tucker Carlson, *Tucker Carlson Tonight*, Fox News, February 22, 2022.

300 *a January 2022 poll*: Andrew Romano, "Poll: As Ukraine Tensions Escalate, 62% of Republicans Say Putin Is a 'Stronger Leader' Than Biden," Yahoo News, January 25, 2022.

300 *"I recognize the liberal left"*: Eliza Relman and John Haltiwanger, "We Asked Republican Senators about Tucker Carlson's Favorite Authoritarian Leader. Their Praise and Dodges Underscore the Danger to the US," *Insider*, August 13, 2021.

300 *Carlson had broadcast his Fox News show*: Benjamin Novak and Michael M. Grynbaum, "Conservative Fellow Travelers: Tucker Carlson Drops In on Viktor Orban," *New York Times*, August 7, 2021.

300 *"It's hard to imagine"*: MR, interview, February 9, 2022.

302 *"Sad to see what's being done"*: Senator Mitt Romney, "Sad to see what's being done to bribe the voters. Biden's student loan forgiveness plan may win Democrats some votes, but it fuels inflation, foots taxpayers with other people's financial obligations, is unfair to those who paid their own way & creates irresponsible expectations," @SenatorRomney, Twitter, August 24, 2022, 12:14 p.m.

302 *"This is not about inflation"*: Senator Mitt Romney, "Everyday Americans are not who will benefit from the prescription drug price setting provisions in Democrats' reconciliation bill. Instead, it's the government that will save money, and these savings will then be used to fund Green New Deal priorities!" @SenatorRomney, Twitter, August 3, 2022, 1:36 p.m.

302 *Romney said he posted*: MR, interview, April 27, 2022.

302 *"After [the Trump] crisis passed"*: George Packer, "Are We Doomed?" *The Atlantic*, December 6, 2021.

303 *They pitched their amendment*: MR, interview, January 11, 2023.

304 *"If you keep on doing things"*: MR, interview, January 11, 2023.

305 *Romney was coming out of a meeting*: MR, interview, May 23, 2022.

305 *Thom Tillis and John Cornyn were leading*: Burgess Everett and Marianne Levine, "How a Centrist, a Liberal and 2 Conservatives Achieved 4-Part Harmony on Guns," *Politico*, June 14, 2022.

306 *As governor of Massachusetts, he'd signed*: Lindsay Whitehurst, "Fact Check: Romney Criticized for Assault-Weapons Ban," Associated Press, June 1, 2018.

306   *he liked to hunt "small varmints"*: Mitt Romney on *Hardball*, MSNBC, April 5, 2007.

306   *"Why do people do this?"*: MR, personal journal, November 18, 2015.

306   *Romney, incensed by the slander*: MR, interview, June 13, 2022.

306   *"Chris was very realistic"*: MR, interview, May 22, 2022.

307   *Ron Johnson protested*: an individual with knowledge of the meeting, text message, June 15, 2022.

307   *Mike Lee complained*: Matt Waldrip, interview, March 20, 2023; an individual with knowledge of the meeting, text message, n.d.

307   *stalking and violent threats*: Casey Tolan, Curt Devine, and Isabelle Chapman, "As Herschel Walker Eyes Georgia US Senate Seat, a Newly Revealed Stalking Claim Brings His Troubled History under Scrutiny," CNN, September 2, 2021.

307   *"Pointing a gun"*: MR, interview, November 3, 2022.

308   *part of a plot by Bill Gates*: Benjamin Wallace-Wells, "The Curious Case of Donald Bolduc," *New Yorker*, September 29, 2022.

308   *"He's said some very unusual things"*: MR, interview, November 3, 2022.

308   *"I don't know that I can disrespect"*: MR, interview, May 5, 2022.

308   *They'd first met years earlier*: MR, interview, February 9, 2022.

308   *the "childless left"*: Spencer Lindquist, "Senate Candidate Blasts 'Childless Left' Who Have 'No Physical Commitment to the Future of This Country,'" *The Federalist*, July 24, 2021.

308   *"a fake holiday"*: J. D. Vance, "'Indigenous Peoples' Day' is a fake holiday created to sow division. Of course Joe Biden is the first president to pay it any attention," @JDVance1, Twitter, October 11, 2021, 10:45 a.m.

308   *"to punish people"*: Mary Papenfuss, "J. D. Vance Wildly Suggests Biden Is Trying to 'Kill a Bunch of MAGA Voters,'" *HuffPost*, April 30, 2022.

308   *"I do wonder"*: MR, interview, February 9, 2022.

309   *he gave a notorious speech*: Dennis Romboy, "Sen. Mike Lee Explains Comparing Donald Trump to Capt. Moroni from Book of Mormon," *Deseret News*, October 30, 2020.

309   *more than sixty leaked text messages*: "READ: Mark Meadows' Texts with Mike Lee and Chip Roy," CNN, April 15, 2022.

309   *Early polls suggested*: Dennis Romboy, "How Close Is the Senate Race between Mike Lee and Evan McMullin in Utah? Here's the Latest Poll," *Deseret News*, July 20, 2022.

309   *in private, he frequently predicted*: MR, interview, September 13, 2022.

309   *In March, he told* Politico: Burgess Everett and Anthon Adragna, "Mitt Romney Says He's Unlikely to Endorse in the Senate Contest between Mike Lee and Evan McMullin," *Politico*, March 8, 2022.

310   *"It's noteworthy here that all forty-eight"*: Mike Lee, interviewed by Tucker Carlson, *Tucker Carlson Tonight*, Fox News, October 11, 2022.

310   *When people in their overlapping circles*: An individual with knowledge of the conversation, interview, n.d.

310 *Lee called the final product "foolish"*: Matt Canham, "Utah's Mike Lee, Mitt Romney Split over Tech Investment to Take on China," *Salt Lake Tribune*, June 8, 2021.

311 *"the legislative equivalent of running"*: Dennis Romboy, "Senate Approves Gun Safety Bill. How Did Mitt Romney, Mike Lee Vote?" *Deseret News*, June 23, 2022.

311 *In August, when it seemed*: Burgess Everett and Marianne Levine, "The Power of 10: Inside the 'Unlikely Partnership' That Sealed an Infrastructure Win," *Politico*, August 10, 2021.

311 *"Maybe," Romney mused*: An individual with knowledge of the conversation, interview, n.d.

312 *"You know, Nancy Pelosi"*: MR, interview, March 1, 2023.

312 *"I've invested a lot of money"*: MR, interview, March 1, 2023.

312 *"Do I want to spend"*: MR, interview, April 24, 2023.

313 *"I listened to Nikki Haley"*: MR, interview, January 31, 2023.

313 *"a lap dog to Trump"*: MR, interview, May 5, 2022.

313 *He liked Tim Scott*: MR, interview, January 31, 2023.

313 *it would be a hoot*: MR, interview, January 31, 2023.

313 *Romney had never met*: MR, interview, April 27, 2022.

313 *"There's just no warmth"*: MR, interview, January 31, 2023.

314 *"He's much smarter"*: MR, interview, March 21, 2023.

314 *"You might point out"*: MR, interview, March 21, 2023.

314 *For months, people in his orbit*: MR, interview, April 24, 2023.

314 *"I was afraid that Biden"*: MR, interview, April 24, 2023.

314 *"I must admit"*: MR, interview, April 24, 2023.

315 *One afternoon in late January*: MR, interview, January 31, 2023.

315 *"The only way you could weaken"*: MR, interview, April 24, 2023.

315 *"shedding thoughtful people"*: MR, interview, June 21, 2021.

316 *"It's almost like you take"*: MR, interview, August 4, 2021.

316 *"I don't recognize"*: MR, interview, June 21, 2021.

316 *In April, Romney privately approached*: MR, interview, April 24, 2023.

EPILOGUE

320 *Tagg built his own*: Town of Wolfeboro, New Hampshire, real estate records.

320 *Romney is an "easy grandparent"*: Matt Romney, interview, August 5, 2022.

322 *"I don't know the answer"*: MR, interview, August 4, 2021.

323 *"How do I look at my life?"*: MR, interview, September 13, 2022.

323 *"He isn't married"*: MR, interview, May 18, 2021.

323 *"She knows I'm fascinated"*: MR, interview, September 13, 2022.

323 *"Even if history"*: MR, interview, September 13, 2022.

Index